PARLIAMENTARY SCRUTINY OF GOVERNMENT BILLS

by the same author

CENTRAL DEPARTMENTS AND LOCAL AUTHORITIES

PARLIAMENTARY SCRUTINY OF GOVERNMENT BILLS

J. A. G. GRIFFITH

Professor of Public Law
in the University of London

PEP

12 Upper Belgrave Street, London

and

THE STUDY OF PARLIAMENT GROUP

LONDON GEORGE ALLEN & UNWIN LTD

Ruskin House Museum Street

First published in 1974

ISBN 0 04 328008 0

Printed in Great Britain
in 10 point Times Roman type
by Alden & Mowbray Ltd
at the Alden Press, Oxford

'Sir Elwyn Jones: I will withdraw the Amendment.

The Chairman: The Amendment cannot be withdrawn, because it is being discussed with No. 65. It would have been possible to have had two Divisions.

Sir Elwyn Jones: One of these days I shall understand these things – after 26 years.'

(Courts Bill 1970–71 Standing Committee A, col. 454)

'It seems to me to be absolutely essential that people should not try to shape our procedure as if perfection would be attained when legislation was most easy. Most Bills, I believe, cost money, lose votes, create officials and worry the public.'

(Mr W. S. Churchill, 293 H.C. Deb., col. 2183; 15 November 1934)

See 'em in the 'ouse o' Commons,
Passin' laws to put down crime.

(Popular song)

'The object of debate in the House is to persuade the other side'
(Second Clerk Assistant to the Select Committee on Procedure, 23 June 1971)

'The most amazing piece of legislation in this amazing Parliament, so noted for its complicated legislation . . . the chef d'oeuvre of all bureaucratic legislation . . . will be held up to ridicule and contempt by the A. P. Herberts of the future . . . most Draconian piece of bureaucratic legislation since the introduction of the Land Commission and betterment levy'.

(Mr Gresham Cooke on off-street parking control, Transport (London) Bill 1968–69, Standing Committee A, col. 398)

'This Clause has been backwards and forwards not only between the Opposition and the Government and between hon. Members opposite and the Board of Trade but also between this House and another place, like a pea in a baby's rattle'.

(Mrs Gwyneth Dunwoody during the debate on the Trade Descriptions Bill 1967–68; 764 H.C. Deb., col. 462)

PREFACE

This book considers only Government bills (not private Members' bills, not subordinate legislation). It is concerned to try to estimate the impact which Parliamentary scrutiny has on Government bills; other influences are referred to only so far as they operate through Parliamentarians as revealed in Parliamentary proceedings.

The method adopted is to describe the ways in which the House of Commons scrutinises Government bills; and to examine in detail the extent of this scrutiny in three recent sessions: 1967–68, 1968–69 and 1970–71. A chapter on the House of Lords considers the extent to which that House exerts its impact. And some conclusions are drawn and proposals made.

I hope that this examination will indicate some of the many directions in which further research into the day-to-day working of Parliament could be conducted. The amount of work to be done on this most famous of institutions is considerable.

I am greatly indebted to Miss Norma Percy who helped me for two years in the research needed for this book. She was responsible for the analysis of Government bills in 1967–68. And, more broadly, her knowledge and understanding of the ways of the House of Commons and of those who people it were a continuing instruction to me. At one time or another, she has read and commented on almost the whole typescript; and so has enabled me to avoid many errors.

I have had much help from many officials of both Houses of Parliament, but above all from Mr M. T. Ryle of the Public Bill Office in the House of Commons. He took great trouble on my behalf and read the whole typescript in earlier or later drafts. To write about an institution without having been a member of it is a dangerous business and it is essential to check both one's facts and one's feelings against the experience of another who knows it well from the inside. Mr Ryle both instructed me and saved me from innumerable blunders. I am most grateful to him.

Many Members of Parliament, including some Ministers and former Ministers, gave me interviews and enabled me to see more accurately how the legislative process appeared from front and back benches and from the chair of committees. My thanks to them.

The staff of the British Library of Political and Economic Science were as helpful as they could possibly have been. I also thank the staff of the Library of the House of Commons where I worked from time to time during periods when the House was not sitting.

Political and Economic Planning co-sponsored the work with the Study of Parliament Group and members of both bodies read parts of the typescript and helped me by their comments. But I add a special and personal note of thanks to Mr John Pinder of PEP and his staff, who, as always, simply removed any administrative difficulties that arose. The Social Science Research Council made money available and I am grateful to them for their confidence.

Much of the typing and re-typing was undertaken by Miss Colleen Etheridge. I do not write the clearest of hands and the text was not straightforward. She did the job accurately and with great good humour and forbearance. Not for the first nor (I hope) for the last time, I am much in her debt.

The faults that remain are mine.

J. A. G. GRIFFITH

CONTENTS

CHAPTER ONE

INTRODUCTION

The making of laws takes a long time. Government bills gestate slowly, being conceived in some policy statement or the administrative failings of earlier legislation; or more grandly, in the digested thoughts of Royal Commissions or inter-departmental committees; or less grandly (and less likely), in the idiosyncracies of individual Ministers or civil servants; or in party committees or election manifestos. Over the months they grow in the womb of Departments while many consultations, both with drafts-men and outside interests, are entered into, which shape the embryos until the time comes for their birth as bills. And then each is handed over to the two Houses of Parliament for scrutiny and, its parents confidently expect, approval.

What follows is concerned with this scrutiny by the House of Commons and, to a lesser extent, by the House of Lords. That Parliament makes an impact on the legislative proposals of Governments is undeniable. That Governments, with their majorities, will at the end of the day almost always have much the greater part of what they want, is common knowledge. But the language which is used to describe the more or the less of the impact is imprecise. We may be told that Governments will get the 'principles' of their bills but that the 'details' may be altered. Or that the two Houses greatly improve the bills. Or that the House of Lords is an important, indeed necessary, revising chamber. Or that Government back-benchers never speak in committee and so exert no influence. Or we may be told that the legislative process in the House of Commons is a farce and a waste of time; or that it is the most efficient part of the scrutiny functions of 'that House.

Further, the procedure of the House of Commons, in particular, affects not only how Ministers, Government backbenchers, and Opposition Members work but also what is done. Erskine May and Standing Orders tell the formal story in great detail but often the informal working of Parliament is only hinted at. Thus, when dealing with the selection of amendments, May says nothing about the pressure that may be brought on the Speaker or the chairmen of committees; and all he says about the grouping of amendments is that it is common practice to allow several amendments to be discussed together although they have not all been selected to be moved.[1] Yet both these examples of the informal working of Parliament are of great importance.

The method adopted in what follows is to attempt a description of the process but passing quickly over the well known, more formal, parts and, by analysing what happened to Government bills during recent sessions, to try to show the quality as well as the quantity of the impact of the Houses on these bills. Tables are included both in the text and in the Appendices giving some basic and relevant statistics. But, of course, in the examination of institutions like the Houses of Parliament, statistics may be more than usually misleading. In considering amendments[2] moved to a bill, what is important is their relative effect on the bill, not their number. This presents its own difficulty for there is no alternative to using general words to describe the greater or less importance of particular amendments. And that involves a degree of personal judgement about which Members amongst themselves sometimes disagree. At the lowest level, it is not uncommon for one Member – probably the Minister in charge of the bill – to introduce an amendment with the words 'This is a purely drafting amendment' and for him to be immediately challenged by another Member who sees, or thinks he sees, something substantive secreted in the proposed alteration.

I hope, however, that I have been able somewhat to overcome this difficulty by describing amendments which I have designated as more, or less, substantive so that the meaning 'substantial' or 'important', always relative, becomes relatively clear. One result of the method I have adopted is to produce a work which has some of the characteristics of a book and some of those of a report.

What happens in Parliament is often not the most formative part of the legislative process. Indeed the presentation of the proposal in the form of a bill, representing it may be many hours of hard labour by Parliamentary counsel, means that ossification is well advanced. The most formative part of the whole process – the point at which the proposal may most significantly be changed – is the time when the Department are consulting with affected interests. This fact has its impact on what takes place in Parliament, for Ministers may consider themselves committed.[3] But except so far as what takes place before a bill is introduced directly affects what takes place in Parliament, I am not concerned with that earlier period.

More perhaps than in most other lawmaking systems, what is contained in a Government bill in the United Kingdom varies from the most to the least important. Bills may radically change the way of life of thousands, even millions, of people. Or they may make some minor adjustment that is effectively unnoticed by more than a few. Bills may be very long and contain hundreds of clauses or they may consist of one or two substantive

[1] Erskine May, *Parliamentary Practice*, p. 442 (18th edition).

[2] Unless the context otherwise requires, 'amendments' includes new clauses and new schedules.

[3] See, for example, the Agriculture (Spring Traps) (Scotland) Bill 1968–69, below, p. 213.

sentences. The long bill may change nothing if it only consolidates the law. The short bill may have considerable consequences.

For both the relatively important and the relatively unimportant measure, the formal procedure in Parliament is the same. But that procedure is, in its working, most flexible. Normally an important bill will be considered at length and an unimportant bill can pass with little examination. Sometimes an important bill of moderate length can, if thought necessary by the Government, and especially if it is not likely to be strongly opposed, pass all stages in both Houses in a few days.[1]

1.1 LEGISLATIVE TIME IN THE HOUSE OF COMMONS

A Government will normally expect to pass between fifty and eighty bills in a session. Table 1.1 shows, for three recent sessions, how the time of the House of Commons and its committees was distributed between bills.

Table 1.1 TIME SPENT BY THE HOUSE OF COMMONS AND ITS COMMITTEES ON BILLS

1967–68	Number of Government bills	Total time	Average time for each bill
Less than 5 hr	22	41 hr 15 min	1 hr 52 min
5–10 hr	10	76 hr 29 min	7 hr 39 min
10–20 hr	11	154 hr 14 min	14 hr 1 min
20–50 hr	10	351 hr 4 min	35 hr 6 min
More than 50 hr	7	812 hr 26 min	116 hr 4 min
Total	60	1435 hr 28 min	
1968–69			
Less than 5 hr	18	44 hr 24 min	2 hr 28 min
5–10 hr	7	45 hr 23 min	6 hr 29 min
10–20 hr	11	167 hr 8 min	15 hr 12 min
20–50 hr	7	232 hr 49 min	33 hr 15 min
More than 50 hr	7	527 hr 3 min	75 hr 17 min
Total	50	1016 hr 47 min	

[1] The second reading of the Commonwealth Immigrants Bill was moved at 4 p.m. on 27 February 1968 in the House of Commons and the bill passed all stages in the Commons and the Lords on the same day. Notification of the Royal Assent was received in the Lords at 9.45 a.m. on 1 March 1968. This example was overtaken by the Northern Ireland Bill the second reading of which was moved in the House of Commons at about 10.10 p.m. on 23 February 1972 and the bill passed all stages in the Commons and the Lords. Notification of the Royal Assent was received in the Lords at 2.11 a.m. on 24 February 1972.

Table 1.1 *(continued)*

	Number of Government bills	Total time	Average time for each bill
1970–71			
Less than 5 hr	34	42 hr 32 min	1 hr 15 min
5–10 hr	12	84 hr 15 min	7 hr 1 min
10–20 hr	11	147 hr 47 min	13 hr 22 min
20–50 hr	9	243 hr 59 min	27 hr 6 min
More than 50 hr	7	667 hr 33 min	95 hr 22 min
Total	73	1186 hr 6 min	

In these three sessions there were ten Consolidated Fund or Appropriation Bills, nine of which have been excluded wholly from this table as the debates are not truly legislative but concerned with matters of administration or policy raised by private Members. But on one occasion an attempt was made to debate the bill in committee.[1] The proceedings in the Joint Committee on Consolidation Bills, etc., are also excluded.[2]

The figures in the table show how large is the proportion of bills dealt with at some speed by the House, between one-half and one-third (74 out of 183) being disposed of in less than 5 hours at an average time for each bill over the three sessions of under 2 hours. At the other end of the scale are the seven bills in each session of major political importance absorbing 55 per cent of the time spent on Government bills in the House. These great diversities create problems when the legislative process is discussed for reforms which are practical politics for non-controversial bills may not be so for bills that arouse party political passions. Much of the debate about legislative reform has tended to concentrate on non-controversial bills especially when the purpose of the reform is to move more business off the floor of the House and into committees of the House. But, as we shall see, such reforms, though they may be worthwhile, have very little effect on the working of the House. Any important changes must be directed to the procedures affecting at least those bills that take between 20 and 50 hours of the time of the House. These may be less controversial than the heavyweights taking more than 50 hours, but they are bills the size and importance of which call for thorough examination in committee.

The time spent by the House on the different stages is shown in Table 1.2.[3]

[1] See 811 H.C. Deb., col. 1773–808 and this is included. Also excluded from the table are three bills that did not receive a second reading in the House of Commons.

[2] See below, p. 37.

[3] The Finance Bill is counted twice in the committee stage because it was recommitted in 1967–68 and split in 1968–69 and 1970–71. In 1968–69 the Parliament (No. 2) Bill was abandoned in committee and so not reported. As above, nine consolidated Fund and Appropriation bills have been excluded.

Table 1.2

	1	2	3	4	5	6	7	8	9	10	11	12	Total
	2R	2R Cttee	Scottish Grand Cttee	Total, cols 1–3	Cttee of whole House	Stand-ing Cttee	Scottish Stand-ing Cttee	Total, cols 5–7	Report	3R	Total, cols 9 and 10	Lords amend-ments in Commons	Total, cols 4, 8, 11 and 12
1967–68													
Number of bills	49	6	5	60	25	30	6	61	60	60	—	13	—
Time spent, hr	170.14	9.22	10.40	190.16	89.36	814.36	75.35	979.47	193.48	24.47	218.35	46.50	1435.28
Percentage of total time	11·9	0·6	0·8	13·3	6·3	56·7	5·2	68·2	13·5	1·7	15·2	3·3	100
1968–69													
Number of bills	39	6	5	50	16	29	6	51	49	49	—	16	—
Time spent, hr	138.33	10.50	17.41	167.4	199.35	352.20	88.37	640.32	167.27	18.59	186.26	22.45	1016.47
Percentage of total time	13·6	1·1	1·8	16·5	19·7	34·6	8·7	63·0	16·4	1·9	18·3	2·2	100
1970–71													
Number of bills	59	10	4	73	34	35	5	74	73	73	—	11	—
Time spent, hr	172.49	16.33	7.28	196.50	183.2	478.47	88.33	750.22	156.50	33.28	190.18	48.36	1186.6
Percentage of total time	14·6	1·4	0·6	16·6	15·4	40·4	7·5	63·3	13·2	2·8	16·0	4·1	100

The three sessions show strong comparisons and few significant differences. The percentage of the time spent on second reading procedures averages at 15·5, in committee at 64·8 and on report and third reading at 16·5, with no great divergences from one session to another. The very small number of hours taken by second reading committees and in the Scottish Grand Committee, considered together (1·4 per cent in 1967–68, 2·9 per cent in 1968–69 and 2 per cent in 1970–71) emphasise how moderate is the saving of time on the floor by the use of these devices. The most striking difference between the sessions is the relatively high percentage of hours spent in committee of the whole House in 1968–69 and 1970–71 as compared with 1967–68. This is explained by the length of debate on the Parliament (No. 2) Bill in 1968–69 which was in committee for more than 87 hours; and on the Industrial Relations Bill in 1970–71 which was in committee of the whole House for more than 106 hours. In 1967–68 there were no such giants, the Finance Bill being longest in committee on the floor and that for less than 18 hours.

Finally the figures show the importance of the committee stage. And also that the time spent on second reading is closely comparable with that spent on report. In terms of the impact which the House can make on bills we shall see that the second reading is of little direct importance and that the report stage is where the Government makes its principal concessions to Parliamentary opinion expressed primarily in committee. But the figures somewhat mislead for while it is unusual for a bill, however unimportant, not to be debated for some time on second reading, the number of bills considered on report is generally less than half of the number of bills considered in committee.[1]

No excuse is needed to justify a discussion of time in the first pages of a book on Parliament. Ministers are the actors and all other Members of Parliament are reactors. Action absorbs time and there are only so many Parliamentary days in a session. Reaction also absorbs time much of it being Government time. So having seen in broad terms how legislative time is used, we must look at the means Governments have to save it.

1.2 METHODS OF CURTAILING DEBATE IN THE HOUSE OF COMMONS

Under this heading, Erkine May[2] discusses closure of debate, the selection of amendments, and allocation of time orders. The second of these is considered separately below.[3]

1.2.1 *Closure*

Standing Order No. 30 provides that after a question has been proposed a Member rising in his place may claim to move 'That the question be now

[1] Therefore for many of the bills included in cols 9 and 10 in Table 1.2, report and 3R stages are purely formal.

[2] *Op. cit.*, Chapter XX.

[3] See p. 70 *et seq.*

put', and unless it shall appear to the Chair that such a motion is an abuse of the rules of the House, or an infringement of the rights of the minority, the question, 'That the question be now put' shall be put forthwith. If that procedural question is decided in the affirmative then the substantive question is put and decided. But not less than 100 Members must vote in the majority for the procedural question to be carried.[1] This is called the ordinary closure. A second type – closure upon the words of a clause or schedule – has now fallen into disuse.

These provisions, which apply to proceedings of the House or of the Committee of the whole House, have been extended to standing committees where the majority effective for the closure is the number prescribed as the quorum.[2]

An analysis of closures moved to Government bills in the House of Commons during three recent sessions is given in Table 1.3. Of the 102 motions that the chair accepted all except one were agreed to, seventy-five after divisions. The exception was the Government's failure to obtain 100 votes in the majority on the last vote on the Parliament (No. 2) Bill 1968–69 but by that time the battle was over and it was known that the Government did not intend to persist with the bill.[3] It was that bill also which largely accounted for the dominance of 1968–69 in the figures for committees of the whole House in the table. The dominance of 1970–71 in the figures for standing committees was the result of the acrimony caused by the Education

Table 1.3 NUMBER OF RULINGS GIVEN BY THE CHAIR ON CLOSURE MOTIONS

	1967–68		1968–69		1970–71		Totals	
	Assent given	Assent with-held	Assent given	Assent with-held	Assent given	Assent with-held	Assent given	Assent with-held
Second Reading	6	—	4	1	8	—	18	1
Cttee of Whole House	3	1	23	1	—	3	26	5
Standing Cttee	8	4	3	4	27	10	38	18
Report	1	—	9	1	3	—	13	1
Third Reading	1	1	—	—	—	—	1	1
Allocation of Time Order	3	—	—	—	2	—	5	—
Lords Amendments	—	—	—	—	1	—	1	—
Totals	22	6	39	7	41	13	102	26
Grand total	28		46		54		128	

[1] S.O. No. 31. [2] S.O. No. 65(3)(b). [3] See below, p. 142–3.

(Scotland) Bill[1] and the Licensing (Abolition of State Mangement) Bill.[2] Closure motions were sought on fourteen Government bills in 1967–68, on ten in 1968–69 and on eleven in 1970–71.[3]

1.2.2 *Allocation of time*

The closure, the selection of amendments and the rules of the House which enable the chair to control filibustering do not in their sum prevent Members from deliberately extending the length of debates beyond that which the Government are willing to accept.[4] And so the power exists to enable a Minister to move an allocation of time order (the guillotine) to allot a specified number of days or portions of days to the consideration of the bill in committee of the whole House or on report. The debate on such a motion may last for 3 hours but not more.[5] It then becomes the duty of the Business Committee to divide the bill into such parts as they see fit and allot to each part so many days or portions of a day. Resolutions of the Business Committee are reported to the House for approval without debate.[6]

Until 1971, the Business Committee consisted of the members of the Chairmen's Panel[7] and not more than five other Members nominated by the Speaker who chose three representing the Government and two representing the Opposition. The Select Committee on Procedure considered timetabling at some length in 1970–71[8] and, in accordance with its recommendations, the Government proposed[9] that the members of the Chairmen's Panel (other than the Chairman of Ways and Means) should be excluded from membership of the Business Committee which now consists of that chairman and not more than eight other Members nominated by the Speaker, in respect of each bill, with a quorum of four.[10] All this relates to proceedings in the House, not in standing committee.

For proceedings in standing committee,[11] Standing Order No. 74 operates. This provides for a business sub-committee consisting of the chairman and seven other members of the standing committee nominated by the Speaker. The House makes an allocation of time order requiring that the bill shall be reported by a certain date. The sub-committee decides the number of sittings, the parts to be taken at each sitting, and the times at which those parts shall be concluded. The report of the sub-committee is to be agreed to by the Standing Committee on Question put without debate.[12]

[1] 18 motions.
[2] 12 motions.
[3] For all these figures, see Return respecting application of S.O. No. 31 (now S.O. No. 30) for each session.
[4] For a recent general account see John Palmer, 'Allocation of time: the guillotine and voluntary timetabling', 23 *Parliamentary Affairs*, 232 (1970).
[5] See S.O. No. 44.
[6] S.O. No. 43.
[7] See below, p. 57–8.
[8] See H.C. 538 of 1970–71 *Report* paras 12–18, Appendices 4 and 10.
[9] 825 H.C. Deb., cols 648–58; 826, cols 349–78.
[10] S.O. No. 43.
[11] For sittings motions and voluntary arrangements see below, p. 61 *et seq*.
[12] E.g. Transport Bill 1967–68 (see 760 H.C. Deb., cols 1647–854, 1863–96).

The principal decision is whether or not to guillotine a bill (the detailed allotment of time is usually of not great significance[1]). When Mr Whitelaw was Leader of the House in November 1971 he said:

> 'I can only say to the hon. Gentleman that the whole business of timetable Motions is something which no Leader of the House embarks upon either happily or quickly, because it is for him personally a particularly nasty and difficult situation, as the House should rightly make it. That situation is one of the great safeguards the House has, and a very important one, and I accept it. It is always something that a Government do when they can show that they have not succeeded in carrying their business in the normal way.'[2]

This comes close to saying that the safeguard of the House is the personal embarrassment of the Leader which at first sight seems not to be much of a deterrent. But, oddly perhaps, Leaders and Chief Whips do take personal pride in getting difficult bills through without a guillotine and feel correspondingly disappointed when they have to resort to one. If the Government want a guillotine motion, their majority in all but the most rare circumstances will ensure that they get it. And, on the principle that the Queen's government must be carried on, this is desirable.

Perhaps a further safeguard against Governments too easily moving for allocation of time orders is the extent to which the Opposition can, in a large number of small ways, make Parliamentary life difficult for the Government. In other words, when the general relationship between Government and Opposition is, within the terms of the political dissent, relatively harmonious, the Government can get on with its job of governing with no more than the usual problem of facing a critical party on the opposite benches. But if this general relationship is sour – and the too hasty seeking of guillotines is one sure way of making it sour – then the Opposition has many ways of worrying the Government. Within the legislative process the Opposition may easily delay proceedings on innocuous and uncontentious bills as part of a campaign. The usual channels can easily be blocked and that informality of dealings between Government and Opposition which enables the parties to live together within one House may harden. The Opposition normally acquiesces in its minority rôle; it accepts the conventions that bind it in defeat. But if it feels strongly that the Government is reducing the conventional rights of the minority, the Opposition may feel free to obstruct the business of governing.

On a contentious bill, especially in standing committee, the Opposition are aware that they live under the shadow of a guillotine. Nevertheless for fear lest they should make the passage of the bill easy for the Government, they commonly seek to ensure that debate on clauses lasts for as long as

[1] But see Sir Robin Turton on European Communities Bill (Allocation of Time) motion (836 H.C. Deb., cols 235–40).

[2] 826 H.C. Deb., col. 377.

is feasible. They sail as close to the wind as they dare, not necessarily spinning out debate on relatively unimportant clauses but certainly extracting full measure from the debate on crucial clauses. They may indeed press the Government so hard that a guillotine becomes inevitable. The Opposition sometimes appear to attach much political significance to forcing the Government first to sit long hours and secondly to introduce the guillotine motion. When the debate on the floor of the House on that motion often took eight hours or so this tactic had some advantages in embarrassing the Government. But when the debate was limited to 2 hours and even now when it has been extended to 3 hours, the embarrassment is much less. It may be doubted whether those outside Parliament who are opposed to the measure are much impressed by the Opposition's cries of protest at the imposition of the guillotine and Opposition Members themselves, who when in Government used the device, seem now to realise that complaints of 'gagging' or 'stifling criticism' are regarded as a part of the Parliamentary game to which few people attach much importance.

At the end of the day, the Government will get its bill and will get its bill more or less in accordance with its schedule, unless, as in the case of the Parliament (No. 2) Bill or the proposed Industrial Relations Bill of 1968–69, the normal forces of party loyalty do not operate.

It is noticeable that when a guillotine is in operation, debate often tightens, and speeches become shorter and more to the point. Moreover, Government backbenchers speak more frequently[1] and although they may do so to embarrass the Opposition by using some of the limited time available, when they do so to make true debating points the general level of argument can be seen to rise markedly.

The proposal has been made from time to time that the decision for an allocation of time order should be made, in the interests of the House as a whole, by a small number of senior members drawn from both sides. At first sight this has obvious attractions for it would vest the decision in those who are seeking to hold the balance between the conflicting claims of Government and Opposition, of front and back benches. But, in practice, it is doubtful if such a system could work. For we are concerned with measures that sharply divide the parties and those 'senior members' are also party members. The proposal implies that objectivity is possible to decide an issue which is, in party terms, highly subjective. If we are looking for an objective view, free of party interest, the Speaker would appear to be the only person cast for the rôle. And yet the danger is immediately apparent that, in the result, he would be drawn into the party conflict by being required to make the decision.

One way of cutting the Gordian knot would be to require the Government by Standing Order, in the case of every Government bill, whether

[1] The Transport Bill 1967–68 was guillotined in committee. Before the guillotine, Government backbenchers made 101 speeches out of a total of 845; after the guillotine they made 133 speeches out of 553 – a percentage increase from 11·9 to 24.

contentious or not, to prescribe the number of days to be allotted to the bill in committee or on report; and to leave to the Opposition to decide how much time should be spent on each part of the bill within the allotted overall time. This would have the advantage, noted above, of sharpening debate. And Governments would no doubt welcome it because it would give them that predictability which above all is what they seek.[1]

But would such a proposal greatly weaken the position of the Opposition? It is easy to overstate the extent to which obstruction by the Opposition causes the Government to change its position. But there can be no doubt that under the present system, when no timetable is operating, the Government are willing to buy time by making concessions. And if the Opposition have no time to sell, as would be the case if all bills were timetabled, their bargaining position is destroyed.[2] Further, if all bills were timetabled it would be impossible for the Opposition to use their weapon of time-spending (or time-wasting if you prefer) on non-contentious bills to bring pressure to bear on the Government.

In the legislature of the United Kingdom, the Government is, in comparison with other Parliamentary legislatures, in a strong position to have its own way. Any proposal which strengthens that position should be looked at most closely. And the present position in which the Government must take positive action – whether by seeking to extend sittings or to apply the closure or to move an allocation of time order – is not to be lightly replaced by a system that would permit the Government in advance to determine the amount of time available to the Opposition for criticism.

With all its defects and its myths and its illogicalities, the present system of timetabling and the resulting balance of power between Government and Opposition in this matter is probably the best that can be achieved. And any improvement in the quality of debate must be looked for in other directions. 'A large part of a backbencher's power lies in the fact that he can take up time. Deprived of this he is deprived of most of his influence.'[3] So also is this true for the Opposition at large.

1 See H.C. 539 of 1966–67, Q214–5 (Mr R. H. S. Crossman).
2 *Ibid.* Q222 (Mr R. H. S. Crossman); Q337 (Mr Whitelaw).
3 Mr G. Lawson (826 H.C. Deb., col. 369).

CHAPTER TWO

SECOND READING

Erskine May calls this 'the most important stage through which the bill is required to pass; for its whole principle is then at issue, and is affirmed or denied by a vote of the House; though it is not regular on this occasion to discuss, in detail, its several clauses.'[1]

The Minister – as the Member in charge of the bill – moves that the bill be now read a second time. An amendment may be moved, by way of opposing the second reading, to leave out 'now' and add 'upon this day six (or three) months'. Or a Member may put down a reasoned amendment that, usually, 'declines to give a second reading' for stated reasons. In practice the carrying of either type of amendment would mean that the bill would be dropped.

A bill may, instead of being debated on second reading in the House, be referred to a Second Reading Committee; or it may be referred to the Scottish Grand Committee.

Under S.O. No. 66 a motion, of which not less than 10 days' notice has been given, may be made by a Minister that a public bill be referred to a second reading committee; but if at least twenty Members rise in their places and signify their objection, the Speaker declares that the noes have it. A second reading committee reports to the House either that they recommend that the bill ought to be read a second time or that they recommend it ought not.[2] Upon a motion being made for the second reading of a bill reported from a second reading committee, the question thereon is put forthwith. A second reading committee is a standing committee and its size and selection are governed by the same rules.[3]

The Select Committee on Procedure in 1964–65 were directed by the House to consider the expediency of appointing such a committee and proposed a draft standing order for its establishment.[4] For 1965–66 and 1966–67 sessional resolutions governed the experiment and the Standing Order was made in November 1967.[5]

[1] *Op. cit.*, p. 485. The Select Committee on Procedure in 1971 detected 'an increasing tendency for detailed matters contained in the clauses to a Bill, rather than the general principles of the Bill, to be debated on second reading' (H.C. 538 of 1970–71, *Report* para 22).

[2] If they recommend that it ought not, they may state their reasons.

[3] See below, p. 47 *et seq.*

[4] H.C. 149 of 1964–65, para 6.

[5] The making of a Standing Order was also recommended by the Select Committee on Procedure in 1967 (H.C. 539 of 1966–67, *Report* para 20).

During the six sessions from 1965–66 to 1970–71 thirty-three bills were sent to second reading committees.[1] All were non-contentious, many being concerned with law reform. On average over these sessions the second reading committee stage lasted 1¼ hours.

No bill can be sent to a second reading committee unless the principal parties in the House are agreed. When in 1967 Mr Crossman, as Leader of the House, was asked by the Select Committee on Procedure why relatively few bills were being sent to second reading committees, he emphasised first, the necessity for co-operation between the parties; secondly, the need for some non-controversial bills to be taken on the floor of the House because of the greater publicity (he instanced the Royal Assent Bill and the Public Records Bill, both of 1966–67); and thirdly, the use that could be made of morning sittings of the House.[2]

Even if the front benches agree, any twenty Members may prevent the committal. In 1966 the Family Provision Bill was objected to – apparently as a protest against morning sittings.[3] In 1968, the Genocide Bill was objected to perhaps because Members wished to speak on the floor of the House rather than in standing committee for greater publicity.[4] And in 1971 objection was taken to the Friendly Societies Bill.[5]

The evidence submitted to the Select Committee on Procedure 1970–71 by the Second Clerk Assistant and the Clerk of Public Bills reviewing the preceding sessions[6] was not encouraging. They said: 'As a device for saving time upon the Floor of the House these procedures must be regarded as having had only limited success'. The bills committed would 'probably have taken more time if they had been debated in the House during the normal time for public business, i.e. 3.30–10.00 p.m.; but if they had been put down as exempted business after 10.00 p.m. or on a Government Friday (as minor non-contentious bills have often been taken in the past) it is possible that pressure from both sides to avoid sitting late might have resulted in less time being taken'.[7] On that basis the total time saved on the floor of the House during a session is of the order of 5–8 hours.

If more time is to be saved by this device, contentious measures will also have to be sent to second reading committees. It is highly improbable that the Opposition would agree. So it would be necessary to empower Governments to move an ordinary motion for this purpose. At present one factor that militates against more non-controversial business being dealt with upstairs is 'the use that can be made of the Floor of the House by Opposition to prevent Government legislation getting through'[8] or getting

[1] See H.C. 538 of 1970–71, Appendix 1 Annex A; and H.C. 638 of 1970–71.

[2] H.C. 539 of 1966–67, Q187,188; nowadays the House rarely sits in the mornings except on Fridays.

[3] 733 H.C. Deb., col. 44; see H.C. 538 of 1970–71, Q509.

[4] 775 H.C. Deb., col. 38; see H.C. 538 of 1970–71, Q7.

[5] 811 H.C. Deb., col. 1220.

[6] More use was made in 1970–71 of second reading committees than in any previous session, ten bills being so committed.

[7] H.C. 538 of 1970–71, Appendix 1 para 3.

[8] H.C. 538 of 1970–71, Q509 (Mr John Silkin).

through quickly. The central problem is that saving time on the floor means saving Government time; and saved Government time tends to be used for more Government business. So the pendulum swings out a little further at the expense of the Opposition.

These arguments against the further extension of second reading committees are somewhat weakened by the working of the Scottish Grand Committee.

Under Standing Order No. 67, if the Speaker is of opinion that the provisions of any public bill relate exclusively to Scotland, he gives a certificate to that effect. On the order for the second reading, a motion may be made by a Minister that the bill be referred to the Scottish Grand Committee, but, if at least ten Members rise in their places and signify their objection, the Speaker declares that the noes have it. A bill so referred is considered in relation to the principle of the bill and is reported to the House as having been so considered. Then it is ordered to be read a second time upon a future day.[1] When the order for the second reading has been read, a Minister may move that the bill be committed to a Scottish standing committee, unless notice of an amendment to the second reading has been given by at least six Members. If the motion of committal is agreed to, the bill is deemed to have been read a second time and is committed to a Scottish standing committee.

The Scottish Grand Committee consists of all the Members representing Scottish constituencies together with not less than ten nor more than fifteen other members nominated by the Committee of Selection having regard to the approximation of the balance of parties in the committee to that in the whole House.[2]

During the three sessions 1967–68, 1968–69 and 1970–71, twenty-one Government bills related exclusively to Scotland. Of these, fourteen were referred to the Scottish Grand Committee and seven had their second reading on the floor of the House. But of those seven, the proceedings on the Housing (Financial Provisions) (Scotland) Bill 1967–68 were wholly formal, and those on the New Towns (Scotland) Bill 1967–68 and the Rent (Scotland) Bill 1970–71 were almost wholly so. Only on four bills was there a normal second reading debate on the floor: these were on the Social Work (Scotland) Bill 1967–68, the Education (Scotland) Bills 1968–69 and 1970–71, and the Teaching Council (Scotland) Bill 1970–71.

One obvious and important difference between the rules applying to second reading committees and those applying to the Scottish Grand Committee is that all Scottish Members are members of the latter. And there will be few non-Ministerial non-Scottish Members who are likely to feel deprived – or, if they feel deprived, have courage to voice their feelings

[1] In contrast to second reading committees, the Scottish Grand Committee only considers the principle; it makes no recommendation.

[2] S.O. No. 68(2). The general election of 1970 resulted in only 23 Scottish Conservative Members out of a total of 71; by tradition, the Scottish Grand Committee does not divide on the second reading of bills.

– by inability to speak on the second reading of a Scottish bill. Certainly bills of considerable importance may be referred to the Scottish Grand Committee as, for example, was the Housing (Scotland) Bill 1968–69.

The fact that a high proportion of bills affecting Scotland have their second reading outside the Chamber and that this is acceptable both to Scottish Members and to others supports the argument for a greater use of second reading committees. And it is doubtful if any real hardship would be done to Members who were not members of those committees. As the Second Clerk Assistant said to the Select Committee on Procedure in 1971: 'A Second Reading Committee can consist of between 16 and 50 Members. On most bills, you will not find more than 50 Members in the Chamber for a Second Reading'.[1]

To return, however, to the crucial question whether it is desirable or practicable for a Government to be given power, by the use of its majority, to insist on second reading debates taking place in committee on politically contentious bills. Such a power might be abused but the House at large and the Opposition in particular have generally been able successfully to impede Governments who abuse its conventions. The convention could be that, of the Government time saved by the increased use of second reading committees, the Opposition would be enabled to decide how part of that time should be used. And, of course, the second reading of the dozen or so major Government bills in each session would still have to be taken on the floor. As in its origins the use of standing committees was limited to non-contentious matters but, after a few years, had to be extended as pressure on the House increased, so now a further modification seems advisable.[2] This should not offend those who deplore the passing of business from the floor to committees upstairs for it should enable the floor of the House to be used more often as a well-populated grand forum for debate.

The House of Commons in its legislative process, while retaining the same forms for bills, is capable of considerable flexibility in their use.[3] Second reading debates vary from the formal, the cursory and the brief, to extended examination of the principles and sometimes of the details, of Government bills. Table 2.1 shows the number of bills and the number of hours for which they were debated.

More than one-third of bills in these three sessions were thus debated on second reading for less than 2 hours. Nearly one-third were debated for between 5 and 7 hours which is the normal period for policy bills, the debate beginning about 4 p.m. and ending at 10 p.m. With the three exceptions of bills debated for more than 7 hours, the remainder were

[1] H.C. 538 of 1970–71, Q9 (Mr R. D. Barlas).

[2] See evidence of Second Clerk Assistant to the Select Committee on Procedure (H.C. 538 of 1970–71, Q2, 6).

[3] In considering the length of debates, the submission and moving of amendments, and the divisions on second reading on the floor of the House during the sessions of 1967–68, 1968–69, and 1970–71, no regard is paid in what follows to the consideration of bills in second reading committees, or in the Scottish Grand Committee; Consolidated Fund Bills are also disregarded unless the contrary is indicated.

Table 2.1

Session	Number of hours debated									Total number of bills
	0–1	1–2	2–3	3–4	4–5	5–6	6–7	7–8	12–13	
1967–68	12	2	6	7	2	11	7	2	—	49
1968–69	5	6	4	8	4	6	6	—	—	39
1970–71	20	5	6	5	4	9	8	—	1	58
Total number of bills	37	13	16	20	10	26	21	2	1	146

debated for between 2 and 5 hours. Those three exceptions were, in 1967–68, the Coal Industry Bill and the Finance Bill, and, in 1970–71, the Industrial Relations Bill.

In 1967–68, fifteen[1] amendments were put down to seven bills. Of these, twelve were not selected. The three selected were all reasoned amendments moved by front-bench Opposition spokesmen and were pressed to a division. They were to the Gas and Electricity Bill,[2] the Race Relations Bill,[3] and the Revenue (No. 2) Bill.[4] Divisions also took place on the motion for the second reading of nine other bills;[5] six of these were straightforward challenges by the Opposition. Of the other three, the Liberals divided the House on the Commonwealth Immigrants Bill 1967–68 and were joined by Labour and Conservative rebels; only the Liberals voted against the Public Expenditure and Receipts Bill (the Labour left abstaining); and only four Opposition Members (including tellers) voted against the International Monetary Fund Bill. In addition, on two occasions – the Finance Bill and the Transport Bill – the Opposition also divided the House on motions seeking to commit the bills to committees of the whole House.

In 1968–69, four amendments – all reasoned – were put down and were selected. They were to the Customs (Import Deposits) Bill,[6] the Education (Scotland) Bill,[7] the Children and Young Persons Bill,[8] and the House of

[1] This is an abnormally high figure, the result of six amendments being put down to the Commonwealth Immigrants Bill and four being put down to the Prices and Incomes Bill. None of those ten amendments was selected. Amendments tabled by Members not on the Opposition front bench ('unofficial' amendments) are not normally selected on second reading.

[2] 765 H.C. Deb., cols 543–660.

[3] 763 H.C. Deb., cols 53–174.

[4] 758 H.C. Deb., cols 664–786.

[5] Finance Bill 763 H.C. Deb., cols 250–412; Transport Bill 756 H.C. Deb., cols 1281–434; Transport Holding Company Bill 756 H.C. Deb., cols 1635–742; Public Expenditure and Receipts Bill 759 H.C. Deb., cols 245–366; Prices and Incomes Bill 765 H.C. Deb., cols 301–430; International Monetary Fund Bill 767 H.C. Deb., cols 955–1028; Industrial Expansion Bill 757 H.C. Deb., cols 1571–696; British Standard Time Bill 757 H.C. Deb., cols 290–366; Commonwealth Immigrants Bill 759 H.C. Deb., cols 1241–368.

[6] 774 H.C. Deb., cols 749–878.

[7] 776 H.C. Deb., cols 271–384.

[8] 779 H.C. Deb., cols 1176–304.

Commons (Redistribution of Seats) (No. 2) Bill.[1] A division took place on each occasion. On the last named bill and on seven others[2] there were divisions on the motion for the second reading; on the Army Reserve Bill the Opposition abstained and the division was forced by Mr Emrys Hughes and Mr William Baxter supported by Mrs Winifred Ewing; on the Development of Tourism Bill, ten Opposition Members only voted against the motion and on the Immigration Appeals Bill there were twenty-six Opposition dissenters; on the Redundancy Rebates Bill, only the Liberals dissented.

In 1970–71, three amendments – all reasoned – were put down and were selected. They were to the Coal Industry Bill,[3] the Family Income Supplements Bill[4] and the Rating Bill.[5] Each was pressed to a division. An amendment put down to the Housing Bill[6] was not selected. On fourteen other bills there were divisions on the motion for the second reading.[7] Two of these fourteen were unusual. The motion for the second reading of the Atomic Energy Authority Bill[8] was carried by 81 votes to 8; the front benches were agreed on the desirability of the Bill, the minority all being Opposition backbenchers. The motion on the Civil Aviation Bill[9] was carried by 177 votes to 30, the minority being drawn all from the Opposition back benches and mostly from the left-wing of the Labour party. On three occasions the Opposition divided the House on motions to commit the bills to committees of the whole House: on the Coal Industry Bill,[10] the Immigration Bill[11] and the Vehicles Excise Bill.[12] This last Bill was a consolidation measure and the Government moved to commit it to the whole House for the committee stage to be taken at once, immediately after the second reading. Some Opposition members protested at the lateness of the hour – it was then 5 a.m. – and seven voted against the proposal.

In practice, it is very difficult for backbenchers on either side to persuade

[1] 786 H.C. Deb., cols 443–572.

[2] Army Reserve Bill 779 H.C. Deb., cols 1503–18; Development of Tourism Bill 778 H.C. Deb., cols 1940–2054; Finance Bill 783 H.C. Deb., cols 289–416; Immigration Appeals Bill 776 H.C. Deb., cols 489–568; Iron and Steel Bill 783 H.C. Deb., cols 678–798; Redundancy Rebates Bill 776 H.C. Deb., cols 1555–604; Parliament (No. 2) Bill 777 H.C. Deb., cols 43–172.

[3] 807 H.C. Deb., cols 1483–606.

[4] 806 H.C. Deb., cols 217–340.

[5] 811 H.C. Deb., cols 109–92.

[6] 820 H.C. Debs., cols 789–848.

[7] Atomic Energy Authority Bill 808 H.C. Deb., cols 1590–658; Civil Aviation Bill 814 H.C. Deb., cols 1172–282; Civil Aviation (Declaratory Provisions) Bill 807 H.C. Deb., cols 236–366; Education (Milk) Bill 819 H.C. Deb., cols 42–168; Education (Scotland) Bill 806 H.C. Deb., cols 409–540; Finance Bill 816 H.C. Deb., cols 438–570; Immigration Bill 813 H.C. Deb., cols 42–173; Industrial Relations Bill 808 H.C. Deb., cols 961–1076, 1126–250; Industry Bill 810 H.C. Deb., cols 347–462; Investment and Building Grants Bill 816 H.C. Deb., cols 1380–506; Land Commission (Dissolution) Bill 808 H.C. Deb., cols 1383–484; Licensing (Abolition of State Management) Bill 815 H.C. Deb., cols 960–1080; Local Authorities (Qualification of Members) Bill 805 H.C. Deb., cols 684–796; Social Security Bill 816 H.C. Deb., cols 50–162.

[8] See note 7 above.

[9] *Ibid.*

[10] See note 3 above.

[11] See note 7 above.

[12] 812 H.C. Deb., cols 1654–6.

the Speaker to accept a reasoned amendment tabled by them. The result is that unless the Opposition front bench put down a reasoned amendment which they can support, backbenchers are forced to vote for or against the motion for second reading, or to abstain.[1]

A summary of amendments, motions and divisions in second reading debate in the House of Commons is given in Table 2.2.

Table 2.2 SECOND READING DEBATES IN THE HOUSE OF COMMONS

	Number of amendments put down	Number of amendments selected (all divided on)	Number of motions for second reading divided on	Number of divisions on motions to commit bill to committee of whole House
1967–68	15	3	9	2
1968–69	4	4	8	—
1970–71	4	3	14	3
Total	23	10	31	5

Erskine May's statement quoted above that second reading is the most important stage for a bill is a highly formalistic view. As we have seen, in only 31 out of 146 bills were the motions for second reading divided on during the three sessions. By any reckoning other than that of an adverse vote, which in modern political terms is extremely unlikely, second reading is much less important than committee or report. As a means whereby the House makes an impact on Government bills its only value is to present an occasion when for the first time in the House[2] a Member or a group of Members can urge the Minister to accept certain changes which they hope to move in committee; and when the Minister may indicate any parts of the bill which he admits may need revision.

The second reading debate also gives the Opposition an opportunity to state its political objections to the bill or parts of it. And the attendant publicity may enable supporters to rally support to their cause. As a political fanfare the second reading has a useful function for the small number of controversial bills.

[1] See, for example, the debate on second reading of the Prices and Incomes Bill 1967–68 (765 H.C. Deb., cols 301–430, especially cols 385–6).

[2] Members may also urge changes on Ministers informally by correspondence, in personal and party meetings, etc.

CHAPTER THREE

COMMITTEE STAGE IN THE HOUSE OF COMMONS

3.1 GENERAL

Standing Orders require that when a public bill (other than a Consolidated Fund or an Appropriation Bill or a bill confirming a provisional order) has been read a second time, it shall stand committed to a standing committee unless the House otherwise order.[1] A motion to commit a bill to a committee of the whole House or to a select committee or to a joint committee of Lords and Commons may be made by any Member – usually immediately after the bill has been read a second time; it must be decided without amendment or debate and, if negatived, the bill stands committed to a standing committee.[2]

A motion to commit a bill to a standing committee in respect of some of its provisions and to a committee of the whole House in respect of other provisions may be made by the Member in charge of the bill. If the motion is opposed, the Speaker, after permitting, if he thinks fit, a brief explanatory statement from the member who makes and from a member who opposes the motion, shall, without permitting any further debate, put the question thereon.[3] After the second reading of the Finance Bill on 28 April 1971 some Members asked that the limitation of debate to two brief speeches should be reviewed and that the possibility of tabling amendments should be considered.[4] The Leader of the House and the Opposition Chief Whip in their evidence to the Select Committee on Procedure 1970–71 agreed that there could be no objection to a short debate of, say, three-quarters of an hour. But both opposed the possibility of amendments. The Select Committee recommended the adoption of this suggestion,[5] but no action has resulted. If the motion to split the committee stage is negatived, the whole bill is committed to a standing committee[6] (see Table 3.1).

[1] S.O. No. 40(1). Consolidated Fund and Appropriation Bills are committed to a committee of the whole House. Provisional order confirmation bills are referred to the Committee of Selection under S.O. 217 (relating to Private Business).

[2] S.O. No. 40(2)(4). For an example of a failure to move committal to the whole House, see 806 H.C. Deb., cols 340–4.

[3] S.O. No. 40(3).

[4] 816 H.C. Deb., cols 565–70. Present practice is to 'split' the Finance Bill but no other.

[5] H.C. 538 of 1970–71, *Report* para 32, 33 and Q649–52, 838, 864–6, 1060–62.

[6] S.O. No. 40(4); further on Finance Bill, see below, pp. 34–7.

Table 3.1 COMMITTAL OF GOVERNMENT BILLS[1]

	To standing committee	To committee of the whole House	To joint committee	To select committee
1967–68	36	28	10	—
1968–69	35	19	4	1
1970–71	40	37	11	1

In practice the decision on which type of committee a bill should be sent to is taken by the Government. In 1945 the Select Committee on Procedure considered a scheme put forward in a document submitted to the Select Committee by the Labour Government.[2] The scheme was conceived to meet the special circumstances of transition from war to peace and anticipated a heavy programme of legislation. One proposal in the scheme (which was approved by the Select Committee) was that substantially all bills should be referred to standing committees. The scheme envisaged that three classes of bills would be considered in committee of the whole House: those which it might be necessary to pass with great expedition; 'one clause' bills not requiring detailed examination in committee; and bills 'of first-class constitutional importance'.[3] As examples of this third class, the scheme instanced those bills which became the Parliament Act 1911 and the Statute of Westminster 1931.[4] The two examples indicate a very limited group and Mr Herbert Morrison, then Lord President of the Council and Leader of the House of Commons, made clear that it did not necessarily include bills which might cause 'acute political controversy'. He said he would not accept the doctrine that 'solely because a Bill is big and controversial, it must be kept downstairs'.[5]

Broadly the ideas behind the scheme of 1945 have been adopted. As we shall see[6] bills debated on the floor of the House include many on which the

[1] This table includes 10 Consolidated Fund and Appropriation Bills. The table contains some double counting. All the bills sent to the Joint Committee (for consolidation, etc., bills) were subsequently committeed to committees of the whole House. The select committee in 1968–69 was for the Transport (London) Bill which was subsequently sent to a standing committee. The Select Committee in 1970–71 was for the Armed Forces Bill which was subsequently sent to a committee of the whole House. In 1967–68 the Finance Bill went first to a standing committee and was then re-committed to the whole House. In 1968–69 and 1970–71 the Finance Bill was split, some clauses going to a standing committee and some to a committee of the whole House. The bill is therefore included under both headings in all the sessions.

[2] This elliptical form of words is necessary because the document had been prepared by a Committee under the War Cabinet of the Coalition Government but not approved by that Cabinet. The Labour Government was not committed to it in detail but thought its conclusions 'well worthy of the consideration of the Select Committee as a basis of discussion' (H.C. 9–I of 1945–46, Q84 (Mr H. Morrison)).

[3] H.C. 9–I of 1945–46, paras 5–7 and Appendix.

[4] H.C. 9–I of 1945–46, Appendix para 5.

[5] *Ibid.*, Q126, 127.

[6] See below, p. 45.

proceedings are formal or very brief; but also include a few bills of great importance which are debated at length; and some which need to be passed with great expedition such as the Commonwealth Immigrants Bill 1967–68 and the Northern Ireland Bill 1971–72. 'Big and controversial' bills are usually sent to standing committees: for example in 1967–68 the Transport Bill and the Prices and Income Bill; in 1968–69 the Post Office Bill; in 1970–71 the Immigration Bill; in 1971–72 the Local Government Bill and the Housing Finance Bill. But standing committees deal also with many bills relatively unimportant in subject matter and requiring little examination.

Two obvious differences between committee stage on the floor of the House and upstairs are that the likelihood of publicity in the press and elsewhere is far greater if the bill is debated on the floor; and that the possibility of Government defeat on amendments is far greater in the smaller standing committee where the Government may have a majority of only one or two or three.[1]

The possibility of Government defeat in committee of the whole House is extremely remote[2] unless the Government majority is very small. But defeats in standing committee do occur for a variety of reasons, one of which is the more vulnerable and exposed position of Ministers confronted directly and closely by those on the opposite benches; as such defeats are regarded as politically less significant, backbenchers are much less reluctant to rebel against their front bench. And so defeats can be brought about by the defection of only one or two members in the small standing committees of recent times.

But for the Government, the principal advantage of sending bills upstairs to standing committees is that time is saved on the floor of the House. The Parliamentary time-table leaves the Government a limited number of days on which to deal with the legislative programme. In 1966–67, 1967–68 and 1968–69, Government legislation took 62·6, 50 and 58·5 per cent, respectively, of the time of each session on the floor of the House.[3] Whether or not the proportion of the time of the House spent on public bills is 'about right' – a rather meaningless view held by the Leader of the House, the Opposition Chief Whip, and the Select Committee on Procedure in 1967[4] – the number of hours available to the Government is limited and can be extended only by longer sittings or shorter holidays, or curtailment of the time spent on other matters. And although the Government controls the timetable and has been known from time to time to deprive private members of some of the time usually allotted to them, it

[1] See below, p. 48. For recent figures relating to motions seeking to keep bills on the floor, see above, pp. 28–30.

[2] At the end of the protracted proceedings in committee of the whole House on the Parliament (No. 2) Bill in 1969, a closure motion, moved by the Government Chief Whip, failed to attract 100 votes in the majority and failed (781 H.C. Deb., col. 945).

[3] The percentages are derived from Addendum to Annex D of Appendix I of Second Report from the Select Committee on Procedure (H.C. 538 of 1970–71, p. 267).

[4] H.C. 539 of 1966–67, *Report* paras 4, 5, Q186, 279.

cannot easily override the rights of the Opposition to insist on proper debate. All the devices for curtailment of debate may be used but they too operate within a conventional frame which cannot be broken without producing a state of affairs in which Parliamentary Government would become almost impossible.

The pressure of events and the shortness of time, then, have led to the great present-day use of standing committees. But standing committees are also more convenient to the Opposition because, apart from the greater possibility of defeating the Government, their smallness and their intimacy make detailed criticism easier and more compelling. This combination of advantage to the Government in time-saving on the floor and of advantage to the Opposition in making criticism more effective results in much the greater part of the committee work being taken upstairs.[1]

Disagreements may arise between Government and Opposition on the decision of the Government to take the bill on the floor of the House or to send it upstairs. So also disagreements may arise over the Government's proposal to split a bill (in present practice, the Finance Bill) and over the particular clauses which are to be sent upstairs or kept on the floor. Such disagreements may begin as arguments between the Government and the Opposition Whips and, if they cannot resolve the dispute, senior Ministers will become involved. The occasions when the House has been divided on a motion by the Opposition to commit the bill to the whole House are rare.[2] And so far the Whips have always been able to agree on the splitting of the Finance Bill.[3]

3.1.1 *Finance bills*

Debates during the committee stage on the Finance Bill range widely and cover a variety of matters from the smallest and most technical to general issues of economic policy. Discussion of reforming the procedure has turned on the wisdom or unwisdom of committing the Bill, in whole or in part, to a standing committee.

The suggestion that a division should be made between matters of 'major importance', which should be taken on the floor, and 'detailed provisions', which could be sent to a standing committee, was made by Mr R. A. Butler, then Leader of the House, to the Select Committee on Procedure in 1958.[4] The distinction between budgetary and administrative clauses was thought by the Treasury not to be practicable and likely to result in a normal year in five-sixths of the Bill remaining on the floor. But that Select Committee suggested that the division might take place if it followed the different 'parts' of the Bill, and recommended the experiment of sending a part or parts to a standing committee.[5] Nothing was then done but the Select Committee on Procedure examined the matter again

[1] The number of bills dealt with in committee of the whole House gives a false impression because so many such bills are dealt with only formally. See below, p. 45.

[2] See above, pp. 28–30.

[3] See H.C. 538 of 1970–71, paras 32, 33.

[4] H.C. 92–I of 1958–59, Appendix 4 para 4.

[5] *Ibid., Report* para 9.

in 1962–63,[1] in 1964–65,[2] and in 1966–67.[3] On that last occasion, the Select Committee chose, or was forced, to avoid a conclusion in these words:

> 'Your Committee have set out the possible courses which have been put to them. They believe that procedural changes will be more successful if undertaken with the general approval of the House. They have therefore not attempted to be dogmatic. Some members strongly believe that the Bill should be sent to a Standing Committee; others think that division of the Bill is practicable.'[4]

That report was made in March 1967. On 14 November of that year, Mr Crossman, as Leader of the House, announced the intention of the Government to send the whole of the Finance Bill of that session to a standing committee, rejecting the alternative proposal of dividing the Bill and retaining some parts or clauses for consideration by the whole House.[5] The proposal was fully debated on a motion to amend Standing Order No. 40 on 6 December 1967. Mr Crossman put forward as his first argument in favour of the change that 'during the 1950s and 1960s the average time spent on the Finance Bill has just about doubled . . . and this has upset the balance of our timetable and produced the chronic annual log jam which causes a string of all-night or late-night sittings'.[6] For the Opposition, Mr Macleod was convinced that 'the Finance Bill should have its Committee stage on the Floor of the House'.[7] Mr Selwyn Lloyd drew a distinction: 'I have said repeatedly that I think it might be possible to send a section of a Finance Bill dealing with very technical tax measures to a Standing Committee, but what I object to is sending the whole Bill there'.[8] The motion was carried by 204 votes to 136.[9] It was clear that no agreement for a voluntary timetable was likely.

On 24 April 1968, the Finance Bill was read a second time and the motion that it be committed to a committee of the whole House, moved by the Opposition, was defeated by 291 votes to 223. So, pursuant to standing orders, it was sent to a standing committee.[10]

Progress in standing committee was so slow that the proceedings were guillotined. On 11 June 1968, the bill was recommitted to the whole House to 'give an opportunity to hon. Members who were not members of the Committee upstairs to raise points or move amendments on the Floor of the House'.[11]

In 1968–69, the procedure was modified. As introduced, the Finance Bill of that year comprised fifty-three clauses and twenty-one schedules.

1 H.C. 190 of 1962–63.
2 H.C. 276 of 1964–65.
3 H.C. 382 of 1966–67.
4 *Ibid., Report* para 21.
5 745 H.C. Deb., cols 249–51.
6 755 H.C. Deb., col. 1447.
7 *Ibid.*, col. 1453; and col. 1461.
8 *Ibid.*, col. 1513.
9 *Ibid.*, col. 1527–30.
10 763 H.C. Deb., cols 407–12; for an account of the technical difficulties which had to be overcome see D. Scott 'The Finance Bill of 1968 in Standing Committee' in 37 *The Table* 75.
11 766 H.C. Deb., cols 43–5.

The Government moved that clauses 7, 8, 36, 38, 43 and 44 and schedule 6 be committed to a committee of the whole House; that the remainder be committed to a standing committee; and that on report the whole bill be treated as if the bill had been reported from the Standing Committee. The motion was agreed to on a division by 261 votes to 17, the minority consisting of nine Liberal members (who also supplied the tellers) and eight Conservative members.[1] In 1969–70, the same procedure was ordered to be followed, this time without a division, but because of the prorogation and dissolution, the Standing Committee was discharged and the whole bill taken on the floor of the House.[2]

In 1970–71 the order made was that clauses 6, 7, 8, 10, 22, 30 and 49 and any new clause relating to purchase tax be committed to a committee of the whole House. There was some discussion about the limitations placed on debate on the question of committal.[3] That discussion took place on 28 April 1971. A few days later when giving evidence to the Select Committee on Procedure, the Leader of the House (Mr Whitelaw) suggested that the debate on committal when a bill was to be split could be extended to three-quarters of an hour;[4] and the Opposition Chief Whip (Mr Mellish) supported the proposal.[5]

The present practice is for the splitting of the Finance Bill to be settled through the usual channels. And the effect of this has been that the Opposition chooses which clauses shall be taken on the floor of the House. Obviously this effect may not always follow, for the Government spokesmen might, for various reasons, dispute the choice. But so far the procedure introduced in 1968–69 has worked well both in its formal and in its informal parts. The practice was to have, as Mr Macleod said, 'what amounts to four economic Supply days on the Floor of the House followed by a discussion in a small and very knowledgeable Committee before returning to Report'.[6]

In 1970–71, for example, the debate on the floor took place on 4 days in May 1971 for a total of just over 26 hours. During that period there were thirteen debates on the chosen clauses, six of which were on Opposition amendments or new clauses, five on clauses stand part and two on amendments moved by Government backbenchers.[7] The debates were on the regulator, surtax rates, corporation tax, the repeal of aggre-

[1] 783 H.C. Deb., cols 405–16. This followed heated debates because an adequate number of copies of the bill was not available; see *ibid.*, cols 266–74, 278–81.

[2] 801 H.C. Deb., cols 352, 1722.

[3] 816 H.C. Deb., cols 565–70.

[4] H.C. 538 of 1970–71, Q649.

[5] *Ibid.*, Q864. It is doubtful, however, whether it would be practicable to allow amendments to be moved to the motion for committal: *ibid.*, Q1060 (Mr K. R. Mackenzie).

[6] Finance Bill 1968–69 Standing Committee F, col. 870. This was said at the end of the Standing Committee debates on the Finance Bill 1968–69 when, even by House of Commons standards, the expressions of thanks to all and of satisfaction by all, were extreme. Certainly Mr Macleod came to accept the value of sending parts of the bill upstairs.

[7] 817 H.C. Deb., cols 216–336, 395–518, 1085–229, 1557–654.

gation provisions for parent and child, the unified system of income tax, the abolition of charge to capital gains tax on death, and an Opposition new clause on rates of purchase tax. In 1971–72 the procedure and practice continued but debates on the floor were taken on 6 (not 4) days and the time totalled 44 hours.[1]

3.1.2 *Consolidation bills*

In every session a select committee of twelve Members is appointed by the House of Commons[2] to join with a committee of twelve peers appointed by the Lords to be the Joint Committee on Consolidation, etc., Bills and to consider consolidation bills; statute law revision bills; bills prepared pursuant to the Consolidation of Enactments (Procedure) Act 1949; bills to consolidate enactments with amendments to give effect to recommendations made by one or both of the Law Commissions; and bills prepared by one or both of the Law Commissions to promote the reform of the law by the repeal of certain enactments which are no longer of practical utility.

Although all bills sent to the Joint Committee are also considered in committees of the whole House, very little time is spent on them at any stage in the House. It is usual for these bills to be introduced first in the House of Lords, as were all twenty-five in Table 3.1 above.

3.1.3 *Proceedings in committee*

'The function of a committee on a bill', says Erskine May, 'is to go through the text of the bill clause by clause and, if necessary, word by word, with a view to making such amendments in it as may seem likely to render it more generally acceptable'.[3] There are two difficulties in this formulation. The first is that it conceals the fact that each clause and each schedule must be put to the committee for its approval whether or not any amendment to the clause or schedule has been moved. The debates on clause stand part are a special characteristic of Commons' procedure in the sense that they are not logically necessary. If detailed examination of a bill is thought desirable, then the power to move amendments is almost an inevitable corollary. But it does not follow that each clause should be debatable. This is not to say that the debates on clause stand part are undesirable but only to notice that they take place, are an important part of the procedure, and are not part of Erskine May's formulation.

The second difficulty is the assumption that the purpose of going through the text of a bill is to make amendments that will render the bill more generally acceptable. This confuses a number of different matters. Amendments may have one or more of a great variety of purposes. Whether moved by the Opposition or by a Government backbencher, an amendment may be intended to cause political mischief, to embarrass the Government, to discover what are the Government's real intentions and whether (in

[1] 835 H.C. Deb., cols 770–892; 836, cols 1146–275, 1328–513, 1580–692; 837, cols 105–80, 246–488, 532–649.

[2] S.O. No. 87A.

[3] *Op. cit.*, p. 494.

particular) they include one or more specific possibilities, to placate interests outside Parliament who are angered by the bill, to make positive improvements in the bill the better to effect its purposes, to set out alternative proposals, to initiate a debate on some general principle of great or small importance, to ascertain from the Government the meaning of a clause or sub-section or to obtain assurances on how they will be operated, to correct grammatical errors or to improve the draftsmanship of the bill. If moved by the Government, the purpose of an amendment is most likely to be to correct a drafting error or to make minor consequential changes, to record agreements made with outside bodies which were uncompleted when the bill was introduced, to introduce new matter, or occasionally to meet a criticism made by a Member either during the second reading debate or at an earlier part of the committee stage, or informally.

Not all of these purposes, if fulfilled, are likely to make the bill 'more generally acceptable'. Apart from the trivialities of minor errors, the occasions of an amendment falling within that phrase are when an Opposition amendment is accepted by the Government or when a Government amendment goes some way to meet an objection. This of course, may, at the same time, make the bill less acceptable to some of the Government supporters. This is not to say that committee debates seldom, if ever, result in the improvement of a bill. It is to say, however, that very many amendments are not put forward with that purpose, and of those that are, not all have that effect.

More importantly, much of what takes place during committee on a controversial bill is an extension and an application of the general critical function of the House and there is little or no intention or expectation of changing the bill. The purpose of many Opposition amendments is not to make the bill more generally acceptable but to make the Government less generally acceptable.

This great variety of functions that a committee may perform reflects also the great differences between the activities of different committees. When several standing committees are sitting at the same time, an observer who moves from one room to another may pass at once from a crowded and heated political debate on some major social problem where tempers are short, Opposition Members obstructive and Ministers intransigent, to a quiet, highly technical discussion conducted by ten or a dozen Members, many of whom, at any point of time, seem not to be wholly absorbed in the proceedings. In mood, in spirit and in purpose, these two sorts of activity are very far apart.

The business of conducting a bill through committee as the Member-in-charge requires a Minister to have a detailed understanding of the provisions of the bill. He must know not only the purpose of each clause and its relation to other clauses and the bill as a whole, but also why the draftsman has used certain words or phrases. Sometimes a Minister's understanding of legislative language is not complete and he is obliged to say that he is advised that the words used and not other words are necessary to achieve the purpose sought. It follows that when amendments are tabled the Ministers must be carefully briefed as to their meaning, their purpose, and their effect. He must know what he can accept either with profit or at least without loss, what he can give way on and to what extent, what he must resist to the end.

For the performance of all these functions, the Minister is advised and instructed by his department. His relationship with his back-bench supporters in committee is of less importance. He wishes, of course, to carry them with him and he hopes to be able to rely on them to support him with their vote in divisions. When the bill is taken on the floor of the House, the relationship is no different from that of a Minister making a statement of general policy on behalf of the Government on any non-legislative matter. If the party machinery has worked well, Members who are interested will have argued the general issues in party groups or, if the issue is important and central to the party's policy, more generally, even perhaps at party conferences. Members may have served on select committees which were concerned with the issue. Or they may, for constituency or other reasons, be wholly familiar with it and need no help from their Minister. And, in the case of standing committees, as we shall see, they may have been nominated for membership of the committee because of the positive help they can give the Minister from the back benches.

At the same time, Members of Parliament are not by nature subservient. Their loyalty to their party may make them hesitate at length before they vote against their front bench in committee, as in the House. And, more often than not, their hesitation will end in their continuing to support their leaders. But this does not mean, when they are Government supporters, that they will speak only when asked to by the Whips[1] or that they will refrain from moving amendments that may cause the Government some embarrassment.[2]

The number of speeches made and amendments moved by Ministers, Government backbenchers and Opposition Members in committee in 1967–68 are shown in Table 3.2. The chief interest in these figures is the indication given of the contribution made by Government backbenchers. On average, in 1967–68, given the state of the parties, the membership of standing committees (and they dominate these figures) was made up of 10 per cent Ministers, 45 per cent Government backbenchers[3] and 45 per cent Opposition members. Although, therefore, the proportion of speeches made by Government backbenchers was appreciably lower than

[1] For an example of an influential Government backbencher, see Mr Onslow in Civil Aviation Bill 1970–71 Standing Committee A; see below, p. 109.

[2] For an example of a Government backbencher fighting a lone battle against his front bench, see Mr Farr in Water Resources Bill 1970–71, Standing Committee D; see below, p. 107.

[3] I have counted the usually silent whip as a backbencher although he is technically a Minister.

Table 3.2

Speeches made by	Ministers CWH	Ministers Standing cttee	Government backbenchers CWH	Government backbenchers Standing cttee	Opposition members CWH	Opposition members Standing cttee	Total
A Number of speeches*	99	2245	156	1245	261	3813	7819
B Total*	2344		1401		4074		7819
C Percentages	30·0		17·9		52·1		100
D Number of speeches moving amendments (including new clauses)	6	433	13	217	55	1437	2161
E Total	439		230		1492		2161
F Percentages	20·3		10·7		69·0		100
G Grand total (B+E)	2783		1631		5566		9980
H Percentages	28·0		16·3		55·7		100

* These two lines do not include speeches made while moving amendments or new clauses (these are included in lines D and E); nor formal short speeches by movers at the conclusion of the debate; nor short interjections nor speeches on sittings motions, or on procedural disputes. They do include speeches made on clause stand part.

the proportion of their membership, it was not inconsiderable and certainly does not justify the general impression often given of an inert bale of lobby fodder. Occasionally, special reasons may increase their participation. When the guillotine is on, speechmaking by Government backbenchers encroaches more on the time of the Opposition than on that of the Government; so Government backbenchers are more likely to speak. Again, some Government backbenchers on some bills, because they differ from the policy of the Government, will be more vocal than they otherwise would have been. The overall percentage participation of Government backbenchers shown in the table is 16·3. But on the Prices and Incomes Bill it was 22·9 per cent and on the Race Relations Bill it was 26·8 per cent. On both these bills there was an active and rebellious group of Government backbenchers.

The extent to which the Minister in charge of a bill, as Minister, will seek to organise his party supporters in standing committee[1] varies greatly from Minister to Minister and from bill to bill. On a contentious and complicated measure, the Minister may call regular meetings to explain the purposes of the different parts of the bill and the way in which he intends to deal with it in committee. And then the opportunity will arise for members to give their views. But this suggests a degree of formality of proceeding which is misleading. Even when such meetings occur, members will approach the Minister informally to give him information, to make suggestions, to urge particular courses of action. Certainly any impression of a tightly knit group of backbenchers meeting, with the Minister, to decide how the bill shall be handled would be false. Apart from the fact that a much looser association normally governs the relationship between Ministers and backbenchers in their ordinary dealings in the House, whether on legislation or other matters, the Minister has a duty to his department and to the Government which transcends his obligation to his party supporters. He is first a Minister and only secondly one of his party's front-bench spokesmen. In this sense the line that separates Ministers from all other Members of Parliament is more strongly drawn than the line that separates the Government side of the House from the Opposition side. Being a member of the Government cuts a Minister off from his party colleagues because, however accountable he may be to his colleagues and to the House, his primary responsibilities are to the Executive arm. In legal terms he is one of Her Majesty's Ministers and not a servant of the House; and this reflects his constitutional and political position also.[2]

Ministers do not, therefore, regard the organising of their supporters in a standing committee as a primary or even as a particularly important part of their duties. To ensure support there is seldom any need to do so; to try to force total unanimity when this does not exist would be folly. Too much emphasis has been placed by too many commentators on the pressures brought to bear on Members of Parliament by the Whips' Office to toe the party line. Of course there are important occasions when the pressures are strong. But the emphasis distorts the general pattern of relationships within a party. Members begin by sharing common beliefs with their party colleagues and it is this, combined with party loyalty, which makes for agreement far more than consideration of the consequences of disagreement.

It is common knowledge that Government backbenchers are not encouraged by whips to take much part in debate because by so doing they take time and it is generally the Government who are anxious to make

[1] If the Committee stage is being taken on the floor of the House and the bill is important, the Minister will consult and take advice from such non-Ministerial colleagues as he chooses.

[2] 'I do not think it takes many Ministers very long to make what is the most important discovery one ever makes in politics; this is that the most important distinction in our whole national political system is the distinction between the Government and the non-Government.' Sir Edward Boyle, *Public Administration*, vol. 43, p. 255 (1965).

progress. 'One of the things', Mrs Shirley Williams has said, 'which makes Parliament worthwhile is that occasionally the vow of silence which Government backbenchers always seem to have to take is broken to give vent to an independent and often extremely valuable opinion'. And the Chairman, stepping out of his rôle, added 'Hear, hear'.[1]

Government backbenchers are not above (or below) complaining about their occasional ill-treatment, as they see it.

> 'The Committee will appreciate that the best one can hope for in putting forward an Amendment, apart from those rare occasions when Ministers accept Amendments – and these Amendments usually come from the Opposition rather than from our side – is an undertaking from the Minister that he will look at the matter again. It is a fact that most of the Amendments which are accepted come from the Opposition for some reason or other. . . . I thought I asked fairly simple questions. The Opposition received answers to complicated questions, whereas I received no answers at all.'[2]

The need to organise is more obvious when in Opposition. There are no departmental advisers to provide information and briefing. On important bills, the affected interests outside Parliament will, as we have seen, be anxious to help in the hope of bringing further pressure to bear on the Government to accept amendments. And if they are powerful they will be well and expertly staffed and will have or will engage lawyers to draft amendments so that all Opposition members need do, if they are so minded, is to sign the amendment provided and hand it in to the Public Bill Office. At times, this servicing by professionals and experts comes close in its drafting and in its briefing to the service provided for the Minister by his department.[3]

Sometimes those who lead for the Opposition will set up working parties of their own drawn from outside affected interests and also draw on teams of lawyers from outside Parliament. These groups may meet regularly to prepare the Opposition case in detail against the bill when it is in committee. And in this way the Opposition provides its own civil service, helped by research departments at party headquarters.

So also those leading for the Opposition may regularly meet with their supporters on a standing committee, or specially selected group if the bill is committed to the whole House, and may seek to divide amongst them the task of moving amendments. But, again, the danger in writing of all these arrangements is to overstate the case. Not infrequently, opposition to a bill is hardly organised at all but carried almost entirely by one or two front-bench spokesmen, with others making back-up speeches when they choose. The organisation, if that is not too strong a word, is then highly informal

[1] National Insurance Bill 1970–71 Standing Committee G, col. 106.

[2] Medicines Bill 1967–68 Standing Committee D, cols 743–4 (Mr Ogden).

[3] A strong case can be made out for saying that the efficient working of Parliament requires that the Opposition is properly serviced out of public funds.

and haphazard. In addition, Opposition backbenchers frequently engage in their own individual activities and put down amendments without, necessarily, informing their front bench.[1]

How far any arrangements are made depends on the nature of the bill, its size and complexity, how far it is a measure in its essentials agreed to by Government and Opposition, and on the personal approach and tactics of those on the Opposition front bench in committee.

Analysis of speeches made on the Town and Country Planning Bill 1967–68 show how heavy a burden was carried by Opposition front-benchers. Four hundred and fifty-three speeches were made by two Members (Mr Graham Page and Colonel Allason) and two other Members (Mr Clegg and Mr Murton) made 112 – out of a total of 630 Opposition speeches. The other four Opposition Members thus spoke only sixty-five times in all.[2] This does not suggest more than a very partial sharing of duties. Yet the opposition to this bill was much more highly organised behind the scenes than is common. The disproportionate amount of work carried by a minority of Opposition Members may be explained on the ground that this is the most efficient way to oppose. The fact is that, on most bills in standing committee, between a quarter and a half of the Opposition Members have no particular interest in the matter before them and do not wish to be involved in more work than is absolutely necessary. At least as many letters get written and speeches (for other occasions) prepared on the Opposition back benches during the long hours in standing committee as on Government back benches. And at any time more Opposition Members than Government Members are likely to be absent from the committee room (though within hailing distance). It is not the Opposition that has to keep a quorum nor maintain its majority. The number of willing hands on the Opposition back benches is therefore considerably diminished. And there is no doubt also a feeling that those who have attained the rank of Opposition front-bench spokesmen might as well pay the price of their ambition by doing most of the work. And these spokesmen may wish to do so for one way to preferment within the party and so, anon, to Ministerial office itself is evidence of active service on the front bench in committee rooms. So, many backbenchers let the front bench do the bulk of the work. And for much of the time the conflict, especially in standing committee, is between two or three champions on each side with the rank and file participating from time to time but in a somewhat desultory, haphazard and unorganised way.

The job of the Minister in charge of a bill in committee, assisted by the committee Whip, is to ensure that it is reported to the House with all its principles and the great mass of its details preserved and, according to the length and complexity of the bill and the extent to which it is contentious,

[1] 'I happened to hear our Chief Whip say to some of his hon. friends that he did not want anyone to take part in the discussion of my amendment' (Mr Arthur Lewis, Industrial Relations Bill 1970–71, 809 H.C. Deb., col. 620).

[2] These figures include speeches made while moving amendments or new clauses.

with reasonable speed. The Government's timetable allows for accidents but if several of its bills are kept longer in committee than had been allowed for, difficulties will begin to arise and the whole programme will be threatened with disruption.

What the Opposition seeks to achieve is more various depending on its attitude not only to the bill itself but also to the Government generally. It follows that the Opposition may be seeking to achieve different objects on different days, at different stages of the bill, on different clauses. And the unexpected often happens. An amendment no bigger than a man's hand may suddenly be used to twist the Government's arm. The personal attitude, real or imagined, of a Minister or an Opposition spokesman may antagonise the other side to such an extent that progress on the bill is effectively ended for a time. If it appears, rightly or wrongly, that the Minister or junior Minister has a brief that he imperfectly understands, perhaps because, through no fault of his own, he has to deal with a subject usually entrusted to others of his colleagues, tempers on the Opposition side may become a little short.[1]

More important than any of these to the progress of a bill, to the attitude of Government to Opposition and Opposition to Government, are political events that may be wholly irrelevant to the subject-matter of the bill. Even a bill supported by both sides of the committee may give rise to angry debates or to obstruction if, for some reason, perhaps in the field of foreign policy or economic affairs, the political atmosphere in the House and outside suddenly thickens and the political fight sharpens. Members on each side begin to show personal distaste for those on the other and the surface courtesy which helps the House to go about its business disappears. Then bills that would otherwise have followed a moderately peaceful or moderately contentious course in committee become the occasion for acrimony and anger. And little progress is made. Even procedural changes, if they appear to be attempts to push Government business through at an unwanted pace, may give rise to obstruction in order to defeat that purpose – as happened in response to morning sittings. On other occasions debate on uncontentious bills may be prolonged to make it more difficult for the Government to make progress on some other, strongly opposed, measure. This took place when the Industrial Relations Bill 1970–71 and the European Communities Bill 1971–72 were before the House.

3.2 COMMITTEE OF THE WHOLE HOUSE

The length of debate in committee reflects the importance of the measure in the eyes of the parties. The pattern for three recent sessions is shown in Table 3.3. Those not debated included nine Consolidated Fund and Appropriation bills; and seven consolidation bills which had been to the

[1] E.g. during some of the debates on the Hovercraft Bill 1967–68 Standing Committee D, cols 53, 62, 65, 77, 85.

Joint Committee. The remaining ten bills were financial measures such as those changing the borrowing powers of public corporation or national insurance contributions and benefits or fixing fees;[1] or concerning the constitution of overseas territories[2] or foreign relations;[3] or which barely admitted of amendment.[4]

Into similar categories fall bills that were debated for less than an hour (often for a few minutes only). Seventeen of these were consolidation bills. The other eight included four financial bills;[5] two constitutional bills for overseas territories;[6] the Education (Handicapped Children) Bill 1970–71 which had been promoted by the previous Government; and Mr Speaker King's Retirement Bill 1970–71.

Table 3.3 NUMBER OF GOVERNMENT BILLS SHOWING TIME SPENT IN COMMITTEE OF THE WHOLE HOUSE

	Not debated	Time debated, hr					Total
		<1	1–3	3–8	8–32	>32	
1967–68	7	9	2	6	4	—	28
1968–69	4	6	3	1	4	1	19
1970–71	15	10	4	4	3	1	37
Total	26	25	9	11	11	2	84

Those bills which were examined at some length by the committee of the whole House are of a quite different order. The bill most debated in 1968–69 was the Parliament (No. 2) Bill (more than 87 hours). Both the subject matter and the contentious nature (within as well as between the parties) of this bill prevented the Government from sending it to a standing committee. The Industrial Relations Bill 1970–71 was kept on the floor of the House for tactical reasons. Also, since compromise and concession were improbable, the Government probably saved time by fighting it through on the floor.[7]

Bills debated for periods between 8 and 32 hours during these three

[1] Air Corporations Bills 1967–68 and 1970–71; National Insurance Bill 1968–69; Medicines Bill 1970–71.

[2] Swaziland Independence Bill 1967–68; Anguilla Bill 1970–71.

[3] Diplomatic and other Privileges Bill 1970–71; Hijacking Bill 1970–1.

[4] Town and Country Planning (London) (Indemnity) Bill 1970–71; Redemption of Standard Securities (Scotland) Bill 1970–71.

[5] International Monetary Fund Bill 1967–68; Miscellaneous Financial Provisions Bill 1968–69; Consolidated Fund (No. 2) Bill 1970–71; Harbours (Amendment) Bill 1970–71.

[6] Tanzania Bill 1968–69; Fiji Bill 1970–71.

[7] This is also true of the European Communities Bill 1971–72 but its subject-matter also would have been sufficient for it to have been kept on the floor; and possible partly splits can be more easily dealt with on the floor.

sessions included the Finance Bills 1968–69 and 1970–71, the Representation of the People Bill 1968–69, and the Customs Duties (Dumping and Subsidies) Amendment Bill 1967–68, all of which were debated for between 20 and 30 hours. Others were the House of Commons (Redistribution of Seats) (No. 2) Bill 1968–69, the Finance Bill 1967–68, the Commonwealth Immigrants Bill 1967–68, the Coal Industry Bill 1967–68 and the Family Income Supplements Bill 1970–71, all debated for more than 10 and less than 20 hours. The Public Expenditure and Receipts Bill 1967–68 and the Housing Bill 1970–71 were debated for between 8 and 10 hours. Eight of these eleven bills were primarily financial;[1] and three were broadly constitutional.

There remain the twenty bills which were debated for periods of 1 hour or more and less than 8 hours. Fourteen of these were broadly financial.[2] Three were Expiring Laws Continuance Bills; and the remaining three were the Mauritius Independence Bill 1967–68, the Atomic Energy Authority Bill 1970–71 and the Armed Forces Bill 1970–71.

Thus of the eighty-four bills considered during these three sessions by committees of the whole House, fifty-one were either not debated or debated for less than an hour. Of these bills, twenty-five were consolidation bills, nine Consolidated Fund bills, seven of a financial character, six affected overseas territories and four were unclassifiable by subject matter. Of the thirteen bills discussed for more than 8 hours, two[3] were of the greatest importance, eight were primarily financial, and two[4] were of general constitutional significance. One was kept on the floor because the Government wished it to be passed very quickly.[5]

The present pattern, imposed by the decision of Governments to take the committee stage of certain bills on the floor of the House, is reasonably consistent and clear. In the majority of cases, the decision is one of convenience which results in many bills being disposed of quickly and with little or no expenditure of Parliamentary time. Simple or popular financial measures, some important, some not, can be moved through an acquiescent House at speed. The device of the joint committee obviates any need to have any further committee stage of more than the most perfunctory kind for consolidation bills. There remain a few measures which either because their nature (for example, affecting the structure of Parliament) demands that all

[1] This includes the Coal Industry Bill 1967–68 and the Housing Bill 1970–71.

[2] Two Family Allowances and National Insurance Bills 1967–68; Overseas Aid Bill 1967–68; Gas and Electricity Bill 1967–68; Transport Holding Company Bill 1967–68; Revenue Bill 1967–68; Redundancy Rebates Bill 1968–69; Sea Fisheries Bill 1968–69; New Towns Bill 1968–69; Consolidated Fund Bill 1970–71; Income and Corporation Taxes (No. 2) Bill 1970–71; International Monetary Fund Bill 1970–71; National Insurance Bill 1970–71; Rolls-Royce (Purchase) Bill 1970–71. The debating of the Consolidated Fund Bill 1970–71 was an attempt to break with tradition and consisted largely of points of order and chairman's rulings (811 H.C. Deb., cols 1773–808).

[3] Parliament (No. 2) Bill 1968–69 and Industrial Relations Bill 1970–71.

[4] Representation of the People Bill 1968–69; House of Commons (Redistribution of Seats) (No. 2) Bill 1968–69.

[5] Commonwealth Immigrants Bill 1967–68.

Members shall be able to participate or because, tactically, the Government wishes to fight them through on the floor, are retained in the whole House.

To the two major categories often spoken of as particularly suitable for debate in committee of the whole House – 'one-clause' bills and those of first-class constitutional importance – are then to be added minor financial measures. And the total number of bills sent to committee of the whole House is, as we have seen, much inflated by the large number of bills there committed with no intention that debate will ensue.

3.3 STANDING COMMITTEES

'As many standing committees shall be appointed as may be necessary for the consideration of bills or other business committed or referred to a standing committee'.[1]

Standing committees are singularly illnamed. It would be more accurate to call them *ad hoc* committees. Each committee is formed separately for each bill so although we may read that Standing Committee A in 1970–71 'considered 6 Bills and held 44 sittings',[2] the reality is that six different groups of Members sitting under four different chairmen were designated successively as Standing Committee A. In 1967–68, eight standing committees were necessary; in 1968–69, seven; and in 1970–71, eight. In addition, in each of these sessions, two Scottish standing committees were necessary to examine Scottish bills.[3] In all but one of the standing committees Government bills have precedence, most private Members' bills being sent to Standing Committee C where they have precedence. It is a duty of the Speaker to allocate bills among the committees,[4] but in so doing he has regard to the priority wished by the Government.[5]

3.3.1 *Members*

The Committee of Selection nominates the members (not less than 16 nor more than 50)[6] to serve on each standing committee and is required to have regard to the qualifications of those members and to the composition of the House. The Committee of Selection consists of eleven members of whom three are a quorum.[7] Its members are nominated each session by the House which in this case means by the party Whips. The chairman is a member of the Government party. It has been the practice for the

1 S.O. No. 60(1).

2 H.C. 638 of 1970–71, p. 12.

3 H.C. 450 of 1967–68; H.C. 9 of 1969–70; H.C. 638 of 1970–71.

4 S.O. No. 60(2)(3)(4).

5 For Scottish committees, see above, p. 26 and S.O. No. 62, 67, 69.

6 S.O. No. 62(1). The quorum is seventeen or one-third of the membership excluding the chairman, whichever is the less (fractions being counted as one): S.O. No. 65(1).

7 S.O. 109. Both the Committee of Selection and the Chairman's Panel (see below, p. 58) are statutorily recognised for it is provided in the Parliament Act 1911 that before the Speaker certifies a bill as a Money Bill he shall consult, if practicable, two members from the panel to be appointed by the committee at the beginning of each session; in practice this is a dead letter.

Deputy Chief Whips of the two main parties to be members of the committee; but this is now less usual than it was.

The Committee of Selection having the power to decide the size of each standing committee, to nominate members (and so to exclude other members), and in so doing to have regard to their qualifications, might have developed into a body important in the relations of the House to the Government. But in practice, particularly in respect of Government bills,[1] it is almost entirely a body which records decisions taken by others. As we have seen, it is required to have regard to 'the composition of the House' which means the party strengths in the House. At the beginning of the 1970–71 session the Conservative party had 330 seats; the Labour party 287 seats; the Liberal party had 6 seats; 1 seat each was held by Members being Independent Irish, Independent Labour, Protestant Unionist, Republican Labour, Scottish Nationalist, and Unity; in addition was the Speaker. This resulted in the allotment of the following numbers of Conservative and Labour Members of standing committees.

Number of Members on standing committee	*Conservative*	*Labour*
16	9	7
20	11	9
25	13	12
30	16	14
35	19	16
40	21	19
45	24	21
50	27	23

If it were wished to include a Liberal Member or one of the independent or unsupported Members, this could be done either by the Government or (more likely) the Opposition giving up one of their places or by increasing the membership of the committee.[2]

Whips may suggest to the Committee of Selection what size a standing committee should be. Otherwise the Committee of Selection will decide. In either case representations may be made (usually for an increase in the size proposed) by the Opposition. The figures for 1967–68, 1968–69 and 1970–71 were as shown in Table 3.4.[3]

Members who are not members of one of the two major parties in the

[1] The functions of the Committee of Selection in relation to Private Members' bills and private bills are far more onerous.

[2] In 1970–71, a Liberal Member (Mr David Steel) was found a place on the standing committee for the Immigration Bill by adding to a committee of 35 one more Conservative member and the Liberal member.

[3] Bills committed to Scottish standing committees are excluded from this table.

Table 3.4

Number of Government bills committed to standing committees of:									
Number of members	16	20	25	29	30	35	37	50	Total
1967–68	—	23	2	—	2	2	—	1	30
1968–69	15	11	1	1	1	—	—	—	29
1970–71	30	2	—	—	1	1	1	—	35
Total	45	36	3	1	4	3	1	1	94

House have great difficulty in obtaining representation on standing committees. On 6 March 1962, Sir David Robertson drew the attention of the Prime Minister to this. Neither he nor Sir William Duthrie had been appointed to the Standing Committee on the Sea Fish Industry Bill despite their strong constituency interests and experience in this matter. The Chairman of the Committee of Selection had written saying:

> 'the fact that you have not been eligible on this Committee is not because I have been thwarted by the Whips; it is because you are unfortunately no longer Members of the Conservative Party.'[1]

As a result of this complaint, twelve senior Members including the Leader of the House, the Deputy Leader of the Opposition and the Leader of the Liberal Party were nominated as members of a sessional Select Committee on Procedure set up to consider any matters referred to them by the House relating to public business.[2] The effect on minorities of the Standing Order (now S.O. No. 62(2)), requiring the Committee of Selection to have regard to the qualifications of Members and to the composition of the House, was then referred to the Select Committee.[3]

The Chairman of the Committee of Selection in his evidence to the Select Committee made clear that his committee worked precisely to the mathematical formula reflecting the composition of the House (which at that time resulted in no Liberal or Independent Members being on standing committees of less than thirty-five members) and that 'the composition of the House' took precedence over 'the qualifications of Members'.[4] The Select Committee recommended no amendment to the Standing Order; but were of opinion that the Committee of Selection ought to feel themselves free to provide for a larger standing committee than that suggested

[1] 655 H.C. Deb., col. 202; and see 653 H.C. Deb., cols 625–6.

[2] 658 H.C. Deb., col. 462 (17 April 1962). The motion for nominating the Members was, most unusually, debated on an amendment (which was withdrawn) to include in the membership of the Select Committee one 'whipless' Member (see 659 H.C. Deb., cols 770–4).

[3] 659 H.C. Deb., cols 774–8.

[4] H.C. 236 of 1961–62, para 4; Q17, 33–4, 44, 54.

to them by the Whips, and that there was no reason why committees should always be nominated in multiples of five.[1]

Until 1960, standing committees were composed of a nucleus of twenty members and an addition of not more than thirty members. From 8 February 1960[2] following the recommendation of the Select Committee on Procedure of 1958–59[3] the requirement was simply 'not less than twenty nor more than fifty members'. Then in December 1968 the minimum number was reduced to sixteen[4] and this has become the norm. Perhaps insufficient time has elapsed to assess what are the various consequences on committee work of the very great reduction in the number of members between 1959 and 1969. But it is clear that minority groups have much less chance of being represented on a committee of sixteen than they had on a committee of forty. The reduction to sixteen seems to have been introduced because of the increasing difficulty in finding Members to man committees; and to have been accepted without protest. The effect on the working of committees may prove to be significant.

In recent years the Liberal Party, as principal minority group, has had so few Members in the House that its claim for representation on standing committees has been arguable only in particular cases and not as a general proposition. And it has usually succeeded in its argument when it has chosen to advance it,[5] and in recent years has secured representation on committees for the most controversial bills.

In January 1973, three Liberal and three Labour Members protested against their non-selection for membership of the Scottish Standing Committee on the Local Government (Scotland) Bill by sitting with the selected members on the first and second sittings of the committee and refusing to withdraw. All were Members of Scottish constituencies. No Liberals had been selected for service on the committee. The Members were reported to the House which empowered the chairman of the committee to instruct the Serjeant at Arms to remove them if necessary. Subsequently the Select Committee on Procedure recommended against giving the chairmen of standing committees greater powers to deal with such situations. They also recommended that the powers granted by order of the House on this occasion should not be regarded as a precedent to be followed.[6]

The Opposition Chief Whip habitually nominates those to serve on a standing committee and expects the Committee of Selection to accept his list without question.

When in power the two principal parties appear to operate in different ways. It was the practice of the last Conservative Government to leave the selection of rank-and-file members to the Chairman of the Committee

[1] H.C. 236 of 1961–62, paras 8, 10.
[2] 617 H.C. Deb., cols 33–4.
[3] H.C. 92 of 1958–59, para 8.
[4] 775 H.C. Deb., col. 1698.
[5] See, e.g. note 2 on p. 48 above.
[6] See First Scottish Standing Committee, first and second sittings on 23 and 25 January 1973; H.C. Deb., cols 666–78; H.C. 202 or 1972–73.

of Selection who is by convention a member of the party in power. A Conservative Member who wished to serve on a particular standing committee and who approached the Whips to urge his candidature was usually referred to the chairman. The Chief Whip under the previous Labour Government, however, seems to have acted as he would when in Opposition and to have presented his list of members to the Committee of Selection for their formal approval only.

In the event the area of difference between the two parties is small. For, first, certain Members are inevitably members of a committee. These are the Minister in charge of the bill; and one or more of his junior Ministers, with perhaps Ministers from other Departments, depending on the size and complexity of the measure.[1] It is the practice for the Parliamentary Private Secretary of the Minister in charge also to be a member; and for a Government Whip to be nominated. Similarly, on the Opposition side, one or more official spokesmen will be members nominated by the Shadow Cabinet;[2] and they will discuss with the Chief Whip which other Members would be helpful on different aspects of the bill because of their particular knowledge or their experience of its subject-matter or their constituency. Such Members who are specialists and experts on particular matters – such as housing and planning, or defence, or health services – appear frequently as Opposition backbench members of standing committees, nominated by the Whips.[3] The Conservative Chairman of the Committee of Selection in deciding who shall be the rank-and-file Conservative members of a standing committee under a Conservative Government will also be in touch with the party Whips and will receive suggestions from them. But the need for a 'team' to support the Minister in charge of the bill is immeasurably less than the need for a team to support the frontbenchers in Opposition. For the Minister is supported and serviced by his Department. This reduces the need for the Government Whips to become involved in selection.

Individual Members may become committee members because (usually being senior) they hold party positions which make their claims almost irrefutable as, for example, being chairman of the relevant Parliamentary party group.

The number of places on a standing committee for which a true com-

[1] For example, Standing Committee B on the Race Relations Bill 1967–68 included in its membership the Home Secretary, an Under-Secretary of State from the Home Office, and two Joint Parliamentary Secretaries from the Ministry of Labour and the Ministry of Housing and Local Government.

[2] The amount of responsibility taken by junior Ministers and junior shadow Ministers may depend on the extent of other duties at that time. For example, the debates on the Immigration Bill in 1971 coincided with the conflicts in Northern Ireland in which both the Home Secretary (Mr Maudling), and his opposite number (Mr Callaghan) were much involved so that, for that reason alone, it was necessary for each to be well supported.

[3] A special expertise may be obtained by chairmanship or membership of select committees of the House, e.g. Select Committee on Nationalised Industries or Select Committee on Race Relations and Immigration.

petition exists may therefore be relatively small. But this is subject to two considerations: first, the larger the committee the greater the number of places to be competed for; and secondly, the keenness of the competition, whatever the size of the committee. For it must not be supposed that Members commonly vie for committee membership. Sometimes this is so. Membership of the Standing Committee on the Finance Bill is sought after, particularly by Conservatives. Opportunities can arise to plead the case (and, if one's own party is in power, with some hope of success) for the relief from taxation of special groups of persons. Committee membership for bills on controversial social issues (such as immigration or housing) is also sought after. Generally there will be no shortage of Conservative candidates for committees on bills concerned with agriculture or of Labour candidates for committees on mining bills or those affecting other regional industries.

But committee members are not easily found for the large number of unexciting bills which pass through the House of Commons each session. Many MPs have other occupations, separate from their Parliamentary membership, which they seek to pursue in the mornings and early afternoons which is when standing committees normally sit.[1] Professional men and women, businessmen and journalists, for example, are often able to continue to act as such although Members. Barristers and solicitors, who total between one-fifth and one-sixth of all Members, are the groups most often referred to as habitual absentees from membership of standing committees and, despite perennial complaints from some other Members, seem to have established almost a recognised right not to be called on.

Again, standing committee work, except for the main protagonists, can be tedious and time-wasting. This is particularly so for Government backbenchers who, although they are often discouraged by the committee whip from speaking as this tends to slow down progress, must be present or at hand in case of divisions. And so the Chief Whip will find the recruitment of members for standing committees more difficult when the party is in power than when it is in Opposition; and usually he has fewer backbench Members to choose from.

In 1967–68 the Committee of Selection seem to have become sufficiently worried, at the congestion of bills and the consequent pressure on a limited number of Members who were willing to man committees, to take evidence from the Leader of the House. He made 'a unique appearance before the Committee of Selection and explained that it was the Government's fault for bringing forward legislation late and thereby crowding the Committee stage'.[2]

It is the responsibility of the Committee of Selection to ensure that Members nominated are actually available and willing to serve, for there is no assurance that a Member whose name has been put forward has

[1] The Boyle Committee in 1971 found that one out of eight Members had a part-time occupation which employed him for more than 20 hours a week (Cmnd. 4836, para 25).

[2] Horserace Betting Levy Bill 1968–69 Standing Committee E, col. 9 (Mr Temple).

already agreed. Indeed, the first intimation he has that he is on a committee may be when he is told so by the Committee of Selection. If the news is unwelcome he may seek to be removed. But normally he will accept his fate as part of his duties as a Parliamentarian and a party member.[1] For obvious reasons, Whips prefer to obtain volunteers rather than pressmen. By knowing the main interests of the Members of their party, they reduce discontent. But on many bills it cannot be eliminated.

During the debate on the sittings motion on the first day of the controversial Licensing (Abolition of State Management) Bill 1970–71, the Opposition Whip said:

> 'Hon. Members on this side were informed as late as last night that they were appointed to it. . . . I have been trying since Monday to get a complete list of the Members of the Committee. Only this morning was I able to obtain a copy. . . . The fact that the Committee of Selection met only yesterday to decide finally upon the Committee's composition, and that the meeting was called for today, shows indecent haste.'[2]

It appeared that the size of the committee, originally fixed at sixteen, had been increased to twenty, at the request of the Opposition.[3] It appeared also that those added late were not all taken wholly unaware.[4] The argument was, as so often happens in Parliament, largely unreal in substance and more directed to mild opening obstruction by the Opposition on a bill much disliked by them. But it serves to show that committees are sometimes put together in a state of some haste when alterations are sought.

It is frequently said that those who nominate Members to serve on standing committees and the Committee of Selection itself, pay particular attention to those who spoke during the Second Reading debate.[5] So far as Government bills are concerned, this seems to be a traditional belief rather than a present-day reality. Or, in so far as it is still true, it is regarded as no more than an indication of the Member's interest in the subject matter of the bill. And a more important indication (for there are many good reasons why a Member may have been unable to speak on Second Reading) will be the pressure he brings to bear on the Chairman of the

[1] As did Mr John Hall although he had heard only the day before that he had been placed on the committee for the Industry Bill 1970–71 and expressed himself not quite accurately, nor perhaps quite seriously, as 'speechless with rage' (Standing Committee E, col. 5).

[2] Standing Committee D, col. 7.

[3] *Ibid.*, col. 10, 41.

[4] *Ibid.*, col. 11, 41.

[5] On 27 November 1972, Mr Sydney Chapman exemplified the situation when he said, during the debate on the second reading of the Land Compensation Bill: 'My diffidence in rising to speak is caused by the fact that the last time I spoke on the Second Reading of a Bill concerning money and housing I was lumbered on the Standing Committee which considered the Housing Finance Bill and cost me precisely 257 hours of my life. I hope that the Whip on duty . . . will take this as an early application for a dispensation from serving on the Standing Committee which considers this Bill.' (847 H.C. Deb., cols 101–2).

Committee of Selection or the Whips in arguing his case for inclusion on the committee. And, more important than either of these, will be the assessment of whether he will be of value as a member of the committee.

Each party claims that it seeks to get 'a fair spread' of opinion within the party represented on the more popular or controversial committees. And each tends to believe that the other is more ruthless. The concept itself is too vague for any precise assessment. But it is certainly true that under the Labour Government 1964–70 the 'Left' was represented on standing committees for bills concerned with housing, prices and incomes, nationalisation and others where their views on certain clauses were known to be opposed to Government policy.[1] No doubt also they felt themselves inadequately represented on other committees. Similarly under the 1970–74 Government the Conservative membership on the Standing Committee for the Immigration Bill 1971 contained Members usually associated with the right wing on this issue, e.g. Mr Enoch Powell, and others usually regarded as liberal, e.g. Sir George Sinclair. It would have been interesting to see how far the 'fair spread' principle would have been applied by either Government or Opposition parties had the European Communities Bill 1971–72 been sent to a standing committee.[2]

The Committee of Selection may discharge members nominated by the Committee and may appoint substitutes.[3] The Committee resolves each session to exercise this power once a bill has begun to be considered by a standing committee only when a Member is incapacitated from attendance by illness or has been appointed to be, or ceased to be, a member of the Government or has changed his office. On one recent occasion when the substitution was made on the ground of illness, the rule was discussed and it was wondered whether it would operate 'if somebody has a cold and is away for a few days'. The Chairman of the Standing Committee undertook to speak to the Chairman of the Committee of Selection.[4]

In 1968–69,[5] standing committees A to G and the two Scottish standing committees considered forty-eight bills[6] and held 246 sittings. In addition

[1] A minority group within the Government party may be willing, on matters where its special political position is at issue, to be troublesome (for example, by putting down amendments on report) if not represented on the committee. And this may predispose the Whips to give them membership on the committee. Certainly the Speaker is open to the argument that he should select an amendment on report tabled by a minority group unrepresented on the committee.

[2] In February 1973, backbenchers on the Government side in standing committee on the Counter-Inflation Bill included Mr Nicholas Ridley and Mr John Biffen, both of whom were known to be critical of the Government's policy; and, with Opposition support, they forced through an amendment which made Part II of the Bill renewable annually. But the Government reversed this on report (851 H.C. Deb., cols 1507–70).

[3] S.O. Nos 62, 68, 72.

[4] Education (Scotland) Bill 1970–71 First Scottish Standing Committee, cols 513–18; see also Industry Bill 1970–71 Standing Committee E, cols 3–16.

[5] See H.C. 9 of 1969–70. These figures include Private Members' bills.

[6] This includes both Government and Private Members' bills.

the Scottish Grand Committee[1] considered five bills at seven sittings, thirteen estimates at six sittings and one matter at one sitting; the Welsh Grand Committee considered two matters at three sittings; and the Second Reading Committee[2] considered six bills at seven sittings.

A total of 478 Members were appointed to serve on these committees. Of these, nineteen were appointed to serve as chairmen (eight of these also serving as members of other committees) but two of the appointed chairmen were not summoned to serve as such. Of the 478 Members, fifty-three served as Ministers.

In considering the duties of Members, we may exclude the eleven chairmen who did not also serve as members, and the fifty-three Ministers. The remaining 414 Members between them were summoned to attend 5979 sittings and attended 4503. This overall rate of about 75 per cent attendance is reflected without much discrepancy throughout the record of individual Members. The burden is less evenly spread among Members as the following shows:

Number of sittings to which summoned	*Number of members summoned*
1–10	208
11–20	88
21–30	66
31–40	35
41–50	13
51–60	2
61–70	1
71–80	1
	414

The normal length of a sitting is 2½ hours. So almost exactly half (208) of the members summoned (414) were summoned to attend for 25 hours or less; and a further 154 members for up to 75 hours. All but one[3] of the seventeen Members summoned to attend more than forty sittings sat for Scottish constituencies and were summoned to attend Scottish grand and Scottish standing committees as well (in most cases) as others.

Excluding the Speaker and the Chairman and Deputy Chairman of Ways and Means, 149 Members of the House of Commons (23·6 per cent) in 1968–69 were not appointed to serve on any of these committees. But of these about thirty held Ministerial office so that the number of Opposition and Government back-bench Members who did not serve was about 119 (18·9 per cent).

[1] See above, pp. 26–7.

[2] See above, pp. 24–6.

[3] The exception was Captain L. P. S. Orr (Ulster Unionist) who was a member of the committees on the Sunday Entertainments Bill (19 sittings) and the Post Office Bill (24 sittings); he attended 32 sittings.

When a standing committee first meets, members may not altogether like the results of the selection process. Opposition Members sometimes express offence at the non-membership of senior Ministers. When the Standing Committee on the Finance Bill met on 11 June 1969, Mr John Nott (Con.) objected to the fact that the Chancellor of the Exchequer was not a member.[1] (The Government spokesmen were the Financial Secretary to the Treasury and a Minister of State.) The chairman on these occasions retreats behind the formal barrier:

> 'The hon. Gentleman must understand that it is no function of this Committee to criticise the selection of Members. This is done by an appropriate Selection Committee. It has no part in our debates. . . . I will not tolerate oblique criticisms of the Selection Committee. . . . Do not let us waste time complaining about [the Chancellor's] absence in speech after speech.'[2]

The failure of the Secretary of State to attend as a member of the Standing Committee on the Education (Milk) Bill 1970–71 was heavily criticised by the Opposition on the ground that it was her 'brain-child'. It was said: 'She knows this is a disgusting, disgraceful Bill and she is deliberately absenting herself from this Committee'.[3]

Mr Sheldon for the Opposition on the Pensions (Increase) Bill 1970–71 protested at the absence of a Treasury Minister[4] and he was able to quote from a speech made in 1969 by the Financial Secretary to the Treasury (then an Opposition spokesman) when he deplored the absence of a Treasury Minister from the committee on the Pensions (Increase) Bill of that year.[5] And indeed the complaint about the absence of certain Ministers has some of the compulsive qualities of a Parliamentary party game.

More surprisingly, on 20 March 1969 objection was made to the non-membership of any shadow Minister to represent the Opposition on the Children and Young Persons Bill. But this was more a riposte to the complaint that the Home Secretary though a Member of the committee was absent. He was said to be 'practically at the opposite end of the world' which was a little unfair and geographically inaccurate, as he was on a Parliamentary delegation to the Caribbean.[6] Thereafter the allegations thickened:

> 'The point which I am making is that it may be said that it does not matter whether the Home Secretary comes to the Committee or not, because the Committee has been packed in such a way that the Bill will not be altered.'[7]

[1] Standing Committee F, col. 13.

[2] *Ibid.*, col. 13, 18 (Mr Jennings). Since it is the Government's decision which Ministers shall be members of a committee on a Government bill, this protection by the Chairman of the functions of the Committee of Selection is unreal.

[3] Standing Committee A, cols 15, 14.

[4] Standing Committee E, cols 3, 4, 5, 6.

[5] 1968–69 Standing Committee F, cols 3–4.

[6] Standing Committee G, cols 4, 5.

[7] *Ibid.*, cols 6–7 (Mr Carlisle).

Another Member hinted at 'a bit of jiggery-pokery in deciding who is to attend on the Government side'.[1] And another asked for an assurance (which he did not get) from the Under-Secretary of State that there had been no attempt by the Home Office to influence the selection of Members of this committee.[2] The Chairman on this occasion contented himself, rather mildly, with reminding the committee that its composition was the responsibility of the Committee of Selection;[3] while the Ministerial spokesman expressed his 'feeling of disappointment that a predilection for political mischief has made its appearance so early in our deliberations'.[4] The real purpose of these Opposition protests was to protract the proceedings of this first meeting of the committee. In the event the Minister agreed that a crucial early amendment would not be decided on before the Home Secretary returned and he was duly present at the second sitting.

The Law Officers, if Members of the House, are entitled to take part in the deliberations of a standing committee, though not members of it, but may not vote or make any motion or move any amendment or be counted in the quorum.[5] So also may any Minister, if a Member of the House, participate in a committee's deliberations on a Finance bill.[6] During the discussion in June 1969 on the Finance Bill in standing committee (referred to above) of which the Chancellor of the Exchequer was not a member, the chairman said:

> 'If the presence of the Chancellor is desired, there is nothing to prevent his coming here, making a statement and answering questions. We have had this before in Committees. I would certainly allow it if the Chancellor consented to come. But no one can force him to do so.'[7]

The creation of large departments – like that of the Environment or Trade and Industry – with several junior Ministers who would otherwise have been in charge of separate departments gave rise in 1970–71 to more complaints at the absence from committees of the Secretary of State as chief Minister.[8] In so far as the Minister in charge of the bill has to refer to his superior before major amendments in the bill can be accepted, this does make stronger the argument of the Opposition for the membership on the committee of the chief Minister. But by 1971–72, the Opposition seemed to have accepted the situation.[9]

3.3.2 *Chairmen*

Standing Orders provide that the Speaker shall nominate, at the commencement of every session, not less than ten Members to act as temporary chairmen of committees of the whole House when requested by the Chairman of Ways and Means.[10] These Members together with the

[1] *Ibid.*, col. 8 (Mr Miscampbell).
[2] *Ibid.*, col. 14 (Mr Lane).
[3] *Ibid.*, col. 4 (Mr G. Rogers).
[4] *Ibid.*, col. 9 (Mr Elystan Morgan).
[5] S.O. No. 63(1).
[6] S.O. No. 63(2).
[7] Standing Committee F, col. 14.
[8] E.g. Industry Bill 1970–71, Standing Committee E, cols 3–16.
[9] E.g. on the Industry Bill 1971–72.
[10] In practice the Chairman of Ways and Means selects the members of the Panel.

Chairman and the two Deputy Chairmen of Ways and Means constitute the Chairmen's Panel.[1] The chairman[2] of each standing committee is appointed by the Speaker from that Panel. And the Panel, of whom three form a quorum, is empowered to consider matters of procedure relating to standing committees and to report their opinion thereon to the House from time to time.[3]

In committee of the whole House the chair is generally taken by the Chairman or Deputy Chairman of Ways and Means and where necessary, as in the case of a bill (like the Industrial Relations Bill of 1970–71) which is many hours in committee, by one or more members of the Chairmen's Panel.

Temporary chairmen are usually reappointed to the Panel at the beginning of each session until they cease to be Members of the House or become Ministers or accept positions on the Opposition front bench. For the session 1969–70, eighteen were nominated, nine being Conservative and nine being Labour Members. Together they presided over 285 sittings of standing committees. The longest serving chairman was Sir Ronald Russell who had been first appointed as Panel member for 1960–61. During the ten sessions which followed, he presided over fifty-eight sittings but was far outstripped by Sir Robert Grant-Ferris[4] who since 1962–63 had presided over 210 sittings. Five members of the Panel had been first appointed in 1964–65, a further eight in 1966–67 and the remaining three in 1968–69. In addition to Sir Robert, three members had presided over more than 100 sittings, the hardest worked being Mr Gurden who during the four sessions 1966–67 to 1969–70 presided over 150 sittings.[5]

It is commonly said that chairmen are drawn from the more senior members and, if Ministers and former Ministers are excluded, this is true within limits. Age and general elections take their toll and it will be seen that in 1969–70, seven of the eighteen temporary chairmen had previously served as such for only three sessions or less. The turnover is not slow. Moreover, six of the eighteen had been Members of the House for ten years or less. We can agree that the most senior members of the Panel are indeed senior Members of the House; but the appellation can hardly be attached to the others.

Temporary chairmen must be acceptable to Members of the House but this means little more than that they can be relied on to continue the tradition of impartiality, which attaches to their job, in applying the rules of procedure and in exercising their considerable discretionary powers. It by no means follows that they must in political terms be men of the centre. Their influence within their parties may, especially when they are senior, be considerable but it is also true that their names are not amongst those

[1] S.O. No. 106.

[2] For longer bills, more than one chairman may be appointed.

[3] S.O. No. 61(1)(4). This rarely happens.

[4] He became Chairman of Ways and Means after the General Election in 1970.

[5] For all these figures, see the annual *Returns of Standing Committees*.

best known to the general public. The possession of a legal qualification[1] may be counted an asset in so far as it suggests a familiarity with procedural rules but other qualities and attributes – patience, humour and knowing how far elastic will stretch before it snaps – count for more. Practising lawyers are in any event habitual absentees from the Palace of Westminster in the mornings.[2]

In contrast to the usual practice when Members are required to serve the House and its committees, the Whips' Office takes no part in the selection of temporary chairmen. Any Member may put forward a name for membership of the Panel and proposals made by existing Panel members carry much weight. No doubt, also, consultation takes place with senior Members of the Panel before new nominations are made. And the proposal to nominate a Member will be put to his party leader before being made formally. But neither the Whips nor the leaders are consulted and it is doubtful whether they have ever sought to prevent an appointment. A Member who is asked to join the Panel may consult others before he decides but essentially this is a House of Commons, not a party, matter.

It is rare for any conflict to appear between a chairman's political views and his official functions. The Immigration Bill of 1970–71 was a highly controversial measure and the proceedings in standing committee tested the skill of the chairmen who served it. The first chairman withdrew after the eighteenth sitting and his place was taken by Mr Gurden. At the close of the twenty-fourth and last sitting, after the usual compliments had been exchanged, Mr Gurden said:

> 'I sought not to serve in this capacity on this Bill, and I hoped I had avoided it, but in trying to avoid it I am reminded, as I have been reminded on other occasions, of the scrupulous fairness and honesty of all Chairmen serving under Mr Speaker, and then I could no longer avoid helping out my colleague who wanted to get away. I appreciate how much all the hon. Members have shown that they know the Chairmen are fair'.[3]

The meaning of this statement is not altogether clear but Mr Gurden's expressed reluctance may have been caused by his feeling that all members of the committee knew that he held strong and definite views about immigration.

Occasionally individual Members are roused to protest when they believe they have been treated unfairly by chairmen. In a Scottish standing committee on the Erskine Bridge Tolls Bill 1967–68, a Member claimed that he had risen to speak before the Chairman (Sir Myer Galpern) had finished putting the Question that Clause 7 stand part of the bill. But the Chairman overruled him saying 'I disagree with the hon. Member entirely'. When, a few minutes later, proceedings on the Bill in committee were

[1] Of the eighteen temporary chairmen in 1969–70, five were barristers and two were solicitors.

[2] See p. 52.

[3] Standing Committee B (27 May 1971), cols 1643–4.

concluded and the Chairman was being thanked for presiding, the Member said:

> 'I want to say to you, Sir Myer, that I dissent from the Motion, and I feel so strongly about your decision this morning, showing, I am quite sure, unnecessary personal animosity to me, that I have no recourse but to report the incident to the Panel of Chairmen.'

The Chairman denied any personal animosity.[1]

The Education (Scotland) Bill 1970–71 inspired more bad temper than any bill, other than the Industrial Relations Bill, during that session. While protesting against the Chairman's decision to accept a closure motion Mr Lawson said: 'I do not think that you are fit to take the chair' and chose to withdraw from the committee rather than withdraw his statement. But when the committee next met he withdrew his statement.[2]

Until recently it had been understood that a chairman would not speak or vote on Report or Third Reading of a bill he had chaired in committee. Something like an exception occurred during the proceedings on the Education Bill 1969–70. For the fifth sitting of the standing committee on 24 March 1970, the designated chairman (Mr John Brewis) had been unable to preside and his place had been taken, as is usual in such cases, by another member of the Panel, Sir Barnett Janner. After the Government were defeated in committee on a crucial clause of the Bill, the House debated the recommittal of the bill.[3] When the standing committee reconvened after the Commons' debate a member of the committee (Mr Fergus Montgomery) attacked Sir Barnett – whom he called the 'alternative' chairman of the committee – for having intervened in the House, making 'a very partial speech' and voting on the two motions before the House. Mr Montgomery said that, if Sir Barnett took the chair again, he would:

> '. . . object most strongly. I believe that the hon. Member has shown partisanship, and I shall have no faith in his impartiality if he comes back to this Committee as Chairman. I should like to know from you what power hon. Members on this side have to remove a member of the Chairmen's Panel who has foolishly intervened in a debate on legislation on which he himself could well have to be an impartial Chairman at a later date.'

Mr Brewis replied that he was the sole chairman of the committee and that the question of appointing another chairman was for the Speaker alone.[4]

In the last few years considerable doubt has been thrown on this principle of the non-involvement of chairmen in the subsequent proceedings on bills they chaired. For the report and third reading of the Industrial Relations

[1] Scottish Standing Committee (7 December 1967), cols 64–5, 79–80. Both the Chairman and the Member (Mr W. Hannan) were Labour members.

[2] First Scottish Standing Committee, cols 282–4, 305–7.

[3] 800 H.C. Deb., cols 424–504.

[4] 1969–70 Standing Committee A Education Bill (recommitted), cols 11–12.

Bill 1970–71, the Opposition Chief Whip did not allow those of his Members who had chaired the committee stage to be paired. They were expected to vote. And this was a view believed to be shared by the Government Chief Whip. This breach of the principle was repeated for the Housing Finance Bill 1971–72. Presumably the attitude of the Speaker is influential. It is his panel from which chairmen are drawn and he might be expected to consider chairmen as officers of the House, and so apart from party conflict, in relation to bills they chaired.

3.3.3 *Sittings*

After a bill has been committed to a standing committee, the Committee of Selection, which normally meets each Wednesday, appoints the members of the committee. At about the same time, the chairman and the clerk are appointed.

The Public Bill Office is responsible for providing clerks for standing and grand committees. The Office is part of the Department of the Clerk of the House and is headed by the Clerk of Public Bills. Under him the Clerk of Standing Committees is responsible generally for ensuring that all necessary arrangements are made for standing committees to be set up when necessary; he appoints the clerk for each committee and is usually himself clerk to any standing committee on the Finance Bill. The Public Bill Office and its clerks provide the expert advice required by Members generally, by the chairman of the committee, by committee members, by the committee at large, and by the House on public bill procedure.

Once a standing committee is constituted, the chairman becomes responsible for fixing the first day of its meeting. The Standing Order states:

> 'A standing committee to whom a bill or other business has been committed shall meet to consider such business on the day and at the hour named by the Member appointed chairman of the committee in respect of that business.'[1]

Before fixing the day of the first meeting of the standing committee, the chairman will confirm with the Minister in charge of the bill that the day is convenient to him, and in practice will follow the Minister's wishes.

The necessary functions, though formal, of the Committee of Selection, the appointment of a chairman and the taking into account of the views of the Department, all take time. Time must also be allowed for the tabling and study of amendments. So it is unusual for the first meeting of a standing committee to take place less than 10 days after the second reading. The Children and Young Persons Bill had its Second Reading on 11 March 1969[2] and committee proceedings began on 20 March to the protests of Opposition spokesmen who complained at the short interval since Second Reading. The Chairman observed that the bill had been printed and

[1] S.O. No. 64(1).

[2] 779 H.C. Deb., cols 1176–1304.

available since 12 February and that he thought that was adequate notice.[1]

The first business of a standing committee is to decide the occasions on which it will sit, the usual custom being to sit from 10.30 a.m. to 1 p.m. on Tuesdays and Thursdays.

Standing Orders restrict the sittings to days on which the House sits and requires the committee not to sit between 1 p.m. and 3.30 p.m.[2] The proceedings begin with a sittings motion to define the days and times but which often provokes discussion and argument, sometimes with the purpose of delaying progress.[3] Thus on the Horserace Betting Levy Bill 1968–69, a Government backbencher opposed the usual Tuesdays and Thursdays motion and moved to leave out 'and Thursdays'. He did not think the bill was sufficiently important (indeed he said he was 'against the whole principle of the Bill'); he was supported by Opposition Members and pressed the amendment to a division which resulted in a tied vote; the Chairman then voted against the amendment.[4] If the Committee does not make the progress which the Government wish to see, further motions may add additional sittings.

Sometimes the Minister, as the Member in charge of the bill, will move at the beginning that the committee should meet more frequently.

Debate in standing committee begins and, for the great majority of bills, is concluded after a number of sittings with both sides content that adequate time has been made available for discussion. But on a small number of bills, and those amongst the most important and politically the most contentious, conflicts arise between the two sides. The Opposition may wish to discuss the bill at greater length than the Government wish (sometimes with an intention to delay the passage of the bill or generally to slow down the Government's legislative programme). Conversations will then take place between the two sides conducted by the Minister and the shadow Minister. This may lead to an informal agreement that debate on the bill will end at or about a future specified date, and there may be subsequent agreements about additional sittings. Normally the shadow Minister will be able, after consultation, to persuade Opposition backbenchers to adhere to agreements though he has no ultimate power to enforce their compliance. But the conversations may not lead to agreement. In such a situation the Minister may move a second sittings motion which will propose additional times for meetings and which he knows will be opposed.

Additional sittings may be proposed for other mornings for 10.30 a.m. until 1 p.m.; or, more probably (or in addition) afternoon sittings begin-

[1] 1968–69 Standing Committee G, cols 3, 4, 7; and see Customs Duties (Dumping and Subsidies) Amendment Bill 1967–68 Standing Committee E, col. 8.

[2] S.O. No. 64(1); for exceptions to general rule see S.O. No. 64(2).

[3] The Second Clerk Assistant and the Clerk of Public Bills suggested to the Select Committee on Procedure that they might like to consider means of curtailing this debate (see H.C. 538 of 1970–71, Appendix 4 para 25). But the Select Committee did not pursue this.

[4] 1968–69 Standing Committee E, cols 3–14, 111 (the Member was Mr Arthur Lewis).

ning at 4 p.m. or 4.30 p.m. After debate which may be lengthy because, *ex hypothesi*, the Opposition is unlikely to be co-operative, the motion will be put and, normally, carried. The particular advantage to the Government of afternoon sittings is that they are open-ended in that they may continue throughout the night and until 1 p.m. the next day.

Occasionally, Opposition amendments may be moved to increase the number of sittings. Thus, on the Coal Industry Bill 1970–71, Mr Foot from the front bench moved an amendment that the Committee should sit, additionally, on Wednesday mornings, although on Second Reading the Opposition had moved a reasoned amendment to the bill. He explained his motion on the ground that the Opposition wished some of the provisions to become law at 'a fairly early date'; but other provisions they found 'deeply offensive and highly dangerous'. So Mr Foot asked for additional sittings 'so that the good purposes of the Bill can be served and the bad points can be at least radically overhauled'. The amendment was defeated.[1] At the fourth sitting of the Committee the Minister moved to add Thursday afternoon sittings and Mr Foot again moved his former amendment. That amendment was defeated as was one by Sir Gerald Nabarro from the Government back benches who was seeking to ensure that the Committee would not be sitting when the House was debating the Industrial Relations Bill. The Government motion was approved.[2]

On a highly controversial bill, especially where the Government move for additional sittings because they are dissatisfied with the progress being made, the debate on that motion can become protracted. Thus to a new sittings motion made at the beginning of the sixteenth sitting on the Education (Scotland) Bill 1970–71, the Opposition put down eleven amendments and the debate lasted for $4\frac{1}{4}$ hours.[3]

The main work of a Committee is to consider amendments proposed by Members from both sides, including the Government front bench, and to dispose of each of them in one of a defined number of ways; and to debate each clause[4] on a separate motion 'That the clause (or the clause as amended) stand part of the bill.'

In considering what impact the House makes on Government bills, the chairman's powers to restrict debate are important.[5] In particular he has power to direct a member to discontinue his speech if the member 'persists

[1] Standing Committee B, cols 3–10. [2] *Ibid.*, cols 155–204.

[3] First Scottish Standing Committee, cols 753–834. Similarly, also because the matter was of acute political controversy, the first sittings motion on the Licensing (Abolition of State Management) Bill 1970–71 was debated for two and a half hours before a motion for the closure was accepted and passed: see Standing Committee D, cols 3–50. This taking of the whole of the first sitting for debate on a sittings motion is not rare. Chairmen have recently let it be known that they would not normally support the continuance of the debate for long during the second sitting.

[4] Unless the chairman rules that the clause has been adequately discussed (S.O. No. 48, 65(3)(c)). Throughout, 'clause' includes 'schedule' unless the context otherwise requires.

[5] Closure and timetabling are considered above, pp. 18–23.

in irrelevance or tedious repetition either of his own arguments, or of the arguments used by other Members in debate.'[1] The use of this power in this drastic form is most unusual but its existence enables the chairman to warn a Member, at first in the politest terms but on subsequent occasions with more force, that the argument he is pursuing, or the topic he is developing, is straying beyond the limits of relevance or is beginning to be repetitious. One of the duties of the clerk to a standing committee is to suggest to the chairman, privately, that a Member is out of order on these as on other grounds. The chairman may also, if of the opinion that a dilatory motion[2] is an abuse of the rules of the House, forthwith put the question from the chair or may decline to propose the question.[3] This power is most often used when the Opposition are seeking to obstruct the progress of a bill; but if a sitting continues late into the night, the chairman frequently accepts a motion to adjourn, thus making it necessary for the Minister to state his intentions.

The chairman has a casting vote when the votes are equal, but not otherwise. And he must exercise it.

The practice in the matter is that the chairman normally votes for the bill as read a second time by the House. So he will vote No on an amendment and Aye on the question 'That the clause stand part of the Bill'. The practice has been departed from on occasions.[4]

On a sittings motion moved by the Minister in charge of the Licensing (Abolition of State Management) Bill 1970–71, a division resulted in an equal number of votes and the chairman voted with the Ayes. He was challenged and said he had so voted not to uphold the *status quo* but because it was a matter which could be reversed at a later stage.[5] An Opposition amendment had been defeated on a previous vote.[6]

Very rarely indeed does a chairman go beyond firmness and insistence that his rulings must, in the last resort, be adhered to. But occasionally he is provoked beyond endurance. The Education (Scotland) Bill 1970–71 was highly controversial. At one point the chairman[7] said:

> 'I am glad to see the hon. Member for South Angus (Mr Bruce-Gardyne) is back. He was guilty of one of the rudest interjections as he left the Room having had his attention drawn to it on previous occasions. I take umbrage at the way in which the hon. Member has treated the Chair in particular, and the Committee in general. I would not even accept an apology from him now, but I want him to know exactly what my feelings are. I regarded his departure from the Room with utter contempt. . . . He had not spoken in Committee, except for one interjection, but he has wandered in and out discriminately and has stood talking on his side of the Committee with his back to me . . .' and so on.

[1] S.O. No. 22, 65(3)(c).
[2] I.e. a motion to adjourn the debate.
[3] S.O. No. 28, 65(3)(c).
[4] May, *op. cit.*, pp. 395–8, 610.
[5] Standing Committee D, cols 49–52.
[6] *Ibid.*, cols 45–6.
[7] He was Mr J. C. Jennings (Conservative) one of the most experienced members of the Chairman's Panel. The Member was also a Conservative.

The Member said that what someone else called 'loud and memorable noises' were caused by an obstruction of his throat.[1] And there the matter rested.

3.3.4 *Amendments – submission and admissibility*

Once the bill has been read the second time, any Member of the House may hand in (usually to the Table or the Public Bill Office) proposed amendments or new clauses at any time so long as the part of the bill to which they relate has not been dealt with by the committee. A number of Members may jointly propose amendments; and identical amendments may be handed in by a number of Members. Any Member may add his name to an amendment of which notice has been given and, if a Minister does so, his name is put at the head of the list. Any Member may hand in an amendment, but if the bill is committed to a standing committee, only a member of the committee can move it. In practice it is unusual for amendments to be handed in by Members of the House who are not members of the committee although they quite often add their names to amendments tabled by committee members.

Notice of amendments is not required by Standing Orders but the chairman usually announces at the beginning of the first sitting of a standing committee that he will not normally accept manuscript amendments (of which no notice has been given).[2]

All amendments are handed in in the name of individual Members but may be accurately described as being either Government amendments or official Opposition amendments or back-bench amendments (from either side). When handed in, amendments are scrutinised by the Clerks in the Public Bill Office to ensure that they are formally correct.[3] The amendments are sent to the printer, published as Notices of Amendments, and so made available to all Members. Before the first sitting of the committee several of these Notices may be published. On the day before the first sitting, a marshalled list is published which numbers the amendments, groups them clause by clause and sets them down in the order in which they would appear in the bill. Amendments subsequently handed in are published as Notices and further marshalled lists will appear incorporating these new amendments in their proper place but omitting any amendments which relate to parts of the bill already dealt with in commit-

[1] First Scottish Standing Committee, cols 547–50.

[2] In the exceptional case of committee stage following immediately after Second Reading, only manuscript amendments are possible (see e.g. Rolls-Royce (Purchase) Bill 1970–71, 811 H.C. Deb., cols 931–7). Manuscript amendments are sometimes accepted in order to alter amendments under discussion where to do so would make them acceptable to the Minister (see e.g. Civil Aviation Bill 1970–71, Standing Committee A, cols 643, 649). They may be substantial and important as when in 1958 the chairman allowed on Official Opposition amendment to leave out Clause 1(1) of the Overseas Resources Development Bill 1957–58 (581 H.C. Deb., cols 1239–40).

[3] Members may seek advice from the clerks to try to ensure that amendments are in order.

tee. Those which appear for the first time in a marshalled list without having previously appeared in a Notice are starred and will not usually be considered by the chairman for selection on that day.[1] Ministers and other members like to have plenty of time to consider amendments, and complaints are made if amendments, either manuscript or starred, are tabled late.[2] Despite the general practice, starred amendments are from time to time accepted (especially in standing committees) when the chairman decides that to do so would be 'for the convenience of the Committee',[3] as for example, on the first day of debate on a bill which has been hurried into committee; or because there are other amendments previously tabled on the same point (thus giving sufficient notice) which were ruled out of order.[4]

A bill of any appreciable size will attract scores or hundreds of amendments. Three major and interrelated tasks are immediately presented to the chairman of a committee: to decide whether any of these amendments are out of order and so not able to be moved in committee; to decide which amendments are to be moved; and to decide which amendments are to be grouped for discussion in committee.[5]

Erskine May[6] lists twelve grounds on which amendments may be held to be inadmissible as being out of order. These grounds are based on longstanding practice and buttressed by collections of precedents, Standing Orders making no provision for the matter save to say that amendments must be relevant to the subject matter of the bill.[7] Put briefly, these grounds are (i) being irrelevant to the subject-matter or beyond the scope of the Bill, (ii) being governed by or dependent upon amendments already negatived, (iii) being inconsistent with the bill as agreed by the committee,[8] (iv) being incomplete, (v) being a negation of the principle of the bill, (vi) being a negation of a clause of the bill, (vii) being unintelligible or ungrammatical, (viii) being vague, trifling or 'tendered in a spirit of mockery', (ix) being offered at a wrong place in the bill, (x) being a proposal for change in

[1] For recent exceptions to this see Civil Aviation Bill 1970–71, Standing Committee A, cols 3, 34, and Highways Bill 1970–71, Standing Committee D, cols 3, 4. If the starred amendment is not reached, it will appear unstarred in the next Notice and be available for selection.

[2] E.g. Medicines Bill 1967–68, Standing Committee D, col. 56 (non-Ministerial amendments); Gaming Bill 1967–68, Standing Committee B, col. 341 (Ministerial amendments).

[3] E.g. Health Services and Public Health Bill 1967–68, Standing Committee D, col. 138.

[4] Countryside Bill 1967–68, Standing Committee A, col. 52.

[5] As will be seen, some amendments, although in order, may be not selected either to be moved or to be grouped.

[6] *Op. cit.*, pp. 508–10.

[7] S.O. No. 42. E.g. an amendment that sought to widen the scope of the Mines and Quarries (Tips) Bill 1968–69 to include provisions relating to amenity was ruled out of order as being outside the scope of the Title and of the Bill (1968–69 Standing Committee B, cols 55–7).

[8] Grounds (ii) and (iii) include amendments that may be in order when put down but become out of order because of decisions taken by the committee.

legislative procedure which would be contrary to constitutional practice, (xi) being an attempt to delay the coming into force of a bill relating to England only until a similar bill should have been passed for Scotland, (xii) being an amendment or new clause creating public charges without a money resolution or ways and means resolution having been passed, or not being covered by the terms of such resolution.

Some of these grounds need explanation. Ground (i) was most recently and most dramatically evidenced when the Chairman of Ways and Means in committee of the whole House ruled out of order a large number of amendments put down by the Opposition to the European Communities Bill 1971–72. The reason given by the Chairman was the nature of the Bill itself, for most of the amendments ruled out of order sought to discuss articles of the treaties. The Chairman said that the amendments were ruled out of order 'because they subject to Parliamentary approval provisions of the Treaties already accepted, and therefore fall outside the scope of the Bill which . . . is concerned with the modification of United Kingdom law needed to implement the Treaties'.[1] The matter was debated at length, both at the beginning of the committee stage[2] and on a motion criticising the Chairman of Ways and Means and saying that his ruling 'gravely infringes the rights of the House and its powers of decision on the issues raised by the Bill, and that, therefore, a full new selection of Amendments should be proposed.'[3] The motion was defeated by 309 votes to 274.[4]

Ground (v) is not always easy of application. It is closely connected with the general powers of a committee and with the limitations by which it is bound. Erskine May says that a committee is bound by the decision of the House, given on second reading, in favour of the principle of the bill, and shall not, therefore, amend the bill in a manner destructive of this principle. When a Member moved an amendment that would have given Commonwealth parentage as a sufficient claim for free entry into the United Kingdom during the debates on the Commonwealth Immigrants Bill 1967–68, the Home Secretary, without directly challenging the chairman's selection, considered that the amendment was 'entirely opposed' to the decision registered by the House on second reading and clearly thought that it should not have been selected.[5] But there is nothing to prevent a committee negativing a clause or clauses, the omission of which may nullify or destroy the bill, and reporting the bill as amended to the House.[6]

An essential clause was negatived during the eighth sitting of the Standing Committee on the Education Bill 1969–70 when the Opposition defeated the first and vital clause of the four-clause bill designed to ensure the universal introduction of comprehensive education. (The Opposition had also amended the clause in one important respect before the whole clause as amended was struck down.) As a result the committee agreed with a Government motion that 'the committee do not proceed further with the

[1] 832 H.C. Deb., col. 526.
[2] *Ibid.*, cols 260–308.
[3] *Ibid.*, col. 432.
[4] *Ibid.*, cols 543–8.
[5] 759 H.C. Deb., cols 1431, 1498.
[6] May, *op. cit.*, pp. 494–5; and see p. 612.

consideration of the Bill'; and made a Special Report to the House that 'as the effective Clause of the Bill has been struck out during the consideration of the Bill in Committee, your Committee cannot with advantage proceed with the Bill'.[1] For a Government bill, the occurrence was without precedent. After debate and division, the House ordered: 'That the Education Bill, so far as amended, be recommitted to the former Committee'; and further ordered, after further debate and another division: 'that it be an Instruction to Standing Committee A that, notwithstanding that they have disagreed to Clause 1 of the Education Bill, they have power to insert in the Bill provisions with a like effect'.[2] When the committee reconvened the Minister moved New Clause 1 which was to put back in the bill the clause as unamended; and the Opposition tabled New Clause 3 which would have put back the Clause as amended. The chairman ruled that New Clause 3 should be discussed with New Clause 1 but that if New Clause 1 were not adopted by the committee then New Clause 3 could be divided on. In the event, New Clause 1 was, after debate and division, read a second time which meant that New Clause 3 fell.[3] All this had taken time and the Committee adjourned on 14 May 1970 for the Whitsun recess until 2 June 1970. But on 29 May Parliament was prorogued and subsequently dissolved for the general election. So the Education Bill was never reported a second time from committee.[4]

Although ground (vi) excludes an amendment to leave out a clause, or to remove its effective words, it is of course proper to speak and vote against the motion that the clause stand part of the bill.[5]

Erskine May summarises ground (xii) by saying that no amendment may be moved in committee on a bill which would increase the charge beyond the limits authorised by the relevant financial resolution as recommended by the Crown and agreed to by the House.[6] A 'charge' may be either a charge on the people (taxation) authorised by a Ways and Means resolution; or a charge on public funds (expenditure) authorised by a Money resolution. Especially since a Treasury circular of 9 November 1937, financial resolutions have usually been drafted more widely so that today amendments are not as frequently ruled out of order on this ground. Nevertheless, for some bills the Minister does move a Money resolution which, when agreed to by the House, materially restricts the scope of amendments. An example arose on the Health Services and Public Health Bill 1967–68 when the resolution covered, *inter alia*, 'any expenditure incurred by the Ministry of Health or the Secretary of State in making

[1] 1969–70 Standing Committee A, cols 321–2, 325, 338.

[2] 800 H.C. Deb., cols 424–504.

[3] 1969–70 Standing Committee A Education Bill (recommitted), cols 3, 4, 16, 77–8.

[4] For a more detailed account see K. A. Bradshaw: 'The Education Bill 1970' in 39 *The Table*, p. 59.

[5] See, for example, Development of Tourism Bill 1968–69, Standing Committee E, col. 355.

[6] May, *op. cit.*, p. 754; and see pp. 695–6. The rule applies equally to amendments moved on report. See, generally, May, *op. cit.*, Chapter XXIX.

payments towards costs incurred by persons appearing to be suffering from severe physical defect or disability, in connection with invalid carriages or other vehicles provided by the Minister or the Secretary of State for or belonging to such persons.'[1] An amendment which sought to empower the Minister to make payments, up to the cost of an invalid carriage, to a person who had purchased or agreed to purchase his own vehicle rather than an invalid carriage provided by the Minister was ruled out of order as being outside the scope of the resolution.[2] It is indeed on provisions which empower the payment of direct grants or subsidies that financial resolutions are drawn most tightly.[3] So an amendment to the Housing Bill 1970–71 was rejected on this ground.[4]

It is the chairman who rules that an amendment is inadmissible. Before doing so he takes the advice of the clerk of the committee and may also consult the draftsman of the bill who can advise on the interpretation of any clause or amendment.[5]

Until a Government bill is introduced into the House and published, no Member of the House of Commons other than Ministers will have seen it.[6] Nor will the clerk of the committee have had prior knowledge of its contents. The draftsman, however, knows the bill more intimately than any other person. For weeks or months he has been engaged on preparing the bill, discussing it with civil servants in the Department concerned, attending conferences, taking his instructions, raising queries and suggesting alternative ways of dealing with the problems which the bill is designed to solve. It is usual for the clerk of the committee and the draftsman to consider together whether any amendments are out of order and for the clerk to advise the chairman accordingly. Only very rarely will the chairman overrule their common advice.[7] Nevertheless the clerk and the draftsman represent different interests. The draftsman is a civil servant while the clerk is an officer of the House. And the function of the draftsman, working closely with officers in the Department, is to put forward views

[1] H.C. Deb., col. 1804.

[2] 1967–68 Standing Committee D, cols 344–5.

[3] During the debate on the Local Government Grants (Social Need) Bill 1968–69 a member began to praise the work done by voluntary bodies and the chairman warned him that any argument that they should receive grants direct from the Government would be outside the Financial Resolution (1968–69 Standing Committee B, col. 18).

[4] 820 H.C. Deb., cols 1687–90; see also Housing (Amendment) Bill 1972–73, Standing Committee D, cols 9–10.

[5] As is explained below, the clerk advises the chairman also on the selection of amendments to be moved and of those to be discussed. What follows applies also to those situations.

[6] Unless, of course, it was first introduced into the House of Lords.

[7] Occasionally a chairman will reveal the problems. During the committee stage of the Finance Bill in 1937 he said: 'I have been in consultation with the advisers of the Chair, and have had considerable difficulty in making up my mind that these Amendments are in order' (325 H.C. Deb., cols 2199). The chairman will normally meet the clerk and sometimes also the draftsman shortly before the first meeting of the committee to take decisions on the amendments submitted at that time. Thereafter they will meet to deal with later clauses and amendments subsequently tabled, as occasion requires.

on behalf of the Government and to advise on the interpretation of the bill; while that of the clerk (and of the chairman) is to ensure that Members have a full opportunity to propose amendments and to comment on the Government's legislative proposals.

It would be wrong to infer from this difference of interest and of function that the draftsman and the clerk are often in conflict. But it is sometimes said that, when there is a difference of opinion, the draftsman with his far greater knowledge of the bill is in too strong a position *vis-à-vis* the clerk (and through him the chairman); and that this may particularly be so on the more complex measures such as the Finance Bill where a detailed knowledge of the implications of particular amendments for other parts of the bill is necessary for a full understanding. It is doubtful whether there is much in this criticism. Draftsmen have a corporate and professional independence that distinguishes them from most other civil servants and they can be relied on to explain the whole matter. Clerks spend much of their time dealing with the complexities of bills. Both draftsmen and clerks acquire a considerable understanding of the others' mysteries. And any greater expertise that the draftsman may have over the clerk is offset by the power of the chairman whose decision is what matters and who, when faced with a difficulty or a conflict between clerk and draftsman, will lean towards the clerk's view and therefore, in almost all cases, allow disputed amendments to stand. This does not mean that clerks and chairmen are unduly lenient towards Members. It means that, when amendments are ruled inadmissible, most likely both clerk and draftsman agree. In any event the decision whether to amend the bill rests with the committee. The chairman will, therefore, in case of doubt about the admissibility of an amendment, give the benefit of that doubt to the member who has tabled it so that the substance of the matter can be debated by the committee.

3.3.5 *Amendments – selection and grouping*

The second task of the chairman concerns the selection of amendments. The Chairman of Ways and Means and the Deputy Chairman in committee of the whole House, and the chairman of a standing committee, have the power to select, from among those which are in order, the amendments, new clauses and new schedules to be moved.[1]

On the face of it this is a power of great importance. The Government have put forward their proposals in a bill and by the law of the constitution that bill must be submitted to both Houses of Parliament where it may be amended. And the assent of each House is necessary before the bill (as amended) can become an Act of Parliament. However much the party system may ensure that the Government in the end will have the bill it wants, the right of individual Members of Parliament to propose amend-

[1] S.O. No. 33(2), 65(3)(a). The Speaker has the same power in respect of any bill under consideration on report (see below, p. 150 *et seq.*).

ments, to have them debated and, if necessary, divided on would seem to be absolute. Yet under this power of selection, a Member may be wholly prevented from moving or even discussing an amendment of which he has given notice; and which is entirely proper, within the rules of the House, to be moved or discussed. Moreover, this power in the case of the chairman of standing committee is given not to a person selected by the House but to a person nominated by the Speaker. Further, chairmen always select all Government amendments to Government bills.[1]

In 1909 the Standing Order governing closures was added to by allowing a motion to be made[2] that with respect to certain words or a certain clause or schedule the chair be empowered to select the amendments to be proposed. The motion was to be put forthwith and decided without amendment or debate and had to be made on each occasion. In approving this proposal after many hours' debate the House accepted an amendment which expressly excluded the chairmen of standing committees from exercising the power.[3]

In 1919, a new Standing Order was approved which empowered the Speaker on report and the Chairman and Deputy Chairman of Ways and Means in committee of the whole House to select the new clauses or amendments to be proposed. This meant that a special motion on each occasion ceased to be necessary.[4] But again, chairmen of standing committees were excluded.

The power was extended to those chairmen in 1934.[5] But at the same time the nomination of chairmen of standing committees was transferred from the Committee of Selection to the Speaker – the origin of the chairmen's panel. The Lord President of the Council (Mr Baldwin) put it, delicately, thus:

> 'I believe that the method of appointment and the new functions . . . of the Members of that Panel will add a weight and dignity to an office [Committee chairman] which has always been esteemed in this House as one of great responsibility, and will make it still more than it has been in the past, an office that may well be desired by Members whose gifts run rather to directing debate than taking part in it.'[6]

The Opposition agreed with the Government's proposals and were indeed likened by Mr Churchill to 'hungry cats purring at the prospect of a brimful dish of cream, about to be handed to them, they hope, at no great distance of time'.[7] But there was opposition apart from Mr Churchill's.

[1] In constitutional terms this is because the Minister, as the Member in charge of the Bill, has the initiative.

[2] Subject to the usual provision that the chair will not assent to the motion if it appears to the chair that the motion is an abuse of the rules of the House or an infringement of the rights of the minority.

[3] 8 H.C. Deb., cols 1212–1317.

[4] 112 H.C. Deb., cols 1077–92, 1213–38.

[5] 293 H.C. Deb., cols 2169–248.

[6] *Ibid.*, cols 2173–4.

[7] *Ibid.*, col. 2179.

Mr Maxton objected to the increased 'mechanisation' the change implied. 'To say to the Chairman, "When you are in that Chair, take what you like and leave all those that you do not like" is to place a tremendous power in the hands of any Member who only sits here with the same qualifications as the rest of us, and who has persuaded some constituency somewhere to be foolish enough to elect him.'[1] The Government won the division by 144 votes to 24.

The power to select amendments, then, was originally given to prevent undue obstruction of the consideration of bills, first on the floor of the House and subsequently in standing committees. Lord Campion said in 1932:

> 'It is usually exercised silently and seldom disputed by Members whose amendments are not selected. Its effectiveness cannot be checked by figures. On a general impression it is most effective on the report stage of Bills, where it is chiefly used by the Speaker to dispose of amendments which have been adequately debated in committee. In committee it is more sparingly used, generally only for amendments which are of little substance or doubtfully in order – seldom for substantial amendments. It cannot deal with obstruction on an important Bill, or be a substitute for the closure. But it is very valuable where a Bill is being debated under the "guillotine", in helping the House to make the best use of the time allotted by concentrating on the most important amendments.'[2]

So far as these comments relate to the committee stage they are as broadly true today as they were 40 years ago. Soon after Lord Campion's summary, the Unemployment Bill was considered in committee under a guillotine. A Member protested that the non-selection of an amendment meant there would be no chance of discussing the means test in the clause on allowance. The Chairman replied:

> 'I have been doing my best in the very great difficulties under which the whole Committee is obviously labouring, with regard to the large number of Amendments on the Paper, to confine discussion as much as possible to those amendments raising definite points. I have tried to select Amendments with a view to having those definite points raised and dealt with by the Minister as quickly as possible, in order that there may be some opportunity of discussing the Question, "That the Clause stand part of the Bill".'[3]

Two strands are apparent in the arguments about the selection of amendments: convenience and the rational ordering of discussion; and

[1] 293 H.C. Deb., col. 2190.

[2] G. F. M. Campion (then Clerk-Assistant of the House of Commons); 'Methods of closure in the Commons', in 1 *The Table* at p. 23.

[3] 286 H.C. Deb., col. 803 (26 February 1934); for the allocation of time motion see 284 H.C. Deb., cols 1129–222.

the saving of time (which at its extreme becomes the prevention of undue obstruction). The strands are not separate. But in committee, for the great majority of bills, it is the first which is the stronger, and the non-selection of certain amendments is not normally used as a weapon to speed business. Indeed to do so would be seen by some as an abdication by the chairman of his duties and a reversal of the rôle which the committee stage is supposed to play in the whole legislative process. For Government bills that stage is intended to enable Members of Parliament (especially, but by no means solely, Members of the Opposition) to challenge the Government, to propose amendment to Government proposals, or to require the Government to explain and justify their bill.

An example of the possible misuse of the power to select was put by Mr Churchill during the debate in committee on the Government of India Bill, 1934–35. It had been agreed that a number of clauses might be put *en bloc* if there were no amendment to any clause. But there arose a case where six clauses were put when there was an amendment tabled to the third of these clauses. Mr Churchill said:

> 'It was an Amendment which you did not select, but it was not an Amendment out of order. If it had been out of order it might be argued that it did not exist at all, but as it was an Amendment that you did not select it came into that category which I think you described as coming within the more questionable area of the selective power of the Chair in respect of amendments. We have always understood that that selective power related to making sure that the particular topic for discussion was taken at the best point which was on the Paper, and by no means related to the shortening of discussion and the excluding of any topics from discussion.'

The Chairman referred to the power of selection as 'a great responsibility, and the purpose of it has not been hedged with any rules or acknowledged usages' but he promised to ensure that Members were given an opportunity to speak on any clause.'[1]

Despite the undoubted extent of the power, and the considerable dangers of its misuse, little has happened in committee to justify the fears. This is largely because the practice of 'grouping' has developed. This allows chairmen to group amendments so that all in the group are discussed together although only the first in the group is moved. To this is added the device of permitting divisions to be taken on amendments discussed but not moved – the permission is that of the chairman but if asked for, and the intention of the grouped amendment is clearly different from that of the moved amendment, it is rarely refused.[2] In the event, therefore, members who have put down amendments generally have the opportunity

[1] 300 H.C. Deb., cols 207, 208.

[2] It is more likely to be refused in committee of the whole House than in standing committee because more time is expended in divisions on the floor.

in committee to speak to their amendments although those amendments have not been selected to be moved.[1]

This grouping of amendments is the third of the tasks that face a chairman before the committee meets for the first time. Again the main burden of the preparatory work falls on the draftsman and on the clerk of the committee.[2] Amendments will be placed in the same group if they deal with the same point though proposing different alternatives or are otherwise linked by subject matter; if they are logically linked; if some are consequential on others. Amendments are printed and considered in the order in which each would appear in the bill. When a number of amendments are grouped, the amendment that is first in order is therefore selected to be moved. This means that the moved amendment may be merely a consequential point of drafting and the substantial amendment will then be one of those included in the same group for discussion.

The grouping of amendments leads sometimes to confusion. When the Countryside Bill was being debated in committee on 19 December 1967, a Member moved Amendment No. 43 and the Chairman suggested that No. 51 (which was in the same terms but related to a later clause) should be discussed at the same time. The Minister said that the Government accepted 'the Amendment' but asked the Member to withdraw it so that the drafting could be improved. He did so. When the later clause was reached, the Minister asked whether Amendment No. 51 was not being taken but the Chairman replied that it had been discussed very thoroughly on Amendment No. 43 and so was not now being called. The Minister said that she had not intended to accept No. 51; and she apologised to the committee.[3]

Amendments may be tabled in very large numbers, sometimes as a form of obstruction. Erskine May says that the power to select amendments is in most cases 'the best method of securing reasonable opportunities for all varieties of opinions'[4] in these circumstances. But it is the grouping of amendments which is the truly effective part of the device because it enables members to speak to those amendments which are not selected to be moved. During three recent sessions the figures were as shown in Table 3.5. Thus of all amendments of which notice was given during these

[1] In the great majority of cases, the only disadvantage that flows from an amendment being selected to be discussed but not to be moved is that it may attract less press publicity.

[2] Grouping of amendments is the task that takes most of the time at the meetings of chairman, clerk and draftsman.

[3] 1967–68 Standing Committee A, cols 353–5, 463–7. On Report both amendments were effectively conceded by the Government (762 H.C. Deb., cols 1276, 1312).

For an example of the complications that can arise when similar amendments from opposite sides of the committee are grouped together although their intentions differ, see Immigration Bill 1970–71, Standing Committee B, cols 3–4, 15–6, 248, 275–6, 1024–34. And see Coal Industry Bill 1970–71 Standing Committee B, cols 282, 305–5, 308–9.

[4] *Op. cit.*, p. 436. Mr Sydney Silverman once argued (unsuccessfully) that the Standing Order empowering selection could not entitle a chairman to refuse to select the only amendment tabled to a motion (655 H.C. Deb., cols 1400–10).

three sessions, 59·8 per cent were selected to be discussed. However, the true percentage of all amendments dealt with is much higher. First, all amendments ruled out of order[1] (and so not available for selection) are included in the total tabled. But their number is not known. Again, some amendments almost duplicate others and are not selected for that reason. More importantly, in addition to the amendments referred to in Table 3.5

Table 3.5 GOVERNMENT BILLS IN STANDING COMMITTEE

	Number of amendments (including new clauses)	(1) 1967–68	(2) 1968–69	(3) 1970–71	(4) Total
1	Selected to be moved and discussed	2161	1256	1000	4417
2	Selected to be grouped and discussed	2013	1279	915	4207
3	Total	4174	2535	1915	8624
4	Of which notice was given ('tabled')	7150	3953	3315	14418
5	Column 3 as percentage of column 4	58·4	64·1	57·8	59·8

in columns 1, 2 and 3, many amendments are formally moved (and agreed to). The very great majority of these are moved by Ministers as part of the tidying up process on a bill and are minor or consequential or drafting amendments. For these three sessions the numbers of such amendments were: for 1967–68, 837; for 1968–69, 678; and for 1970–71, 278. Sometimes those amendments are grouped for discussion with other amendments (and so appear in column 2 above) and then are moved formally when their place in the bill is reached. Because of this, it is not possible to add them to those totalled in column 3 without some double counting.

So, for 1967–68, a further analysis was made to discover how many of these amendments formally moved were not selected to be grouped for discussion. The number was found to be 394 (out of the total of 837). This figure can be added to the total of 4174 in the table to give a new total of 4568 amendments dealt with in committee. And the percentage of 58·4 rises to 63·9.

[1] It seems not unreasonable to suppose that a number of Mr Arthur Lewis's amendments to the Industrial Relations Bill 1970–71 fell into this category, e.g. Amendment No. 340 which would have inserted: 'object of this Act is to ensure that workers and employers in industry, Parliament, the Law Courts, legal profession do not take time off from their normal employment to attend Ascot, the Derby, golf tournaments, race meetings and grouse shooting and that their holidays and periods of recess from work in any one year do not exceed four weeks'.

It may also be relevant to take into account non-Ministerial amendments that were not dealt with because of the operation of the guillotine. In 1967–68 the Transport Bill and the Finance Bill were guillotined and many amendments fell as a result. If those amendments are discounted, then 81 per cent of the amendments tabled were dealt with.

It is not common for the grouping of amendments – which is entirely within the discretion of the chair – to be discussed in committee, but during the debates on the Education (Scotland) Bill in 1971, the Chairman not only defended his decision but entered on 'horse-trading' with the member concerned which resulted in a different grouping being adopted.[1] Later in the same debates the Chairman said:

> 'Amendments are grouped for the convenience of the Committee. Discussion on groupings cannot take place in Committee. . . . But I have laid it down that when the lists are published, hon. Members can always approach me with a view to amending a grouping.'[2]

From time to time, members argue that while it is wholly for the chairman to decide which amendments are selected, his ruling should not prevail over the wish of the committee when grouping is under discussion. One chairman put it thus:

> 'It is for the chairman to decide these matters, unless there is a consensus that his decision is undesirable or inappropriate . . . [Grouping] is for the convenience of the Committee. The Chairman is the interpreter of that convenience until there is a consensus to show that he is wrong.'[3]

I am not sure whether that is quite the same as the statement of another chairman, this time in committee of the whole House:

> 'If the Committee wishes it so, it is absolutely entitled to have it so. All the Chair tries to do is to help the Committee and facilitate matters. If the right hon. Gentleman would like to move his Amendment alone, we shall take it alone.'[4]

The non-selection of amendments leads occasionally to protest. On 5 June 1951 when the House began its consideration of the Finance Bill in committee, the chairman announced that he had ruled the first amendment to Clause 1 out of order and did not propose to select any of the other Amendments to that clause but invited Members to make their points on the Question 'That the Clause stand part of the Bill'. This decision caused some concern but the chairman adhered to his ruling and after debate the

[1] 1970–71 First Scottish Standing Committee, cols 536–8. But contrast this with the chairman's insistence at cols 863–6 that his ruling on grouping must prevail.

[2] *Ibid.*, col. 1184; see also cols 1205–7. For a submission for change in grouping made formally in committee by an Opposition spokesman see Industry Bill 1970–71 Standing Committee E, cols 179–81.

[3] Licensing (Abolition of State Management) Bill 1970–71, Standing Committee D, cols 491, 493.

[4] Rolls-Royce (Purchase) Bill 1970–71, 811 H.C. Deb., col. 938.

clause was agreed to following a closure motion.[1] The Opposition then put down a Motion of Censure: 'That this House views with concern the decision of the Chairman of Ways and Means so to exercise his powers of selection as to exclude Amendments to Clause 1 of the Finance Bill, which would have permitted the House to debate and pronounce upon specific burdens imposed upon individuals and industries'. This was debated on 21 June 1951 when the Opposition made clear that while they were not challenging the bona fides of the Chairman, they were challenging his judgement. After debate the Motion was put and negatived without a division.[2]

The Finance Bill is often a source of complaint partly because of the practice of chairmen not to select amendments which deal with matters discussed in recent years.[3] On 1 July 1937 a Member asked whether the chairman could give guidance 'as to what steps it would be proper to take if Members of the Committee desired to know on what principles Amendments were accepted or rejected'. He was, however, told (as no doubt he expected to be) that the question of which amendments were to be selected was one that had been left entirely in the discretion of the chairman who was not bound to give any reason for his selection.[4] Generally, amendments to the Finance Bill, especially new clauses tabled by backbenchers, are less likely to be selected to be moved or grouped for discussion than amendments to other Bills.

More recently, in 1969, much debate arose over the non-selection of certain amendments and the grouping of others.[5] The occasion was the committee stage of the Parliament (No. 2) Bill which was there discussed for more than 87 hours. Twenty-one amendments were moved and a further fifty-one were grouped and discussed with them. Nearly 300 new clauses and amendments were tabled. All this was part of a highly skilled and successful campaign to obstruct the bill and force its abandonment.

During the discussions on this bill, the chairman expressed himself willing to listen to any representations made to him privately and this is indeed the more common practice. But arguments are sometimes made about selection in the committee itself. On innumerable occasions chairmen have observed and the committee has been obliged to accept that selection of amendments and their grouping for discussion are matters wholly within the discretion of the chair. And any criticism is out of order.[6] On the other hand selection, when made known beforehand, is always said to be pro-

[1] 488 H.C. Deb., cols 811–908.

[2] 489 H.C. Deb., cols 721–46.

[3] In this matter of selection of amendments as in much else, proceedings on the Finance Bill are *sui generis*, selection being much more strict.

[4] 325 H.C. Deb., cols 2290–1.

[5] 777 H.C. Deb., cols 1324–37; see also *ibid.* cols 1419–25; 778 cols 219–20, 1472–4; 780, cols 229–33; 781, cols 248–9. For debate on European Communities Bill, see above, p. 67.

[6] For a recent example, see Licensing (Abolition of State Management) Bill 1970–71, Standing Committee D, col. 54, where a Member was rebuked for saying the procedure seemed 'more like that of the Reichstag or the Kremlin'.

visional and so it is open to Members to ask for the chairman's reconsideration. This happened for example at the beginning of the committee on the House of Commons (Redistribution of Seats) (No. 2) Bill in July 1969. The Opposition spokesman explained that the amendments he and others had put down were intended to deal with three separate groups of subjects and he hoped that these might be dealt with separately both for discussion and for Division.[1]

It is usual for Members to make their protests about non-selection in sorrow rather than in anger though one Member placed on record his 'protest at the selection of Amendments in such a way as to prevent the Committee from discussing the merits of the Bill' and, when challenged, replied 'It is not I who am out of order; it is the Deputy Chairman'.[2]

The chairman not only refuses, in the great majority of cases, to respond to any criticism of his decisions, he also normally refuses to give publicly any reasons for those decisions. At times he seems to be even refusing also to distinguish between not calling an amendment because the amendment is out of order and non-selection for other reasons. Erskine May lists some examples (none being more recent than 1923) of the Speaker and chairmen giving and not giving reasons.[3] A recent example of explanations being given for non-selection arose on the Merchant Shipping (Oil Pollution) Bill 1970–71. The Chairman said:

> 'Nearly all of the Amendments which have been tabled are selected and are in order. Those which are not are Amendment No. 10 in page 6, line 40, leave out paragraph (c), which would make the Bill rather ridiculous if it were agreed to, and new Clauses Nos. 2 and 3 which are beyond the scope of the Bill, which deals with the civil liability of owners and others in respect of pollution caused by the discharge of oil and not with the prevention of pollution, which is the subject dealt with by new Clause 3, for instance.'[4]

To the controversial Education (Milk) Bill the Opposition tabled an amendment which would have added the words 'without charge' to the provision that regulations should not require a local education authority to provide milk for those over seven years' old. The non-selection of the amendment was challenged and the Chairman replied:

> 'The decision has not been taken without a good deal of consideration. I would ask the right hon. Gentleman to consider the effect of the Amendment as drafted. Besides inserting a qualifying restriction as to the provision of free milk, it would leave Section 49 of the Act of 1944 to operate as originally enacted. That is leaving a duty to provide all milk

[1] 786 H.C. Deb., cols 1170–1; and see 783 H.C. Deb., col. 1229 (Finance Bill 1968–69) and 795 H.C. Deb., cols 1422, 1459 (Commonwealth Immigrants Bill 1967–68).

[2] 432 H.C. Deb., cols 388–90 (Mr W. J. Brown during a debate on the Pensions (Increase) Bill on 23 January 1947).

[3] May, *op. cit.*, p. 442.

[4] Standing Committee G, col. 3.

for all pupils in maintained schools, both primary and secondary. The Amendment is thus in conflict with the Long Title of the Bill, which is to restrict the duty to provide milk.'[1]

The non-selection of amendments which are not out of order presents fewer problems in committee than it does on report. Indeed most amendments (except to the Finance Bill) which are in order are either moved or grouped for discussion, unless they are so ill-drafted as to verge on unintelligibility or are silly or are plainly intended to be purely obstructive or are fully covered by other amendments.[2] More commonly a chairman's power of selection is so used that even Mr George Rogers's high opinion of himself might command support: 'One measure of my extreme generosity', he said in May 1969, 'is that I cannot remember another Bill with so many Amendments when only two substantial Amendments were not selected by the Chairman'.[3]

Standing Orders provide that the Speaker or a chairman 'may, if he thinks fit, call upon any Member who has given notice of an amendment, new clause or new schedule to give such explanation of the object thereof as may enable him to form a judgement upon it'.[4] This power is not often used[5] and a Member may be refused when he asks to be allowed to explain.

Very occasionally the chairman in committee[6] seeks to meet the problem positively by suggesting an alteration which will make the amendment acceptable. The Gaming Bill 1967–68 provided that no person should take part in gaming in any street or other place to which the public had access except, amongst other things, that dominoes or cribbage could be played on licensed premises, Amendment 26 proposed: 'Clause 6 page 3 line 31, after "cribbage" insert "darts or shove halfpenny".'

Possibly carried away by the seriousness of the whole matter, the Chairman said:

'We now come to Amendment No. 26. I must confess that I have been in

[1] 1970–71 Standing Committee A, cols 14–15; for a similar though shorter explanation see cols 217–18.

[2] An unusual reason for non-selection of amendments was given during the debate on the Transport Bill 1967–68. The chairman said he had selected none of the amendments to Part VI of the Bill because, he said: 'I understand by devious means that there may be a statement from the Government'. The statement was that the Government proposed to drop the whole of Part VI. See Standing Committee F, cols 2808–12 and below, p. 132.

[3] 1968–69 Standing Committee G, col. 643 (Children and Young Persons Bill).

[4] S.O. No. 33(3), 65(3)(a). See 343 H.C. Deb., cols 1451–2 (Czecho-Slovakia (Financial Assistance) Bill 1938–39). For examples of explanations given on Report see 318 H.C. Deb., cols 1693–4 (Public Order Bill 1935–36); 303 H.C. Deb. col. 1719 (Housing (Scotland) Bill 1935–36); 296 H.C. Deb., cols 1363–4, 1388 (Electricity (Supply) Bill 1933–34).

[5] For a recent example, see Mineral Workings Bill 1970–71 Standing Committee E, col. 8. Erskine May, *op. cit.*, p. 442, cites two examples in 1909 and 1921.

[6] He may more frequently seek to do so privately – and the clerks in the Public Bill Office regularly help Members in this way.

some difficulty. As hon. and right hon. Gentlemen know, the selection of Amendments is entirely a matter for the chair. The chair does not normally have to explain its actions, but there are certain occasions, I feel, when the chair should take the Committee along with it.

'In Amendment No. 26 "darts" must be left out because that is a game of skill and not of chance, according to the definition in Clause 49. With regard to shove halfpenny, I have had some difficulty in deciding whether that is a game of skill or chance. Perhaps the hon. Member for Southend East (Sir S. McAdden) can persuade me on this, but before we deal with the Amendment as a whole, I shall have to be convinced on whether shove halfpenny is a game of chance or skill, or a bit of both.'

After explanation had been given (not by the hon. Member for Southend East but by the hon. Member for Gosport and Fareham who suggested that it was a game of skill with some element of chance) the Chairman said: 'In order to save time, I agree to allow the Amendment to read as follows: Clause 6, page 3, line 31, after "cribbage", insert "shove halfpenny".'[1] So the great wheel turns.

The House of Commons operates throughout so many of its functions on the informal as well as the formal level. The informal eases the formal and it is unusual for major conflicts on procedural questions to take place on the floor of the House or in committee room unless private discussions have failed. This is particularly true when the conflict is between Members on the one hand and the Speaker or chairmen on the other. The provisional selection of amendments by the Speaker or the chairmen may, especially on report, give rise from time to time to feelings of injustice. And the Opposition Chief Whip (or any other Member) may, as we have seen, approach the person responsible for the selection and make representations. The relative importance which the official Opposition attaches to amendments, the extent to which this is communicated to the Speaker or chairman, and the consequences of the communication are best left to be described when we consider the report stage.[2] For the moment it is worth noting that informal approaches may be made at the time of committee stage also, and even, though exceptionally, in the committee itself. As when the Opposition spokesman at the beginning of this stage indicated certain clauses and a schedule in the Finance Bill, 1968–69, as being regarded by the Opposition as particularly important and said to the Chairman: 'We hope your selection of Amendments, Mr Jennings, will be appropriately lavish when we come to those Clauses'.[3]

As has been said, chairmen will, in standing committee, usually allow[4] a division to be taken on an amendment selected to be discussed but not

[1] 1967–68 Standing Committee B, cols 72–75. [2] See below, p. 150 *et seq.*

[3] 1968–69 Standing Committee F, col. 6.

[4] The decision is theirs. As the chairman said during the debate on the Education (Scotland) Bill in 1971: 'I must make it clear that when Amendments are grouped, it is entirely for the Chairman to decide which he will allow to be moved formally for a Division' (1970–71 First Scottish Standing Committee, col. 1183).

moved, if this is requested; and may do so in committee of the whole House. Sometimes a chairman will postpone his decision on whether to allow a division until he has heard the debate. But he must be on his guard against undue obstruction. For example, when the Commonwealth Immigrants Bill was in committee of the whole House in December 1961, a number of amendments had been put down which sought to exclude from immigration control the citizens of independent Commonwealth countries. The first of these amendments concerned Ghana. It was selected to be moved and the Chairman (Sir Gordon Touche) informed the committee that he thought it would be convenient to discuss it with the other eight amendments concerning other countries. After over two hours of debate the closure was moved successfully and the amendment was divided on and rejected.[1] Opposition Members then sought divisions on the other amendments. Arguments were used: 'It would really be very extraordinary if we recorded our division . . . on Ghana and not on Nigeria, Canada, Australia and other great and equal countries of the Commonwealth' (Mr Gordon Walker). 'Surely this is a very extraordinary Ruling. . . . What power has the Chair first to select an Amendment for discussion and then to deny the Committee the right to divide on it? I submit that it certainly has not that power' (Mr Jay). 'A discussion was opened on the invitation of the Chair, not because someone on the back benches or the front benches rose and said "Is it permissible for us to make reference to other Amendments that you have selected, Sir Gordon?" There was no suggestion that they were not selected' (Mr Hale). When the Chairman denied that the other amendments had been 'selected', he was asked: 'How does one debate an Amendment which has not been selected or called. . . . It is surely the most unusual procedure to refuse the Committee the right to express its opinions on the other Amendments' (Mr G. Brown).[2]

The Chairman's view was the other amendments 'have not been selected, cannot be moved and, consequently cannot be voted upon'.[3] Erskine May states: 'For the sake of convenience, and with the consent of the committee, the chairman frequently permits debate to range over several amendments which raise different aspects of the proposal in the actual amendment under consideration. This latitude in debate is usually allowed on the understanding that, if the later amendments are called, they may be

[1] After some confusion, as one of the tellers for the Noes announced the result as Ayes 268, Noes 193 when he meant the other way round and so led the chairman into contradictory statements (650 H.C. Deb., cols 1455–6).

[2] 650 H.C. Deb., cols 1457, 1458, 1459. The debate then developed into a wide argument with the Chair and eventually 'Grave disorder having arisen in the Committee, the Chairman left the Chair to report the circumstances to the House. Mr Deputy Speaker resumed the Chair and suspended the Sitting for half an hour.' The Chairman was, as it happened, also Deputy Speaker and, on resumption, further argument continued on the position of the Mace and the rightness of the suspension. The dispute lasted from 6.48 p.m. until 9.35 p.m. (650 H.C. Deb., cols 407, 1455–1500).

[3] *Ibid.*, col. 1461.

divided on, if desired, but not discussed.'[1] This last sentence is somewhat opaque but arises from the rule that an amendment cannot be divided on unless it is moved; and what is moved may normally be discussed. What is sought to be achieved by this 'understanding' is that the later amendment may be moved for the purpose of a division only. None of this helps to answer the questions: may a division always be insisted on? and what are the conventions (if any) that govern this matter?

One chairman summarised his understanding of the answers thus, on 23 March 1964:

> 'If a subsequent Amendment hung on the Committee's division on the first Amendment, that would certainly be called and be voted on. Otherwise, the practice of the Chair, carrying out the duty imposed upon it, is that certain Amendments shall be selected and certain Amendments should be grouped together; and in that case if one side or the other is particularly anxious to register a Division, the Chair, in its discretion, may allow a Division on a further Amendment although it has been discussed together with a block of other Amendments.'[2]

As the Chairman made clear, this discretion is additional to that under which a chairman may indicate, when he announces the amendments he proposes to select, which grouped amendments may be called for the purpose of a division.

The power of selection thus governs the whole matter. When Erskine May speaks of 'the consent of the committee' in the quotation above, it must be remembered that if the committee do not consent the result may be that the amendments proposed to be grouped will not be discussed at all. And similarly if Members should show signs of unwillingness to abide by the 'understanding' that they will not seek to discuss further those amendments which are called for division only, it is possible that those amendments might not be called. But, on the other hand, as Sir Gordon Touche discovered, when he refused divisions to an Opposition angered no doubt by the moving of the closure on amendments to a bill which concerned so politically explosive an issue as race relations, the chair is often wiser to yield. Moreover, when a Member does formally move an amendment which had been discussed as a grouped amendment, it is not, on that account alone, out of order to debate it further although the 'understanding' is thereby broken and the chairman may deprecate the proceeding.[3]

The rule that the chairman's decision on the selection of amendments

[1] *Op. cit.*, p. 507.

[2] 692 H.C. Deb., col. 53–4 (Sir William Anstruther-Gray, then Deputy Speaker). A division will be refused if the later amendment has fallen, e.g. because the earlier amendment on which it depended was negatived, e.g. Development of Tourism Bill 1968–69, Standing Committee E, col. 821.

[3] E.g. 679 H.C. Deb., cols 1495, 1499, 1521–6 (Finance Bill 1962–63 on Report). The Opposition denied there had been any breach.

shall not be challenged is justifiable if designed to prevent argument in committee. It is also justifiable on the ground that the fairest way to restrict debate and to make it more coherent is to vest the power of decision in an impartial person and to trust him to exercise his discretion properly. Nor is there any appreciable general criticism in recent times of the way in which this power is exercised – though it is the grouping of amendments that removed the basis of criticism. But this rule is separate from the rule that the chairman shall give no reasons and this latter rule is far less easily justifiable. It would seem to be a small but desirable reform to require the chairman to state on what ground he had found any amendment to be out of order; and why he had decided that an amendment should be neither selected to be moved nor grouped for discussion. It would be not necessary for the chairman to make such a statement in every case but only if a Member who had given notice of such an amendment asked for an explanation. And the statement could be made in writing so that no time of the committee would be lost. In practice, the chairman's informed and private explanation would no doubt suffice in the great majority of cases. But a formal request requiring a formal answer should be made possible.

Until quite recently, a member of a committee would not normally know beforehand whether amendments of which he had given notice had been selected for debate. This information could not be obtained until either he was called to move his amendment or the chairman called a later amendment and it became clear that his had been passed over.

From time to time complaints were made by members who might have spent much time preparing themselves to no purpose. To the suggestion that chairmen should announce their selection in advance or (at least) at the beginning of the relevant sitting the standard reply was that there were difficulties because the course of debate might change the decision.

Thus in 1937 on the Finance Bill, a member said:

> 'I should also like to ask about the notice which is given to the House collectively in advance as to which Amendments are in fact going to be called and which are not. Further to the point, I should like to draw attention to the fact that some days ago I was informed through an unofficial channel that an Amendment which stood in my name on the Order Paper was not to be called. I heard it purely by chance. A number of other hon. Members have made extensive preparations for their speeches and have found that their Amendments have not been called. In these circumstances I desire to submit that it would be for the convenience of the Committee and hon. Members as a whole if some method were established which would inform hon. Members in advance of what Amendments would be called. What I wish to know is what method could be adopted.'[1]

1 325 H.C. Deb., cols 2290–1 (Mr Garro Jones).

The Deputy Chairman replied that on most occasions this would be attended with great disadvantages. He continued:

> 'It is sometimes possible on occasions like this for hon. Members to ask privately whether their amendments are to be called, and if possible the Chairman gives them an answer, but that is not always possible because the selection or otherwise of Amendments may depend upon the course of the discussion of some previous Amendments, which it may be impossible for the Chairman to anticipate.'[1]

This objection turned on the extent to which any such advance information would be regarded as binding on the chairman.

On 3 July 1958 the Chairman of Ways and Means told the Select Committee on Procedure his own practice on the Finance Bill which was then in committee. The point had come during the previous week when selection had to be made of new clauses that had been tabled. He said that he had intended to hold his conference to decide on 30 June (the day before that on which the first new clause was in fact moved)[2] but he was asked by the Government to hold it earlier because they did not want to prepare briefs on clauses which would not be called.[3] So he had his conference on 26 June. Thereafter many Members asked him what new clauses were to be called. He said: 'I cannot tell you how many people have been to my room in the last few days about new clauses, but there have been dozens of them'. But he distinguished between 'anything I say in my room' (which is 'never a promise') and anything put on the Order Paper ('then I could not change my mind'). He continued: 'The position is: These are the ones that I hope to select, and people come and say "Look here, we would rather have this one than that one," and I say to them, "By all means".' His questioner said: 'I thought we might save you some of that lobbying if it did become public, but I can see the difficulty' and the witness replied, 'I think you must keep a free hand, really'.[4]

This amount of activity (including lobbying and the trading of one amendment for another) and the quite drastic rejection of amendments is likely to happen at committee stage only on the Finance Bill[5] and sometimes on a few other bills of that magnitude, and especially in committee of the whole House. More commonly it occurs before and during report and I return to it below.[6]

[1] 325 H.C. Deb. col. 2291. Cp. the chairman of a Committee in 1943 who, when asked what amendments he proposed to call, said that this was 'not usual nor indeed always possible' (391 H.C. Deb., col. 393).

[2] 590 H.C. Deb., cols 1280–6.

[3] This must mean to prepare briefs for Ministers to enable them to reply to amendments which were not to be called.

[4] H.C. 92–I of 1958–59, Q695–7.

[5] E.g. on 11 May 1971 the Chairman on the Finance Bill in committee of the whole House said: 'Following upon representations which have been made to me by right hon. and hon. Members on both sides of the Committee, I have decided to vary my provisional selection of Amendments for this first debate'. (817 H.C. Deb., col. 216.)

[6] See p. 152 *et seq.*

The Select Committee recommended that chairmen should announce this selection publicly, both in the House and in standing committee at the beginning of each sitting on the committee and report stages of bills. But the committee recognised that if this were done the chair must reserve the right to alter the selection as the debate progressed and so the preliminary announcement could not be regarded as binding the chair.[1] The Government accepted this recommendation.[2]

Today the practice is for chairmen to announce their provisional selection of amendments at the beginning of the committee and report stages. When the debate will continue during many sittings (especially on a substantial bill in standing committee) the chairman's first announcement will cover amendments to the early clauses only and subsequent announcements will be made later. A list of the selected amendments is available for each meeting in the committee room or the lobbies; and, for standing committees meeting the next morning, is normally obtainable the previous evening from the Public Bill Office. The 'provisional' character of the selection means that the chairman can change his mind at any time before the proper place in the Bill is reached for the amendment to be moved. Not only can an amendment be selected to be moved which has not been provisionally selected; one which has been provisionally selected may at the chairman's discretion be subsequently excluded.[3] More usual is the discussion exemplified by the debate on the Immigration Bill in March 1971 when the chairman first ruled that Amendment No. 9 could be referred to only briefly while Amendment No. 6 was under discussion. But subsequently when the mover of the motion and an Opposition front-bench spokesman and the Minister asked for Amendment No. 9 and two others to be fully discussable with Amendment No. 6, the chairman agreed to 'succumb to the blandishments of the Committee'.[4]

The change in recent years is exemplified by the words of the Chairman on the Finance Bill, 1968–69, in contrast to the words of the Chairman in 1937 quoted above. On 11 June 1969 the Chairman said: 'I have also arranged that an hour before each Committee meeting the selection of Amendments be placed outside the Committee Room door, on the notice board outside the Tea Room downstairs and any other appropriate place that is available'.[5]

Although the modern practice is clearly an improvement on the old, a Member may not know until very shortly before the committee meets whether his amendment has been selected. This, in its turn, depends on when the chairman confers with his advisers and makes his decisions. And the earlier he does so, the shorter is the time available to Members to draft and to give notice of their amendments. The problem arises most

[1] H.C. 92–I of 1958–59, *Report* para 14.

[2] 615 H.C. Deb., col. 1463 (16 December 1959).

[3] E.g. Licensing (Abolition of State Management) Bill 1970–71, Standing Committee D, cols 171–5, 189–95.

[4] Standing Committee B, col. 130.

[5] 1968–69 Standing Committee F, col. 6.

acutely during the week or ten days between second reading and the first and second meetings of the committee, though the practical period during which amendments must be prepared can be said to begin with the publication of the bill (which, of course, precedes the second reading). One possibility would be to fix final dates for the giving of notice of amendments to named clauses so that the chairman would be able to publish his selection of amendments to be moved or grouped for discussion 24 hours before the appropriate sitting of the committee. Those final dates would have to be determined (and perhaps extended) from time to time depending on the progress of the committee, and the chairman would still, as now, retain his right to admit starred or manuscript amendments.[1] But the change would mean that Members would be relieved of the uncertainty which from time to time presently afflicts them. Such a reform would be most valuable on the Finance Bill, both in standing committee and on the floor, and on all bills taken in committee of the whole House. Alternatively, the chairman might make his selection earlier than he does at present, while still leaving the possibility of later considering the selection of further amendments.

Certainly there seems to be a strong case for requiring the selection of amendments for committee of the whole House (and on report) to be concluded and made public at least 24 hours before the debate takes place (instead of the late morning of the day of debate).

The disadvantage of reform on these lines is that Members would have to submit amendments one day earlier than at present. But, on the face of it, it would seem that the advantage to Members of earlier information about selection would greatly outweigh that disadvantage.

3.4 COMMITTEE STAGE ON GOVERNMENT BILLS 1967–68, 1968–69, 1970–71

3.4.1 *Introduction*[2]

An amendment moved in committee is disposed of in one of a limited number of ways. First, it may be withdrawn by the member who moves it by the unanimous leave of the committee. Thus a single dissentient voice prevents withdrawal. And if, after the mover has begged leave to withdraw, any member rises to continue the debate, the amendment cannot be withdrawn. Not infrequently it happens that a Government backbencher, having moved an amendment to elicit some information or undertaking from the Government, is denied leave to withdraw by Opposition Members who wish to force a division on the question.[3] Secondly, an amendment

[1] For starred and manuscript amendments, see above, pp. 65–6.

[2] For detailed figures, see Appendix 1.

[3] Very occasionally the Government benches may refuse leave to withdraw to Opposition amendments as on the Countryside Bill 1967–68 when the Minister said it was 'the function of this Committee to try to reach decisions when it can. . . . I felt we had discussed the . . . Amendment very fully.' (Standing Committee A, cols 120, 127.)

may be negatived by the voice of the members, without a division being taken. Thirdly, an amendment may be agreed to by the assent of the committee without a division. Fourthly, an amendment may be negatived as the result of a division. Fifthly, an amendment may be agreed to as the result of a division. In all these cases the question proposed is 'that the amendment be made'[1] but if the amendment is withdrawn the question is not put.

Amendments, if selected by the chairman, may be moved by any member of the committee who for this purpose falls into one of three groups: a member of the Government, a backbencher on the Government side, or a member of the Opposition. The Opposition has its front bench and its back bench but the distinction is here unhelpful as in many cases the Opposition backbencher who moves an amendment does so not only with the approval but often at the request of his front bench. This concerns the wider question of the way in which Government and Opposition organise their committee members on a bill.[2]

Table 3.6

Amendments (including new clauses) moved by	1967–68		1968–69		1970–71			
	CWH (24 bills and recommitted Fin. Bill)	St. Cttee (35 bills and Fin. Bill)	CWH (15 bills and pt. Fin. Bill)	St. Cttee (34 bills and pt. Fin. Bill)	CWH (32 bills and pt. Fin. Bill)	St. Cttee (39 bills and pt. Fin. Bill)	Total 182 bills	%
Ministers	6	433	16	272	24	156	907	20·5
Government backbenchers	13	217	16	63	15	112	436	9·9
Opposition Members	55	1437	92	797	95	598	3074	69·6
Total	74	2087	124	1132	134	866	4417	100
Grand total	2161		1256		1000		4417	

The total number of amendments to Government bills moved and discussed[3] in three recent sessions in committee and the distribution between Ministers, Government backbenchers and Opposition Members is shown in Table 3.6. It will be seen that the total number of bills in each session (sixty in 1967–68; fifty in 1968–69; seventy-two in 1970–71) bears little relation to the total number of amendments moved. The reason for the large number of amendments in 1967–68 (almost as many as the other two

[1] S.O. No. 32. [2] See above, p. 41–4.

[3] This excludes those moved formally and agreed to, some of which will have been previously grouped and discussed. The table excludes the 10 Consolidated Fund and Appropriation Bills.

sessions combined) was that a few bills in that session were large and contentious. Thus 464 amendments were moved to the Transport Bill which, as considered by the Standing Committee, consisted of 169 clauses and eighteen schedules contained in 260 pages. More than 200 amendments were moved to the Town and Country Planning Bill and to the Countryside Bill; and more than 100 to five other bills[1] of the same session. In 1968–69, to only three bills were more than 100 amendments moved[2] and in 1970–71; to only two bills.[3]

Table 3.6 shows the high proportion of amendments moved in committee by Opposition Members (69·6 per cent). Relatively few Opposition amendments are concerned with purely drafting points (though many are concerned with relatively minor matters), whereas many of those moved by Ministers are, so that the proportion for non-drafting amendments is still higher. As is shown by the full table in Appendix 1, this proportion is fairly constant for all bills.

The number of substantial amendments moved by Ministers in committee is often a reflection of the extent to which Parliamentary Counsel as draftsman had been able to prepare the bill before it was introduced into the House. If the Minister was obliged, because of the pressures on the Parliamentary timetable, to introduce the bill before the draftsman was reasonably satisfied with its form and shape and with the details of its language, then Government amendments may be more plentiful.

Sir Noël Hutton, then First Parliamentary Counsel, said of Government amendments:

> 'It is only after a Bill has been published that comments come in, sometimes from the public, and of course there are comments made in the House, which lead to amendments being made. Some government amendments, no doubt, arise from the fact that the Bill has had to be introduced a bit earlier than one would have liked in order to get it complete. It is common ground . . . that you have to take the tide when it serves and that if you do not get a Bill this Session you may not get it next Session or the one after that, so it must go in when the time is ripe. So if it is not possible to get everything sewn up in detail before the Bill is introduced, the only thing is to go on injecting the detail afterwards.'[4]

Sometimes an amendment will be moved by a Minister in committee as a direct result of a point made on second reading – as for example, the removal of the punishment on summary conviction by magistrates' courts of three months' imprisonment under the Gaming Bill 1967–68.[5] So also the Government reviewed the penalties originally provided for

[1] Medicines Bill (153), Finance Bill (159), Social Work (Sc.) Bill (119), Sewerage (Sc.) Bill (105), Gaming Bill (104).

[2] Finance Bill (213), Housing Bill (149), Post Office Bill (112).

[3] Civil Aviation Bill (124), Finance Bill (129).

[4] Evidence to Select Committee on Procedure (H.C. 539 of 1966–67, Q376).

[5] 758 H.C. Deb., cols 1190–1; Standing Committee B, col. 94.

infringements under the Fire Precautions Bill 1970–71 and removed limitations as a result of what was said on second reading.[1] And the Government abandoned their proposal to establish an Expert Committee as well as an Advisory Council under the Misuse of Drugs Bill 1970–71, after reconsideration following the suggestion of a Government backbencher made during the second reading.[2]

The practice may create difficulties. At the beginning of the first debate in committee – on the sittings motion – of the Oil in Navigable Waters Bill 1970–71, a spokesman for the Opposition intervened:

> 'We have been presented with Government Amendments and new Clauses of such magnitude that, if they are accepted, as they are likely to be because they are Government Amendments and new Clauses, the Bill will be vastly different from the Bill which received a Second Reading. . . . This great change in the scope of the Bill means that a virtually new Bill which has not had a Second Reading is being placed before the Committee. There are only four operative clauses in the Bill. The Government's four new Clauses vastly change the Bill.'[3]

The Opposition may, as the Minister said, have been making heavy weather of the matter on this occasion.[4] If the procedure moves forward as it is designed to do, Government amendments will normally be introduced either on report or as new clauses at the end of, and sometimes as a result of, proceedings in committee.

The number of amendments moved by Government backbenchers while only one-seventh of those moved by Opposition members is nearly half those moved by Ministers. As very few amendments moved by Government backbenchers are merely drafting, the number of 436 is an appreciable proportion of the whole.[5]

Table 3.6 also shows that relatively fewer amendments are moved to bills committed to the whole House than to bills sent upstairs. In the three sessions, 182 bills (including three Finance Bills) were considered in committee. Of these, seventy-four (including the whole or part of the Finance Bills) were taken on the floor of the House and to those 332 amendments were moved. To the remaining 111 bills (again including the whole or part of the Finance Bills) considered in standing committee, 4085 amendments were moved. The vast difference between an average of four amendments to

[1] Standing Committee A, cols 71–82; for another example, see Rating Bill 1970–71 Standing Committee D, cols 347–53, where a Government backbencher both raised the point on Second Reading and moved the Amendment in committee where it was accepted by the Government.

[2] Standing Committee A, cols 6–7.

[3] Standing Committee D, cols 3, 4. Following the decision to select Foulness as the site for London's third airport, a very long new clause on the regulation of noise and vibration was introduced into the Civil Aviation Bill 1970–71 (see Standing Committee A, cols 767–96).

[4] *Ibid.*, col. 16.

[5] See below, p. 94 *et seq.*

each bill on the floor and an average of thirty-six amendments to each bill in standing committee is largely explained by the considerable number of bills taken on the floor to which no amendments are moved (see Table 3.7).

So to 51·2 per cent of the bills, no amendments were moved; and to another 26·2 per cent, only one or two or three amendments were moved. This confirms the analysis already made which shows how very few contentious bills are taken on the floor. The one bill in Table 3.6 to which

Table 3.7 NUMBER OF GOVERNMENT BILLS SHOWING NUMBER OF AMENDMENTS (INCLUDING NEW CLAUSES) MOVED IN BILLS COMMITTED TO THE WHOLE HOUSE*

	No debate and no amendments	Debate but no amendments	1–3 amendments	4–30 amendments	Over 30 amendments	Total
1967–68	7	6	8	7	—	28
1968–69	4	3	6	6	—	19
1970–71	15	8	8	5	1	37
Total	26	17	22	18	1	84

* For 1967–68, the figures include the re-committal of the Finance Bill; for 1968–69 and 1970–71, the figures include that part of the Finance Bill committed to the whole House. The Consolidated Fund and Appropriation Bills are included in this table.

more than thirty amendments were moved was the Industrial Relations Bill 1970–71. The seventy amendments moved to that Bill, with the thirty moved to the Representation of the People Bill 1968–69 and the twenty-one moved to the Parliament (No. 2) Bill 1968–69 together account for 52·1 per cent of all the amendments moved to all the bills taken on the floor of the House during these three sessions.

Normally, however, the Government will postpone the moving of its amendments, or the bulk of them, until report stage. Essentially the making of statutes by Governments is a continuous process which begins when the idea for a bill originates whether in an election manifesto, or in the report of a commission or in the administrative shortcomings of existing provisions or in the pressure exerted by certain groups to which the Government is beholden. As the ideas begin to take shape and a place is found for the proposal in the legislative programme, consultations begin with the interests and instructions begin to flow from the Department to Parliamentary Counsel. The Treasury and other related departments having been satisfied, then, several conferences later, the bill will emerge in a more or less complete form and be printed and read a second time. Now that the affected interests can see in precise legislative language what they had known as partial, relatively unspecific, proposals they will learn how far their earlier representations have been successful. And in so far as they have not, these interests, and others not previously consulted, will begin to bring pressure to bear directly on Ministers and Departmental officials and on any other Member of the House (and, if the bill has been sent upstairs, especially on members of the Standing Committee) who may be helpful.[1] Some interests will turn more naturally to Conservative members, others to Labour members. But they will go where they feel the results are likely to be most beneficial; and they will frequently approach the Members on both sides.

The willingness of Opposition Members to be the mouthpiece of outside interests without too much understanding sometimes has hilarious results. For example:

> 'This is a drafting Amendment. I regret to have to tell the Committee – a dreadful confession to make – that I am not quite sure, in the literary sense, of its purpose. I have been looking, without success, for the very eminent note which I have received from some legal gentleman who assured me that these words were necessary to make the Clause better than it now is. . . . I should be grateful if the Under-Secretary, who has had the advantage of all the legal advice of the Home Office, would tell me whether that point, which I admit I put down without great faith in it, has any sense.'[2]

Here again, later on the same Bill:

> 'I recall that when we put down the Amendment, it seemed to us to cover a very important point. What that point is momentarily eludes me. I fancy, however, that the Minister will himself discover the point, and we shall be very interested to hear what he has to say.'[3]

The Government being under pressures (often conflicting) from such interests, from its own supporters both inside and outside Parliament, and from Opposition Members, is not in too great a hurry to amend its pro-proposals in the earlier stages of the Parliamentary part of the legislative process. It tends therefore to maintain its position, though (as we shall see) after promising on occasion to look again at that position, until the committee stage is concluded and then, after further consultation, to decide what, if any, amendments to propose when the bill is considered on report or subsequently.

Mr Graham Page, speaking with 18 years of Parliamentary experience told the Select Committee on Procedure in 1971 of what he regarded as:

[1] This simultaneous approach to both the Departments and Parliamentarians is commonly adopted by public authorities (such as associations of local authorities or other similar bodies). See, for example, the action of the Association of River Authorities on the Countryside Bill 1967–68, Standing Committee A, cols 389–406.

[2] Gaming Bill 1967–68, Standing Committee B, cols 245–6 (Mr Mark Carlisle).

[3] *Ibid.*, col. 624 (Mr William Deedes).

'one of the grievous faults of legislation at the present time which is becoming more prevalent. The Government will never accept an Amendment or ever put their own Amendment on the Order Paper in Committee stage. I am sure this is one of the conventions or practices which has grown in past years and is delaying legislation. Speaking as a Minister, I would very much like on many occasions in Committee to be able to put Amendments on the Order Paper or to accept Amendments which I think are sound. But in our procedure with parliamentary draftsmen, consultations outside the House are usually left until after the Committee stage.'[1]

Mr Page went on to say that he thought Ministers should come to the Committee having already had 'full consultation' and really knowing the attitude of those outside the House.[2] This of course might tend to make the Ministers more inflexible and 'unable to make the slightest amendment or concession in Committee or on Report'.[3]

Much would seem to depend on how far Ministers give firm commitments to outside interests before the committee stage or, indeed, before the Bill has been introduced at all. Ministers do sometimes use language like 'breaking faith' – which suggests a considerable degree of commitment. If they insisted more, in their dealings with outside interests, on reserving their final position, consultation might be more difficult but would be less restricting.

The fate of amendments which were moved to Government bills and discussed in three recent sessions is shown in Table 3.8.[4]

The withdrawal of an amendment generally means that the mover either is satisfied with the Minister's explanation or wishes to give the Minister an opportunity to reconsider. An amendment which is moved by a Government backbencher and negatived, may, especially if the amendment is divided on, indicate a revolt. But an amendment moved by an Opposition Member and negatived generally indicates nothing more than the wish of the Opposition to express their dissent. An amendment agreed to without a division generally indicates Ministerial acceptance whereas one agreed to after a division may amount to a Government defeat.

3.4.2 *Amendments moved by Ministers*

Ministers do not propose amendments to Government bills and then withdraw them. Logically there is no reason why a Minister should not be persuaded by the arguments against his own proposal that he should think

[1] H.C. 538 of 1970–71, Q452. Clearly he does not mean that there are no consultations before committee stage but that consultation on matters arising during committee is usually not concluded until after the stage is completed.

[2] *Ibid.*, Q453.

[3] *Ibid.*, Q1058 (Mr K. R. Mackenzie, Clerk of Public Bills). Sometimes Ministers will say in committee that they will move an amendment on report because to do so in committee would give members too little time for consideration, e.g. Medicines Bill 1967–68, Standing Committee D, col. 514.

[4] See next page.

again and so not press the proposal at that time. But in practice, this rarely happens.[1] Nor do Ministers, when they propose amendments, expect to be defeated. The one occasion during the three sessions when a Ministerial amendment was defeated was during the debate in Standing Committee on the Finance Bill 1968–69. This Bill disallowed in certain cases yearly interest as a deduction for tax purposes (Clause 18). But it retained the right to deduct interest on loans for the purchase of improvements of land (Clause 19). And then the Bill made further provision in Schedule 13 to exclude the operation of Clause 19 for certain transactions which might be used for tax evasion. In Standing Committee the Minister of State moved an amendment replacing part of Schedule 13 with new,

Table 3.8

Number of amendments (including new clauses) moved* by	1967–68			1968–69			1970–71			Total
	W	N	A	W	N	A	W	N	A	
Ministers	—	—	439	—	1	287	—	—	180	907
Government backbenchers	160	55	15	45	23	11	89	23	14	436
Opposition Members	765	678	49	420	426	43	318	336	39	3074
Total	925	733	503	465	450	341	407	360	233	4417
Grand total	2161			1256			1000			4417

Notes: W means Withdrawn; N means Negatived (whether on division or not); A means Agreed to (whether on division or not).

* This excludes those formally moved which are almost exclusively Ministerial amendments and the great majority of which are consequential or drafting. For tables including these amendments, see Appendix 1.

more elaborate, provisions to the same purpose. At the end of a debate in which the amendments were strongly attacked from the Opposition benches, the committee divided Ayes 13, Noes 13, and the chairman voted against the amendment as is the usual practice.[2] There was no crossvoting, the Liberal member of the committee voting with the Noes. The four non-voters out of the committee of thirty included one of the three

[1] It happened during the committee stage of the Industrial Relations Bill, 1970–71 in the House of Lords (see 319 H.L. Deb., cols 653–61); and during the report stage of the Misuse of Drugs Bill 1970–71 in the House of Lords (see 316 H.L. Deb., cols 23–30).

[2] See above, p. 64. On the motion that the Schedule be the 13th Schedule to the Bill, the committee again divided Ayes 13, Noes 13, but this time, as is also usual, the chairman declared himself with the Ayes.

Ministers and three Government supporters; two of these supporters were recorded as having attended the sitting, so their abstention was probably deliberate.

Most Government amendments moved in committee in the Commons are the result of extra-Parliamentary activity or of pressure exerted by Members privately,[1] Ministerial reaction to Parliamentary activity being usually recorded on report. And, surprisingly, this appears to be not less true of Government bills first introduced in the House of Lords.

During the three recent sessions there were seven bills, first introduced in the Lords where the number of amendments moved by Ministers in committee in the Commons totalled ten or more,[2] to a total of 162 such amendments. Only four of these were directly attributable to debates in the House of Lords. Two reversed amendments to the bills made in the Lords – one to restore large burghs as local authorities for the purposes of the Social Work (Scotland) Bill 1967–68[3] and the other to reverse the amendment to the Family Law Reform Bill 1968–69 which in the Lords fixed the age of marriage without parental consent at 20 years instead of 18.[4] The other two amendments were consequential to unimportant amendments made in the Lords.[5] More significant than these cases were the many amendments moved by Ministers in the Commons which were clearly the result of discussions with outside interests and with individual Members; and many more which were drafting or consequential. Because of the period which had elapsed between the introduction of the Bills in the Lords and the committee stage in the Commons, the ordinary processes of legislation were more advanced and more was therefore able to be done in committee in the Commons. One wonders whether it is so unthinkable as is usually supposed for controversial bills to be introduced in larger numbers in the Lords and whether to do so might not make committee stage in the Commons more efficient and Members better informed.[6]

3.4.3 *Amendments moved by Government backbenchers*

1967–68 In 1967–68, fifty-five amendments moved by Government backbenchers were negatived, twenty-seven without a division and twenty-eight

[1] Government reaction may, of course, be evidenced by Ministerial acceptance of amendments moved by their own backbenchers or by Opposition Members.

[2] In 1967–68, Civil Aviation Bill (13 amendments moved by Ministers); Social Work (Sc.) Bill (67); Trade Descriptions (No. 2) Bill (10). In 1968–69, Family Law Reform Bill (11); Town and Country Planning (Sc.) Bill (25). In 1970–71, Courts Bill (25); Friendly Societies Bill (11).

[3] Scottish Standing Committee, cols 4–70.

[4] Standing Committee B, cols 35–58.

[5] Both were to the Trade Descriptions (No. 2) Bill 1967–68, Standing Committee A, cols 242–4, 304–7.

[6] Under S.O. No. 58A agreed to by the House of Commons in August 1972, the scope of financial measures which, having been brought from the House of Lords, may be considered by the Commons, was extended (see 842 H.C. Deb., cols 1656–61).

on a division. Of the fifteen amendments agreed to, five were on a division. The remaining 160 amendments were withdrawn (see Table 3.8 above).

A common reason for the negativing without a division of an amendment moved by a Government backbencher is that the mover intended to withdraw his amendment having heard the Minister's explanation but failed to indicate this clearly so that it could not be said the committee agreed to its withdrawal. But frequently also, the mover may have decided to register his dissatisfaction by refusing to withdraw.

Withdrawal requires a positive request by the mover of the amendment. Silence most frequently indicates an unwillingness to press the amendment to a division but may indicate also an unwillingness to make that request. So the question on the amendment will be put and negatived. Eleven of the twenty-seven amendments negatived without division in 1967–68 fell into this 'silent' category.[1] Very similar are the occasions, of which there were three in 1967–68,[2] where there is nothing to show why the mover did not withdraw but where it seems that the mover is more or less satisfied with the Ministerial explanation. On six occasions the withdrawal of amendments was prevented by the refusal of committee members to give leave or by speeches subsequent to the request for leave.[3] In two cases it appears that the absence of the mover of the amendment and so the impossibility of withdrawal resulted in amendments being negatived;[4] in both, the debate was interrupted by adjournment until the next sitting and the probability was that the mover was absent at the resumption. On one occasion, the mover expressed herself dissatisfied with the Ministerial reply and so did not withdraw.[5] Similarly, on another, the mover said 'I shall not press[6] the Amendment, but I shall not surrender either. It can be defeated openly and honestly. We each have a case. Let the Committee decide.'[7]

None of these twenty-four amendments raised points of great importance. The other three were more controversial and the movers were dissatisfied. The purpose of the Revenue Bill 1967–68 was to reduce the amount of

[1] Countryside Bill, Standing Committee A, cols 949–52, 1259–61; Gaming Bill, Standing Committee B, cols 15–8; Transport Bill, Standing Committee F, cols 2382–8; Health Services and Public Health Bill, Standing Committee D, cols 275–7, 277, 569–70; Medicines Bill, Standing Committee D, cols 569–70; Sewerage (Sc.) Bill, Scottish Standing Committee, cols 235–6; Social Work (Sc.) Bill, Scottish Standing Committee, cols 389–93.

[2] Health Services and Public Health Bill, Standing Committee D, cols 365–7; Medicines Bill, Standing Committee D, cols 540–3, 835–41.

[3] Countryside Bill, Standing Committee A, cols 355–76; London Cab Bill, Standing Committee D, cols 22–30; Transport Bill, Standing Committee F, cols 1432–55; Medicines Bill Standing Committee D, cols 306–14; Prices and Incomes Bill Standing Committee F, cols 1081–9; Town and Country Planning Bill Standing Committee G, cols 846–8.

[4] Medicines Bill, Standing Committee D, cols 559–63, 783–91.

[5] Finance Bill, Standing Committee A, cols 648–53.

[6] I.e., presumably, to a division.

[7] Medicines Bill, Standing Committee D, cols 823–5 (Mr Ogden).

payments under the Selective Employment Payments Act 1966 with exceptions for development areas and Clause 1 reduced payments from 1 April 1968. An amendment moved by Mr Henig sought to postpone this date by one year and it is clear from the debate that he and other Government backbenchers were unhappy at the Ministerial position and so the amendment was not withdrawn.[1] Rather similarly, Clause 3 of the Prices and Incomes Bill 1967–68 increased the duration of standstills which might be imposed on prices and charges and on awards and settlements. Mr Mikardo moved an amendment to challenge this extension and did not attempt to withdraw it.[2] This was a movement from the left wing of the party. So also was an amendment moved by Mr Heffer to the Public Expenditure and Receipts Bill, Clause 1 of which provided for an increase in national insurance contributions by employed persons. The amendment sought to impose this burden instead onto employers. The mover was supported by Mr Allaun, Mr Mendelson, Mr Mikardo, Mr Foot, Mr Orme, Mr Dickens and others and after long debate, the amendment was negatived.[3] Of all these amendments moved by Government backbenchers and negatived without a division, only this last could be said to come close to a threat of non-support for the Government.

In 1967–68, twenty-eight amendments moved by Government backbenchers were negatived on a division.

On five of these twenty-eight occasions, the mover was refused leave to withdraw and a division was forced by the Opposition. As in four of the divisions the mover abstained and in the fifth he (Sir Myer Galpern) voted against his own amendment, none amounts to a genuine challenge to the Government from its own backbenches. The four occasions were on the Countryside Bill,[4] the Gaming Bill,[5] the Medicines Bill,[6] and the Finance Bill;[7] the fifth was on the Teachers Superannuation (Scotland) Bill.[8] This last amendment resulted in a long debate which took place on a previous Opposition amendment with which Sir Myer's amendment was grouped for discussion but subsequently divided on. The effect of Sir Myer's amendment would have been to allow a teacher who, having retired and drawn his pension, returned to teaching, to receive both pension and his full pay. The question had been debated on several occasions previously. The Minister undertook to re-examine the proposal but the Opposition refused leave to withdraw and the division followed.

On twelve occasions the Government backbenches divided the committee when the likelihood was that the Opposition would, in sufficient numbers to ensure a Government majority, either support the Government or abstain. So Mr Pavitt voted alone in favour of an amendment he moved to the Medicines Bill.[9] The Prices and Incomes Bill produced much dissension

[1] 759 H.C. Deb., cols 43–64.
[2] Standing Committee F, cols 387–90.
[3] 759 H.C. Deb., cols 954–1014.
[4] Standing Committee A, cols 346–54.
[5] Standing Committee B, cols 119–22.
[6] Standing Committee D, cols 686–702.
[7] Standing Committee A, cols 1387–92.
[8] Scottish Standing Committee, cols 45–6.
[9] Standing Committee D, cols 721–8.

amongst Government supporters. On amendment 51, Mr Mikardo[1] and Mr Ted Fletcher divided the committee but no one else voted with them. The bill provided that the Treasury might by order applying to any description of companies specified prohibit those companies from declaring ordinary dividends without first obtaining the consent of the Treasury. The amendment proposed that all companies should be prohibited from declaring ordinary dividends, without obtaining that consent, at a rate greater than that paid for the preceding financial year. The Opposition abstained.[2] Mr Mikardo moved another amendment to the same bill affecting Northern Ireland. This time, he and Mr Fletcher were joined by Mr Ogden and Mr Shaw while several Opposition members voted with the Government.[3] Twice on the Race Relations Bill those on the left of the Government backbenches divided the committee. The first was on an amendment moved by Mr Whitaker to extend the bill to Northern Ireland. Nine Government backbenchers were defeated by two Ministers, three Government backbenchers and eleven Opposition members.[4] The second amendment was moved by Mr Lyon and sought to allow the Race Relations Board to claim, on behalf of a person who had been discriminated against, damages that would be assessed not only on actual cash loss but also on damage to feelings. Six Government backbenchers were this time defeated by two Ministers, four Government backbenchers and ten Opposition Members.[5] On the Finance Bill, Mr Haseldine (Labour and Co-op) moved an amendment which, with those grouped with it, sought to exclude from selective employment tax the wholesaling and retailing of food in development areas. It was defeated by 4 votes to 20, four Government backbenchers voting in the minority against three Ministers and seventeen Government backbenchers, Opposition Members abstaining.[6]

To the Public Expenditure and Receipts Bill, in committee of the whole House, Mr Peter Jackson moved an amendment to postpone the reduction in the provision of school milk until the national food survey had conducted an up-to-date report. After debate lasting nearly 2¾ hours the amendment was defeated by 150 votes to 37, six Liberals voting with the Government backbenchers in the minority.[7] Twice on the Race Relations Bill, Government backbenchers were joined by Opposition backbenchers who were also voting against their own front bench. Mr Bidwell moved an amendment to exclude the provisions that enabled an employer to discriminate for the purpose of securing or preserving a reasonable balance of persons of different racial groups. This was defeated by 14 votes to 10, the minority being composed of seven Government and two Opposition backbenchers and a Liberal member, and the majority of two Ministers, five Government

1 He abstained on the vote for the Second Reading of the Bill (765 H.C. Deb., cols 390, 419–22).

2 Standing Committee F, cols 777–96.

3 *Ibid.*, cols 1101–8.

4 Standing Committee B, cols 674–82.

5 *Ibid.*, cols 729–30.

6 Standing Committee A, cols 2005–46.

7 759 H.C. Deb., cols 1054–106.

backbenchers and seven Opposition Members.[1] The other amendment sought to exclude the exemption of the merchant marine from the provisions of the Bill on discrimination in employment. This was defeated by 18 votes to 9, one Liberal and one Opposition backbencher joining seven Government backbenchers in the minority against two Ministers, six Government backbenchers and ten Opposition Members.[2]

The Commonwealth Immigrants Bill provided three more instances. First, Mr Paget moved an amendment to exempt from Clause 1 of the bill any who needed special protection and rights of entry because their liberty or livelihood was threatened in the country of residence. After long debate the closure was agreed to by 186 votes to 40, the minority being composed of members of all parties. The amendment was then defeated by 196 votes to 71, the minority consisting of forty-four Government backbenchers, fifteen Opposition backbenchers, eleven Liberals and one Scottish Nationalist.[3] Secondly, a new clause providing that nothing in the bill should be construed so as to limit or deny political asylum was refused a second reading by 122 votes to 44, again with all three parties represented in the minority.[4] Thirdly, another new clause to provide a right of appeal from an immigration officer to a magistrates' court met the same fate by 127 votes to 26. On this occasion the rebels from Government and Opposition backbenches were joined, in addition to the Liberals, by a senior Opposition frontbencher.[5]

All these twelve amendments moved by Government backbenchers and negatived on a division were substantial and represented revolts often led by the Tribune group but also on occasion supported by Liberals and some Opposition rebels. Prices and incomes, SET, race relations and immigration control are all issues that divide the Labour Party in and out of office and the latter two frequently result in Liberal and some Conservative opposition to Government policy whichever party is in power.

The third group of eleven amendments takes those dissents a stage further. Here we find Government backbenchers dividing the committee in circumstances where a defeat of the Government was a real possibility. The principal scene of battle was the Prices and Incomes Bill. On nine occasions (in addition to those already referred to)[6] such divisions occurred at the instance of Mr Mikardo and Mr Ted Fletcher. First, the bill provided that although sections 1 to 3 of the Prices and Incomes Act 1967 should cease to have effect at the end of 1969 orders or directions previously made or given should not be affected. The amendment sought to terminate such orders or directions also at the end of 1969. It was defeated by 18

[1] Standing Committee B, cols 508–36.

[2] *Ibid.*, cols 559–70 (Mr Whitaker's amendment 167).

[3] 759 H.C. Debs., cols 1553–600 (the two tellers for the Ayes were Government backbenchers).

[4] 759 H.C. Deb., cols 1663–72.

[5] *Ibid.*, cols 1671–90 (the frontbencher was Mr Iain Macleod).

[6] See above, pp. 96–7.

votes to 15, the two Government backbenchers voting with thirteen Opposition Members in the minority.[1] Secondly, another and similar Mikardo amendment was defeated by 18 votes to 16, the same fifteen being joined by another Opposition Member.[2] Thirdly, Mr Mikardo sought to prevent the continuance in force of a number of sections of the Prices and Incomes Act 1966. The purpose of this amendment was, in the mover's words, 'to take away from the Minister the right to be rough with the trade unions in respect of wage claims which they put in and which have been agreed . . . and to be rough with them in respect of wage claims on which there is no agreement'. The amendment was defeated by 17 votes to 16 (the same 16 as before).[3] The fourth Mikardo amendment sought to bring to an end the effectiveness of certain sections of the Act of 1967 6 months earlier than provided for. This was defeated by 18 votes to 16, as before.[4] Fifthly, Mr Fletcher moved to reduce from 3 months to 30 days the period for which the Secretary of State could postpone the making of a wage regulation order; and this was defeated by 17 votes to 15, two of the regular Opposition votes not voting in this division but one Liberal (Mr Hooson) joining the minority.[5] Mr Mikardo sought to reduce a similar period of postponement but was defeated by 16 votes to 12, the two Government backbench rebels being joined by ten Opposition Members.[6] The seventh amendment was similar and the voting was the same.[7] Eighthly, Mr Mikardo sought to leave out all reference to agricultural wages orders in Schedule 2 (that dealing with deferments and postponements of wages orders) with, again, the same result.[8] And finally Mr Mikardo moved an amendment to postpone the coming into effect of the Bill until 12 August 1968. This was defeated by 18 votes to 16, Mr Mikardo and Mr Fletcher being rejoined by their full complement of Conservative Opposition supporters.[9]

The other two occasions in this group were on the Town and Country Planning Bill and the Race Relations Bill. The first was an amendment moved by Mr Wellbeloved the effect of which would have been to require local planning authorities to 'define' action areas and not merely to 'indicate' them. The amendment was defeated by 8 votes to 6, only Mr Wellbeloved voting with the Opposition.[10] The second concerned a provision in the Race Relations Bill that permitted certain discriminatory advertisements for employment and Mr Whitaker moved an amendment to delete it. This was defeated by 12 votes to 9, one other Government backbencher supporting the mover in the minority.[11]

1 Standing Committee F, cols 339–82.
2 *Ibid.*, cols 1109–10 (Amendment 38); for debate, see previous note.
3 *Ibid.*, cols 177–8; for debate see cols 114–76.
4 *Ibid.*, cols 339–40; for debate see cols 55–112.
5 *Ibid.*, cols 673–96.
6 *Ibid.*, cols 723–4; for debate see previous note.
7 *Ibid.*, cols 755–6; for debate see note 302.
8 *Ibid.*, cols 726–56.
9 *Ibid.*, cols 1091–102; the Act came into force on the date of royal assent, 10 July 1968.
10 Standing Committee G, cols 74–90.
11 Standing Committee B, cols 441–54.

On five occasions in 1967–68, amendments moved by Government backbenchers were agreed to on a division.

The Transport Bill provided that, in a designated area, it should be the duty of the National Bus Company (and its equivalent in Scotland) to co-operate with the Passenger Transport Executive for that area in the re-organisation of bus services. An amendment proposed to make this duty reciprocal. The Minister accepted the amendment but the Opposition resisted it and divided the committee which agreed to the amendment by 16 votes to 11.[1]

The other four amendments were defeats for the Government. The Town and Country Planning Bill required local planning authorities to make surveys of their areas but did not require that in doing so they should examine the relationship between the development and planning of their separate areas and the development and planning of the whole of the United Kingdom and their region. The amendment sought to add this requirement. The Minister argued that the Bill as drafted adequately covered the point but the amendment was agreed to by 11 votes to 6, four Government backbenchers voting in the majority.[2]

A more serious defeat was inflicted on the Government during the passage of the Medicines Bill. Part V of that bill empowered the Minister to make regulations with respect to the labelling of containers and packages of medicinal products, the display of distinctive marks on containers and packages, leaflets, the colour, shape and distinctive marks on products and other matters, for certain purposes set out in the bill. Clause 82 laid down the offences and the penalties. These provisions regulating the marking of products and of containers and packages clearly might conflict with registered trade marks or designs in that the regulations might, for example, require certain symbols to be used which were so registered. Clause 82(4) therefore provided that in any proceedings for infringement of trade marks or designs, it should be a defence to prove that the act constituting the infringement was necessary in order to comply with regulations made under the bill. This sub-clause caused something of an uproar in the industry and brought the Ministry of Health into conflict with the Board of Trade. Mr English moved an amendment to delete the sub-clause and the Opposition did so also. The Minister agreed that the sub-clause was too wide and said he proposed to amend it on report. His opponents on both sides of the committee insisted on pressing the motion to a division and the amendment was agreed to by 9 votes to 8 although only Mr English voted with the Opposition in the majority.[3]

The other two occasions were on the Race Relations Bill. Clause 2 made it unlawful for the providers of goods, facilities and services to discriminate but sub-clause (3) provided that the clause should not render unlawful anything done in good faith for the benefit of a particular section of the public which had the effect of promoting the integration of members of

[1] Standing Committee F, cols 1249–58.
[2] Standing Committee G, cols 6–28.
[3] Standing Committee D, cols 613–30.

that section into the community. Mr Rose moved to delete this sub-clause. Other amendments sought to limit the effect of the sub-clause to education. The Under-Secretary of State resisted the amendments but Mr Rose's was agreed to by 15 votes to 8. Two Ministers, three Government backbenchers and three Opposition Members were defeated by ten Government backbenchers, four members of the Conservative Opposition and one Liberal Member.[1] Finally, Clause 25(4)(5) excluded from the operation of Part II of the Bill (in most cases) the Crown; prescribed public bodies; and other authorities acting for the purpose of employing constables. Mr Lyon in what he called a probing amendment (which would normally be withdrawn) moved to delete these sub-clauses. The Secretary of State strongly resisted the arguments used to support the amendment but it was agreed to by 17 votes to 9. One Opposition Member voted with the Government but the majority included six Government backbenchers, one Liberal and ten Opposition Members.[2]

Ten amendments in 1967–68 moved by Government backbenchers were agreed to without a division. Of these, three were drafting or clarificatory in effect.[3] Six others were of minor importance, two of which were to the Countryside Bill. The first of these added land held inalienably by the National Trust to areas for which traffic regulation orders might be made for the purpose of conserving or enhancing the natural beauty of the area, or of affording better opportunities for the public to enjoy the area for recreation or the study of nature.[4] The second concerned the duty of farmers who have ploughed a footpath or bridleway to make good its surface within a specified period. Clause 22(2) of the bill empowered the highway authority to extend the period and to order the temporary diversion or stopping up of the path or way. The amendment sought to delete the power to stop up; and was accepted by the Minister.[5] Two connected amendments were to the Justices of the Peace Bill and were concerned further to protect the interests and enlarge the functions of magistrates' clerks.[6] To the Prices and Incomes Bill, Mr Mikardo (as I have noted) moved many amendments in association with Mr Fletcher. Amendment 49 sought to make clear that when a standstill was in operation and a settlement was about to emerge the Government could not then reimpose the standstill for a further period as 'a sort of cat and mouse game'. The Under-Secretary of State accepted the amendment – taking Mr Mikardo 'aback breathless with surprise'.[7] The last of this group of amendments of minor importance agreed to was moved by Mr Ron Lewis to the Transport Bill to ensure that rural district councils might, with other

[1] Standing Committee B, cols 239–62.

[2] *Ibid.*, cols 790–804; as a result, five Government amendments fell.

[3] Countryside Bill 1967–68 Standing Committee A, cols 528–31, 883 (Amendment 149) 1370 (Amendment 150); Transport Bill 1967–68 Standing Committee F, cols 2655–6.

[4] Standing Committee A, cols 721–4.

[5] *Ibid.*, cols 1252–7.

[6] Standing Committee E, cols 42–5, 45–7.

[7] Standing Committee F, cols 423–30.

local authorities, be entitled to make objections to the grant of operators' licences.[1]

Finally one more important amendment was agreed to, Clause 2 of the Race Relations Bill 1967–68 made unlawful discrimination by persons concerned with the provision of goods, facilities and services and gave examples of what was intended. One of the examples was the services of any business, profession or trade. To this Mr Whitaker successfully moved to add 'or local or other public authority' and he was supported by members of all three parties represented on the committee.[2]

In addition to these ten agreed amendments, fifteen others standing in the name of Government backbenchers were agreed to on formal motions. These were mostly consequential but one was of importance. Clause 10 of the Gaming Bill established the Gaming Board and provided that it should consist of a chairman and two other members appointed by the Secretary of State. An amendment from the Opposition benches proposed to leave out 'two' and insert 'six' and with this was discussed a Government backbench amendment tabled by Mr Paget to leave out 'two'. The latter was accepted and the former withdrawn.[3]

1968–69 The twenty-three occasions in 1968–69 when Government backbench amendments were negatived are separable into five occasions when no division was taken and eighteen occasions on division.[4]

The five occasions referred to above when no division resulted were on the Housing Bill, the Representation of the People Bill and, thrice, on the Parliament (No. 2) Bill. The Housing Bill instance was an amendment moved from the left wing of the Labour party (Messrs Dunnett, Allaun and J. Silverman) in an attempt to limit rent increases when improvements were made. The Minister made a concession, the mover begged leave to withdraw but further speeches were then made and so, procedurally, the amendment could not be withdrawn.[5] On the Representation of the People Bill, Mr G. R. Strauss moved an amendment to reverse the *Tronoh Mines* decision[6] on election expenses but failed to persuade the Minister.[7] The Parliament (No. 2) Bill was, of course, a fertile mother of revolt being indeed in almost continuous labour for nearly 90 hours. Two of the three amendments[8] were negatived without division on the amendment but after division on a closure motion. One of those and another, also moved by Mr Sheldon, were part of the successful campaign to force the Government by attrition to withdraw the bill. In these last four instances the movers were dissatisfied with the Minister's reply.

The eighteen occasions when Government backbench amendments were

[1] Standing Committee F, cols 2366–9.
[2] Standing Committee B, cols 213–14, 238.
[3] *Ibid.*, cols 100–10. [4] See Table 3.8 above on p. 93.
[5] 1968–69 Standing Committee F, cols 501–9.
[6] *R.* v. *Tronoh Mines Limited and others* [1952] 1 All E.R. 697.
[7] 775 H.C. Deb., cols 465–86. [8] 778 H.C. Deb., cols 221–78, 644–96, 1637–87.

negatived after divisions were on the Children and Young Persons Bill (twice), the Customs (Import Deposits) Bill, the Finance Bill, the Housing Bill (twice), the Nurses Bill, the Post Office Bill, the Representation of the People Bill, the Transport (London) Bill and the Parliament (No. 2) Bill (eight times).

Some of these can be explained quickly. Mr Archer moved both the amendments on the Children and Young Persons Bill. On the first, the Opposition spokesman replied to the Minister's explanation, the committee divided equally (Mr Archer not voting) and the Chairman cast his vote against the amendment.[1] On the second, Mr Archer began by saying he did not propose to press it to a division but an Opposition Member who had associated himself with the motion opposed its withdrawal and, the motion being divided on, Mr Archer voted against it.[2] Neither of these amendments was of much importance. The mover of the amendment to the Customs (Import Deposits) Bill (Mr Houghton) said it was 'a purely constituency matter' and concerned the effect on one small family business of the need to pay a 50 per cent deposit on the import of high density, high molecular weight, polyethylene. Opposition amendments were grouped for discussion with Mr Houghton's amendment which was divided on, Mr Houghton not voting.[3] Mr Heffer moved an amendment to the Finance Bill which he asked leave 'extremely reluctantly' to withdraw but Opposition Members forced a division, Mr Heffer not voting.[4] Mr Silverman moved the second reading of a new clause to the Housing Bill dealing with students' residences. He was denied leave to withdraw his motion and the clause was read a second time but on the question that the clause be added to the bill the motion was lost, Mr Silverman not voting.[5]

In none of those five instances did the Government backbencher who moved the amendment vote against the Government. The eight divisions on the Parliament (No. 2) Bill were on four amendments proposed by Mr Sheldon and one each proposed by Messrs English, Hamilton, Tuck and Lee. Of those, Mr English and Mr Tuck voted for the bill on second reading while the others voted against. All, except Mr Sheldon on one occasion, voted for or acted as tellers for the votes on their amendments and were supported by other Government backbenchers.[6]

We are left with five other occasions when individual Government backbenchers moved amendments and voted against their party. On the Housing Bill Mr Wellbeloved did so when he moved a new clause which would have given tenants the option to purchase their houses before an application for a qualification certificate could be entertained by a local authority. The mover and three other Government backbenchers were defeated by a

[1] 1968–69 Standing Committee G, cols 400–10.

[2] *Ibid.*, cols 456–66.

[3] 774 H.C. Deb., cols 1597–620.

[4] 784 H.C. Deb., cols 501–28.

[5] 1968–69 Standing Committee F, cols 855–66.

[6] 777 H.C. Deb., cols 1338–420, 1487–90; 778 H.C. Deb., cols 479–546, 1740–92, 1833–56 and 780 H.C. Deb., cols 229–302, 417–56; 781 H.C. Deb., cols 359–84, 393–426, 432–54, 504–36.

combination of seven Government and four Opposition votes.[1] On the Nurses Bill, Mr Pavitt moved to ensure that one of the persons elected to the General Nursing Council should be a man, was denied leave to withdraw, and voted for his amendment in the division.[2] On the Representation of the People Bill, Mr Strauss moved that the voting age should be reduced not to 18 but to 20 years of age and on the division was one of the tellers for the 121 Ayes (almost all Opposition Members) against 275 Noes drawn from both sides of the House.[3]

Finally two amendments were moved of greater political significance. The first was moved by Mr Raymond Fletcher on the London (Transport) Bill to empower the London Transport Executive, in short, to manufacture buses for sale to outside persons. The amendment was defeated by five Opposition Members and three from the Government benches outvoting four Government rebels.[4] On the Post Office Bill, Mr Dobson moved an amendment on a clause concerned with staff pensions to add 'Any scheme for the payment of pensions, allowances or gratuities shall be determined in consultation with the staff concerned'. On the vote, after much debate, Mr Dobson and five other rebels against the Government were defeated by the Minister, two Government supporters and four Opposition Members.[5]

On three occasions amendments moved by Government backbenchers were agreed to after a division. Two of these were to the Administration of Justice Bill. Both were moved by Sir Eric Fletcher.[6] These were Government defeats but law bills are often treated as non-partisan so defeats have less significance. The bill proposed to increase the power of the county court in actions of contract and tort to award the plaintiff damages to the new figure of £750. Any litigant could still commence his action in the High Court if he chose but in order to discourage plaintiffs in small cases from doing so it had been provided that if a litigant proceeded in the High Court but was awarded less than a specified amount he would get his costs not on the High Court but on the lower county court scale. The bill proposed to increase that specified amount from £400 to £600. Sir Eric's first amendment proposed £500 and this was carried by 11 votes to 2, only the Solicitor General and the Government Whip voting against,[7] and six Government backbenchers supporting Sir Eric.

The second amendment to this bill concerned the right of a litigant who had been unsuccessful before a judge of first instance, in certain circumstances and after having obtained a certificate from the judge, to appeal

[1] 1968–69 Standing Committee F, cols 901–18. See below, p. 140.

[2] 1968–69 Standing Committee D, cols 15–20.

[3] 774 H.C. Deb., cols 309–436; there was a two-line whip for Government backbenchers. See below, p. 142.

[4] 1968–69 Standing Committee A, cols 177–190.

[5] 1968–69 Standing Committee D, cols 992–1048.

[6] From 1964 to 1966 he was Minister without Portfolio, spokesman in the House of Commons for the Lord Chancellor's Department, and assisted the Law Officers.

[7] Standing Committee D, cols 15–38.

directly to the House of Lords 'leapfrogging' the Court of Appeal. One of the conditions in the bill was that both parties should consent to this procedure and it was this condition which Sir Eric's amendment sought to delete. Again he was successful, this time by 6 votes to 3, being supported by two Government backbenchers.[1]

The third amendment moved by a Government backbencher and agreed to after a division was to the Development of Tourism Bill. The bill proposed that a person who incurred certain expenditure in providing a new hotel should be entitled to receive a grant 'after the completion of the hotel'. Mr Carol Johnson moved to delete those quoted words to enable interim payments to be made. He was supported by members of the Opposition who refused him leave to withdraw. The amendment was carried by 7 votes to 5. There was no crossvoting, Mr Johnson voting against his own amendment.[2]

On eight occasions in 1968–69 amendments moved by Government backbenchers were agreed to without a division. One of these was drafting only,[3] six were accepted by Ministers as small but sound and useful points which improved the bill,[4] and one was controversial and important. This last arose on the Agriculture (Spring Traps) (Scotland) Bill 1968–69 when Mr Manuel moved an amendment that prevented the Secretary of State from postponing the abolition of gin traps beyond 1 April 1973. The Minister accepted this at once although he had previously defended the power contained in the bill to defer indefinitely. The amendment was agreed to but only after debate lasting 1¾ hours.[5] This major change by the Government of policy on the bill was clearly made before the discussion on Mr Manuel's amendment which, if not put down by him at the Minister's request, was used by the Minister to implement that change.

1970–71 The twenty-four occasions in 1970–71 when Government backbench amendments were negatived are separable into fifteen occasions when no division was taken and nine occasions on division. Of the fourteen occasions when such amendments were agreed to, thirteen were without a division. (See Table 3.8 on page 93 above.)

Of the fifteen occasions when amendments were negatived without a division, five took place on the Finance Bill, five on the Immigration Bill, two on the Industrial Relations Bill and one each on the Highways Bill, the Atomic Energy Bill and the Rolls-Royce (Purchase) Bill.

Sir Brandon Rhys Williams moved an amendment to Clause 12 of the Finance Bill seeking to delete the provision in the existing law under which

[1] *Ibid.*, cols 101–12.

[2] Standing Committee E, cols 355–62.

[3] Education (Scotland) Bill 1968–69 1st Scottish Standing Committee, cols 595–6.

[4] Housing Bill 1968–69 Standing Committee F, cols 723–7, 797–8, 818–20, 891; Finance Bill 1968–69 Standing Committee F, cols 840–1; Town and Country Planning (Scotland) Bill 1968–69 1st Scottish Standing Committee, cols 302–3.

[5] 1968–69 1st Scottish Standing Committee, cols 37–72.

an annuity started to run from the date on which a person reached the age of seventy whether or not he wished to receive it. And, despite the explanation given by the Financial Secretary to the Treasury, Sir Brandon did not withdraw.[1] Mr Bruce-Gardyne wished to apply to shares or securities of all unquoted companies the provision whereby estate duty was payable by instalments; and to replace the existing 'hardship' discretion exercised by the Inland Revenue. He remained unsatisfied by the Ministerial reply.[2] Mr Dykes moved a new clause which would have made maintenance payments to a separated or divorced woman rank as earned income. This was not the first time such a clause had been moved. The Conservative Government of 1960 and the Labour Government of 1966 had both rejected the proposal. And, so it was again, despite speeches from both sides in its favour.[3] Mr Dykes moved another new clause to exempt in part from liability for capital gains tax contractual savers under SAYE. The Government expressed sympathy but recommended rejection.[4] Finally Mr Parkinson moved a new clause to give exemption from estate duty to property passing to charities. Two other new clauses of a surtax nature were debated at the same time; but the motion was negatived.[5]

Of the five amendments moved by Government backbenchers and negatived without a division during proceedings in committee on the Immigration Bill in 1971, four were moved by Mr Enoch Powell, who, we may assume, was dissatisfied with the Minister's reply. The first of these was to exclude the Republic of Ireland from the common travel area and it enabled Mr Powell to discourse on the failure of the Government to deal with the fundamental problem of citizenship.[6] His second amendment sought to exclude from the category of those having the right of abode, by having been settled in the United Kingdom for a period of 5 years or more, any whose 5 years ended before April 1962.[7] His third amendment related to Clause 23 which empowered the Secretary of State to make grants to any voluntary organisation that helped persons with their rights of appeal under the bill. Mr Powell sought somewhat to limit the effect of the clause.[8] Finally, under the clause dealing with contributions for expenses of persons returning abroad, Mr Powell proposed to generalise the discretion of the Minister and so limit his power to deal on a case-by-case basis with the making of contributions to Commonwealth citizens.[9] The fifth amendment under this bill was moved by Mrs Knight who sought to increase the maximum fine for assisting illegal entry from £400 to £1000 – or least to elicit from the Government the expression of 'sentiments' that the offence was not regarded as minor. This she obtained and expressed herself satisfied but, probably through oversight, failed to respond to the Minister's hope that she would withdraw her amendment.[10]

The moving of amendments to the Industrial Relations Bill by Govern-

[1] 1970–71 Standing Committee H, cols 225–30. [2] *Ibid.*, cols 722–30.
[3] *Ibid.*, cols 805–23. [4] *Ibid.*, cols 853–64. [5] *Ibid.*, cols 823–40.
[6] 1970–71 Standing Committee B, cols 3–23. [7] *Ibid.*, cols 268–76.
[8] *Ibid.*, cols 1208–10. [9] *Ibid.*, cols 1297–304. [10] *Ibid.*, cols 1270–6.

ment backbenchers could not have been an activity popular with the front bench despite the operation of the guillotine. Mr Normanton was at pains to express his full support for the bill when he moved amendment No. 716 concerned with industry-wide agreements. And indeed he sought to withdraw it but leave was refused by other Members.[1] The other amendment to this bill was moved by Dame Irene Ward and concerned bargaining units and the interests of professional workers. She also sought leave to withdraw but the guillotine had already begun to operate and so the amendment was negatived.[2]

Mr Neave moved an amendment to the Atomic Energy Authority Bill to entitle staff recruited to work for the Science Research Council after 1 April 1969 to join the Authority's pension scheme. The Minister was not willing to accept the proposal.[3] On the Highways Bill Mr Maude sought to exclude a power to stop up private access from the highway where that access was likely 'to interfere unreasonably with' traffic on the highway. He thought this was unnecessarily wide; and he was neither altogether happy nor wholly convinced by the Minister's reply. He said that he was not prepared to carry the amendment to a division. But neither did he withdraw it.[4] Finally, Mr Emery sought to insert a terminal date for the provision of moneys by Parliament for the carrying on of any undertaking acquired under the Rolls-Royce (Purchase) Bill. This was a political issue of some importance to a section of the Conservative Party. Leave to withdraw was refused.[5]

The nine occasions when amendments moved by Government backbenchers were negatived on a division included three on the Finance Bill, two on the Water Resources Bill and one occasion on four other bills.

Sir Brandon Rhys Williams proposed to halve the Government's tax on liquified petroleum gases in the Finance Bill. The Government stood firm and so did Sir Brandon. But he was unable to carry any of his colleagues with him in the division and the amendment was defeated.[6] On both the other two occasions on the bill, the movers (Mr Dykes and Mr Tugendhat) sought to withdraw their motions but were prevented by the Opposition. Mr Dykes voted against his amendment[7] and Mr Tugendhat abstained.[8]

In the debates on the Water Resources Bill, Mr Farr played the part of the lone ranger. His first amendment sought to set up a special parliamentary committee to exercise certain Ministerial powers but when he divided the committee he found himself the only Aye vote.[9] Undeterred, he moved a second amendment on a similar point and found himself in an identical position.[10]

[1] 810 H.C. Deb., cols 1607–16.
[2] 811 H.C. Deb., cols 428–36.
[3] 809 H.C. Deb., cols 412–18.
[4] 1970–71 Standing Committee D, cols 8–12.
[5] 811 H.C. Deb., cols 943–6.
[6] 1970–71 Standing Committee H, cols 35–54.
[7] *Ibid.*, cols 556–84.
[8] *Ibid.*, cols 888–900.
[9] 1970–71 Standing Committee D, cols 29–44.
[10] *Ibid.*, cols 43–76.

As to the other four occasions. On the Highways Bill, Mr Maude sought to extend to 3 months the period within which objections to a major scheme might be made. The Minister promised to look again but without much enthusiasm, a division followed, Mr Maude voted for his amendment and a tied vote resulted in the Chairman supporting the Noes.[1]

Mrs Knight moved an amendment to the Immigration Bill to exclude from entry an au pair girl unless there was a signed agreement between her and the head of the family. She obtained support from the Opposition who refused her leave to withdraw and the amendment was defeated, the mover abstaining.[2] Sir Brandon Rhys Williams moved an amendment to the National Insurance (Old Persons' and Widows' Pensions and Attendance Allowance) Bill to reduce the lapse of time requirement for attendance allowances from 6 months to 1 month. Leave to withdraw was prevented by an Opposition frontbencher whom Sir Brandon had chided for not supporting him.[3] Sir Brandon voted against his own amendment. Finally, Mr Sutcliffe moved an amendment to the Investment and Building Grants Bill in an attempt to preserve the power to make an investment grant under Part I of the Industrial Development Act 1966 for the continued development of a mine. It was concerned 'probably exclusively and certainly substantially' with Cleveland Potash. The amendment was defeated, the mover voting with the Opposition.[4]

In the result, therefore, of the nine amendments moved by Government backbenchers and negatived on division, the mover voted for his own amendment (and therefore against his Ministerial front bench) on five occasions, abstained on two occasions and voted against his own amendment on two occasions.

We must now look at the thirteen occasions when amendments moved by Government backbenchers were agreed without a division and at the one occasion when it was agreed on a division. Six of the thirteen were on the Finance Bill, two on the Civil Aviation Bill, and one each on the Fire Precautions, Highways, Immigration, Industrial Relations, and Rating Bills.

The six occasions on the Finance Bill were on six new clauses, two moved by Mr Green, and one each by Sir Brandon Rhys Williams, Mr Dixon, Mr Knox and Mr Coombs. Those by Mr Green concerned, first, the increase from 1 to 2 years of the time limit, within which, following a change in the membership of a partnership, the partners might elect to have the profits of their business taxed as though there had been no change;[5] and, secondly, in relation to stamp duty, to enable a composition to be made in respect of transfer duty on certain loan capital.[6] Sir Brandon successfully moved a new clause concerned with the exemption from pool

[1] 1970–71 Standing Committee D, cols 63–70.
[2] 1970–71 Standing Committee B, cols 564–98.
[3] 803 H.C. Deb., cols 1598–608.
[4] 1970–71 Standing Committee E, cols 75–60.
[5] 1970–71 Standing Committee H, cols 883–5.
[6] *Ibid.*, cols 885–7.

betting duty of voluntary contributions to charities and certain other bodies.[1] Mr Dixon's increased from £1 to £2 the limits on expenses on gifts from which deductions might be made.[2] Mr Knox's new clause concerned the exemption of interest on damages for personal injuries.[3] And Mr Coombs successfully moved an amendment concerned with the replacement of business assets.[4]

None of these six amendments, all accepted by the Government, was of much importance though none was negligible. They are typical of the kind of amendments more frequently moved by Conservative than by Labour backbenchers, which seek to achieve some small relief for a relatively small group and are from time time to time adopted by the Treasury. Often such amendments are drafted by the Government and farmed out to their own backbenchers to table in their own names.

The two amendments on the Civil Aviation Bill were moved by Mr Onslow, the vice-chairman of the Conservative Aviation Committee since 1967. He played a very large part, for a backbencher on the Government side, in the proceedings of this committee.[5] Not infrequently he seemed to know rather more about the bill than his own Ministerial front bench. The first amendment concerned the duty of the Civil Aviation Authority to perform its functions in a manner which it considered was best calculated, as the bill said, 'to encourage British airlines to' provide air transport services, etc. The amendment replaced these quoted words by 'secure that British airlines', etc. At first the Minister resisted the amendment but on being pressed agreed to reconsider. The debate on the amendment was adjourned at the usual hour and when the committee met again 2 days later the Minister accepted the amendment.[6]

Mr Onslow's second amendment was to replace 'aviation' by 'air transport'. The Minister thought the change would very slightly narrow the coverage of what was intended but would improve the bill.[7]

On the Highways Bill, Mr Maude moved that most common of all amendments to leave out 'may' and insert 'shall' in a clause which concerned the indication on certain maps of the centre line of highways. The purpose of the amendment was 'to get my hon. Friend to say in what circumstances he thinks he would not publish a map with this information on it'. The Under-Secretary of State said he could not answer the question and so accepted the amendment – somewhat, I imagine, to Mr Maude's surprise.[8]

Mr Powell in the Immigration Bill persuaded the Government to replace 'somebody' by 'a person' but, as he said, this was not one of the most

[1] *Ibid.*, cols 899–902.
[2] *Ibid.*, cols 906–8.
[3] *Ibid.*, cols 908–10.
[4] *Ibid.*, cols 927–30.
[5] In addition to the two amendments he moved successfully, seven other consequential or drafting amendments standing in his name were formally moved and agreed to.
[6] 1970–71 Standing Committee A, cols 34–53.
[7] *Ibid.*, cols 71–2.
[8] 1970–71 Standing Committee D, cols 85–6.

important amendments which the committee had to consider.[1] Mr Holland proposed that the Secretary of State in preparing the code of industrial relations practice should have regard, *inter alia*, to the need for providing practical guidance with respect to the establishment and maintenance of effective means of 'negotiation, consultation and communication' rather than 'information and communication'; and the Solicitor-General agreed.[2] In the Rating Bill, Mr MacArthur successfully moved an amendment to exempt from rating (as agricultural land), in Scotland as in England, land used for breeding, rearing, grazing or exercising horses.[3]

Finally, to the Fire Precautions Bill, Mr Moate moved an amendment to make clear that where a person appeals against the refusal of a fire authority to issue a certificate, he may continue to operate his business without committing an offence until the final determination of his appeal. The Minister accepted this as a desirable clarification.[4]

The one occasion when an amendment moved by a Government backbencher was agreed on a division resulted in a Government defeat. This was a famous Parliamentary occasion. The Immigration Bill provided that a person had the right of abode in the United Kingdom if he was a Commonwealth citizen and was the child or grandchild of a person having at any time had citizenship of the United Kingdom and Colonies by his birth in the United Kingdom. Mr Powell moved to leave out 'or grandchild'. A division on the previous amendment to leave out the whole of that provision had resulted in a tie (18–18) in which Mr Powell had voted with the Opposition. The Chairman's casting vote was declared for the Noes. Now Mr Powell, on his motion, was joined by the Opposition and one of his colleagues (Sir George Sinclair) while another of his colleagues (Mr Deedes) abstained. So the amendment was carried, against the Government, by 19 votes to 16.[5]

This defeat of the Government was brought about because, for different reasons, there was a strong wish on the part of the Opposition, Mr Powell and Sir George Sinclair to remove the grandpatrial provision. Mr Powell and Sir George are near to the opposite ends of political opinion within the Conservative party on matters of race and immigration. They combined not in a common cause but in a common effect.

3.4.4 *Amendments moved by Opposition Members*

Table 3.8 (p. 93) shows that of 3074 amendments moved by Opposition Members during 1967–68, 1968–69 and 1970–71, 1503 were withdrawn, 1440 were negatived and 131 were agreed to. Those negatived are occasions when the Opposition wish to record their dissatisfaction with some part of the Government proposals as contained in the bill. They also indicate that

[1] 1970–71 Standing Committee B, cols 1131.
[2] Industrial Relations Bill, 809 H.C. Deb., cols 1012–14.
[3] 1970–71 Standing Committee D, cols 347–53.
[4] 1970–71 Standing Committee A, cols 98–9.
[5] 1970–71 Standing Committee B, cols 127–248, 275–6.

the Opposition either feel there is no likelihood of persuading the Government to change its mind then or at any subsequent stage or do not expect to return to the matter on report (otherwise, in either case, the amendments would be withdrawn)[1] or both.[2] Forcing an amendment to a division indicates a stronger Opposition dissatisfaction than allowing the amendment to be negatived without a division.

An Opposition amendment being agreed to without a division indicates Government acceptance. This may happen for one (or more) of a number of reasons. It may be that the Government accept that the amendment improves the bill either by making a positive new provision or by removing an anomaly that the Government had overlooked. It may be that the amendment is to correct a minor drafting error. It may be because the Government, for tactical reasons, wish to give way on this amendment perhaps to strengthen their position in opposing other amendments. It may be that the Government do not wish to appear wholly unbending in committee. A willingness to yield sweetens the atmosphere in committee and makes less likely obstruction by the Opposition.

Withdrawals of amendments may, as we shall see, lead to Government concessions, generally on report. Those apart, it is to the amendments agreed to that we must look in seeking to estimate the impact on Government bills of debate.

1967–68 In 1967–68, forty-six amendments were agreed to without a division. These were to the Agriculture (Miscellaneous Provisions) Bill (3),[3] Commonwealth Immigrants Bill (1),[4] Countryside Bill (4),[5] Finance Bill (4),[6] Gaming Bill (3),[7] Medicines Bill (8),[8] Race Relations Bill (1),[9] Restrictive Trade Practices Bill (1),[10] Sewerage (Scotland) Bill (10),[11] Social Work (Scotland) Bill (3),[12] Town and Country Planning Bill (4),[13] Transport Bill (3),[14] Trustee Savings Bank Bill (1).[15]

[1] Although it not infrequently happens that Opposition members deny a Government backbencher's request to withdraw an amendment (and so force a division), it is most unusual for Government members to use that tactic on Opposition amendments.

[2] It does sometimes happen that the Opposition do not withdraw, at the same time announcing their intention (which may or may not be fulfilled) to raise the matter on report.

[3] Standing Committee B, cols 144–6, 405–6, 505–7.

[4] 759 H.C. Deb., cols 1421–31.

[5] Standing Committee A, cols 69–77, 562–5, 1118–21, 1146.

[6] Standing Committee A, cols 1246–7, 1282–3, 1265–8, 1759–62.

[7] Standing Committee B, cols 272–3, 393–4, 414–5.

[8] Standing Committee D, cols 51–6, 101–4, 138–9, 301–3, 455–70, 727–8, 731, 908.

[9] Standing Committee B, cols 369–77.

[10] Standing Committee H, cols 217–21.

[11] Scottish Standing Committee, cols 52–3, 77, 127–30, 223–4, 224–5, 232–3, 253–4, 261–2, 281–2, 419–20.

[12] Scottish Standing Committee, cols 165, 276–7, 322–4.

[13] Standing Committee G, cols 71–4, 583, 1305–6, 1308–9.

[14] Standing Committee F, cols 369–72, 1307–11, 1517–22.

[15] Standing Committee F, cols 23–4.

Of these forty-six amendments, all but eight are classifiable as drafting, clarificatory or of very minor significance. The eight are diverse in character and their subject-matter does not fall into groups or categories.

Perhaps the most important amendment in this group was that moved by Mr Turton to the Commonwealth Immigrants Bill. The Bill provided that section 1 of the Commonwealth Immigrants Act 1962, dealing with exemption from control enjoyed by citizens of the United Kingdom and Colonies holding United Kingdom passports, should be restricted to persons having certain specified connections with the United Kingdom. As originally drafted it applied to a person who or whose father or grandfather was born or naturalised in the United Kingdom or was adopted or registered as a citizen in the United Kingdom. The amendment extended 'father or grandfather' to include mother or grandmother, and this was accepted by the Solicitor-General.[1]

It is not common for a complete new clause to be successfully moved by an Opposition backbencher but Mr Godber did so to the Agriculture (Miscellaneous Provisions) Bill. Section 49 of the Agriculture Act 1967 provided that, with certain exceptions, any transfer of land in the area of a rural development board required the board's written consent. The new clause exempted from this requirement transfer to or from a river authority or an internal drainage board and this was accepted.[2] To the same bill an amendment was moved in the closing moments of the eighth sitting to extend the power of the Minister to make grants for break crops so as to include those grown for the feeding of stock. When the committee met two days later it was made clear that the Government had during the adjournment expressed its willingness to accept a modified version of the amendment which the same Opposition Member (Mr Stodart) then moved.[3]

Mr Godman Irvine successfully moved an amendment to the Countryside Bill that required highway authorities to consult with the owner or occupier before erecting signposts along footpaths or bridleways.[4] Mr Dean persuaded the Minister to denude himself of the power by Order to increase or reduce the minimum number of members of the Medicines Commission under the Medicines Bill.[5] And Mr Macmillan, helped by the period between two sittings of the committee, persuaded the same Minister in the same bill to agree to the deletion of eleven lines of some importance. The bill sought to indicate by what criteria a document, advertisement or representation might be adjudged 'misleading' and said that for the purpose of determining any question arising out of this indication regard should be had to 'appropriate professional opinion' which was then further described. Mr Macmillan suggested that this was an attempt to interfere with the conduct of the courts which might be called on to interpret the bill and to

[1] 759 H.C. Deb., cols 1421–31.

[2] Standing Committee B, cols 505–7.

[3] *Ibid.*, cols 401–6.

[4] Standing Committee A, cols 1118–21.

[5] Standing Committee D, cols 138–9.

decide whether or not a document, advertisement or representation was misleading. The Minister eventually agreed to 'leave this to the courts to determine. I have no doubt that they will have regard to the kind of expert opinion set out in this clause.'[1] On an amendment to the Sewerage (Scotland) Bill, the Under-Secretary of State agreed with Mr Noble that local authorities should not be empowered to 'abandon' public sewers or drains.[2]

Finally Mr Eldon Griffiths moved an amendment to the Race Relations Bill. He argued that the bill as it stood could be interpreted to mean that a coloured person could not be dismissed for misconduct or inefficiency if work for which he was qualified was available for him. He was supported by Mr Heffer, by Mr Hogg, and by the CBI. The Under-Secretary of State was sympathetic but said that the Parliamentary draftsmen were not absolutely certain that the amendment did what the mover wanted it to do. But he accepted it on the understanding that he might have to make changes on report.[3]

In addition to amendments moved by the Opposition and accepted by the Government, some of those tabled by Opposition Members, discussed, accepted and made after being formally moved, were of some importance. Into this category falls an amendment tabled by Mr Nigel Fisher to the Medicines Bill. That bill provided that no person should import any medicinal product except in accordance with a product licence. This did not apply if the import took place within 12 months ending with the first appointed day. Mr Fisher's amendment extended this period to 24 months and this the Minister accepted.[4]

On three occasions in 1967–68, Opposition amendments were agreed to on a division. The first was on the Medicines Bill when Mr Macmillan moved an amendment to ensure that when a licensing authority was dealing with an application for a product licence, efficacy by comparison with other products was not to be taken into consideration. After the Minister and others had contributed, Mr Macmillan spoke again and was still on his feet when the sitting ended. On the resumption of the debate at the next sitting, Mr Macmillan pressed the amendment immediately to a division and the Government troops being even fewer in attendance than those of the Opposition the amendment was agreed to by 6 votes to 5 in a committee of twenty members.[5] Another snap vote, this time after dinner, resulted in another defeat for the Government on the Prices and Incomes Bill. The amendment limited the period within which orders requiring the reduction of prices or charges would be imposed. It was agreed to by 12 votes to 11 in a committee of thirty-five members, two of the four Ministers being absent.[6]

The third defeat for the Government on an Opposition amendment was on the Countryside Bill. The proposal was to add 'National Parks and'

[1] Standing Committee D, cols 455–70.
[2] Scottish Standing Committee, cols 127–30.
[3] Standing Committee B, cols 369–77.
[4] Standing Committee D, cols 253–60.
[5] Standing Committee D, cols 274–88.
[6] Standing Committee F, cols 515–16.

to the title of the Countryside Commission. It was agreed to by 12 votes to 11. Five Government backbenchers voted with seven Opposition members to defeat three Ministers, three Opposition Members and five Government supporters.[1] The new Commission proposed by the bill was to absorb the National Parks Commission set up by the National Parks and Access to the Countryside Act 1949. During the debate on the second reading of the Countryside Bill the view was expressed that the new body should be called the National Parks and Countryside Commission[2] but this was at once disputed on the ground that (broadly) national parks were neither national nor parks.[3] The National Parks Commission itself hoped that its title would be included in the title of the new Commission because 'The expression "National Parks" has become part of the national consciousness, and around it there has grown a strong and widespread feeling of loyalty and dedication'.[4] The Minister resisted the amendment on the ground that it would be misleading. Mr Channon thought it was 'a classic example of a Standing Committee debate'. It was certainly unusual in the way it divided the parties.

1968–69 On thirty-eight occasions in 1968–69 Opposition amendments to Government bills were agreed to without a division. These were to the Children and Young Persons Bill (1),[5] Development of Tourism Bill (2),[6] Finance Bill (7),[7] Housing Bill (6),[8] Housing (Scotland) Bill (4),[9] Immigration Appeals Bill (1),[10] Mines and Quarries (Tips) Bill (1),[11] Nurses Bill (1),[12] Post Office Bill (3),[13] Representation of the People Bill (1),[14] Town and Country Planning (Scotland) Bill (8),[15] Trustee Savings Bank Bill (1),[16] and Transport (London) Bill (2).[17]

With two exceptions, all these amendments were either drafting points or very small improvements to the bills. The first exception was the amendment moved by Dame Joan Vickers to the Immigration Appeals Bill.[18] The bill authorised a police constable or an immigration officer, on a

[1] Standing Committee A, cols 19–40.
[2] 753 H.C. Deb., col. 1451 (Mr Carol Johnson).
[3] *Ibid.*, cols 1459–60 (Mr Jopling).
[4] Standing Committee A, cols 19 (quoted by Mr Ramsden in moving the amendment).
[5] Standing Committee G, cols 384–5.
[6] Standing Committee E, cols 3–58, 156–7.
[7] Standing Committee F, cols 246, 417, 506–7, 575, 679–80, 786, 810–11.
[8] Standing Committee F, cols 437–40, 524–6, 587–8, 624, 778–9, 821.
[9] 1st Scottish Standing Committee, cols 79–85, 95–6, 227–8, 279–80.
[10] Standing Committee A, cols 133–6.
[11] Standing Committee B, cols 26–7.
[12] Standing Committee D, cols 11–13.
[13] Standing Committee D, cols 197–205, 605–6, 1119–21.
[14] 775 H.C. Deb., cols 287–90.
[15] 1st Scottish Standing Committee, cols 3, 172–4, 276–7, 309–10, 397–9, 468–9, 475–6.
[16] 787 H.C. Deb., cols 1678–81.
[17] Standing Committee A, cols 33, 307–11.
[18] Standing Committee A, cols 133–6.

warrant of a Justice of the Peace to enter, if need be by force, any premises where it was suspected would be found a person liable to arrest under section 13 of the Commonwealth Immigration Act 1962. The amendment was to leave out the immigration officer and was accepted by the Minister on the ground that there was no need for an immigration officer to have this power. The second exception arose on the first amendment to the Development of Tourism Bill. As originally drafted the bill provided for a British Tourist Authority and a Welsh and a Scottish Tourist Board. The amendment, moved by Mr Emery, was to create also an English Tourist Board.[1] Six Opposition Members and five Government supporters spoke in favour of the amendment after which the Minister moved the adjournment of the sitting so that he might consult his colleagues. During the five days between the adjournment on the Thursday and the next meeting of the committee on the Tuesday following, the Minister was informed that the British Travel Association now accepted, as it had not done previously, the need for an English Board. Mr Emery who moved the amendment said:

> 'The most difficult thing in the world is to get any Government, of whatever complexion, to change the major structure of a Bill once it has been presented. Governments can frequently be got to do this before a Bill is actually before us in print, but to have made so major an Amendment and to have altered the whole structure of the Development of Tourism Bill is a major achievement for us.'[2]

Both sides agreed that 'there cannot be any party politics in this matter.'[3]

An Opposition amendment agreed to after a division usually represents a Government defeat. The five occasions when this occurred in 1968–69 were during proceedings on the Children and Young Persons Bill, the Development of Tourism Bill (thrice) and the Horserace Betting Levy Bill. In no case did a Government supporter vote against the Government.

Clause 12 of the Children and Young Persons Bill provided that a supervision order made by a court might require the supervised person to comply with certain directions of the supervisor but that it should be for the supervisor to decide whether and to what extent he exercised any power to give such directions. This meant, it was argued, that the supervisor could ignore the decision of the court; and the amendment sought to remove that possibility. It was carried by 7 votes to 6.[4]

The first of the three amendments to the Development of Tourism Bill proposed to retain the name of British Travel Association instead of the proposed British Tourist Authority partly on the ground that 'Authority' is 'a horrid word. . . . It is an autocratic word; it is an authoritarian word; it is a dictatorial word; it is an arrogant word. Above all it is an unfriendly word.' The amendment was carried by 9 votes to 8.[5]

[1] Standing Committee E, cols 3–58. [2] 1968–69 Standing Committee E, col. 53.
[3] *Ibid.*, cols 7, 28. [4] Standing Committee G, cols 319–34.
[5] Standing Committee E, cols 58–66.

The second amendment to this bill reduced from ten to five the minimum number of letting bedrooms which a hotel must have in order to qualify for a grant. The Minister opposed this change on economic grounds – 'a very considerable increase in public spending'. But it was carried by 7 votes to 5.[1] Thirdly, on the same clause an amendment was successfully moved (by 7 votes to 5) to replace a condition qualifying a hotel for receipt of grant that it provided breakfast and an evening meal by 'breakfast or self-catering facilities'.[2]

The Horserace Betting Levy Bill empowered the Secretary of State to determine a scheme for the bookmakers' levy or to direct that the current scheme should continue. An amendment required him to have regard to the extent of the need for certain contributions and to the capacity of bookmakers to make these contributions. It was agreed to by 9 votes to 8.[3]

The first four of these adverse votes were caused by the absence from that sitting or that vote of Government supporters. There was no cross-voting or apparently deliberate abstention. The fifth occasion is more doubtful. As we have already seen,[4] Mr Arthur Lewis expressed himself frequently as being against the whole principle of the Horserace Betting Levy Bill. On this occasion he said, 'I am not in favour of the Bill at all, and that is why I am opposing the Amendment'.[5] But he did not vote against it, the voting was Ayes 9, Noes 8, and the amendment was agreed to. Deliberate abstentions are not common in standing committee and impossible to itemise unless Members state their intention. The fact that a Member is listed as having attended a sitting does not mean that his failure to vote was a refusal to do so. On this occasion, it is probable but not certain that Mr Arthur Lewis decided not to vote and so caused a defeat for the Government.

1970–71 In 1970–71, thirty-four Opposition amendments were agreed to without a division. These were on the following bills: Civil Aviation Bill (10), Coal Industry Bill (1), Courts Bill (5), Family Income Supplements Bill (2), Highways Bill (4), Hospital Endowments (Sc.) Bill (2), Immigration Bill (2), Industrial Relations Bill (1), Law Reform (Jurisdiction in Delict) (Sc.) Bill (1), Misuse of Drugs Bill (1), Recognition of Divorces and Legal Separation Bill (1), Sheriff Courts (Sc.) Bill (1), Social Security Bill (2), Water Resources Bill (1).

Of these thirty-four occasions, fifteen can be disregarded as being of minimum importance being concerned with drafting, clarification and printing errors.[6] A further seventeen were of some minor importance. And two were of more significance though neither was major.

[1] 1968–69 Standing Committee E, cols 363–8. [2] *Ibid.*, cols 369–90.
[3] *Ibid.*, cols 101–22. [4] See above, p. 62. [5] *Ibid.*, col. 113.
[6] Civil Aviation Bill 1970–71, Standing Committee A, cols 350, 451–4, 454, 660; Courts Bill 1970–71, Standing Committee A, cols 85–7, 322–3, 443; Highways Bill 1970–71, Standing Committee D, cols 91–2; Hospital Endowment (Sc.) Bill 1970–71, 1st Scottish Standing Committee, cols 16–8, 176–9; Immigration Bill 1970–71, Standing

The seventeen of minor importance included six which were procedural in character. Thus under the Civil Aviation Bill, amendments were accepted to extend the period for consultation on charges schemes from 30 to 60 days;[1] to extend the time for objections from 28 to 42 days;[2] to provide for disqualification of a member of the Airworthiness Requirements Board if he absented himself from meetings for 3 rather than 6 months.[3] The Courts Bill provided that a majority verdict in civil proceedings was not to be acceptable by a court unless the jury had deliberated for at least 2 hours; an amendment left the period to the discretion of the court.[4] Two amendments to the Highways Bill specified minimum period for the submission to the Secretary of State of details of alternative routes.[5]

Twice in the Civil Aviation Bill, auditors were required to be chosen from recognised bodies of accountants.[6]

There remain nine heterogeneous amendments of minor importance. Under the Coal Industry Bill the Secretary of State was empowered to call for reports on the National Coal Board's diversified activities. Reports were to include particulars 'of the advantages (if any) which are foreseen as resulting from continuance of the activities'. The Government accepted the addition of the words 'and financial consequences' after the bracket.[7] An amendment to the Courts Bill made statutory the right of a person to be exempted from jury service where a Court had, on an earlier occasion, excused him from service for an unexpired period.[8] An amendment provided that family income supplements in the bill of that name should not count as earnings of a debtor for attachment on maintenance orders.[9] In the Highways Bill a local authority was empowered to acquire land which 'in their opinion' was required in connection with the construction or improvement of a highway or for authorised works. The amendment deleted those quoted words.[10] In the Immigration Bill an amendment made certain orders of the Secretary of State liable to annulment in either House of Parliament.[11] One general principle of the Industrial Relations Bill was that of 'developing and maintaining orderly procedures in industry for the peaceful settlement of disputes'. An amendment added 'and expeditious' after 'peaceful'.[12] The Misuse of Drugs Bill provided that the Secretary of State could give 'such directions as he thought fit' for the safe custody of

Committee B, cols 878–9; Law Reform (Jurisdiction in Delict) (Sc.) Bill 1970–71, 1st Scottish Standing Committee, cols 3–4; Recognition of Divorces and Legal Separations Bill 1970–71, Standing Committee B, cols 15–16; Water Resources Bill 1970–71, Standing Committee D, cols 13–14; Social Security Bill 1970–71 Standing Committee F, cols 239–40.

[1] Standing Committee A, cols 275–9. [2] *Ibid.*, cols 811–12.

[3] *Ibid.*, cols 812–13. [4] Standing Committee A, cols 389–92.

[5] Standing Committee D, cols 72–4, 153–4.

[6] Standing Committee A, cols 683, 822–3.

[7] Standing Committee B, cols 423–6. [8] Standing Committee A, cols 385–6.

[9] Family Income Supplements Bill, 806 H.C. Deb., cols 1385.

[10] Standing Committee D, cols 136–8.

[11] Standing Committee B, cols 985–9.

[12] 809 H.C. Deb., cols 669–74.

drugs; an amendment replaced this by 'directions' simply.[1] The Sheriff Courts (Scotland) Bill provided that the Secretary of State might 'direct' a sheriff to act in another sheriffdom. The amendment replaced that word with 'authorise', the argument being that 'direct' appeared to be a possible encroachment by the Executive upon the judicial function. Prayed in aid were the Bill of Rights and, for Scotland, the Claim of Right of 1689.[2] Finally, an amendment marginally extended the period of repayment of supplementary benefit under the Social Security Bill.[3]

The first of the two more important matters concerned the powers of the Secretary of State under Clause 4(3) of the Civil Aviation Bill to give directions to the Civil Aviation Authority in relation to matters affecting the national interest. The clause provided that if such directions conflicted with the requirements of the bill then, with certain exceptions, those requirements were to be disregarded. Speakers on both sides of the Committee urged the deletion of the whole sub-clause and the Secretary of State, who had other powers to give directions under the clause, accepted this amendment.[4] It was, as Mr Millan said, 'a minor triumph at least'.[5] The second matter concerned those entitled to family income supplement. The amendment, moved by Mr Barnett, ensured that they included persons who in fact provided for a child even though they might not be under a legal obligation to do so.[6]

The five occasions in 1970–71 when Opposition amendments were agreed to on a division were on the following bills: Coal Industry Bill, Licensing (Abolition of State Management) Bill, Mineral Workings Bill, National Insurance Bill, and Oil in Navigable Waters Bill.

Four of these were significant amendments. Clause 7 of the Coal Industry Bill gave powers to the Secretary of State to direct the Board to discontinue or restrict any of their activities, dispose of any part of their undertaking, dispose of any assets held by them, call in any loan made by them or exercise any power they might possess to revoke any guarantees given by them; also to exercise any control over any subsidiary to the same effect; also to take specified steps with a view to altering the way in which the activities of the Board or any subsidiary were organised. The clause further provided that the Secretary of State should consult with the Board before giving any such direction. The amendment added to this last provision a requirement that, if the Board objected to a direction, the direction should have no effect unless incorporated in an order and approved by resolution of each House of Parliament.

This was the most contentious clause in the bill being concerned with 'hiving off'. Four Government backbenchers spoke, in varying degrees of strength, in favour of the amendment–mainly because it reinforced Parliamentary accountability of nationalised industries. The Minister

[1] Standing Committee A, cols 107–9.
[2] 1st Scottish Standing Committee, cols 68–75.
[3] Standing Committee F, cols 506–7. [4] Standing Committee A, cols 173–6.
[5] *Ibid.*, col. 176. [6] Family Income Supplements Bill, 806 H.C. Deb., cols 115–34.

opposed the amendment while promising to 'look closely at the matter again and take into account fully the points which have been raised on both sides of the Committee'. In the division, two Government backbenchers (Sir Gerald Nabarro and Mr Skeet) voted with the Opposition and one abstained. So the Government was defeated and the amendment carried.[1]

The Mineral Workings Bill required contributions to be paid by ironstone operators to the Secretary of State at a rate to be specified by him. The amendment was to add that the rate should contain no charge for the cost of restoring land worked before 1 April 1971. The Government opposed the amendment but was defeated, without any crossvoting taking place.[2]

Clause 7 of the National Insurance Bill was designed to limit the rate of unemployment benefit payable to a person over the age of sixty who was receiving an occupational pension of more than £18 a week; and to disqualify altogether a person receiving such a pension of £30 or more. An amendment was carried against the Government giving a right of appeal to the National Insurance Tribunal. Three Government backbenchers spoke against the clause and abstained.[3]

The Oil in Navigable Waters Bill proposed to increase the maximum fine for offences connected with the discharge of oil from £1,000 to £5,000. An amendment proposed £50,000. The Minister agreed that £5,000 was inadequate and undertook to introduce a further amendment to increase the sum but was unwilling to say to what figure. Three Government backbenchers (Mr Laurance Reed, Mr Maxwell-Hyslop and Mr Wilkinson) voted with the Opposition to defeat the Government.[4]

The fifth and less important amendment concerned a provision in the Licensing (Abolition of State Management) Bill which imposed restrictions on the 'sale and supply' of intoxicating liquor. The amendment proposed this should read 'sale or supply' and the Minister accepted this. The division took place because four Opposition backbenchers disagreed with their front bench.[5]

3.4.5 *Amendments withdrawn, assurances and undertakings*

Table 3.8 (page 93) shows that the number of Opposition amendments withdrawn is much the same as the number negatived. Amendments moved by Government backbenchers are twice as often withdrawn as negatived.

Amendments may be withdrawn for one of several reasons, which apply as much to Government backbenchers as to Opposition Members. An amendment may be moved primarily to enable questions to be asked in the

[1] Standing Committee B, cols 642–68.

[2] Standing Committee E, cols 27–62. Three Government backbenchers who were recorded as having attended the sitting did not vote. But they may not have been present when the vote was taken.

[3] Standing Committee G, cols 165–92. On clause stand part, the clause was disagreed to (see below, p. 136).

[4] Standing Committee D, cols 45–66. [5] Standing Committee D, cols 57–66.

hope that Ministers will answer them.[1] The meaning of words in the clause may not be clear, their extent may be imprecise. Is it certain they could not or would not be used to cover this situation or that? Why should they not be interpreted thus and, if they were, would this not be undesirable or anomalous? All these are or begin by being probing questions. The answers are often satisfactory and the amendment is, with the leave of the committee, withdrawn. Sometimes an amendment seems to be moved for no reason other than that the mover wishes to speak. He seeks neither information nor concession. He does not look for support or condemnation. And he may conclude by saying that the committee has had an interesting debate on a matter of some interest but that nothing is further from his mind than to press the motion to a division. Amendments may be tabled and may be selected on other grounds when the intention is primarily to obstruct the business of the committee though that may not be apparent at the beginning.

The response of the Minister to the debate on the amendment will commonly affect the mover. Certain phrases are used by Ministers which can be categorised in descending order of positive acceptance of the amendment. Thus the Minister may promise to introduce his own amendment at a later stage to meet the point made. Occasionally he may be able to say that another Government bill will be the appropriate place for remedying the defect. Or he may promise to introduce regulations, or other form of statutory instrument, for that purpose. Thirdly, he may assure the mover that the difficulty can and will be solved by administrative action or inaction. These four responses amount to an undertaking that something will be done substantially to satisfy the mover who will then withdraw. The Minister may be persuaded that the amendment should probably be met but may not be ready when it is moved to give a firm promise. He will then promise to consider the matter favourably – in these or similar words.

A very common form of words that does not commit the Minister to any positive response is that the Minister undertakes to 'look again' at the point. His immediate response to the mover may be that he cannot accept the amendment for reasons which he then gives. But if the point is pursued at length and especially if it is clear that there is some sympathy for the amendment on the Government back benches, the Minister may give way to the extent of promising to reconsider.[2]

[1] E.g. 'On a Bill like this, which we on this side regard as non-controversial in principle, the purpose of this Amendment to the Clause, and indeed, the four other Amendments to the Bill, is not to try to change the Bill, as I am sure the Minister of State will realise, but to give the Government some notice of points which we wish to raise so that they can be prepared, where necessary, to give details.' (Mr Gordon Campbell during debate on the Erskine Bridge Tolls Bill on 5 December 1967 in Scottish Standing Committee, cols 4, 5).

[2] Occasionally the Minister comes close to saying that he will reconsider if the amendment is withdrawn (see for example Health Services and Public Health Bill 1967–68, Standing Committee D, col. 326), but usually the promise is more delicately made.

Giving way in these circumstances is a significant part of Parliamentary procedure. For it emphasises once again how valuable a weapon for the Opposition, and indeed for Government backbenchers, is the use of time. The Government is always short of time and will frequently be willing to concede this far in order to get on with the debate. But Ministers may find that the time they are saving by promising in committee to 'look again' will be lost on report. For, unless the Minister puts down an amendment on report to meet the point (in which case the time taken on report need be no more than a few moments) the Speaker is likely to select for debate on report the same amendment put down by the Opposition or a Government backbencher. Much of the skill of debate in committee is directed to forcing the Minister to promise to reconsider. Incidentally, this contributes in part to keeping the tone of committee debate relatively quiet. For if an amendment is moved aggressively and is responded to aggressively the result is likely to be a refusal by the Minister to give any such undertakings and probably a division. And then the Speaker is far less likely to select the amendment on report. Indeed one may say that whenever an amendment is moved aggressively, this indicates that the mover knows he will be most unlikely to persuade the Minister to accept the amendment or anything like it at any stage of the bill's passage. All that remains in these circumstances is to lambast the Government and its iniquitous policy.

It is therefore frequently very important, especially for the Opposition, to press the Minister in committee to the point where he gives an undertaking but not to press him so hard that he refused to consider the matter. This relates in its turn to all that goes on outside the committee room. So long as the Minister can be kept from taking a final and adverse stand, pressure on him may be continued privately by members of the committee, by other Members of the House and by outside interests. Once he has finally declared himself in committee, while he may still be persuaded to change his mind, the difficulties in the way of this are considerable.

The most frequently stated reason for withdrawal of an amendment is that the mover, having heard the Minister's explanation, does not wish to press the matter further. It may be that he is genuinely satisfied whereas before he had been doubtful. Or it may be that he wishes merely to force the Minister to make a public statement of the meaning of that part of the clause although he has little doubt that the interpretation he had put on it was the Minister's interpretation also. Similarly the mover may say that he wishes to withdraw because all he sought was a discussion. Where the Minister's reply is complex or introduces new material which the mover and his friends had not thought of, the mover may withdraw so that he may reconsider the matter himself. Occasionally the withdrawal is in favour of another similar amendment, especially if the Minister has indicated his preference for and sympathy with that other. And finally the mover may withdraw while at the same time stating his dissatisfaction with the Minister's reply, perhaps with the threat, express or implied, of seeking to raise the matter again at a later stage.

Table 3.9 REASONS FOR WITHDRAWAL OF AMENDMENTS IN COMMITTEE

Reason	Opposition	Government backbenchers	Total	Percentage
Mover having heard Minister's explanation	262	55	317	34
Mover to reconsider	62	5	67	7
Mover sought discussion only (includes probing)	57	9	66	7
Mover not satisfied but not willing to press to a division	69	16	85	9
Mover prefers another amendment	29	8	37	4
Ministerial promise to look again	148	27	175	19
Ministerial promise to table own amendment	52	10	62	7
Ministerial promise to reconsider favourably	42	9	51	6
Ministerial promise to meet point administratively	31	18	49	5
Ministerial promise to meet point by regulations	10	2	12	1
Ministerial promise to meet point in different bill	3	1	4	1
Total	765	160	925	100

Note: In a small number of instances the evidence for the reason is slight and has had to be deduced from the surrounding circumstances.

In detail the figures for 1967–68 were as shown in Table 3.9.

Ministers, as I have said, may in answering questions give certain assurances. These may range from interpretations of the meanings of words to promises that certain types of administrative action will or will not be taken under the powers given by the bill's provisions. An example of the first arose during the debates on the Finance Bill 1968–69 already referred to on the right of payers of interest on loans for the purchase of property to deduct these payments for tax purposes. The Opposition sought an assurance that this would cover incidental expenses. The Minister replied that as the loan would be less than the purchase price the question could not arise.[1] But he added:

'. . . assume the unheard of case of the loan being fully equal to the whole of the purchase price and in addition covering the variety of incidental expenses. . . . I can say with the authority of a Treasury Minister within the Revenue – though of course I have none over the

[1] The statement was made on report.

courts – that if ever such a case came along the incidental expenses would be interpreted by the Revenue as being part of the cost of the property.'[1]

The reference to the courts is significant for in these cases the Minister is saying how the Department interprets the clauses it is proposing. Her Majesty's judges applying their own rules of interpretation might come to a different conclusion and then the Minister's assurance would be of little value.

Assurances that certain actions and not others will be taken by the Government when the bill becomes law are sometimes doubted by Members not avowedly on the ground that the good faith of Ministers is questioned but either that other Ministers in other Administrations may take different views or that the Minister may find himself unable to fulfil his assurances.

Thus in the debates on the London Cab Bill 1967–68 a Government backbencher (Mr R. Fletcher) moved an amendment to require the Home Secretary before making an order increasing the length of obligatory journeys to consult representatives of owners and drivers of cabs. On four occasions during the second reading debate the Under-Secretary of State had given an assurance that this would be done; in standing committee earlier on the day the amendment was moved, he had given a fifth and he now in response to the amendment gave a sixth assurance.

But as another Member said:

'These provisions will continue for many years, and by the time the Act is operating, in a few years' time, the Ministers concerned and the civil servants in the Ministry will all have changed. When the years have passed and these matters are mentioned, people will not re-read the Second Reading debate; not even the extreme eloquence of the Under-Secretary in that debate will bring them back to read it. They will look at the Act, and that is where the principles should be laid down. I am not accusing the Under-Secretary of wishing to renege on the assurance he has given, but he is an able Minister and may one day find himself in another job. The Secretary of State has changed within the last hour or two and of course when the next General Election comes, there will also be a change of Government.'[2]

The Minister rather lamely pointed to the difficulty of knowing who were the representatives but promised to look at it again and Mr Fletcher sought leave, unsuccessfully, to withdraw his amendment which was negatived

[1] 787 H.C. Deb., col. 780.

[2] 1967–68 Standing Committee D, col. 24 (Mr Worsley). As also Mr English said on another bill in the same committee: 'We can all quote innumerable cases where Clauses have been left in broad form because a Minister has given an assurance and where, 20 years later, a different Minister has said that the circumstances are now different and he will interpret the Clause in its literal meaning.' (Medicines Bill 1967–68 Standing Committee D, col. 695.)

without a division.[1] On report the requirement to consult was written into the Bill.[2]

Ministerial assurances were matters of considerable political importance during the debates on the Commonwealth Immigrants Bill 1967–68. On 28 February 1968 a Government backbencher (Mr Paget) moved an amendment that sought to ensure that certain Kenyan Asians, who needed special protection because they had been expelled or had lost their livelihood, should not be subject to the immigration control proposed by the Bill.[3] The Home Secretary (Mr Callaghan) had given a number of assurances. For example, he said, 'I was asked what we would do about a man who was thrown out of work and ejected from the country. We shall have to take him. We cannot do anything else in those circumstances.'[4] Now it was sought to write these assurances in to the bill. Mr J. P. Mackintosh said 'A verbal assurance is not adequate. No one doubts the Home Secretary's word, but this must be written in to the bill so that it can be read by those who will be affected by this Measure.'[5] And the same point was made by other members of the committee. Behind the insistence on writing the assurance in to the bill was perhaps the consciousness that, in the opinion of many, the main provisions of the bill themselves broke an assurance earlier made to the Kenyan Asians. Or as Mr Hogg said:

> 'The lesson that I draw from the bitterly humiliating events to which we have been subjected is that one must never make promises that one does not intend to perform, and one must never make a promise that one cannot perform when the time for performance is due.'[6]

From this he concluded that the assurance ought not to be written into the bill. The Government would not be moved and the committee divided on the amendment: Ayes 71, Noes 196. With the Ayes voted forty-three Government backbenchers.[7]

Three years later on the Immigration Bill 1970–71 Mr Callaghan, now on the Opposition benches, was involved in a similar question. Speaking of the rights of immigrants already in this country the Under-Secretary of State said:

> 'My right hon. Friend has given an absolute assurance, although it is not enshrined in the Bill, that their rights will be exactly the same as they are at the present time regarding their wives and dependent children coming here.'[8]

He was asked by Mr Clinton Davis 'with all the innocence of a new Member' to what extent that undertaking bound the Minister's successors

[1] 1967–68 Standing Committee D, cols 22–30. [2] 756 H.C. Deb., cols 1011–15.
[3] 759 H.C. Deb., col. 1553. [4] *Ibid.*, col. 1501. [5] *Ibid.*, col. 1571.
[6] *Ibid.*, col. 1582. [7] *Ibid.*, cols 1597–1600.
[8] 1970–71 Standing Committee B, col. 296.

and was told, it 'certainly binds this Government'.[1] Mr Callaghan argued that the undertaking should be written into the bill for 'an undertaking by a Minister, put into rules which are not subject to assent by Parliament, cannot clearly be as good and right as those of a Statute'.[2]

Frequently Ministers seek statutory powers which are wider than those required for the immediate task and, when Opposition spokesmen seek to limit those powers, Ministers plead the need for flexibility while giving assurances that they will not use the powers to the full. This dialogue persisted through many sittings of the Health Services and Public Health Bill 1967–68 – what Mr Maurice Macmillan referred to as 'a constant demand for powers justified by the statement that they are not going to be used'.[3] The Minister moved an amendment in committee to meet this complaint on one clause[4] and again on another clause on report.[5]

A similar criticism was made by Mr Macmillan about the Medicines Bill 1967–68 when he said:

> 'I was very disturbed by the reference the Minister continually made to his intentions under the Bill. Although these themselves were reassuring in the extreme, the fact that the Bill has been so drafted that it requires this type of reassurance seems to me to make the Minister's intentions for the more distant future virtually irrelevant to the powers which he is taking under the Bill. In all this, it is not what this Minister may intend to do that we are putting on to the Statute Book, but the wording of the Bill itself. In practice, the interpretation depends, not on the Minister or the Ministry, but, as the Minister himself said, on the courts.'[6]

The Minister may often refuse to agree to an amendment or to give it further consideration, but he will rarely accept an amendment of any substance without first considering the matter within his Department.[7] Amendments may be put down at such short notice that the Minister cannot consider them fully before the committee sits; and in any event, they may not be selected. The speeches which members make during the debate on an amendment may give it more weight than it appeared, at first sight, to carry. The Minister will of course be briefed by his Department on the answer he should immediately give but this brief may itself suggest procrastination so that all aspects, including the debate in committee, can be considered. Most importantly, on all bills of any substance, outside interests affected by the bill, especially those already consulted by the department, may have to be consulted again before a decision on the

[1] 1967–68 Standing Committee D, col. 297. In 1973, Ministers claimed that immigrants who had entered illegally were not protected by the bill.

[2] *Ibid.*, col. 298. [3] Standing Committee D, col. 316. [4] *Ibid.*, col. 277–9.

[5] 762 H.C. Deb., col. 134–6 (clause 30 misprinted in Hansard as 40).

[6] 758 H.C. Deb., cols 1618–19.

[7] During the debates in committee on the Leasehold Reform Bill 1966–67, the Minister, under pressure, recommended acceptance of an amendment removing rateable value limits. But further pressure from within the Cabinet and by affected interests made him withdraw on report (see E. Rowlands, Appendix 17 to H.C. 538 of 1970–71).

amendment can be come to. During the debates on the Medicines Bill 1967–68 – a prolific source of examples on this matter because its provisions regulated an industry – Mr Maurice Macmillan criticised the Minister on the number of occasions when it seemed necessary for him to look again at matters raised by amendments and suggested that this reflected the speed and lack of consideration with which the Bill had been introduced.[1] The Parliamentary Secretary replied:

> 'It is appropriate that we should listen to what Hon. Members have to say and then, if a reasoned case has been made, give further consideration to the matter. It would be discourteous to hon. Members and to outside organisations if we were to be dogmatic'.[2]

During the debates on this same bill, the Minister complained:

> 'My experience of this Committee has taught one that it is very dangerous either to make a concession or to ask to look at something again; to do so seems only to prolong the argument. The last time my hon. Friend made a substantial concession, at the last Sitting, the argument continued for 80 minutes afterwards.'[3]

But this perhaps reflects more the Minister's sense of timing. To give way too early may serve to encourage further pressure.

To assess the impact of withdrawals on the Government, it is necessary to see how far the Government modified its views in subsequent proceedings, especially on report. This is considered below.[4]

3.4.6 *Clause stand part*

In committee, after all selected amendments (if any) to each clause have been disposed of, the question is proposed that that clause, or that clause as amended, stand part of the bill; or that that schedule (or that schedule as amended) be the schedule to the bill.[5]

The purpose of this debate is to consider the clause as a whole and there is some logic in this especially if the clause has been amended. Further it is argued that sometimes there are points which need to be made and questions to be asked which are not easily able to be framed as specific amendments. On the other hand such a debate on a vital clause, especially in a bill that has few clauses, can easily turn into a debate on the general principles of the bill, and become a repetition of the second reading debate. Further, defeat of a vital clause though procedurally permissible (as was seen on the Education Bill 1969–70)[6] effectively reverses a decision taken by the whole House at second reading.

Standing Orders provide that if, during the consideration of a bill in committee, the chairman is of opinion that the principle of a clause or

[1] Standing Committee D, cols 274–5. [2] *Ibid.*, col. 279. [3] *Ibid.*, col. 238.
[4] See pp. 167–82. [5] There may, of course, be many schedules to a bill.
[6] See above, pp. 67–8.

schedule and any matters arising thereon have been adequately discussed in the course of debate on the amendments proposed thereto, he may, after the last selected amendment has been disposed of, forthwith put the question that the clause stand part or this schedule be the schedule.[1]

When this power is exercised, it prevents further debate on the clause. Sir Harry Legge-Bourke has justified it in these terms:

> '. . . My own experience in taking the chair in Standing Committees has taught me that this is a most important right to preserve for the Chairman. I have exercised it on more than one occasion, and on only one occasion do I recollect it being challenged. To me, this is essential if we are not to get wildly repetitive in clause stand part debates.'[2]

What constitutes 'adequate discussion' is entirely at the discretion of the chair and indeed it would be impossible to provide rules for its exercise. A few examples may be given of its use.

In 1968–69 the Standing Order was invoked on Clause 10 of the Vehicle and Driving Licences Bill after discussion on amendments had continued for 1 hour and 40 minutes. That clause provided that, subject to a number of exceptions, a person who for any period kept a vehicle in respect of which duty had at any time become chargeable should be liable to pay duty for that period. In other words, liability to pay duty was to be continuous and put the onus on individuals to notify the Minister when they did not intend to use the vehicle for a period. The Opposition had put down an amendment which would have wrecked the whole clause but it had not, presumably because of that consequence, been selected. During the debate on the first selected amendment the Chairman warned that if the debate continued to range widely (and he thought it was impossible to stop it doing so) then there would not also be a debate on clause stand part. A Government backbencher who also disliked the clause and whose speech had caused the Chairman's intervention suggested that if he sat down at once, the Minister could reply and then the committee could go straight to the debate on clause stand part. The Chairman agreed to this 'subject to what the Committee thinks'. However, the debate continued, was adjourned for the Christmas recess and was resumed. After some time, the Chairman announced that he did not intend to allow a debate on clause stand part. After this amendment had been negatived, the Minister moved an amendment that was agreed to and the Chairman invoked the standing order.[3]

Clause 3 of the Iron and Steel Bill 1968–69 put a limit on borrowing by and investment in the British Steel Corporation of £500m to £650m. The first amendment sought to reduce the first figure to £450m and a long discussion followed that 'slid over', as the Parliamentary Secretary said,

[1] S.O. No. 48, 65(3)(c).

[2] H.C. 538 of 1970–71, Q585. On 26 February 1968 in committee of the whole House on the Public Expenditure and Receipts Bill a temporary chairman (Mr Victor Yates) had to declare an attempted objection out of order (759 H.C. Deb., cols 1105–6).

[3] Standing Committee A, cols 152–68, 174–92.

'into a virtual Second Reading debate'. At one point the Chairman said he would have to reserve his opinion as to whether there would be a debate on clause stand part but that he 'would not dream' of pronouncing on this until he had heard the whole of the debate 'which is the evidence on which I shall decide the matter'. At the next sitting there was a different chairman. The second selected amendment was to reduce the figure of £650m to £550m and the Chairman hoped that Members would not repeat the arguments used on the first amendment. The third amendment proposed to insert a requirement that no order should be made under the clause unless the Minister had first presented a report to the House. When that amendment was disposed of, the committee had debated the clause for over 5 hours and the Chairman invoked the standing order and when the ruling was challenged refused, after referring to the words of his predecessor, to allow discussion.[1]

Protests against the chair's ruling after 17½ hours' debate on Clause 1 of the Parliament (No. 2) Bill 1968–69 were no doubt part of the general war of attrition being waged on that occasion.[2] So also, both left-wing Labour Members and the Opposition front bench protested against the Chairman's ruling on Clause 3 (the school milk clause) of the Public Expenditure and Receipts Bill 1967–68.[3]

A chairman then may warn members of this possible consequence of widening the debate on amendments. He may frequently seek to come to an understanding with the committee and this may take the more elaborate form of his allowing the debate 'to go a little wide' on amendments so long as there is no repetition of the arguments during the debate on clause stand part.[4]

The standing order is undoubtedly a valuable and sometimes a necessary device. Chairmen use it sparingly. And if it did not exist, chairmen might sometimes resort to the use of other, less appropriate, means of keeping debates within proper limits.

An apparent anomaly, already referred to, does arise. The principle of the bill has been agreed to on Second Reading and so amendments are inadmissible which are equivalent to a negative of the bill or which reverse that principle. So also an amendment to leave out a clause, or to leave out the only effective words or the words upon which the rest of the clause is dependent, or to negate the clause, is inadmissible.[5] Yet it is always possible to vote against the Question that the clause stand part and so to strike out the clause.

A criticism often made of committee proceedings is that 'Committees tend to spend a lot of time on the earlier clauses and to race through the

[1] Standing Committee A, cols 171–282.

[2] 777 H.C. Deb., cols 1338–49; 778, cols 219–351, 363–414.

[3] 759 H.C. Deb., cols 1048–108; see also Family Allowances and National Insurance Bill 1967–68, 765 H.C. Deb., cols 925–7.

[4] E.g. Education (Sc.) Bill 1968–69, First Scottish Standing Committee, col. 338.

[5] May, *op. cit.*, p. 509; see above, pp. 67–8.

later ones'[1] with the implication that if less time could be spent on the earlier clauses there would be a more even spread and that this could best be effected by reducing the time spent on clause stand part. In 1967 the Clerk of Public Bills suggested 'tentatively' to the Select Committee on Procedure that the Question that the clause stand part should not be put automatically but only if an amendment were moved to leave out the clause. The decision whether or not to select such an amendment would be for the chairman and would pose the same problem which he has under S.O. No. 48 but it would be 'rather less invidious' not to select it than to invoke the standing order.[2] The Select Committee preferred their own proposal for the appointment of a steering committee which would be able to take into consideration representations made to them and, in the light of those representations and the selection of amendments, report recommendations about the progress of the bill to the committee or (on report) to the House.[3]

The Select Committee returned to this question in 1971 when the Clerk of Public Bills emphasised that the purpose of his suggestion was to discourage second reading debates in committee on the vital clause of a bill but not to diminish the rights of Members to challenge other clauses. The present understanding is that Members who table amendments to leave out a clause do so in order to draw attention to the fact that they intend to oppose the clause during the debate on the Question that clause stand part. And such amendments are ruled out of order and never selected. Under the proposal of the Clerk of Public Bills, an amendment to leave out a vital clause would be out of order and could not be called though such an amendment might be selected if the clause were not vital to the bill.[4] The Select Committee, however, did not deal with this matter in their report.

The two principal defects in the present practice on clause stand part are the second reading debates on the vital clauses and the (partly consequential) disproportionate amount of time spent on the earlier clauses. The first of these defects may apply to any bill. The second applies most seriously to longer bills, especially those which deal with a number of major issues of policy grouped under the different parts of a bill. In a short bill, the first clause normally contains the principle of the bill and the other clauses depend on it. For such a bill it is natural and desirable that far more time should be spent on the first clause than on the others. In contrast, a long bill may contain six or even ten vital clauses each proposing an important statutory change and spread throughout the bill. When the last two or three of these are rushed through, Parliamentary scrutiny becomes a farce.

A solution to both these defects might be, for any bill containing more than, say, twenty clauses, first, for an order to be made which would lay down the sequence in which clauses (with, where appropriate, associated

[1] H.C. 539 of 1966–67, Q78 (Mr K. R. Mackenzie, Clerk of Public Bills).
[2] *Ibid.*, Q93. [3] *Ibid.*, *Report* paras 24, 17.
[4] H.C. 538 of 1970–71, Appendix 1 paras 13–16; and see Q264–71.

schedules) were to be debated in committee;[1] and to ensure thereby that the most important clauses were debated first. Secondly, a debate on any clause as a whole should be possible only if the chairman selected an amendment to leave out that clause; and this he would normally not do on important clauses.

The effect of this change would not necessarily be to save time if only because Members would quickly find ways of drafting amendments to meet many of the points now raised on clause stand part. But it should have the effect of reducing the number of second reading points (and of repetition of points made on amendments) by reducing the opportunity for raising them and by enabling the chairman to deal with attempts to raise them on amendments, where they are more obviously out of order than on clause stand part. And it should also have the effect of concentrating the time of the committee on the more important aspects of the bill.

1967–68 In 1967–68, there were 119 divisions on Government bills and the Question that the clause (or the clause as amended) stand part or that this schedule (or this schedule as amended) be the schedule to the bill. Forty-seven of these were on the Transport Bill (of which thirteen[2] were taken after the guillotine had fallen) and twenty were on the Finance Bill in standing committee (of which thirteen[3] were after the guillotine). Ten divisions were on the Prices and Incomes Bill; eight on the Town and Country Planning Bill; five each on the Industrial Expansion Bill and on the Law Reform (Miscellaneous Provisions (Scotland)) Bill; three each on the Finance Bill in committee of the whole House, the Race Relations Bill, the Sewerage (Scotland) Bill, and the Social Work (Scotland) Bill; two each on the Countryside Bill, the Medicines Bill and the Public Expenditure and Receipts Bill; and one was on each of the British Standard Time Bill, the Commonwealth Immigrants Bill, the Gaming Bill, the Restrictive Trade Practices Bill, the Revenue (No. 2) Bill, and the Trade Descriptions Bill.

Divisions on bills are part of the ordinary Parliamentary process and tell us little about the impact of that process on Government legislation. Divisions on clause stand part indicate a wish, normally on the part of the Opposition, to register dissent. So it is to be expected that controversial legislation will attract many such divisions. Voting against clauses after the guillotine has fallen enables the Opposition both to express its dislike of the clauses and to make the Government pay the price, in inconvenience, for its curtailment of debate. The forty-seven divisions on the Transport Bill, the twenty-three divisions on the Finance Bill, and the ten divisions on the Prices and Incomes Bill fall into this category of divisions on highly controversial legislation.

[1] As, to some extent, already is the practice on the Finance Bill; and occasionally on other bills also.

[2] Standing Committee F, cols 2706, 2708, 2710, 2712, 3074, 3076, 3078, 3274.

[3] Standing Committee A, cols 1804, 1806, 1808, 1810, 1812, 1814, 2110, 2112.

The great majority of divisions on clause stand part were expressions of party differences on the whole or particular parts of Government bills. Thus the five clauses of the short Industrial Expansion Bill on which the Opposition divided the committee were a reflection of its general disapproval of a measure over which they had divided the House on Second Reading.[1] Often bills which are in their main principles agreed measures give rise to controversies on particular peripheral questions of policy. The Town and Country Planning Bill was of this kind. The eight clauses on which the Opposition divided the committee were typical points of difference between the parties: compulsory purchase, limitations on the duration of planning permission, and restrictions on the exercise by public authorities of the power to dispose of land.[2]

Exceptionally, divisions may occur because of the feelings of small minorities. Liberals, left-wing Labour Members and some Opposition backbenchers came together to form the minority of 76 on clause 1 of the Commonwealth Immigrants Bill.[3] Liberals and left-wingers joined with Sir Cyril Osborne to divide the committee on clause 1 of the Public Expenditure and Receipts Bill; on clause 3 the Liberals and Sir Cyril went it alone.[4]

In 1967–68 the Government were defeated once only on clause stand part. Clause 39 of the Gaming Bill restricted advertising about gaming. It was not a particularly happy or easily comprehensible clause and was both ridiculed and called hypocritical. Mr Paget and Mr Weitzman voted with the Opposition in standing committee and the clause was rejected by 8 votes to 7.[5]

On a number of occasions clauses were negatived with the assent or at the request of the Government. Clause 9 of the Civil Aviation Bill sought to empower an aerodrome authority, when default was made in the payment of airport charges, to detain and sell the aircraft. The drafting of the clause and the extent of the powers given were criticised. The Minister, having first asked the committee to reject an Opposition amendment, said he would like to have 'a sharp and detailed look at the whole clause' and he moved the early adjournment of the second sitting of the committee. On the third sitting, at the opening of the clause stand part debate, the Minister agreed to withdraw the clause and table a new clause. Debate followed on procedure and on the way to deal with consequential amendments and clause 9 was formally negatived. At the seventh sitting the new clause was moved and at the eighth sitting it was agreed to.[6] Clause 20 of the same Bill was negatived on the Government's initiative because the

[1] See 757 H.C. Deb., cols 1571–696; and Standing Committee E, cols 75–8, 221–2, 255–6, 285–6, 409–10.

[2] Standing Committee G, cols 641–60, 671–2, 741, 772–3, 985–8, 987–94, 1031–40, 1270–98.

[3] 759 H.C. Deb., cols 1599–602. [4] 759 H.C. Deb., cols 1041–4, 1105–8.

[5] Standing Committee B, cols 462–88.

[6] Standing Committee G, cols 62–115, 253–97.

powers of the Board of Trade there provided for were covered by the Industrial Expansion Bill.[1]

Clause 23(1) of the Countryside Bill provided: 'If the occupier of any field or enclosure through which there is a footpath or bridleway permits any bull exceeding the age of ten months to be at large in the field or enclosure he shall be liable on summary conviction to a fine not exceeding £50'; and there were seven other sub-sections. Amendments were moved and the committee adjourned in due course. At the next sitting the Joint Parliamentary Secretary said:

> 'It is an astonishing position. We were faced with a unanimous recommendation from the Gosling Committee, upon which are represented all the country interests. We have, with our draftsmen, done our best to produce a clause which would give that recommendation legislative effect. The net result seems to be that we have satisfied nobody.'

The Government withdrew the clause.[2]

Clause 56 of the Social Work (Scotland) Bill empowered a court to refer the case of a child pleading or found guilty to the reporter of the local authority to arrange for the disposal of the case by a children's hearing; so also for a person between 16 and 17½ years of age. Clause 57 dealt with a similar situation. The Under-Secretary of State having tabled two new clauses to replace them, the committee negatived clauses 56 and 57.[3] Clause 59 made certain provision for the custody of children and the abolition of remand homes. This also was disagreed to at the Minister's request as being unnecessary because of other provisions.[4]

The most dramatic request by the Government for the deletion of provisions occurred when the Minister asked Standing Committee F to remove the whole of Part VI (clauses 90 and 113 and schedules 11 and 12) from the Transport Bill. This Part was to impose charges in respect of heavy goods vehicles, and fees in respect of carriage by road of large or heavy loads. The Government changed their mind and instead raised a similar sum of money by increasing duties on goods vehicles in the budget.[5] From the same bill clause 81 also was deleted at the Government's request. This concerned holding and subsidiary companies and was replaced, as a result of discussions with the industry, by a new clause.[6]

Finally, the Family Allowances and National Insurance (No. 2) Bill 1967–68 consisted of two substantive clauses of which clause 2 abolished entitlement to unemployment, sickness and injury benefits for the first 3 days of a period of interruption of employment. Mr James Griffiths

[1] Standing Committee G, cols 165–6. [2] Standing Committee A, cols 1292–332.

[3] Scottish Standing Committee, cols 522–4; for new clauses see cols 574–82.

[4] *Ibid.*, cols 529–30.

[5] Standing Committee F, cols 2808–12; for budget statement see 761 H.C. Deb., col. 283.

[6] Standing Committee F, cols 2755–6; for the new clause see cols 3387–8.

had attacked this proposal during the budget debate.[1] During the debate on the second reading of the Bill, Lord Balniel for the Opposition said this clause would be opposed and he put down an amendment to delete it.[2] The Minister promised on second reading to look again at the proposal, and in Standing Committee she announced that it would not be proceeded with, partly as a result of conversations she had had with the CBI and the TUC.[3]

When pressure is seen to be exerted in committee on the Government to change its mind and delete clauses, it can be safely assumed that the pressure has also been exerted outside the committee room by individual members and probably by interested organisations. On three of the occasions referred to – clause 9 of the Civil Aviation Bill, clause 23 of the Countryside Bill and clause 2 of the Family Allowance and National Insurance (No. 2) Bill – the Government yielded because of this pressure from both inside and outside the committee. On the other hand the changes to the Social Work (Scotland) Bill were primarily the result of second thoughts within the Department on how to improve the measure. The major changes to the Transport Bill were the result of arguments between the Treasury and the Department in which Members of Parliament, other than Ministers, took no part and could have taken no part as the issue became overladen with the secrecy that surrounds Budget proposals. The minor change to the Transport Bill (the deletion of clause 81) resulted mainly from discussions with affected interests.

1968–69 During the course of the 1968–69 Parliamentary session there were thirty-six divisions on clause stand part. Six of these divisions were on the Education (Scotland) Bill, five on the Iron and Steel Bill and on the Parliament (No. 2) Bill, four on the Housing Bill and on the Post Office Bill, three on the Finance Bill, and one on the Air Corporations, Decimal Currency, Electricity (Scotland), Family Law Reform, Law of Property, Medical, Representation of the People, Town and Country Planning (Scotland), and House of Commons (Redistribution of Seats) (No. 2) Bills.

The Government were defeated on three occasions. The first was on one of the divisions on the Education (Scotland) Bill. This concerned section 16 of the Education (Scotland) Act 1962 which empowered the owners or trustees of certain denominational schools to which an Act of 1918 would have applied, with the consent of the Secretary of State, to transfer the school to a local educational authority. Clause 3 of the bill proposed to repeal that section on the ground that it was out of date. The motion that clause 3 stand part was negatived by 7 votes to 14, six Government

[1] 761 H.C. Deb., cols 950–1 (25 March 1968).

[2] 762 H.C. Deb., cols 194–206; Mr Griffiths returned to the attack (cols 206–11) as did others.

[3] 765 H.C. Deb., cols 927–30, 941–5.

backbenchers crossvoting.[1] Secondly, clause 2 of the Air Corporations Bill empowered the Board of Trade to provide for the investment of public dividend capital in BEA as was already permissible for BOAC. The motion that clause 2 stand part was defeated by 5 votes to 4, with no crossvoting.[2] Thirdly, the dispute on clause 1 of the Decimal Currency Bill centred on two questions: gold coins as legal tender; and the retention of the 6d piece, an amendment to which was defeated only by the casting vote of the chairman. The motion that the clause stand part was defeated by 6 votes to 5, no member crossvoting.[3]

When we look at the other bills on which there was only one division, the least controversial include, first, the Family Law Reform Bill. On that bill the division took place on clause 14 which provided that in the disposition of property references to children should be presumed to include illegitimate children. This was opposed on the ground that the change would give rise to far more difficulties than it would help to solve.[4] Secondly, the Law of Property Bill was another law reform bill. The division was on clause 26 which enabled the Lands Tribunal more easily to discharge restrictive covenants – a change regarded as 'political' by its opponents.[5] Thirdly, in the Medical Bill, there was a division on clause 19 which empowered the General Medical Council to request information from registered persons for statistical purposes and which was seen by some as sinister.[6] The opposition to clause 1 (the only vital clause) in the Electricity (Scotland) Bill was highly individualist since only one member voted against the clause – and that because he had been disappointed in the way an amendment moved by him was received.[7] More controversial was clause 21 in the Town and Country Planning (Scotland) Bill which enabled persons appointed by the Secretary of State to determine planning appeals, as this was thought to be 'inappropriate to Scotland'.[8]

In the committee of the whole House there were two divisions on clause stand part in this group of bills. The first was on clause 15 of the Representation of the People Bill which concerned non-resident and property qualifications in local government.[9] This was a clear party political issue as was, supremely, the other: a division on clause 1 of the House of Commons (Redistribution of seats) (No. 2) Bill which, under the guillotine and without debate on clause stand part, suspended that redistribution in an atmosphere of considerable party acrimony.[10]

1970–71 In 1970–71 there were 125 divisions on clause stand part but of these ninety-one took place on the Industrial Relations Bill as the

[1] First Scottish Standing Committee, cols 335–60.
[2] Standing Committee D, cols 72–86. [3] Standing Committee A, cols 82–90.
[4] 1968–69 Standing Committee B, cols 132–4.
[5] 1968–69 Standing Committee F, cols 110–22.
[6] 1968–69 Standing Committee D, cols 44–8.
[7] 1968–69 Second Scottish Standing Committee, cols 25–46.
[8] 1968–69 First Scottish Standing Committee, cols 345–68.
[9] 775 H.C. Deb., cols 367–80. [10] 786 H.C. Deb., cols 291–8.

Opposition kept the Government marching through the lobbies during the small hours of the morning after the guillotine had fallen.

Of the remaining thirty-four divisions, six took place on each of the Immigration Bill and the Social Security Bill, three on each of the Coal Industry Bill and the Licensing (Abolition of State Management) bill. All these were controversial bills. So also was the Industry Bill which gave occasion for two divisions; and the Civil Aviation (Declaratory Provisions), the Education (Milk), the Education (Scotland), the Family Income Supplements, the Investment and Building Grants, the Land Commission (Dissolution), the Local Authorities (Qualification of Members), and the Rating Bills, each of which produced one division.

The other six divisions occurred during the debate on five bills. The first two divisions were on the Courts Bill. Clause 18 provided that the salaries of Circuit judges should be such as might be determined by the Lord Chancellor with the consent of the Minister for the Civil Service but no provision was made for Parliamentary scrutiny. The Under-Secretary of State was obviously not altogether happy. Nor was the former Attorney-General who however abstained on the vote.[1] A similar point arose on clause 19 which concerned pensions of Circuit judges but only Mr Clinton Davis voted against it.[2] The third division was on clause 49 of the Finance Bill which proposed to abolish a charge to capital gains tax on the death of an individual imposed by the Finance Act 1965. The Opposition front bench divided the committee.[3] Clause 13 of the Misuse of Drugs Bill produced a curious division. The clause concerned directions prohibiting prescribing, supply, etc., of controlled drugs by practitioners in certain cases. Where a doctor contravened regulations, the Secretary of State was to be empowered to give him prohibitory directions. Both Labour and Conservative Governments thought the General Medical Council – the profession itself – should exercise this control but the profession did not wish to. Hence, clause 13. Mr Deedes argued strongly against the clause. Other Government backbenchers also expressed considerable doubts. In the event only one Opposition Member (Mr Clinton Davis) joined Mr Deedes in voting against the clause which was supported by seven Members from the Government benches and four from the Opposition.[4]

The second reading of the Vehicles (Excise) Bill (which was a consolidation bill) was moved at 4.57 a.m. and agreed to at once. But Opposition Members forced a division on the motion that the bill be committed to a committee of the whole House (with the intention that it be immediately considered) because of the lateness of the hour. Defeated on this, the Opposition divided the House on clause 1 stand part. On clauses 2–6, Opposition Members called for divisions. *Hansard* records in each case:

'*The Committee proceeded to a Division, and the Chairman stated that he thought the Ayes had it; and, on his decision being challenged, it*

[1] 1970–71 Standing Committee A, cols 256–70. [2] *Ibid.*, cols 278–80.
[3] 817 H.C. Deb., cols 1571–608. [4] Standing Committee A, cols 119–46.

appeared to him that the Division was unnecessarily claimed, and he accordingly called upon the Members who supported and who challenged his decision successively to rise in their places, and he declared that the Ayes had it, seven members only who challenged his decision having stood up.'

A compromise was then come to and the remaining clauses of the bill were put and agreed to.[1]

The sixth and last division occurred on clause 1 of the Water Resources Bill where Mr Farr pursued his one-man show already referred to and divided the committee.[2]

None of these 125 divisions resulted in a defeat for the Government. On four occasions the proposal that a clause stand part was negatived without a division. Clause 38 of the Civil Aviation Bill was a 'general duty' clause of a type often inserted in nationalisation statutes but of little significance. The Minister suggested its deletion.[3] Clause 9 of the Family Income Supplements Bill enabled the Supplementary Benefits Commission to recover from a husband or father the cost of any supplementary benefit paid to a family where the husband or father was liable to maintain the child. Miss Mervyn Pike, supported by Mrs Knight, both from the Government back benches, claimed that this requirement worked unfairly for an unsupported woman claiming FIS. The Secretary of State accepted the argument and agreed to the deletion of the clause.[4] Clause 1 of the Misuse of Drugs Bill was deleted in committee because the Government introduced another version as a new clause.[5] In none of these cases, therefore, was the negation of the clause a Government defeat.

The fourth case arose on clause 7 of the National Insurance Bill and has already been referred to.[6] An amendment was carried which showed a lack of support on the Government back benches for the whole clause, and the motion that the clause as amended stand part was negatived without a division.

3.4.7 *Crossvoting*

1967–68 In 1967–68 crossvoting took place on twelve bills and on seventy-eight occasions. Thirty of these were on the Race Relations Bill and eighteen on the Prices and Incomes Bill; seven on the Commonwealth Immigrants Bill; five on the Finance Bill; four on the Town and Country Planning Bill; three on the Public Expenditure and Receipts Bill and the Social Work (Scotland) Bill; two on the British Standard Time Bill, the Gaming Bill and the Medicines Bill; and one was on each of the Countryside Bill and the Sewerage (Scotland) Bill. Six of these occasions have already been referred to as they resulted in Government defeats.[7]

[1] 812 H.C. Deb., cols 1654–65. [2] Standing Committee D, cols 14–30.
[3] Standing Committee A, cols 607–9. [4] 806 H.C. Deb., cols 1365–7.
[5] Standing Committee A, cols 4–40. [6] See above, p. 119.
[7] See above, pp. 100, 101, 113–4, 131.

There were five voting groups in committee on the Race Relations Bill: the two front benches and, on the back benches, the Labour left, the liberal Conservatives and the Conservative right wing. The extraordinary result was that there was crossvoting on all but three of the thirty-three divisions during the thirteen sittings of the committee. On nineteen occasions, some Opposition Members voted contrary to their front bench;[1] on four occasions, Government backbenchers alone defected;[2] and on seven occasions some members of both the principal parties voted against their colleagues. These seven occasions resulted on two occasions in Government defeats. As already noted, Mr Rose's amendment 25 to the Race Relations Bill was supported by ten Government backbenchers, and five Opposition Members (including one Liberal) against two Ministers, three Government backbenchers, and three Opposition Members.[3] So also Mr Lyon's amendment 117 was agreed to by six Government backbenchers and eleven Opposition Members (including one Liberal) against three Ministers, five Government backbenchers and Mr Ronald Bell.[4] On two of the other five occasions, the Labour left and the liberal Conservatives joined to oppose both front benches;[5] on another occasion two Members of the Labour left were supported by the Conservative front bench and others against the Government and its supporters including one Conservative right winger.[6] On the fourth occasion the Labour left, a right-wing Conservative and a liberal Conservative opposed both the front benches.[7] Finally on one occasion the Labour left were joined by one right-wing Conservative against both front benches and their supporters.[8] In the result, the Government had its way on all these five occasions.

Reference has already been made to the opposition from the Labour left in the persons of Mr Mikardo and Mr Ted Fletcher to many of the provisions of the Prices and Incomes Bill.[9] They divided the Committee on eleven occasions on their own amendments. On nine of these, they were supported by Opposition Members;[10] once the Opposition abstained;[11] once the movers were joined by two other Government backbenchers while the Opposition voted with the Government.[12] On one occasion Mr Mikardo and Mr Fletcher voted for an Opposition amendment.[13] On four occasions they joined the Opposition in voting against the motion that a

[1] Standing Committee B, cols 51–2 (twice), 91–2, 119–20, 197–8, 303–4, 333–4, 369–70, 459–60, 459–62, 471–2, 505–6, 609–12, 685–6, 699–700, 727–8, 729–30, 809–10. (division No. 30)

[2] *Ibid.*, cols 239–40, 641–2, 681–2, 729–30 (division No. 29).

[3] See above, p. 100–1. [4] See above, p. 97.

[5] Standing Committee B, cols 501–2, 569–70; see above, p. 98.

[6] *Ibid.*, cols 453–4; see above, p. 99. [7] *Ibid.*, cols 535–6; see above, p. 98.

[8] *Ibid.*, cols 555–6. [9] See above, pp. 96–7, 101.

[10] Standing Committee F, cols 177–8, 339–40, 379–82, 695–6, 723–4, 755–6 (twice), 1101–2, 1109–10.

[11] *Ibid.*, cols 795–6. [12] *Ibid.*, cols 1107–8.

[13] *Ibid.*, cols 423–4.

clause stand part;[1] and once Mr Mikardo alone joined the Opposition in voting for the adjournment of the committee.[2]

On the Commonwealth Immigrants Bill in committee of the whole House, some Opposition Members voted with some Government backbenchers and some Liberals on two procedural motions,[3] on a Liberal amendment,[4] on two new clauses moved by Government backbenchers,[5] on a clause stand part;[6] and on a Government back-bench amendment.[7] The Opposition had a free vote on these occasions and they voted on both sides of the divisions, as did Government backbenchers.

In standing committee on the Finance Bill, on the motion that the clause for instituting a national lottery stand part, the Noes (in the minority) consisted of seven Opposition Members (including one Liberal) and two Government backbenchers, the Ayes being Ministers and Government backbenchers.[8] On two other occasions on this Bill, Government backbenchers voted against their Ministers: two so voted on clause 46 (for SET) stand part;[9] and were joined by two others on an SET amendment, the Opposition abstaining.[10] One morning, shortly after 6 a.m., the adjournment of the committee was moved by an Opposition Member, supported by eleven Government backbenchers, and defeated by a combination of sixteen Opposition Members (including the mover) and four Government backbenchers, the Minister present abstaining.[11] The fifth occasion was on the same bill, perhaps not truly crossvoting. It occurred, after the guillotine had fallen, on a motion that a schedule be the sixteenth schedule to the bill. All the Opposition Members, except Mr Anthony Grant, abstained, and the motion was carried by 27 votes to 1.[12]

In addition to the Government defeat on the first division on the Town and Country Planning Bill,[13] there was crossvoting on three occasions. On an amendment moved by a Government backbencher, the mover voted with the Opposition;[14] on an Opposition amendment, one Government backbencher voted with the Opposition;[15] another, grouped with it, was immediately divided on with two Government backbenchers supporting the Opposition and one abstaining so that the result was a tie and the chairman cast his vote against.[16]

The Labour left twice divided the committee of the whole House on the Public Expenditure and Receipts Bill. On clause 1 stand part, the Opposition abstained and the Noes (in the minority) consisted of twenty Government backbenchers, eight Liberals and Sir Cyril Osborne; there were also probably some twenty abstentions on the Government side.[17] On the next

[1] Standing Committee F, cols 335–6, 447–8, 767–8, 775–6. [2] *Ibid.*, cols 601–2.
[3] 759 H.C. Deb., cols 1541–4, 1595–8. [4] *Ibid.*, cols 1627–30.
[5] *Ibid.*, cols 1669–72, 1687–90; see above, p. 98, notes 4, 5.
[6] *Ibid.*, cols 1601–2. [7] *Ibid.*, cols 1597–600.
[8] Standing Committee A, cols 2111–12; but this was a free vote.
[9] *Ibid.*, cols 1945–6 (Mr Pavitt and Mr Haseldine). [10] *Ibid.*, cols 2045–6.
[11] *Ibid.*, cols 1373–4. [12] *Ibid.*, cols 1813–14. [13] See above, p. 100.
[14] Standing Committee G, cols 89–90. [15] *Ibid.*, cols 709–10. [16] *Ibid.*
[17] 759 H.C. Deb., cols 1041–4.

division (on school milk) there was a similar result on an amendment which was defeated but the minority consisted of twenty-eight Government backbenchers, eight Liberals and Sir Cyril Osborne and again there were a large number of Government abstentions. Again the Opposition abstained.[1] On this clause stand part, Sir Cyril voted with the Liberals, the Labour left and the Opposition abstaining.[2]

The first division on the Social Work (Scotland) Bill was on a Government amendment to restore to the bill its original provision that large burghs as well as counties and cities should be social work authorities. This had been amended in the House of Lords when the bill was first introduced. One Government backbencher supported the Opposition and there were a number of abstentions.[3] On clause 3 stand part, some Opposition divided the committee and one Government backbencher voted with them.[4] Thirdly, on this bill, two Opposition Members divided the committee on clause 42 stand part when one of them had risen too late to ask a question.[5]

During the debate on the British Standard Time Bill one Government backbencher voted twice with the Opposition in an attempt to exclude Scotland.[6] The Government defeat on the Gaming Bill has been referred to;[7] on an Opposition amendment to clause 12, one Government backbencher supported it.[8] On the Medicines Bill, in addition to the Government defeat,[9] Mr Pavitt divided the committee on his amendment to clause 87 on advertisements and representations directed to practitioners but found no one to support him.[10] The crossvoting on the Government defeat on the Countryside Bill has been noticed.[11] Finally Mr Noble moved a long amendment to the Sewerage (Scotland) Bill concerning the expenses of local authorities and supported by the Association of County Councils. In the division Mr Maclennan voted with the Opposition.[12]

Race relations, including immigration, and prices and incomes accounted for fifty-one of the seventy-eight occasions in 1967–68 when crossvoting occurred. On the Race Relations Bill the most consistent and most frequent rebels were the liberal Conservatives while on prices and incomes the representatives of the left wing of the Labour party made all the running. The pattern of crossvoting was unsurprising during this session and expressed minority views without causing any great upsets.

1968–69 In 1968–69, crossvoting took place during the debates on eleven Government Bills and on a total of seventy-seven occasions. But fifty-four of those occasions were on sixteen substantive and thirty-eight procedural motions on the Parliament (No. 2) Bill while the remaining twenty-three

[1] *Ibid.*, cols 1103–6. [2] *Ibid.*, cols 1105–8.
[3] Scottish Standing Committee, cols 69–70. [4] *Ibid.*, cols 133–4.
[5] *Ibid.*, cols 489–90. [6] Standing Committee A, cols 77–80, 105–6.
[7] See above, p. 131. [8] Standing Committee B, cols 243–4.
[9] See above, p. 100. [10] Standing Committee D, cols 727–8.
[11] See above, pp. 113–4. [12] Scottish Standing Committee, cols 367–8.

occasions were during the debates on the Family Law Reform Bill (four times); the Horserace Betting Levy Bill, the Post Office Bill, the Representation of the People Bill, and the Housing Bill (each thrice); the Education (Scotland) Bill, and the Administration of Justice Bill (each twice); the Medical Bill, the Nurses Bill and the Transport (London) Bill (each once). On three occasions, already referred to, the crossvoting led to Government defeats: once on clause 3 stand part of the Education (Scotland) Bill and twice on the Administration of Justice Bill.[1]

On fifteen of these twenty-three occasions the crossvoting was that of Government backbenchers voting against their front bench. These included those three Government defeats just mentioned where the defectors numbered six, seven and three respectively. But they were not, as we have seen, of much political significance. On four occasions only does a genuine party split appear.

Clause 46 of the Housing Bill provided for the conversion of controlled tenancies to regulated tenancies. On the motion that this clause stand part, Mr Allaun led the left wing of the Government supporters into strong revolt against a policy which they had continously resisted and which he described as 'political dynamite'. The motion was agreed to by 7 votes to 3 (Mr Allaun being joined by Mr Dunnett and Mr Julius Silverman), Opposition Members of the committee abstaining.[2] Later Mr Wellbeloved moved his new clause to the same bill on the tenants' option to purchase, was supported by Messrs Allaun, Dunnett and Silverman, but was defeated by 11 votes to 4.[3] The other two occasions were also on a contentious issue which often marks off the left wing of the Labour party from its front bench: the powers of nationalised industries to compete with private interests. The first arose on clause 13 of the Post Office Bill which restricted the manufacturing powers of the Post Office and its subsidiaries. On the motion that this clause stand part, five Government backbenchers defected and the Government was saved from defeat by the adherence of eight Opposition Members.[4] The second was Mr Raymond Fletcher's amendment to enlarge the powers of the London Transport Executive where again the Government was saved by Opposition votes.[5]

I have already referred to crossvoting on Mr Dobson's amendment to the clause on the Post Office Bill concerned with staff pensions which once again the Government defeated only with Opposition help;[6] and to Mr Pavitt's campaign for male chauvinism on the Nurses Bill where he and two colleagues were overwhelmingly defeated.[7] On the remaining six of these fifteen instance, only one Government supporter in each case voted against his front bench.[8]

On four occasions, Opposition members voted on opposite sides of

[1] See above, pp. 104, 133–4. [2] Standing Committee F, cols 383–414.

[3] *Ibid.*, cols 901–18; see above, pp. 103–4. [4] Standing Committee D, cols 561–2.

[5] London (Transport) Bill 1968–69, Standing Committee A, cols 177–90; see above p. 104.

[6] See above, p. 104. [7] See above, p. 104.

divisions. The first concerned the rights of registered and certificated teachers under the Education (Scotland) Bill, clause 19 of which amended section 85 of the Education (Scotland) Act 1962. Mr Bruce-Gardyne spoke strongly against the motion that this clause stand part but was able to persuade only one other Opposition backbencher to vote against it. Eight other Opposition Members (including one Liberal) voted with thirteen Government supporters on the other side.[1] The other instances occurred during the debates on the Family Law Reform Bill. Clause 1 of the bill provided for the reduction of the age of majority from 21 years to 18. Law reform bills may be traditionally non-partisan, but they are often controversial. Dame Joan Vickers moved an amendment (which she said was 'probing' but which Mr Waddington hoped was not only so) to leave out 18 and insert 20. The debate that followed resembled a second reading debate on Part I of the bill and resulted in the amendment being negatived, Dame Joan Vickers and Mr Waddington being joined by two other Opposition backbenchers (Mr Bruce Campbell and Mr John Hunt) and opposed by the Attorney-General, six Government supporters and three Opposition Members.[2] Clause 2 of the Bill dealt with the age at which persons could marry without parental consent. As originally introduced into the House of Lords, the bill provided that the age should be reduced from 21 years to 18. But an amendment in the Lords raised this to 20. In Standing Committee B in the House of Commons, the Attorney-General moved an amendment to reinstate the age of 18 years. Mr Campbell, Dame Joan Vickers and Mr Waddington voted against the amendment but nine Members (including two Opposition backbenchers) voted in favour.[3] The third amendment was to clause 13 in Part II of the bill concerning the property rights of illegitimate children. Three Opposition backbenchers and one frontbencher were defeated by the Attorney-General, eight Government supporters and one Opposition backbencher.[4]

Also on four occasions crossvoting resulted in both Government supporters and Opposition Members voting together on opposite sides. In one division on the Family Law Reform Bill, on an Opposition amendment that proposed to give the mother rights to the estate of an intestate bastard to the exclusion of the father, six Government supporters and one Opposition Member defeated one Government backbencher and four Opposition Members.[5] On an amendment to the Horserace Betting Levy Bill, requiring certain Ministerial powers to be exercisable by statutory instrument, eight Government supporters and two Opposition Members defeated one Government supporter and three Opposition Members.[6] In the Post Office Bill, an Opposition Member sought to extend the penalty for obscene and other improper use of telecommunication services to include imprisonment for 1 month. He was supported by one Opposition

[1] First Scottish Standing Committee, cols 609–26.
[2] Standing Committee B, cols 5–32. [3] *Ibid.*, cols 35–58.
[4] *Ibid.*, cols 82–106. [5] *Ibid.*, cols 105–10.
[6] 1968–69 Standing Committee E, cols 51–82.

Member and four Government backbenchers against eight Government supporters and four Opposition Members.[1] In committee of the whole House on the Representation of the People Bill, the amendment moved by Mr Strauss to raise the voting age from the 18 years proposed in the Bill to 20 years was defeated by 121 votes to 275. Ten Government backbenchers voted against their front bench, up to twenty-five abstained, and thirty-four Opposition Members supported the Government.[2]

Crossvoting in committee of the whole House is normally of less significance. The Government has its majority and a defection of a few of its supporters is not likely to affect the issue. In any event it is most improbable that a sufficiently large number of dissident Members will maintain their dissent when the likely result is the clear and positive defeat of the Government in the House. Nevertheless the possibility is not wholly remote. Had the Labour Government persisted in its intention to introduce an Industrial Relations Bill in 1969 to give effect to its White Paper *In Place of Strife*[3] the discontent amongst its own supporters might have been considerable and the Opposition, although it might have favoured the general intention of the bill, could have been in the position of bringing down the Government. That Government, however, had a majority which was probably large enough to have given the Government an adequate margin. When a similar position was arrived at on the European Communities Bill 1971–72, during the currency of Mr Heath's Government, with its nominal majority of little more than twenty, a genuine threat existed.

Finally, there were the many occasions when Government supporters and Opposition Members were to be found voting together on opposite sides on the Parliament (No. 2) Bill. Here rebellious Government backbenchers averaged during the many divisions about fourteen and Government majorities were normally of the order of seventy-five.[4] Nevertheless, forcing the Government to withdraw the bill was a remarkable and rare achievement. The issue was special and, in the Parliamentary sense, domestic. But it was an issue of Government policy and the withdrawal was a defeat for the Government. On these few occasions when sufficient backbenchers on both sides of the House unite, their power is considerable. And one occasion that is likely to unite them is when the front benches agree. As David Marquand has said,[5] there was insufficient enthusiasm on the part of Government supporters to sustain the Government through all-night sittings or through the Whitsun recess. And the very fact that, at least in theory, the front benches were agreed on the principles of the measure removed it from the arena of party politics and made it less a

[1] 1968–69 Standing Committee D, cols 1108–20.

[2] 774 H.C. Deb., cols 309–436; and see J. P. Mackintosh 'The influence of the backbencher, now and a hundred years ago', in *Manchester Statistical Society* (1969–70) at p. 20 (his figures include tellers). The Opposition had a free vote.

[3] Cmnd. 3888.

[4] See J. P. Mackintosh, *Manchester Statistical Society* (1969–70), p. 22.

[5] *New Society* (24 April 1969).

question of confidence in the Government. In these circumstances party loyalty was an inadequate weapon.

The combination of front-bench agreement and fundamental lack of faith in the reform proposed – because it was seen by many as a temporising measure not truly facing up to the problems of a Second Chamber and what to do about it – resulted in the Government's being unable to sustain that concentrated and long drawn out support that would have been necessary to defeat the opposition from the back benches on both sides of the House.

In summary therefore of crossvoting in 1968–69, of the twenty-three occasions apart from the Parliament (No. 2) Bill, only seven were of any general political, significance. Of these, five were expressions of political difference within the Labour party, two being concerned with the position of tenants under the Housing Bill,[1] two being concerned with the powers of nationalised industries to compete with the private sector,[2] and one being concerned with the rights of employees in a nationalised industry to be consulted on pension schemes.[3]

Of the other two occasions, one was the defeat of the Government on clause 3 of the Education (Scotland) Bill[4] and the other was the amendment to fix the new voting age at 20 years rather than at 18.[5] There were revolts on non-legislative questions in the House of Commons[6] in 1968–69 and some of these were significant. But it can hardly be said of the crossvoting on the committee stage of bills that minority groups within the parties made their presence felt by their voting or that their actions made any measurable impact on the legislative process. All this must be made subject to the undoubted and far-reaching consequences of the actions of minority groups on both sides of the House of Commons which resulted in the abandonment of the Parliament (No. 2) Bill. That was without doubt a famous victory.

1970–71 In 1970–71, there were seventeen occasions of crossvoting on divisions in committee. Three of these resulted in Government defeats: on the Coal Industry Bill (Mr Skeet and Sir Gerald Nabarro),[7] the Immigration Bill (Mr E. Powell and Sir George Sinclair),[8] and the Oil in Navigable Waters Bill (Mr Maxwell-Hyslop, Mr Laurance Reed, Mr John Wilkinson).[9]

On twelve occasions, the crossvoting was by a single Government backbencher: Sir Gerald Nabarro (thrice) on the Coal Industry Bill[10] on a

[1] See above, p. 140. [2] *Ibid.* [3] *Ibid.*

[4] See above, pp. 133–4 note. [5] See above, p. 141.

[6] See J. P. Mackintosh, *op. cit.*, pp. 20–1. He also records absentions of 18 to 23 by Government supporters on Selective Employment Tax on the Finance Bill (see 784 H.C. Deb., cols 256–354).

[7] Standing Committee B, cols 667–8; see above, pp. 118–9.

[8] *Ibid.*, cols 275–6; see above, p. 110.

[9] Standing Committee D, cols 65–6; see above, p. 119.

[10] Standing Committee B, cols 201–2.

sittings motion; Sir Brandon Rhys Williams on clause 2 of the Finance Bill;[1] Mr Angus Maude twice on the Highways Bill;[2] Mr Powell on a motion to leave out the whole of the paragraph which contained the 'grand-child' provision in the Immigration Bill;[3] Sir George Sinclair on a procedural motion on the same Bill;[4] Mr Farr once on clause 1 stand part and twice on amendments to Water Resources Bill;[5] and Mr Sutcliffe on the Investment and Building Grants Bill[6] where he moved his amendment to enable a grant to be paid to Cleveland Potash.

The other two occasions were, first, when Mr Deedes and Mr Clinton Davis voted together and without support against most of the rest of the committee on the motion that clause 13 stand part of the Misuse of Drugs Bill,[7] and secondly when four Opposition Members voted against most of the rest of the committee on an amendment to the Licensing (Abolition of State Management) Bill.[8]

Finally, *Hansard* would have us believe that on an amendment to the Finance Bill in standing committee moved by Mr Taverne for the Opposition, one Minister, four Government and six Opposition backbenchers voted for the amendment; and two Ministers, four Government and six Opposition backbenchers (including Mr Taverne) voted against.[9] But other records suggest that the printer somewhat confused the voting though not the ultimate issue and that, in fact, Ministerial support was not divided nor, indeed, did any backbencher vote contrary to his front bench.

With the exception, therefore, of the three occasions when it resulted in Government defeat, crossvoting in 1970–71 was of little political significance.

[1] Standing Committee H, at 53–4; see above, p. 107.
[2] Standing Committee D, cols 63–4, 69–70; for the second of these see above, p. 108.
[3] Standing Committee B, cols 275–6; see above, p. 110.
[4] *Ibid.*, cols 959–60.
[5] Standing Committee D, cols 29–30, 43–4, 75–6; see above, pp. 107, 136.
[6] Standing Committee E, cols 75–90; see above, p. 108.
[7] Standing Committee A, cols 145–6; see above, p. 135.
[8] Standing Committee D, cols 65–6; see above, p. 119.
[9] Standing Committee H, cols 117–18.

CHAPTER FOUR

REPORT STAGE IN THE HOUSE OF COMMONS

4.1 GENERAL[1]

At the end of the consideration of a bill committed to the whole House, the chairman reports the bill to the House stating whether it has or has not been amended.[2] If there is no amendment, it is ordered to be read the third time forthwith or on an appointed day. If the bill has been amended, the Member in charge names a day on which the bill, as amended, is to be taken into consideration;[3] in a case of urgency it may be agreed that the bill be considered immediately after the report.[4]

The rule that a bill committted to the whole House and not there amended shall not be considered on report is founded in the practice of the House and is not specifically provided for in Standing Orders. Presumably the basis of the rule is that, as all Members have had the opportunity to participate in committee and have decided not to amend the bill, there is no need for the House out of committee to consider the bill again at this stage. The 'report' becomes a formal statement made by the chairman. Nevertheless the rule, however logical, has one important consequence. For it may result in a Government resisting all amendments (including, perhaps, small amendments needed to clarify meaning or to correct drafting errors) because, to save time or political difficulty, the Government wish to avoid the consideration of the bill on report. This seems to have happened on the European Communities Bill 1971–72.[5]

A bill that has been considered by a standing committee, whether amended or not, must be considered on report by the House;[6] but if no Member moves a new clause or an amendment, no question arises on this stage and the Speaker calls on the Minister in charge of the bill who names a day for the third reading or moves 'that the bill be now read the third time'.

The order in which the bill is proceeded with is new clauses, amendments to the bill, new schedules, amendments to the schedules. Although not

[1] For detailed figures see Appendix 2.

[2] S.O. No. 20, 50; Erskine May, *op. cit.*, pp. 521 *et seq.*

[3] So every bill is reported but not every bill is considered on report. The 'report stage' is commonly used to mean consideration of a bill on report.

[4] See S.O. No. 51.

[5] See the debate on Third Reading (840 H.C. Deb., cols 1862–988).

[6] S.O. No. 52.

obligatory, it is highly desirable to give notice of important amendments.[1] Amendments are to the bill not to the particular clauses though they are considered in the order in which they would stand in the bill. But no question is put for each clause standing part of the bill. No amendment which could not have been proposed in committee without an instruction from the House may be proposed on report unless it has been authorised by a resolution of the House[2] and so the rules of order respecting admissibility of amendments in committee apply on report.

The most obvious differences between consideration of bills in committee and consideration of bills on report are that, on report, new clauses are taken first instead of last, there is no motion and so no debate on clause stand part and Government amendments predominate. This last difference can best be seen by referring to Table 4.1.

Table 4.1

Number of amendments (including new clauses) moved* by	Committee					Report				
	1967–68	1968–69	1970–71	Total	%	1967–68	1968–69	1970–71	Total	%
Ministers	439	288	180	907	20·5	379	249	237	865	55·7
Government backbenchers	230	79	127	436	9·9	42	10	37	89	5·7
Opposition Members	1492	889	693	3074	69·6	251	207	141	599	38·6
Total	2161	1256	1000	4417	100	672	466	415	1553	100

* This table excludes amendments moved formally.

The great increase in the percentage of Government amendments moved on report as compared with committee and the corresponding reduction in the percentages for Opposition (and less significantly, Government backbench) amendments reflect a real difference between the two stages. In committee the Government is very much on the defensive, countering arguments, giving explanations, sometimes meeting points. On report the Government puts forward its proposals for change. No doubt this oversimplifies the matter for in committee the Government proposes amendments and new clauses which may be important; and on report the Opposition also seeks once again to change the bill. But the broad distinction holds and on report as in committee all Government amendments are selected. Opposition amendments are more stringently examined by the Speaker on report, before selection, than by chairmen in committee.

When bills are reported from committee of the whole House without amendment and when, to bills reported from a standing committee, no

[1] Notice must be given of new clauses (S.O. No. 49).

[2] S.O. No. 54.

amendments or new clauses or new schedules are moved, no question arises for the House to debate. For Government bills[1] in three recent sessions, the figures were as shown in Table 4.2.

Table 4.2

	Number of Government bills	Number of Government bills considered on report
1967–68	63	30*
1968–69	53	27
1970–71	76	35
Totals	192	92*

* One other bill (Water Resources) was considered on report in committee.

The nature and function of the report stage differ for bills that are committed to the whole House from bills that are sent to standing committee. Most obviously, any Member may take part in proceedings in the whole House but only committee members may take part in standing committee (except that any Member of the House may table an amendment to a bill in standing committee though not a member of the committee; and a member of the committee may move it).

During the many discussions, in the Select Committee on Procedure and elsewhere, that have taken place in recent times on the legislative process, aspects of the report stage have been much criticised. The third Report from the Select Committee on Procedure in 1945–46 was highly influential both for what the Select Committee recommended and for what they failed to recommend. Sir Gilbert Campion was the Clerk of the House and in a famous submission he analysed the proceedings of the House and made a number of radical proposals. He suggested that, apart from the Scottish Standing Committee, there should be two large standing committees consisting of seventy-five to one hundred members, each of which should, for the committee stage of bills, consist of at least three sub-committees of twenty-five members to whom fifteen should be added in respect of each bill. Each sub-committee would report its bills, not to the House, but to its parent standing committee which should consider the bills as does the House on report stage.[2] The Select Committee rejected this proposal primarily on the ground that the removal of the report stage from the floor of the House would be, in the words of the Speaker, 'a drastic interference with the right of private Members'.[3]

[1] Including Consolidated Fund and Appropriation Bills.
[2] H.C. 189–I of 1945–46, p. xli. [3] *Ibid.*, p. vii.

When the Select Committee on Procedure looked at the problem again 21 years later, they had before them a note by the then Speaker (Mr King). He began with a double negative which might be thought unenthusiastic. He considered the report stage 'not unimportant', first, because the bill emerging from committee was often a much modified bill and the Opposition might have a new attitude to parts of it; secondly, because the report stage offered to the Opposition the last chance to secure what they thought were important changes in the bill; thirdly, because the deliberations of the committee had often been of considerable effect on the thinking of both sides and this was revealed at report stage; and fourthly, because undertakings given by the Government during discussions were at report stage honoured by concessions or were further discussed.[1] The Select Committee contented themselves with a suggestion that bills referred (as it proposed) to a committee for second reading might well be considered on report by that committee.[2]

The last proposal was embodied in a Standing Order in 1967[3] but only one bill has since been referred to a committee for the report stage.[4] Statistics produced for the Select Committee on Procedure in 1970–71 showed that in three sessions a total of only 16 hours would have been saved even if all the eligible bills, i.e. those referred to second reading committees, had been sent to a committee for report stage.[5] That Select Committee spoke more strongly than had Speaker King 4 years before. They were 'convinced of the importance of the report stage' especially because the number of Members of the House appointed to standing committees was now smaller than it had been.[6]

It is commonly said that the report stage today is a repetition of the committee stage.[7] It is more formal because, for example, Members (other than the Member in charge or the mover of an amendment[8]) may speak only once on a motion. Experienced Members have suggested that the nature of this stage in the legislative process has changed in recent years: that since bills have been sent to standing committees it has become a stage when the House for the first time can 'have a cut at the detail of the Bill';[9] that the debates on report have deteriorated in the 20 years before 1967 and have become much more repetitive;[10] that the 'old days' (which seems here to mean before 1940) report was 'mostly the discussion of an amendment made in Committee, or a discussion of an amendment that was consequential to an amendment made in Committee, or a discussion of an amendment which followed a promise made in Committee'.[11]

The Clerk of Public Bills[12] to whom these propositions were put as

[1] H.C. 539 of 1966–67, Appendix 1. [2] *Ibid.*, *Report* para 26.

[3] Now S.O. No. 73; it applies also to bills considered by the Scottish Grand Committee in relation to the principle of the bill.

[4] Water Resources Bill 1967–68. [5] H.C. 538 of 1970–71, *Report* para 34.

[6] *Ibid.*, para 35. [7] E.g. May, *op. cit.*, p. 523. [8] S.O. No. 55.

[9] H.C. 539 of 1966–67, Q109. [10] *Ibid.*, Q112 (Mr R. H. Turton).

[11] *Ibid.*, Q113 (Mr R. H. Turton). [12] Mr K. R. Mackenzie, CB.

questions was cautious in his replies, perhaps thinking that impressions unverified by research were often inaccurate. And later he put a paper to the Select Committee in which he examined them. He quoted Campion in 1929 to the effect that 'originally' the main business of the report stage were the amendments proposed by the committee, and fresh amendments were not numerous; and that the change predated the introduction of standing committees. Mr Mackenzie also showed that from 1945–46 to 1964–65 report stages had not tended to become longer, as might have been expected if Mr Turton's impressions were correct.[1] However, evidence given before the Select Committee in 1970–71 again indicated that on report bills were being debated for longer than had previously been the case.[2] The reason for this most recent enlargement of report stage is not at all clear. Speaker King thought that 'with every new Parliament we have a keener Parliament than we had in the previous one. There are no dumb Members of this Parliament.'[3] In 1971, the Leader of the House thought there was 'no doubt that the selection has been more generous' but it is not clear what period he was referring to.[4] So also Mr Douglas Houghton thought 'one could be highly selective on Report'[5] and earlier Mr Crossman had spoken of the desirability of more vigorous policing on the report stage.[6]

Amendments are moved in committee, as we have seen, often with the intention of persuading the Minister at least to give an undertaking that he will 'look again' at the point raised. And as Sir David Renton has put it: 'it is the tendency of Ministers to purchase progress in Committee by giving undertakings to consider at Report'.[7] In his view that practice should not be discouraged even if it meant a slightly longer report stage. But it leads inevitably to some repetition of debate unless the Minister moves an amendment on report which wholly satisfies the Members of the committee. Sir David also suggested that 'the ever-growing complexity of legislation' made for longer report stages. So also the process of legislation itself – the discussion on second reading and in committee – stimulates outside interest and so Members may be approached and feel obliged to put down amendments on report to meet difficulties put to them by constituents and other bodies.[8] Finally Sir David agreed that individual Members sometimes use report stage 'to air a particular point or grievance'.[9]

[1] H.C. 539 of 1966–67, Appendix 7.

[2] H.C. 538 of 1970–71, *Report* para 35. In 1967–68 and 1968–69 the number of statutory pages of Government bills considered per sitting on report was 57 and 58, respectively. Previously, since 1945–46 the lowest number had been 70. See H.C. 538 of 1970–71, Q61–2, 84–6 and Memo 10.

[3] H.C. 538 of 1970–71, Q325–6. [4] *Ibid.*, Q673.

[5] *Ibid.*, Q783. [6] H.C. 539 of 1966–67, Q186.

[7] H.C. 538 of 1970–71, Q272. Lord Maybray-King (formerly Speaker King) divided undertakings into two groups. One was 'We will look at this again, because it is very good'. The other was 'We will look at this again, because we want to get the business through for today' (Q324).

[8] *Ibid.*, Q273. [9] *Ibid.*, Q274.

Apart from the occasions when Ministers undertake in committee to reconsider points raised, they may have second thoughts on clauses or parts of clauses as the result of pressure from within or outside Parliament, and so initiate amendments of substance on report. Or Ministers may have been defeated in committee and amendments or new clauses may be put down to reinstate words lost or to remove words inserted in committee.

All this reconsideration makes for repetition. A distinction should be drawn between reconsideration of matters discussed in committee – which is a main purpose of the report stage – and the repetition on report of debate, of argument, of words even, used before in committee. It is against this latter activity that much of the criticism is directed. Such repetition is more likely to occur when the issue is controversial[1] and is therefore more difficult to exclude because Parliamentary debate on bills is both an exercise which may be directed towards improving a bill or, as the Opposition would say, mitigating its worst effects, and an exercise in party politics. Outsiders, especially those who see themselves as above the petty squabbles of politicians, may have little patience with arguments, from either side, which are based on party doctrine. But a representative asssembly which does not, from time to time, debate the major ideological differences which separate parties fails in one of its important purposes.[2]

4.2 SELECTION OF AMENDMENTS ON REPORT STAGE

Under Standing Orders the Speaker has power to select the amendments, new clauses or new schedules to be proposed.[3]

On the report stage of a bill, amendments, new clauses and new schedules are tabled. Erskine May says: 'While amendments which were rejected in committee may be moved again, and attempts may be made by amendments to restore the original text of the bill, the power of selection of amendments, conferred upon the Speaker by S.O. No. 33 . . . is a check upon excessive repetition of debates which have already taken place in committee: and this power is usually exercised more freely by the Speaker on consideration than in committee by the chairman'.[4]

We saw that the like power conferred on chairmen of committees did not, save exceptionally, operate to curtail discussion unduly and that expression of dissatisfaction with the operation of the Standing Order was infrequent. On report stage the power is real and casts its shadow before as well as after, affecting the tactics employed, especially by the Opposition, during committee.

[1] *Ibid.*, Q607.

[2] The Select Committee on Procedure 1966–67 were 'satisfied that a return to a matter already discussed in Committee is almost always the result of undertakings given in Committee that further consideration would be given to it'. H.C. 539 of 1966–67, *Report* para 25.

[3] S.O. No. 33(1). As above 'amendments' unless the context otherwise requires includes new clauses and new schedules.

[4] May, *op. cit.*, p. 523.

The Standing Order strikes unevenly in that all Government amendments are selected without question. (So they are in committee but the unevenness is less apparent there.) The power to select is that of the Speaker who acts on the advice of the Clerk.

To the Select Committee on Procedure in 1966–67 the Speaker submitted a note which indicated 'broad and important principles' which governed his selection and rejection of amendments on report stage. Those which might or would be selected included: all Government amendments; all involving some undertaking by the Government;[1] new 'compromises' or 'halfway' proposals; important issues carefully debated in committee but still containing vital matters worthy of a 'last look'; new matters brought in by members of the committee or non-members; new developments that had occurred during the passage of time since the committee examined the bill. Those which might or would be rejected included: those out of order; those adequately discussed in committee, particularly those rejected on a division by the committee;[2] those shown to have been treated lightly by the committee; and those not regarded by the chair as significant enough to be selected. The Speaker said:

> 'In all this the Chair is advised by the Clerk of the House and by Officers and Officials with special knowledge of the Bill and of its passage through Committee. Every line of Committee proceedings is painstakingly reviewed; and discussed, when necessary, at a Conference called by Mr Speaker.
>
> 'The final decisions and selections are, however, his own, and in these he must use both all advice rendered to him – his knowledge of procedure – his awareness of the rights of both government and Opposition – his knowledge of the House – and any special circumstances attending any particular Report stage. (Even then, the Speaker describes his selection as *provisional*, to give an opportunity for last minute submissions to be considered on their merits). . . .
>
> 'The Report stage is in my opinion an exceedingly important one, and I see no reason for changing the present procedure for the selection of amendments.'[3]

Four years later that Speaker, then retired, gave evidence again to the Select Committee and re-emphasised the importance he attached to this stage in the legislative process.[4]

It is the practice for the Clerk of the Committee on the bill to note for the Clerk of the House against each amendment put down for the report

[1] But see above, p. 119 *et seq*.

[2] If the division in committee produced significant crossvoting or if it was rejected only by the casting vote of the chairman, it will be selected even though discussed *ad nauseam* on Second Reading and in Committee; see Highways Bill 1970–71 Standing Committee D, cols 43–65, and 813 H.C. Deb., cols 472–86 (reduction of period for objecting to orders or schemes from 3 months to 6 weeks).

[3] H.C. 539 of 1966–67, p. 87. [4] H.C. 538 of 1970–71, Q324.

stage whether the matter was discussed in committee, whether or not it was there debated at length, and what was its fate; and this provides the basis for the Clerk of the House to recommend to the Speaker whether the amendment should be selected or not. In 1919 when the power to select was first introduced, one safeguard proposed was that the Speaker 'should have recourse to the Chairman of the Standing Committee'. Replying to this, the Attorney-General said: 'I imagine that that is the first thing he would think of'.[1] Whether or not this was ever the practice in the past, it certainly is not so now. Once the chairman of a committee has reported the bill, he ceases to influence its passage.

In 1971 the Clerk of the House told the Select Committee on Procedure that every amendment put down on report was looked at by at least three experienced officials, one of whom would be the draftsman. If there was any doubt about an amendment (this presumably includes whether or not to select it), it was then looked at by five experienced officials and the Speaker was given advice. The party allegiance of the Member who put down the amendment was not relevant.

The officials know by the afternoon of the day before which the bill or any amendment is to be considered on report roughly what advice they are putting to the Speaker. He makes his final decision the next morning. There is therefore an opportunity for Members – and this applies particularly to the Opposition front bench – to make representations directly or indirectly to the Speaker about his selection of amendments and about the particular importance they attach to particular amendments.[2] The clerks will not normally approach Members unless instructed to do so by the Speaker. Members, including the Opposition front bench, often take the initiative but sometimes they do not. And the Clerk of the House mentioned the Immigration Bill of 1970–71 as a case where the Speaker sought the views of the Opposition. On that occasion the advice to the Speaker had been not to select a particular amendment because it had been negatived on division in standing committee but the Opposition argued that nevertheless the Minister had given an undertaking that the drafting would be looked at on report. The Speaker's ruling was that he would select it 'provided that the Opposition surrendered another amendment of equal importance which the Speaker had selected'. And this was done.

I have argued above[3] when referring to the selection of amendments for the committee stage that there would be considerable advantage in making public the selection at least 24 hours before debate begins. The case for so doing on report stage is stronger as the need for time in which to make representation is greater.

It was clear from the evidence of the Clerk of the House to the Select Committee on Procedure in 1971 that the Speaker welcomed the making of

[1] 112 H.C. Deb., W. 1082 (Sir G. Hewart).

[2] This does not mean that every Member can make an oral case to the Speaker. Nor does he always agree to receive delegations.

[3] See above, pp. 85–6.

representations so that his decision might be better informed.[1] This was confirmed by the present Speaker.[2]

The principle of the 'last look' has been much discussed. It is more accurately an exception to another more general principle that what has been fully discussed in committee should not be discussed again on report, unless there is reason to believe that the debate – or its outcome – might be different. And the exception is justifiable only on the ground of the great importance of the subject. The Second Clerk Assistant and the Clerk of Public Bills suggested to the Select Committee on Procedure in 1971 that if it were wished to eliminate this discussion on report the only way would be by recommending that such amendments should be selected only where there was reason to suspect (because of casting vote or crossvoting in committee) that the House might wish to reverse the decision of the committee.[3]

To the same Select Committee the former Speaker gave two examples of allowing the House another look. One was whether a majority jury decision should be valid. The other was to decide whether the basic unit in decimal currency should be 10s or £1.[4]

The arguments and discussion which centre on the desire, on the one hand, to eliminate or reduce repetitiveness and, on the other, to protect the rights of the whole House (and so of backbenchers who were not members of the standing committee which considered the bill) frequently are hindered by the use of phrases which seem to determine the whole matter. Thus it is said that report is merely a tidying-up stage.

So the Speaker has said:

> 'I take the view that the Clause cannot be selected because it was discussed in Committee and there was a Division on it. The purpose of Report, as the hon. Member will know, is not to do over again the work of the Committee but to tidy up the Bill after the Committee has made certain Amendments to it.'[5]

Yet this phrase seems quite inadequate to cover much that goes on on report.

And in 1967 the leader of the House (Mr Crossman) disputed this classification:

> 'A Minister who gives an assurance: "If you wait until the Report stage you will find my new clause" – you may have 10, 12 or 14 new clauses in the Report stage, which is a pretty massive tidying-up. . . . There are issues where the Opposition must be allowed the right to fight it stage by stage and, by using the rules of the House, to get themselves another chance to resist, and I think this is justified in big cases".'[6]

[1] H.C. 538 of 1970–71, Q969–80. [2] *Ibid.*, Q882.
[3] H.C. 538 of 1970–71, Appendix 1 paras 19, 20; and *ibid.*, Q76–82.
[4] *Ibid.*, Q324.
[5] 572 H.C. Deb., col. 1388 (Coal Mining (Subsidence) Bill; 4 July 1957).
[6] H.C. 539 of 1966–67, Q242–3.

A simple example of repetition or possibly of the 'last look' occurred during the Decimal Currency Bill 1968–69 debates. In Committee there was a debate lasting over 2 hours on the proposal to repeal section 5(1)(d) of the Decimal Currency Act 1967 which concerned compensation. The Government were firm in their view but the Opposition amendment was withdrawn in the hope that the Government would reconsider.[1] On report an identical Opposition amendment was selected, debated for some 20 minutes and negatived on division.[2]

The 'tidying-up' principle is flatly contradicted when the Government introduces wholly new proposals on report or when the Speaker selects other amendments which raise new issues. This is sometimes protested against,[3] but it happens not infrequently.

In the end the argument turns on questions like: when is repetition justifiable? how important must an issue be to allow a last look on report? is the importance of an issue to be determined in relation to other matters in the same bill or in relation to matters in other bills? It is impossible to lay down answers to such questions. But, however vaguely, climates of opinion – and at present the climate seems to indicate an atmosphere of boredom with repetitious detail – affect the judgement of those who advise the Speaker, and influence the Speaker himself.

The making of representations to the Speaker, now encouraged by the Select Committee on Procedure,[4] still leaves the decision wholly within the Speaker's discretion. No one seems seriously to challenge this or to suggest that some other method or persons should be engaged in deciding what amendments, other than those proposed by the Government, should be discussed. At first sight, on the assumption that the purpose of selection is to limit the time spent on report and to make debate more coherent, the Opposition would seem to be the best persons to decide what non-Government amendments should be discussed. This may indeed happen under guillotine, or where there is agreement on the number of days to be spent on report. It is unsatisfactory for the Opposition to have to forgo discussion on an amendment they regard as important as a condition of being allowed discussion on an amendment they regard as even more important. In 1919 the suggestion was made of associating a few of the most experienced Members of the House with the Speaker and the Chairman of Ways and Means as a consultative committee on the exercise of 'this very far reaching power'.[5] The Attorney-General opposed this on the ground that the selection of amendments had to take place during the course of debate because only 'as the controversy develops' could the relative importance of amendments be seen.[6] Today, of course, with the very few exceptions, the selection is made before the debate is begun and indeed the former Speaker said in 1971 that what distressed him when

[1] 1968–69 Standing Committee A, cols 262–312. [2] 780 H.C. Deb., cols 1913–20.

[3] E.g. see 784 H.C. Deb., col. 689 (Housing Bill, 1968–69).

[4] H.C. 538 of 1970–71, *Report* para 36.

[5] 112 H.C. Deb., col. 1078 (Sir R. Adkins). [6] *Ibid.*, col. 1083 (Sir G. Hewart).

he had selected a new point on report had been to find as the debate proceeded that it was merely 'a rehashing, a redressing or a retrimming of an old point'.[1]

During the debate in 1919 an amendment was moved to the proposed new Standing Order[2] which would have required the Speaker to consult with a committee of not less than ten Members selected by him. Mr Locker-Lampson who moved this claimed it was really only an extension of a practice which had been going on for many years for amendments put down for committee. This was opposed on the ground that it was too formal, and negatived.[3] But again this was on the assumption that amendments would be selected or rejected as the debate developed which is now, save where the Speaker very occasionally accepts manuscript amendments, not what is done. The price paid today for pre-selection is, as Lord Maybray-King said, that the Speaker sometimes finds he has selected the wrong amendment.[4]

If informal consultation develops, the need for a special committee may never arise. But there would seem to be a case for enabling the official Opposition to underline the amendments they have tabled so that the Speaker would know by looking at the number of lines what relative importance was attached to them.

Certainly the present practice is not obviously fair and predictable even to Members with great experience of Government business. Mr John Silkin has said (with, perhaps, deliberate overstatement):

> 'The Report Stage has always struck me as being a bit of a lottery when it comes to the selection of amendments. It seems to me to come through the divine workings of providence, really. You can never be certain that any amendment that you would like selected, as far as an Opposition is concerned, is going to be selected and a lot that an Opposition does not think will be selected are to its intense surprise and sometimes to its embarrassment selected. . . . I could remember discussing the question on one occasion with Mr Macleod, when he was leading for the Opposition on it and we were considering certain Opposition amendments that had been selected and he was as staggered that they had been selected as I was. In fact, he was really rather cross they had been. So that I think possibly some guiding principles would not be out of place.'[5]

When the Speaker has made his selection any queries raised in the House are usually dealt with by a refusal to answer them. The interchange commonly goes like this:

> 'Mr John Smith: On a point of order. May I draw your attention to Amendment No. 296 which is supported by hon. Members from both the

[1] H.C. 538 of 1970–71, Q324 (Lord Maybray-King).

[2] This referred to committee of the whole House and report stage and made selection of amendments a general power; see above, p. 71.

[3] 112 H.C. Deb., cols 1213–14, 1216–17.

[4] See note 1 above. [5] H.C. 538 of 1970–71, Q533, 548.

Liberal and Tory Parties. It is the only Amendment to Clause 9, and unless it is debated, since the Committee stage was taken upstairs, the House will have had no opportunity –
Mr Deputy Speaker: Order. I cannot hear anything further on that point of order, since the selection of Amendments is a matter for Mr Speaker, and the Amendment has not been selected for debate.'[1]

Or;

Mr Frank Allaun: I do ask you very seriously to consider the calling of new Clauses 6 and 7, neither of which were discussed in Committee on the following grounds –
Mr Speaker: Order. I am not prepared to discuss with the hon. Gentleman the selection of Amendments. The Chair gives quite a lot of consideration to the selection of Amendments. In doing so, it is bound to displease many people on the Report Stage. . . .
Mr Allaun: . . . Surely it is derogatory to the proper functioning of Parliament, and its good name, if such important matters are not to be discussed here in the House of Commons.
Mr Speaker: The hon. Gentleman is challenging the Ruling which I have made. I have made a selection and I must stand by that selection.[2]

At the beginning of the debate on the Coal Industry Bill 1970–71, the spokesman for the Opposition (Mr M. Foot) made a long submission to the Speaker. He said that he thought the selection made was astringent 'in the sense that many Amendments which some of us had, mistakenly, thought would have been called are not to be called'. He said that on all previous occasions, the Committee stages of coal industry bills had been taken on the floor of the House but that in this instance many Opposition Members representing mining constituencies were denied the right to participate in the discussion in committee and now were denied the right to press their amendments on report. Mr Foot said that 'on one Bill after another' the Government had sent bills upstairs which by convention should be taken on the Floor of the House. The Speaker replied:

'Selecting Amendments is one of the most difficult jobs which the Chair has to do. This is the first time I have had to do it. I looked carefully at the list of Amendments and tried to take into account all the various factors to ensure that there is a series of wide-ranging debates. I am told that I have been rather more generous in my selection than has usually been the case in the past.'[3]

It may be that amendments are out of order and ineligible for selection on that ground. On the National Insurance (No. 2) Bill 1968–69, the only amendments put down were ruled out of order because they sought to bring in additional classes of persons whereas the scope of the bill was

[1] 787 H.C. Deb., cols 768–9 (Finance Bill 1969).
[2] 784 H.C. Deb., cols 684–5 (Housing Bill 1968–69).
[3] 812 H.C. Deb., cols 861–2.

confined to the rate or amount of contributions and benefit. On this occasion the Speaker was almost apologetic in his refusal.[1]

Occasionally, however, arguments do prevail. Mr Speaker, having told a Government backbencher who asked for reconsideration of the non-selection of a new clause on the Development of Tourism Bill 1968–69 that his mind was 'fairly well made up' on the day's selection was asked by an Opposition frontbencher (Sir Keith Joseph) to reconsider three or four other amendments which had not been selected. Sir Keith argued, without being interrupted, that the first two amendments were new points not raised in committee and that others related to 'a near-undertaking' given by the Minister in committee. Mr Speaker said, on all but one of the arguments, that he had noted what was said but gave no commitment at that time.

The opposite view was then put by a Government backbencher. He said there was

> 'a growing feeling in the House that, on Report of many important Bills of great complexity, we are engendering an atmosphere in which there is a regurgitation of the Committee proceedings to such inordinate length that a great deal of time and the patience of the House are wasted. . . . A great many of us would welcome the greater vigilance of the Chair to prevent the regurgitation of ancient debate – the regurgitation of ancient vomit as some might call it – keeping the House sitting at inordinate hours late at night on matters which have been adequately discussed in Committee.'

The Speaker stated his dilemma:

> 'I realise that the Opposition always want to discuss more on Report than the Chair wishes them to do, and the Government always want less discussed on Report than the Chair permits. This is the classic duty of Mr Speaker, as an unhappy Solomon in the midst of two contending forces.'[2]

When the House further considered the bill on report, the Speaker added to his list of selections two of the amendments urged on him the previous day by Sir Keith Joseph.[3] For which he was warmly thanked.[4]

In 1968, very strong objection was taken by some left-wing Labour backbenchers to the non-selection of certain amendments to the Prices and Incomes Bill 1967–68. Mr Michael Foot was supported by Mr Orme, Mr Mikardo and Mr Park; and from the opposite benches by Sir Douglas Glover, Mr Robert Carr and Mr Biffen. The difficulty, said the Speaker,

[1] 786 H.C. Deb., cols 1733–4. [2] 785 H.C. Deb., cols 1012–16. [3] *Ibid.*, col. 1237.

[4] *Ibid.*, cols 1281–2. Another recent extension of the provisional selection occurred when the Education (Scotland) Bill 1970–71 was considered. When protest still continued, the Speaker said that he had taken 'very experienced advice' and had been told he had been 'unusually generous' (815 H.C. Deb., col. 1091).

was that there were 'three strands of opinion in the House' but he promised to reconsider his selection.[1] When he had done so, he said that most of the non-selected amendments had been rejected because they had been debated at length, and negatived, in committee. To meet the dissident Government backbenchers, the Speaker added one amendment to his list of selected amendments, allowed another to be taken separately instead of being grouped, and changed the grouping of a third.[2]

The usual refusal of the Speaker to explain his selections and non-selections can make difficulties for him. In 1947 during the committee stage on the Town and Country Planning (Scotland) Bill, an Opposition amendment sought to provide that for the purposes of an issue of an industrial development certificate by the Board of Trade what should be regarded was not the 'distribution of industry' but the 'development of industry in Scotland'. The Joint Under-Secretary of State resisted the amendment but after further debate said:

> 'All I want to do is get on with the Bill. I would like to give an assurance . . . that next week or the week after, I will go into the question, consult with the learned Lord Advocate, and report this discussion fully to the Secretary of State for Scotland. We will also speak to the Board of Trade, and put this before them.'

The mover of the amendment withdrew it 'in view of what the Joint Under-Secretary has said and that we shall have a chance of discussing this as some other stage of the Bill.'[3]

On report, there being no Government amendment put down, the Opposition put down their amendment again but it was not selected. The Deputy Speaker said, when questioned, that the hon. Member 'was not entitled to discuss the reasons of Mr Speaker'; he also denied that the matter was for the Government – it was 'one entirely for Mr Speaker's discretion'. And the Opposition spokesman had to be content with saying that of course it would be impossible for them to accept assurances in future.[4]

In this case, the Opposition were seeking to blame the Government; the Government denied blame[5] and so, by inference, passing the responsibility on to the Speaker; and the Deputy Speaker[6] was refusing to give any explanation. However valuable may be the principle of the unchallengeability of the Speaker's ruling, strict adherence to that principle in cases of this kind seems unhappy.

[1] 767 H.C. Deb., cols 259–67.

[2] *Ibid.*, cols 297–8.

[3] 1946–47 Standing Committee on Scottish Bills, cols 1356–7.

[4] 439 H.C. Deb., cols 1914–15.

[5] The Minister said: 'I have not denied the right of hon. Members to discuss the Amendment. I have nothing to do with it.' (*Ibid.*, col. 1915.)

[6] He is in a difficult position as he must defend and cannot change the Speaker's selection.

Finally, any reform which seeks to enable the Opposition to debate the amendments of its choice within the time available should ensure that backbenchers on both sides are not overlooked. Representations made by the Opposition front bench will always carry weight. But backbenchers also need to have their wishes regarded and the present procedures make less allowance for this.

4.3 REPORT STAGE
1967–68, 1968–69, 1970–71

In terms of the impact of the House on Government legislation we must analyse those amendments which appear to reflect this impact. These include amendments successfully moved, first, by the Opposition and, secondly, by Government backbenchers. They also include Government amendments made in response to Opposition or Government backbench pressure in committee. And they include, as possible sources of revolt, amendments moved by Government backbenchers which were negatived. Finally, there are those amendments which resulted in Government action in the House of Lords; we will postpone consideration of these until we deal with that House.

Table 4.3 AMENDMENTS (INCLUDING NEW CLAUSES) MOVED AND DISCUSSED ON REPORT*

	1967–68	1968–69	1970–71	Totals
Moved by Ministers	*379*	*249*	*237*	*865*
Agreed to without division	360	234	166	760
Agreed to on division	18	15	71	104
Withdrawn	1	—	—	1
Moved by Government backbenchers	*42*	*10*	*37*	*89*
Agreed to without division	4	3	2	9
Agreed to on division	1	—	—	1
Negatived without division	15	5	5	25
Negatived on division	7	2	4	13
Withdrawn	15	—	26	41
Moved by Opposition Members	*251*	*207*	*141*	*599*
Agreed to without division	13	6	9	28
Agreed to on division	1	—	—	1
Negatived without division	78	74	42	194
Negatived on division	80	69	60	209
Withdrawn	79	58	30	167
Totals	672	466	415	1553

* This excludes those amendments moved formally.

4.3.1 *Amendments successfully moved by Opposition Members and Government backbenchers*

1967–68 Opposition Members successfully moved fourteen amendments in 1967–68. Thirteen of these were agreed to without a division and one on a division.

Of the thirteen, four were to the Town and Country Planning Bill, two to the Social Work (Scotland) Bill and to the Industrial Expansion Bill, and one to each of the Civil aviation Bill, the Consular Relations Bill, the Erskine Bridge Tolls Bill, the Finance Bill, and the Gaming Bill. Six of these amendments were very minor or drafting points. In the Industrial Expansion Bill words agreed to be unnecessary were deleted.[1] In the Social Work (Scotland) Bill the word 'grants' was inserted in place of 'sums'[2] and 'may' instead of 'shall'.[3] A paragraph letter[4] and a reference to the Bill[5] were inserted in the Town and Country Planning Bill and '(if any)' was removed from the Gaming Bill.[6] Four amendments were minor matters of some substance. In the Erskine Bridge Tolls Bill, the period of 21 days' notice of an order for the suspension or reduction of tolls was reduced to 14 days; in committee the Opposition had suggested 7 days – now the difference between them and the Government was happily and accurately split.[7] The word 'industrial' was removed at one point from clause 2 of the Industrial Expansion Bill, some Government supporters thinking it was a frivolous amendment and the Minister thinking it made no effective difference.[8] In the Town and Country Planning Bill an amendment was accepted which again the Government thought would make no real difference – 'the only possible compulsory purchase order which is not covered is in section 11 of the Pipelines Act, 1962' – but 'for the sake of peace and quiet at this time of the night, this is a good gesture'.[9] To the Consular Relations Bill, an Opposition Member kindly moved an amendment to the title to accord with Government amendments which would otherwise have been ineffective.[10]

A technical company law amendment of some substance was moved as a short new clause by Mr Patrick Jenkin to the Finance Bill. Sub-paragraph (3) of paragraph 4 of schedule 17 to the Finance Act 1965 used the words 'three companies' and the amendment was to replace these by the words 'company and that other company'. It concerned dividend stripping and the rules in the schedule prescribed special treatment for dealings between associated companies. The rules required that not only the selling and the buying company must be associated but also the company in whose shares

[1] 762 H.C. Deb., cols 472–3. [2] 768 H.C. Deb., cols 1470–1.

[3] *Ibid.*, col. 1537 – on this occasion there was no effective difference between these two words.

[4] 765 H.C. Deb., col. 808. [5] *Ibid.*, col. 820.

[6] 766 H.C. Deb., col. 185. Sometimes the insertion of these two words can be significant but was not on this occasion.

[7] 756 H.C. Deb., cols 1003–5. [8] 762 H.C. Deb., cols 429–34.

[9] 765 H.C. Deb., cols 725–6. [10] 761 H.C. Deb., cols 1848.

the dealings were being made. The effect of the amendment was to apply the rules to a company in no way associated with the transferor and transferee companies.[1]

I have already referred[2] to the clause in the Civil Aviation Bill which empowered the detention and sale of aircraft on the failure to pay airport charges. The bill laid down a period of 28 days beginning with the day on which the aircraft was detained after which the aircraft could be sold if the charges remained unpaid. An Opposition amendment extended this period to 56 days and the Government accepted this 'on the clear understanding that no precedent is being set' – whatever that meant.[3]

Finally, the Town and Country Planning Bill empowered a local planning authority to serve a stop notice prohibiting any person from acting in a way contrary to the terms of an enforcement notice. The stop notice might be withdrawn by serving further notices and the stop notice would then, under the bill as reported by the standing committee, cease to have effect from the date of that further notice. The amendment was to provide that that last date should be 'the date of the service' of that further notice. This was accepted.[4]

On one occasion there was that rare occurrence of an Opposition amendment, moved on report, being agreed to after a division. But it was in many ways unusual not least in being a free vote on both sides and therefore not a Government defeat. The form of the amendment was to leave out clause 50 of the Finance Bill which provided:

> 'If, with a view to raising money to be paid into the Consolidated Fund, arrangements are made in such manner as Parliament may hereafter determine for the holding of a national lottery, nothing in any enactment relating to lotteries shall make those arrangements unlawful.'

In Standing Committee this clause fell under the guillotine and was agreed to by 24 votes to 9, two Government backbenchers voting with the Opposition. On report, after a debate lasting for more than 4 hours, the amendment was carried by 166 votes to 76.[5]

Five amendments moved by Government backbenchers were agreed to, four without a division and one on a division. Two of the four were to the Medicines Bill. Clause 2 of that bill listed the 'activities' which were to be represented by at least one person who was to be consulted before the Ministers appointed the members of the Medicines Commission. One of these activities was 'the pharmaceutical industry, except so much of it as relates to retail sale'. Mr English moved an amendment to leave out from 'industry' to the end of the phrase. He had moved a similar amendment in

[1] 767 H.C. Deb., col. 1543. As a result of this amendment, the sub-paragraph begins 'A company acquiring from another company (neither of them being a dealer) a holding in a third company at a time when the company and that other company are associated . . .'.

[2] See above, p. 131. [3] 768 H.C. Deb., cols 1903–5.

[4] 765 H.C. Deb., cols 685–7. [5] 767 H.C. Deb., cols 1156–244.

committee but had withdrawn it. And a similar Opposition amendment had been disagreed to on a division.[1] On report, Mr English was supported by two members of the Opposition. The Minister's view was that another activity which was listed – 'the practice of pharmacy' – covered retail pharmacy but he accepted the amendment.[2] Clause 58 of the Bill empowered Ministers to make regulations dealing with medicinal products. Mr English moved an amendment which, in his opinion, limited that power. The Government accepted it though advised that 'it makes no change in the meaning at law'.[3]

Clause 5 of the Justices of the Peace Bill was declaratory of the position of justices' clerks and the Attorney General accepted an amendment restating a Practice Direction made in 1953 which said that clerks might properly call the justices' attention to a question of law.[4] And clause 75 of the Town and Country Planning Bill empowered the Minister, in the interests of amenity, to authorise the change to a footpath of what was a highway. Mr Blenkinsop moved to insert 'or bridleway' after 'footpath'. The Government accepted this though it caused some surprise on Opposition benches as it had been thought that the object of the provision was to provide pedestrian precincts and when Mr Allason read the amendment he had visualised 'camels being led through a bazaar'.[5]

The amendment moved successfully by a Government backbencher on a division was, like that successfully moved on a division by an Opposition backbencher,[6] not a Government defeat. Mr W. O. J. Robinson moved the second reading of a new clause to the Health Services and Public Health Bill. The purpose of the new clause was to apply to the services provided under Part IV of the National Health Service Act the provisions relating to the Crown use of patents contained in certain sections of the Patents Act 1949. It implemented a recommendation of a Committee of Inquiry – the Sainsbury Committee – which had reported the previous year. The Government accepted the new clause but the Opposition divided the House against. It was read a second time by 167 votes to 116.[7] The question was of some importance to the pharmaceutical industry as it gave the Government a somewhat privileged position.

1968–69 Opposition Members successfully moved six amendments all being agreed to without a division. Two of these were on the Children and Young Persons Bill, one each on the Finance Bill, the Housing (Scotland) Bill, the Law of Property Bill, and the Mines and Quarries (Tips) Bill.

The first of those on the Children and Young Persons was designed to ensure that a probation officer who had in the past acted in relation to one member of a household might be selected as supervisor for another

[1] Standing Committee D, cols 56–80. [2] 766 H.C. Deb., cols 1402–6.
[3] 767 H.C. Deb., cols 69–75. [4] 762 H.C. Deb., cols 1451–2.
[5] 765 H.C. Deb., cols 786–7. [6] See above, p. 161.
[7] 762 H.C. Deb., cols 79–108.

member.[1] The second was designed to restrict reporting of cases in magistrates' courts. The Government had said in committee that they would look at this again[2] but had not put down an amendment on report. Nevertheless they now accepted the amendment.[3]

It is unusual for a non-Ministerial amendment to a Finance Bill to be accepted by the Government. The present example, however, was scarcely a major breakthrough as it was to suggest that the words 'the deceased's having become absolutely and indefensibly entitled to the property' should read 'indefeasibly'. The Minister agreed.[4]

The amendment to the Housing (Scotland) Bill extended from 7 to 14 days the period within which a lessee was required to inform his lessor that he had been served with a notice requiring him to repair the house, if the lessee wished to recover any part of his expenses from the lessor. The question of the period was discussed in committee and the Minister had promised to look at it again.[5] Now he accepted 14 days.[6] To the Law of Property Bill the amendment was to leave out 'may' and insert 'shall' thus, in this case, making mandatory the payment of costs and expenses of any person suffering loss in certain circumstances as a result of the abolition of the Yorkshire Deeds Registry. The Solicitor-General had shown sympathy to the point in committee[7] and supported the amendment on report.[8]

Finally on the Mines and Quarries (Tips) Bill the amendment related to the length of notice which authorised persons were required to give before exercising their right of entry. The bill had provided 24 hours and the amendment proposed 'at least 48 hours'. The discussion in committee on this point had been somewhat lengthy[9] and the Minister had promised to look again. Now he accepted the amendment.

Government backbench Members successfully moved three amendments all being agreed to without a division. One was to the Housing (Scotland) Bill and two were to the Town and Country Planning (Scotland) Bill. The first of these was to provide that a Ministerial power to make orders should be subjected to negative not affirmative resolution procedures. The Minister in committee had promised to look at this again[10] and now accepted it.[11] One of the two amendments to the Town and Country Planning (Scotland) Bill concerned publicity in connection with the preparation of structure plans and was welcomed by the Minister as a clarification.[12]

[1] 784 H.C. Deb., cols 1137–41. [2] 1968–69 Standing Committee G, cols 360–5.

[3] 784 H.C. Deb., cols 1142–4. Probably the Government had 'farmed out' the amendment to the Opposition.

[4] 787 H.C. Deb., cols 1011–12.

[5] 1968–69 First Scottish Standing Committee, cols 209–11.

[6] 786 H.C. Deb., cols 179–80.

[7] 1968–69 Standing Committee F, cols 78–80. [8] 788 H.C. Deb., cols 507–8.

[9] 1968–69 Standing Committee B, cols 69–86.

[10] 1968–69 First Scottish Standing Committee, cols 85–8.

[11] 786 H.C. Deb., cols 150–1 (Amendment No. 16).

[12] 784 H.C. Deb., cols 1557–60, 1589.

The other amendment to that bill was a new clause moved by Mr George Willis, a former Minister of State in the Scottish Office. The clause provided that compliance with an enforcement notice did not discharge it; that any provision in an enforcement notice requiring a use of land to be discontinued should operate as a requirement that it should be discontinued permanently; that any development by way of reinstating or restoring buildings works demolished or altered in compliance with an enforcement notice should be subject to that notice and the person responsible guilty of an offence. In England and Wales, the Town and Country Planning Act 1962 covered this situation and Mr Willis's amendment was, *mutatis mutandis*, a copy of that provision. Mr Willis recounted that he had had the Scottish position pointed out to him by the Midlothian County Council and had then written to the Minister. But the reply he had received was slipshod and said that the problem had not arisen in Scotland. Mr Willis produced evidence in the debate on report that it had. And the Minister accepted it providing a manuscript amendment could be made to correct a small drafting error. The Speaker indicated his willingness to accept the manuscript amendment and the clause was read a second time and added to the bill.

This most unusual example of the impact of a backbench Member on the legislative process was not universally welcomed. One Member thought the Minister was acting rather casually. Another found it 'a most extraordinary way of legislating. I do not know whether it has ever happened before'. Members wanted to know if the Minister was supported by his Departmental advisers; and at what time he had made up his mind to accept the amendment. 'Sensible and properly thought-out legislation will not be produced,' it was said, 'if the Minister comes to a conclusion merely on the basis of one instance brought forward at this late stage when previous evidence has been to the contrary'. Was it right for Parliament to legislate in this way 'on the sudden whim of the Minister?' and much more to the same effect.[1]

The impression given to the reader of this debate is that Members were thrown off their balance by the extraordinary experience of seeing a backbencher successfully move an important amendment in language which suggested he was not in collusion with the Minister; or perhaps of seeing a Minister, under criticism from a former colleague, in effect admitting his error and immediately remedying it. It seems that when a backbench Member succeeds in exercising his right to promote an amendment to the extent of having it accepted, some Members see this as the *failure* of the legislative process.

1970–71 Opposition Members successfully moved nine amendments, all being agreed to without a division. Four of these were to the Civil Aviation Bill, two to the Courts Bill, and one each to the Immigration Bill, the Industrial Relations Bill and the Misuse of Drugs Bill.

[1] 784 H.C. Deb., cols 1529–42.

The first amendment to the Civil Aviation Bill concerned the power given to the Secretary of State by order to require that the property of the Civil Aviation Authority should be placed at the disposal of the Secretary of State 'or of such persons as may be specified in the order'. In committee it had been urged that the quoted words should be left out because 'such persons' might not be answerable to Parliament. The Minister had promised to look carefully at this and he now accepted the amendment.[1] The second amendment concerned the power of the Authority to withhold information and required the Authority to take into account the public interest when deciding whether or not to withhold. Again the point had been argued in committee and the Minister had expressed sympathy. The amendment moved on report was a modification of that moved in committee and was accepted by the Minister.[2] Thirdly, on the 'hiving off' power, the bill empowered the Secretary of State to give directions for this purpose not only to the British Airways Board but also to a subsidiary in which private interests had a joint ownership. The amendment was to exclude these joint subsidiaries. It had been argued in committee where the Secretary of State had been unimpressed but now the proposal was accepted.[3] Finally on this bill, a provision empowered the Secretary of State by directions for the purpose of 'hiving off' to override certain requirements of the Bill relating to the financial duty of the Board not to make a loss. Again this was a committee and indeed a second reading point and the Minister, 'as the least dogmatic of all persons' announced himself finally converted.[4]

The two amendments to the Courts Bill concerned one point. The Lord Chancellor was empowered to remove a Circuit judge from office on the ground of 'inability or misbehaviour'. The Opposition proposed 'incapacity' instead of 'inability' and the Government accepted this.[5] The second amendment applied the same change to Recorders.[6]

Under the Immigration Bill, a non-patrial commits an offence under clause 24(1)(a) if he enters the United Kingdom in breach of a deportation order or without leave. Mr Steel had argued in committee that 'knowingly and wilfully' should be inserted but withdrew his amendment because of the general agreement that 'wilfully' was inappropriate. Now he sought to insert 'knowingly' alone both in that paragraph and twice elsewhere in the clause. The Solicitor General accepted the amendment in two of the three places.[7]

The one non-Ministerial amendment made to the Industrial Relations Bill was to a new clause concerned with the cancellation of registration by the registrar on the request of the organisation 'evidenced in such manner as the registrar may direct'. The amendment was to leave out those quoted words which first appeared in the Trade Union Act (1871) Amendment Act 1876. The Solicitor General said there was nothing sinister about the use of the words and to prove it he accepted the amendment.[8]

[1] 820 H.C. Deb., cols 218–20. [2] *Ibid.*, cols 226–8. [3] *Ibid.*, cols 315–17.
[4] *Ibid.*, col. 318. [5] 815 H.C. Deb., cols 540–1. [6] *Ibid.*, col. 553.
[7] 819 H.C. Deb., cols 672–7. [8] 814 H.C. Deb., col. 346–52.

Finally an amendment was moved to the Misuse of Drugs Bill to replace 'retail pharmacist' by 'a person lawfully conducting a retail pharmacy business' throughout the bill. This was not, said the mover 'merely a matter of establishing a status symbol for those who practise pharmacy or of suggesting that chemists are a lesser breed. It is based on the responsibilities that pharmacists have under the law.' The Government accepted the proposal.[1]

In addition to these nine amendments moved by non-Ministerial Members, the Minister, in moving new clause 1 to the Highways Bill, accepted two amendments tabled by the Opposition (but not selected to be moved) relating to the provision of picnic sites and public conveniences.[2]

Government backbenchers successfully moved two amendments on report stage in 1970–71; to the Civil Aviation Bill and to the Finance Bill. In neither case was there a division.

I have already referred to the influence exerted by Mr Onslow on the proceedings in committee on the Civil Aviation Bill.[3] On report he moved to delete a power given to make regulations for the recovery from any person of costs or expenses incurred in connection with a hearing held for the purpose of certain functions of the Civil Aviation Authority. This point had first been raised by an Opposition Member. The Minister accepted the deletion and managed to do so as if the credit were his own by saying 'Today the proceedings are following rather closely those in Committee, where, if sensible points were made, I did my best to consider them and if possible, to accept them'.[4]

The amendment to the Finance Bill was of a different order. It was a full new clause and sought to exclude from duty under the Vehicles (Excise) Act 1962 certain mechanically propelled vehicles used by severely disabled persons who could not drive themselves. The sponsors of the new clause were drawn from both major parties. The subject was not new and the mover (Mr Marten) quoted at length from the speech on a similar motion made in 1969 by Mr Maurice Macmillan who in 1971 was Chief Secretary to the Treasury. The debate on the new clause lasted for more than 2½ hours and twenty-four Members spoke in favour of the clause before the Chancellor of the Exchequer rose to accept it. Mr Paget said that the mover had 'a very remarkable Parliamentary victory'.[5]

In addition, two amendments tabled by a Government backbencher and grouped for discussion with an Opposition amendment (which was negatived) were accepted by the Government and formally moved. They arose out of the requirement in the Merchant Shipping (Oil Pollution) Bill for compulsory insurance against liability for pollution and were to increase penalties on conviction of offences from £15,000 to £35,000 in one case and from £200 to £400 in another.[6]

[1] 808 H.C. Deb., cols 578–9.
[2] 813 H.C. Deb., cols 439–52.
[3] See above, p. 109. [4] 820 H.C. Deb., cols 228–9.
[5] *Ibid.*, cols 1128–71. [6] 821 H.C. Deb., cols 118–27.

4.3.2 *Government amendments moved on report stage in response to points made in committee by Opposition Members and Government backbenchers*

1967–68 In 1967–68, there were 174 such amendments of which twenty-one were made in response to points made by Government backbenchers, eighteen in response to points made by both Opposition and Government backbench Members and 135 in response to points made by Opposition Members alone.[1] The Sewerage (Scotland) Bill accounted for twenty-two of this total, the Countryside Bill for twenty-one, the Finance Bill for eighteen, the Medicines Bill and Race Relations Bill for sixteen each, the Transport Bill for fifteen, the Town and Country Planning Bill for eleven, the Gaming Bill for ten, and thirteen other bills for the remaining forty-five matters.

The Sewerage (Scotland) Bill was a comprehensive measure of sixty-one clauses and was generally regarded as being long overdue or, as Mr Richard Noble put it, 'long adorning the pigeonholes in St Andrew's House'.[2] It imposed new and extensive duties on local authorities. And the Scottish Standing Committee met on eleven occasions to consider it. Five of the twenty-two amendments had some substance. The first concerned the procedure for giving notice and for objections where a local authority proposed to construct works. It ensured that the local authority drew attention to the right to object.[3] The second amendment ensured that before a local authority exercised its powers to take over private sewage treatment works it first sought the owner's agreement.[4] The third provided that a person should not be guilty of the offence of passing forbidden matter into drains unless he did so knowingly.[5] Fourthly, clause 18 of the bill provided for the transition from the existing rating arrangements where the cost of sewerage fell substantially on special district sewer rates charged in special drainage districts to the new system in which the cost of sewerage would fall on the general county rate. As considered in standing committee, county councils were authorised to collect district rates over a period of 5 years, the amount diminishing over that period and then ceasing. The matter was considered at length in standing committee[6] and the Government on report amended the period to 7 years.[7] Finally an amendment provided that orders preserving or amending local Acts under clause 55 should be made by statutory instrument and be made subject to negative prayer.[8]

Five of the amendments to the Countryside Bill were of some substance. Welsh Labour Members and Mr Gibson-Watt on second reading asked for a Welsh Countryside Commission but the Government showed no

[1] These figures, and those for 1968–69 and 1970–71, exclude a number of consequential amendments formally moved and agreed to.

[2] Scottish Grand Committee 1967–68, col. 12. [3] 762 H.C. Deb., cols 1457–9.

[4] *Ibid.*, cols 1478–9. [5] *Ibid.*, cols 1498–9.

[6] Scottish Standing Committee 1967–68, cols 327–72.

[7] 762 H.C. Deb., cols 1479–94. [8] *Ibid.*, cols 1500–1.

signs of yielding.[1] As a result of the proceedings in standing committee and, no doubt, of outside pressure, the Government yielded to the extent, on report, of proposing in a new clause the appointment by the Commission of a committee for Wales. After the defeat on division of an opposition amendment to the new clause, this was agreed to.[2] Another new clause empowered local authorities, when creating country parks on the coast or on the banks of waterways, to provide facilities for waterborne recreation.[3] Thirdly, an amendment enabled MPs to be Commission Members so long as they were not paid.[4] Fourthly, an amendment introduced a power of compulsory acquisition in relation to land other than common land which was in the neighbourhood of common land; it simplified the procedure for obtaining Ministerial authority for taking land out of a common; and it made clear that the power to acquire commonable and other rights in or over common land did not apply to rights vested in statutory undertakers. The Opposition had 'grave doubts' about these powers but accepted the Minister's assurance that only rarely would they be used.[5] Fifthly, the Minister proposed an amendment to leave out subsection (b) of the clause relating to areas of special scientific interest. The effect of this was to enable access agreements or orders to be made in respect of these areas.[6]

Of the eighteen amendments moved by the Government in response to committee points (all made by Opposition members) on the Finance Bill, only four were drafting. The remainder, as is common with amendments to such bills, were all minor in the sense that they applied to small groups of people but were often substantial in their effect on those groups. Thus new clause 92 concerned double taxation relief where there was group investment in an overseas company.[7] Another amendment exempted 16-mm cine cameras from purchase tax because they were used either in education or in industry for training purposes.[8] The third took out of aggregation (with parents' income) a child's income arising from sums awarded for personal injury; and retained the *de minimis* exception for a child's income not exceeding £5 arising from parent-child settlements.[9] Clause 16 and schedule 9 dealt with life policies, life annuity contracts, and capital redemption policies. The Government put down a large number of amendments of which ten were in response to committee points. As Mr Patrick Jenkin said: 'These are highly technical matters and . . . they have for the most part been very fully discussed with interests outside.[10] I therefore do not think that we would be failing in the duty resting on Parliament in passing legislation like this if we were not to discuss it as fully as might be appropriate in other circumstances.'[11] I propose to follow

[1] 753 H.C. Deb., cols 1512–13. [2] 762 H.C. Deb., cols 1088–110.
[3] *Ibid.*, cols 1111–18. [4] *Ibid.*, col. 1268. [5] *Ibid.*, cols 1278–81.
[6] *Ibid.*, cols 1282–3. [7] 767 H.C. Deb., cols 1335–8.
[8] *Ibid.*, cols 1549–61. [9] *Ibid.*, cols. 1617–24.
[10] Particularly the Life Offices' Association.
[11] 767 H.C. Deb., cols 1706–8, 1712–14, 1717 *et seq.*

Mr Jenkin's example. Four further cases of technical committee points being taken by the Minister concerned clause 18,[1] schedule 10[2] and 11[3] and clause 35.[4]

The examination of the Medicines Bill 1967–68 both in committee and on report is an example of Parliamentary scrutiny at its technical best. The outside interests were strong but the Government also were well informed. The issues were not party political though the differences of opinion did sometimes reflect attitudes of mind which made for political differences. Of the sixteen Government amendments put down in response to points made in committee all but four were of some substance. Part II of the bill contained comprehensive provisions for licences and certificates relating to medicinal products. In standing committee an Opposition Member had argued that the export business of the pharmaceutical industry might be lost if exporters had to go through a licensing procedure which their competitors in other countries did not have to face. As a result of this and other pressures (some of whom counter-vailing) a new clause was introduced on report empowering the Minister to postpone the licensing obligation where certain conditions were fulfilled.[5] The power of the Minister to specify descriptions or classes of medicinal products requiring a prescription before sale or supply was made subject to consultation with the appropriate committee or the Medicines Commission.[6] Orders specifying certain non-medicinal substances as subject to the bill were required to be laid in draft and approved by Parliamentary resolution.[7] While these may be regarded as being the more important amendments a further nine were also of some significance.[8]

As we have seen, proceedings on the Race Relations Bill were lengthy, controversial and liable to lead to disagreements within party ranks. There was, however, in committee general dissatisfaction (not generally for the same reasons) with the definition of discrimination in clause 1, and the first amendment moved in committee (with which seven other amendments were grouped) stood in the names of two Government backbenchers, two Opposition Members and a Liberal. After a debate which lasted for nearly all the first sitting of the committee, the Home Secretary agreed to look again.[9] And on report he proposed a new clause to replace clause 1 as introduced. This also was received with a considerable lack of enthusiasm but was agreed to, without a division.[10] The temporary exemption from the major provisions of the bill for employers was enlarged to apply to those employing twenty-five (originally ten) persons.[11] And another amend-

[1] *Ibid.*, cols 1737 (Amendment 75). [2] *Ibid.*, col. 1728 (Amendment 76).
[3] *Ibid.*, cols 1743–5. [4] *Ibid.*, cols 1779–82. [5] 766 H.C. Deb., cols 1382–90.
[6] 767 H.C. Deb., cols 66–7. [7] *Ibid.*, cols 91–2.
[8] 766 H.C. Deb., cols 1390–8, 1427–30, 1442–3; 767, cols 59–65, 68–9, 78, 84–5, 86, 94–6.
[9] Standing Committee B, cols 7–50.
[10] 768 H.C. Deb., cols 223–46; amongst other things it was said that the new definition introduced the concept of 'separate but equal' into English law.
[11] *Ibid.*, cols 377–84.

ment exempted from vicarious liability an employer who proved that he took reasonable steps to prevent his employee from acting contrary to the provisions of the Bill.[1] New clause 2 protected future as well as existing charitable instruments and acts done thereunder.[2] An amendment to clause 3 on discrimination in employment made clear that no offence was committed if an employer 'chose applicant A rather than applicant B because applicant B lacked the talent, education, experience or aptitude of applicant A'.[3] An attempt by the Government to meet some Opposition opinion that resident landlords should be given greater freedom to discriminate was not altogether successful.[4] Another amendment permitted discrimination by a house-seller who was also the owner-occupier and who neither used an estate agent nor publicised the sale.[5] On these and similar amendments, Government concessions to the Opposition displeased some of their own supporters. Five other amendments were of less importance but worthy of reference.[6]

To the mammoth Transport Bill, the Government moved only fifteen amendments on report in response to committee points. But controversial bills, however large, are often likely to yield fewer concessions. Five of those fifteen amendments were of more than minor importance. As introduced, the bill provided that a driver of a heavy vehicle should not on any working day drive for more than 9 hours. The Opposition pressed in committee[7] for an increase and on report the Minister proposed 10 hours.[8] The second amendment is best explained in the Minister's words when he said that an Opposition frontbencher in committee 'expressed completely unfounded fears about the possibilities that some of the duties of the nationalised transport authorities on research and development might lead them into spheres outside the industry. . . . The purpose of the amendment is to place restrictions on the use of development to meet the point made in Committee.'[9] Thirdly, a long new amendment (partly a redraft) made it possible to control passengers as well as vehicles on roads where road works made damage or danger likely. 'This Amendment', said the Minister 'is further evidence of the extent to which the Government have listened to the arguments put in Committee and have responded to them. One of the things which saddens one is the extent to which the Opposition have treated this generosity with such churlishness.'[10] All this is in the Parliamentary game. New clause 1 was in response to pressure from Government backbenchers in committee. Under the Road Traffic Act 1960 public service vehicle licences were issued to 'fit persons'. The new clause spelled out in far greater detail what fitness meant and gave

[1] *Ibid.*, cols 407–9. [2] *Ibid.*, cols 243–6. [3] *Ibid.*, cols 321.
[4] *Ibid.*, cols 324–50. [5] *Ibid.*, cols 360–77.
[6] *Ibid.*, cols 288–9, 323, 384–5, 405–6, 406–7.
[7] Standing Committee F, cols 2890–916; and see debate on previous clause.
[8] 765 H.C. Deb., cols 1900–9; and see, for further amendment on meaning of 'working day', cols 1926–8.
[9] *Ibid.*, cols 1619–20. [10] *Ibid.*, cols 1991–3.

rights of representation to trade unions, the police and local authorities. The Opposition did not like this proposal and unsuccessfully divided the House against it.[1] So also on new clause 2, inspired by Government backbenchers and opposed by the Opposition to a division. It empowered local authorities to run contract carriages inside their districts and, with Ministry approval, outside also.[2]

The Town and Country Planning Bill went to standing committee in a state, if not of disrepair, then of underpreparation. It bore the signs of a bill that because of the legislative timetable had been introduced earlier than the draftsman would have liked. On report new clauses 1 and 2 replaced clause 3 as introduced; and new clauses 3 and 4 replaced clause 5. The changes in new clause 1 sprang, said the Minister, 'entirely from suggestions made by hon. Members in Committee'[3] and improved the publicity in connection with the preparation of structure plans.[4] New clause 2 concerned the procedure on approval or rejection of structure plans by the Minister, meeting the point that a structure plan might need to be re-submitted. It also slightly altered the nature and extent of the Minister's obligation to consider objections.[5] New clause 3 enabled local planning authorities to begin work on local plans before structure plans had been finally approved by the Minister.[6] Consequential on new clause 3 but also to meet an Opposition point in committee an amendment provided that a local planning authority should not adopt a local plan unless it conformed generally to the approved structure plan.[7] The four-year rule for serving enforcement notices has long been disputed and in this Bill, as introduced, the rule was abolished for breaches taking place after 20 December 1963. But as a result of pressure in committee the Minister, on report, introduced an amendment to confine the abolition to a limited group of cases where, broadly, the breach consisted in a material change of use. The Opposition were still unhappy and divided the House.[8] Compensation for statutory undertakers became a much debated subject. New clause 10 introduced by the Minister in committee proposed 50 per cent of entitlement in certain cases and this was agreed to[9] and became clause 60. On report the Minister moved new clause 5 to replace clause 60, in view of what had been said in committee. This new clause empowered the Minister to make regulations to specify 'descriptions of development'. Where the development was covered by the regulations, 50 per cent compensation would be payable; where it was not, none would be payable. The Opposition were not content and the new clause was adopted only after a division.[10] There were a few minor amendments to the bill as a result of committee points.[11]

[1] *Ibid.*, cols 1247–62. [2] *Ibid.*, cols 1263–96. [3] *Ibid.*, col. 42.
[4] *Ibid.*, cols 41–8. [5] *Ibid.*, cols 49–52. [6] *Ibid.*, cols 51–60. [7] *Ibid.*, col. 259.
[8] *Ibid.*, cols 663–78. [9] Standing Committee G, cols 1150–72.
[10] 765 H.C. Deb., cols 73–96. In the House of Lords the Government were defeated and a clause giving no compensation (save in one case) was agreed to: 296 H.L. Deb., cols 105–18. The Government accepted their defeat: 770 H.C. Deb., cols 1485–7.
[11] 765 H.C. Deb., cols 260–1, 261–2, 739, 755.

In the debates on the Gaming Bill in committee there was general agreement that there must be some limitation of hours. As the Joint Under-Secretary of State said: 'There can be no question whatsoever of 24-hour gambling'.[1] The Opposition, on report, moved that no premises should be open for more than 12 hours out of 24. The Government tabled an amendment that gave the Secretary of State power to make regulations for this purpose and that was accepted.[2] The effect of a group of amendments 'in which the Government have been substantially influenced by the Committee' was to remove the right of appeal to the Secretary of State from decisions of the Gaming Board in respect of the issue and revocation of certificates of fitness to persons engaged in gambling.[3] Another amendment removed from the courts the power to disqualify persons convicted of certain offences – that power was transferred to the Board – while retaining their power to disqualify premises.[4] Finally a group of amendments gave more power to the Board to scrutinise all applications, for the 'privilege' of running gaming establishments, before they were allowed to go forward to the justice and without the Board having to account for its decisions.[5] And indeed schedule 2 of the bill, and now of the act, concerning the grant, renewed, cancellation and transfer of licences is an extremely strong example of regulatory powers.[6]

Of the forty-five other amendments moved by Ministers in thirteen bills in response to committee points, nine were of some substance. Clause 5 of the Civil Evidence Bill concerned the advisability of statements produced by computers and allowed certificates to be put in as evidence. An amendment on report created an offence for wilful mistatement in such a certificate.[7] In the London Cab Bill one amendment required the Secretary of State to consult cabowners and drivers before extending the six-mile compellable limits.[8] And another extended the provisions of the clause prohibiting the display of words such as 'taxi' or 'cab' or 'for hire' on private hire-cars; and made additional provision for advertisements. The Opposition declared themselves content but at least one Government backbencher thought the two front benches were 'ganging up to do something quite ridiculous' and were attempting to delete the word 'mini-cab' from the English language in London.[9] In committee on the Prices and Incomes Bill fears were expressed that a standstill order made by the Minister might be so made as to prolong the effect, though not the legal force, of the standstill; and that an order might be made to operate from a period considerably in the future. An amendment was put forward on report to remove both these fears.[10] To the Social Work (Scotland) Bill the Minister moved an amendment to say that bona fide representatives of the Press could

[1] 766 H.C. Deb., cols 107. [2] *Ibid.*, cols 100–11, 157. [3] *Ibid.*, cols 123–31.
[4] *Ibid.*, cols 160–1. [5] *Ibid.*, cols 314–22.
[6] For minor amendments see 766 H.C. Deb., cols 112, 155–7, 163–72, 313–14, 355–6, 359–61. The whole debate has a moralising, puritanical air.
[7] 769 H.C. Deb., cols 447–9. [8] 756 H.C. Deb., cols 1011–15.
[9] *Ibid.*, cols. 1015–29. [10] 767 H.C. Deb., cols 531–4.

attend children's hearings. In the event the fulfilment of the undertaking given in committee was not rapturously received.[1]

An amendment to the Trade Descriptions Bill enabled local weights and measures authorities, in addition to making test purchases of goods, to authorise their officers to secure the provision of such services, accommodation or facilities as might appear expedient for the purpose of determining whether the provisions of the bill were being complied with.[2] One amendment to the Agriculture (Miscellaneous Provisions) Bill subjected Ministerial regulations to the affirmative procedure;[3] and another confined a power of entry to check whether the statutory provisions were being observed to persons authorised by Ministers and local authorities and excluding the police.[4]

Finally, new clause 1 of the Civil Aviation Bill provided for facilities for consultation at airports not managed by the British Airports Authority and designated by the Board of Trade. In standing committee, the Opposition moved a new clause with a similar purpose which was negatived although the Minister promised to look at the matter again.[5] New clause 1 on report, moved by that Minister's successor in office, was debated for 2¼ hours, was welcomed by the Opposition as accepting the spirit of their view expressed in committee, and was agreed to. The consultation was to be with users of the aerodrome, local authorities, and other organisations representing local interests, and was primarily concerned with the problem of noise.[6] Mr Onslow said of this bill:

> 'It was introduced as a standard Departmental rag-bag, but in course of its passage it turned into something quite different. It became virtually a Private Member's Bill in Goverment time, and with very great help and co-operation from the Minister's predecessor and his understanding attitude in Committee,[7] the Committee can claim to have succeeded greatly in improving and extending this legislation.'[8]

1968–69 In 1968–69 the number of these amendments (including new clauses) was 115. Six of these were in response to points made by Government backbenchers; six in response to those made by both Opposition Members and Government backbenchers; and the remainder in response to those made by Opposition Members. The Finance Bill accounted for twenty-six of these amendments, the Housing Bill for twenty-three, the Children and Young Persons Bill for seventeen, and fourteen other bills for fewer than ten amendments in each case. Substantial bills which produced few such amendments included the Development of Tourism Bill

[1] 768 H.C. Deb., cols 1521–7. [2] 764 H.C. Deb., cols 522–3.
[3] 759 H.C. Deb., cols 459–60. [4] *Ibid.*, cols 465–8.
[5] Standing Committee G, cols 297–318.
[6] 767 H.C. Deb., cols 1966–67; 768, cols 1835–73.
[7] The Minister's predecessor was Mr J. P. W. Mallalieu.
[8] 768 H.C. Deb., cols 1922.

(five), the Post Office Bill (eight), the Representation of the People Bill (seven) and the Transport (London) Bill (six).

The Finance Bill 1969 was considerably amended on report particularly by the introduction by the Government of six new clauses. For the Opposition Mr Iain Macleod said:

> 'I wish sincerely to thank the Chief Secretary for the way in which he has responded to what we tried to do in Committee. We can look back with some pleasure on the exercise, which has resulted in something that is unique in my experience of Finance Bills – that we have had no fewer than six Government Clauses which trench on the single basic point of disallowance of interest. It shows how worth while was the Committee stage.
>
> 'Each of the six points had its origin in Amendments moved from this side of the House, and I freely acknowledge that on a number of points we had support from other quarters of the Committee. I am grateful for what the Chief Secretary has done in meeting in full the undertakings that he gave to us.'[1]

As originally introduced, the Finance Bill had introduced a new principle under which interest on a private loan or overdraft was, except for transitional arrangements and where the loan was in connection with the acquisition or improvement of land, to be treated as part of an individual's disposable income and distinguished from a business expense. The new clauses extended the exceptions to include loans applied in acquiring interest in a close company and in a partnership; loans to purchase machinery or plant used by a partnership; loans to pay estate duty; and loans made on or before 15 April 1969.[2]

The remaining twenty amendments to the Finance Bill were spread throughout the bill: two under customs and excise (bingo duty[3] and gaming machines[4]); ten under income tax and corporation tax (including five under disallowance of interest as a deduction[5] and five under avoidance of tax)[6]; three under estate duty;[7] four under capital gains and betterment levy;[8] and one under selective employment tax.[9]

Only one of these was a major amendment to meet a major criticism made in committee. This was Amendment No. 201. The effect was that if a beneficiary at the time of his death had had no income for 7 years from a discretionary trust, there was to be no charge on that beneficiary;

[1] 787 H.C. Deb., col. 438. [2] *Ibid.*, cols 425–534.

[3] *Ibid.*, col. 721 (Amendment 92). [4] *Ibid.*, cols 724–9 (Amendment 7).

[5] *Ibid.*, cols 834–5, 835–6, 836–40, 898–903, 904–5 (Amendments 275, 218, 47, 301, 231).

[6] *Ibid.*, cols 912–14, 914–26, 926–9, 929–42, 941–3 (Amendments 144, 204, 206, 209, 210).

[7] *Ibid.*, cols 973–6, 976–85, 1012–13 (Amendments 201, 168, 182).

[8] *Ibid.*, cols 1031–7, 1038 (Amendments 135, 136, 137).

[9] *Ibid.*, cols 1047–57 (Amendment 143).

and other similar cases. Most of the other amendments were comparatively minor but nevertheless each represented a concession which to the individuals or companies affected had value. One amendment was not acceptable to the Opposition who divided the House against it.[1]

Of the twenty-three Government amendments moved to the Housing Bill 1968–69 to meet points made in committee, the great majority[2] fell into the category of 'small but valuable' for which much of the credit was given to the Opposition Member for Hemel Hempstead (Mr James Allason). Three new clauses and one amendment were more substantial. New clause 3 concerned certain long leases where the rent reserve, apart from services, was over two-thirds of the rateable value. Following the discussion in committee the Government consulted the Law Commission and put forward this new clause, substantially on the same lines as that proposed by Mr Allason, the effect of which was to take out of Part VII of the Rent Act, which dealt with premiums, long tenancies which fulfilled certain conditions.[3] New clause 4 appeared in response to views expressed by, amongst others, Mr Frank Allaun from the Government backbenches. The problem was that of the protection of poor tenants who wished to prevent landlords from carrying out improvements which would then entitle them to raise rents.[4] He did not approve of the Government's solution. New clause 5 was designed to extend the provisions for compensation for 'blighted' land after publication by a local authority of their proposal to acquire land. The Opposition gave the clause a second reading but divided the House on an amendment.[5]

The other substantial amendment was to delete four clauses that would have required conditions to be observed for a period of years after an improvement grant or a standard grant was given. The principal condition in the bill as considered in committee was that for 3 years after the completion of the works for which the grant was made, the dwelling should be let or kept available for letting when not occupied by the applicant or a member of his family (with other special exceptions). In committee, the substantive clause was debated for about 30 minutes and the three consequential clauses not at all.[6] On report the Government amendment to delete the four clauses was agreed to virtually without debate.[7] There clearly was agreement between the two front benches on the desirability of this deletion but, in view of the dangers felt by the left wing of the Labour party about the possible abuse of improvement grants, it is surprising that no opposition was voiced to the deletion.

Seventeen amendments were made under this heading to the Children

[1] Amendment 209, see above, p. 174 note 6.

[2] 785 H.C. Deb., cols 617–18, 631–2, 634–5, 1727, 1769–74, 1813–14, 1815–16, 1843, 1845–6, 1846–7, 1847–8, 1849–50, 1850–1, 1851, 1862–3, 1863–4, 1873 (Amendments 7, 9, 20, 23, 46, 68, 71, 86, 88, 89, 93, 96, 99, 103, 104, 114, 115, 116, 151).

[3] 784 H.C. Deb., cols 771–86.

[4] *Ibid.*, cols 789–816.

[5] 785 H.C. Deb., cols 491–506.

[6] Standing Committee F, cols 153–63.

[7] 785 H.C. Deb., cols 1727–9 (Amendment 24).

and Young Persons Bill, of which five were relatively important. New clause 1 (restrictions on criminal proceeedings for offences by young persons) was a revised version of what was originally clause 5. That clause 5 provided that before any offender aged 14 and under the age of 17 could be prosecuted the consent of a juvenile court magistrate had to be obtained and the local authority had a right to be heard by the magistrate, thus ensuring that the police normally consulted the local authority before deciding to apply to the magistrate for consent to a prosecution. New clause 1 omitted the requirement of magistrate's consent but in other ways ensured that the police would consult the local authority before proceeding. The new clause was given a second reading but doubts remained and the Opposition divided the House on an amendment.[1] A second new clause applied the criminal legal aid system to care proceedings under the bill.[2] Thirdly, Amendment No. 14, in response to a Government backbench argument in committee, enabled care proceedings to be brought in the case of a child under the age of 5 without the child being brought into court.[3] A new sub-section (Amendment No. 18) to clause 3 provided for the payment in care proceedings of compensation usually by the parents, for offences by children under the age of 14.[4] Finally, Amendment No. 63 made it possible in certain cases for the court to impose a sanction on a person aged 17 for breach of a requirement of a supervision order.[5]

In the Development of Tourism Bill, the Government moved new clause 1 to require hotels and other establishments to display or otherwise notify their room charges.[6] The Opposition divided the House on an amendment. In the Education (Scotland) Bill, the Minister moved one amendment to leave out a clause which restricted the right of parents to appeal regarding the selection of a course of secondary education for their children;[7] and another to remove the right of parents to be present at any psychological examination of their children.[8] Amendment No. 2 to the Immigration Appeals Bill was an important clarification. The bill empowered appellate authorities to review the exercise of discretion by the Home Secretary or immigration officers, within the framework of the immigration rules. The amendment was to make clear that refusal by the Home Secretary to make an exception to those rules in favour of a particular immigrant could not be reversed on appeal.[9]

The Government moved new clause 1 to the Mines and Quarries (Tips) Bill replacing clause 4 in the bill as first printed. Clause 4 had provided that the Mines Inspectorate should be given notice after mine or quarry

[1] 784 H.C. Deb., cols 975–1014. Doubts about the original clause 5 and the new clause 1 were also expressed by one Government backbencher (Mr Peter Archer); for committee discussion, see 1968–69 Standing Committee G, cols 223–37.

[2] *Ibid.*, cols 1013–16. [3] *Ibid.*, cols 1059–60. [4] *Ibid.*, cols 1065–71.

[5] *Ibid.*, cols 1141–2. [6] 785 H.C. Deb., col. 1015–50.

[7] 783 H.C. Deb., cols 595–601 (Amendment 8).

[8] 784 H.C. Deb., cols 1257–8 (Amendment 10). [9] 780 H.C. Deb., cols 689–91.

refuse was deposited on a new site, or tipping resumed on a closed tip. The new clause required notice to be given beforehand.[1] Amendment No. 5 to the same bill was designed to ensure that the penalty of imprisonment for offences relating to tips should be able to be imposed only where the contravention involved the risk of death or personal injury and not where the risk was of injury to property only. The Opposition were not wholly satisfied that the amendment achieved this purpose but accepted it.[2]

The Post Office Bill was a major measure of the session 1968–69 resulting in an Act of 142 sections and eleven schedules. But, on report, only eight amendments were made. I have already referred[3] to the arguments in committee on clause 13 restricting the carrying on by the Post Office and its subsidiaries of certain activities, how five Government supporters then voted against clause stand part and how the Government were saved by Opposition votes. On report the Government introduced new clause 1 to replace clause 13. Opposition speakers expressed the view that this new clause was weaker in its restrictions than the former clause 13 and that the Minister had yielded to pressure from his own backbenchers. The Minister replied that he had thought many of the observations made in committee by Government backbenchers were 'extremely valuable'; that he had considered the matter with the Post Office Board; and that the Board had advised him that the Post Office Corporation (to be brought into existence under the bill) should have powers to increase its manufacturing capacity to meet its own requirements, after consultation with the Minister, rather than having to obtain the Minister's approval in each case. Hence the new clause. The Opposition divided the House on the closure motion and on the second reading of the new clause. A third division followed on an Opposition amendment to the new clause and a fourth on the adding of the clause to the bill. The whole debate on the clause lasted for over 4 hours.[4] None of the other seven amendments moved in response to committee points was substantial though several were acknowledged by the Minister to make minor improvements to the bill.

Section 97 of the Representation of the People Act 1949 made illegal, not for the first time, the incurring of election expenses on account of bands of music, torches, flags and banners. In the bill of the same name in 1968–69, the Government introduced a clause modifying the Act of 1949 but both sides of the committee pressed them to go further and so on report section 97 was wholly repealed and replaced by new clause 1.[5]

Both sides also successfully persuaded the Government to extend postal voting to those prevented from voting 'by reason of religious observance'.[6] And both sides successfully persuaded the Government to remove a pro-

[1] 776 H.C. Deb., cols 388–91.
[2] *Ibid.*, cols 415–20.
[3] See above, p. 140.
[4] 782 H.C. Deb., cols 1167–1252.
[5] 775 H.C. Deb., cols 1398–401.
[6] *Ibid.*, cols 1440–4 (Amendment 1).

vision making it an offence for any person, in managing or editing a broadcast about a particular constituency, to favour any of the candidates taking part in the broadcast.[1] The other four amendments were in response to Opposition points and were minor.[2]

The Town and Country Planning (Scotland) Bill saw three further important results of joint pressure by Opposition and Government backbenchers. On report, the Government introduced new clause 1 which enabled Joint Planning Inquiry Commissions to be set up to inquire into matters affecting both Scotland and England.[3] Amendment No. 30 was designed to enable the Government to see what could be done to give greater publicity to applicants for planning permission.[4] A further amendment, arising from an Opposition point in committee, provided for a right of appeal on a question of law from a decision of a sheriff relating to compulsory acquisition of a listed building in need of repair.[5]

1970–71 Amendments and new clauses totalled seventy-six of which eleven were in response to Government backbench points and nine in response to points made by both Government backbenchers and Opposition Members, the remainder being in response to those made by Opposition Members alone. The Highways Bill accounted for fourteen of such amendments, the Hospital Endowments (Scotland) Bill and the Immigration Bill for ten each, the Finance Bill for eight, the Civil Aviation Bill for six, and the Fire Precautions Bill for four; and thirteen bills for three or fewer amendments.

Moving the first two amendments to clause 17 of the Highways Bill, the Joint Under-Secretary of State said: 'These are the first of a long, helpful and constructive set of Government Amendments' and the Opposition spokesman replied: 'I should like to express my thanks and to say that if on all the subsequent Amendments we do not say how grateful we are, the Minister will understand that that is not through any lack of goodwill, but simply because we want to save time. We are very grateful'.[6] The Bill was essentially an administrative measure involving little controversy and, on third reading, the Opposition again thanked and congratulated the Minister emphasising that it was 'easy for someone to table a home-made Amendment, but to give validity to the point involves the Minister and his advisers in a great deal of work. . . . The parliamentary procedure is only the tip of the iceberg.'[7] None of the fourteen amendments debated (with many consequential amendments not debated) was of substantial importance though new clause 3 gave local authorities the right to defend or institute proceedings under section 116 of the Highways Act 1959 without obtaining the *fiat* of the Attorney General and so removed a control;[8] and

[1] *Ibid.*, cols 1444–6 (Amendment 3).
[2] *Ibid.*, cols 1446–7, 1447–8, 1448–9, 1460–1 (Amendments 7, 8, 9, 21).
[3] 784 H.C. Deb., cols 1512–6. [4] *Ibid.*, cols 1517–21, 1617–18.
[5] *Ibid.*, col. 1608 (Amendment 24). [6] 813 H.C. Deb., cols 486, 487.
[7] *Ibid.*, col. 508. [8] *Ibid.*, cols 454–5.

two affected rights to compensation.[1] The remainder were matters of detail, some clarificatory, some drafting. Without doubt the bill was, in its passage through the House of Commons, improved in many minor and mostly technical ways.

The Hospital Endowments (Scotland) Bill was a measure of ten substantive clauses providing for the constitution of the Scottish Hospital Trust. The report stage lasted 31 minutes during which time ten Ministerial amendments were moved to meet points raised by the Opposition in committee. Two of these amendments were in the form of new clauses, the first of which, dealing with the duty of the Trust to obtain advice on investment, replaced a paragraph in the schedule. That paragraph merely required the Trust to appoint such agents as might be specified in regulations for that purpose. The new clause was more explicit and avoided the need for regulations.[2] The second new clause concerned the audit of Trust accounts and included the usual list of recognised accounting bodies. This again replaced a much less explicit provision in the bill and had been asked for also by those bodies.[3] The third amendment required the Trust to give reasonable access to the accounts to Boards of Management and Regional Hospital Boards.[4] Of the remainder, three were clarificatory[5] and one was consequential;[6] one required affirmative procedure to govern the making of schemes and regulations;[7] one inserted a maximum and a minimum number of members of the Trust for appointment by the Secretary of State.[8] Finally an amendment empowered the Trust to advise Boards of Management and Regional Hospital Boards on investment and management of endowments not transferred to the Trust.[9]

The Immigration Bill was, of course, highly controversial. Mr S. C. Silkin for the Opposition moved new clause 2 on provisions for representations and inquiry in respect of deportation orders and with this were discussed a number of Government amendments two of which Mr Silkin agreed came 'some way to meeting us';[10] and Mr Steel saw another Government amendment as being made in response to an amendment he had moved in Committee though he was reluctant to support it in its proposed form.[11] Government amendments to clause 2 changed the bill where patriality was acquired by descent.[12] A Government proposal introducing negative procedure on statements concerning immigration rules was again considered by the Opposition to have gone only 'some way' to meeting the problem of Parliamentary control.[13] The fine for harbouring an illegal entrant or an immigrant who overstayed was raised from £200 to £400

[1] *Ibid.*, cols 468–71 (Amendment 3 grouped with Amendment 2); col. 488 (Amendment 16).
[2] 809 H.C. Deb., cols 1221–2. [3] *Ibid.*, cols 1223–4. [4] *Ibid.*, col. 1225.
[5] *Ibid.*, cols 1225–6, 1227–8, 1230–2. [6] *Ibid.*, col. 1233. [7] *Ibid.*, cols 1228–30.
[8] *Ibid.*, cols 1232–3. [9] *Ibid.*, cols 1226–7.
[10] 819 H.C. Deb., cols 368–97. He is referring to Amendments 47 and 49.
[11] *Ibid.* He is referring to Amendment 46. [12] *Ibid.*, cols 445–50.
[13] *Ibid.*, cols 479–500.

in response to views expressed by both sides in committee.[1] And a number of other minor amendments were made in response to committee points.

Of the eight occasions when amendments were made to the Finance Bill, seven were made in response to points raised in committee by Government supporters. This departure from the usual pattern where the great majority of points met are made in committee by Opposition not Government Members occurs on the Finance Bill under Conservative, not Labour, Governments. Indeed, Conservative backbenchers traditionally press for tax reliefs for groups of taxpayers (whichever party is in power) far more than do Labour backbenchers.

With one exception – a purely drafting amendment[2] – all the changes made in the Finance Bill were small in range but nevertheless changed the liability of groups of people. Possibly the most important was new clause 35 concerning claims for deferment of part of surtax for 1972–73. This replaced a clause in the bill as originally drafted which had been subjected to some criticism as being too harsh.[3] The second amendment was in response to a request by Government backbenchers asking, within the context of tax relief on annuity premiums, whether it would be possible to give the self-employed a facility similar to the lump sum death-in-service benefit available to employees through approved occupational pension schemes; whether a man could be allowed to make provision for his dependants; and whether a self-employed woman should not be able to provide for her husband or other dependant. The Minister claimed that the amendment he proposed 'more than met the undertaking' given in committee.[4] Thirdly, in connection with the computation of annuities, the formula for determining amount of a lump sum benefit was discussed in committee and the Government proposed a new version on report.[5] Also on annuities, additional provision was made for those born before 1916.[6] Another small amendment provided that repayment of contributions to occupational pension schemes made after a man's death should not be subject to tax.[7] Sixthly, an undertaking was given in committee to an Opposition Member to consider the availability of capital allowances in a situation where a trader sold a machine which he had bought for use in his trade before having actually used it. Under the existing law and the bill as originally drafted, no capital allowance was payable. This was remedied.[8] Finally an amendment concerned with the abolition of the charge to capital gains tax on death added a provision to include also the termination of an interest other than by death.[9]

The six amendments to the Civil Aviation Bill contained nothing of great importance. Clause 3 of the bill imposed duties on the Civil Aviation Authority to perform its function in relation to 'British airlines' in accordance with certain general principles there specified and the quoted

[1] *Ibid.*, col. 681. [2] 820 H.C. Deb., col. 1367 (Amendment 28).
[3] *Ibid.*, cols 935–46. [4] *Ibid.*, cols 1271–2. [5] *Ibid.*, cols 1279–80.
[6] *Ibid.*, cols 1285–6. [7] *Ibid.*, col. 1297. [8] *Ibid.*, cols 1435–6.
[9] *Ibid.*, cols 1443–4.

words were defined as undertakings providing air transport services and appearing to the Authority to be controlled by United Kingdom nationals. The amendment made clear that 'British airlines' had to have their principal place of business in the United Kingdom and to be controlled by United Kingdom nationals or be approved by the Secretary of State.[1] A second amendment required the Secretary of State to consult with the Authority before directing the Authority to pay to him any reserve funds.[2] Thirdly, an amendment required the annual report of the Authority to include details of all directives made by the Secretary of State;[3] and another required the inclusion in the report of differences of view between the Authority and the Airworthiness Requirements Board.[4] Fifthly, some maximum fines for breach of bylaws were increased.[5] And lastly and perhaps most importantly an amendment provided that the Secretary of State could not make an order merging the BOAC and BEA unless the British Airways Board so recommended after formal review.[6] In certain circumstances this could have been a significant limitation on Ministerial power.

The four amendments to the Fire Precautions Bill were trivial. Of three amendments to the Local Authorities (Qualification of Members) Bill, one had some importance. This was a new clause giving a right to any person to inspect nomination papers so as to be able to discover the basis on which someone standing for election to a local council was eligible.[7] The Opposition had urged this in committee.

Two Government amendments to the Water Resources Bill were in response to arguments from both sides in committee. One was clarificatory[8] and the other lengthened the period for objections to an order from 28 days to 6 weeks.[9] The third amendment was of less importance.

There remain seven bills, each with two amendments, and four bills, each with one amendment. Most of these are trivial, or drafting, or clarificatory. A few had rather more importance. The first (strictly arising out of an Opposition amendment tabled for report) concerned a provision in the Coal Industry Bill which empowered the Secretary of State to direct the National Coal Board to take specified steps for altering the way in which any of its activities were organised. The Government amendment added a proviso that such a direction should not prejudice the proper discharge by the Board of its duties.[10]

The Government amendment specifically made in response to an Opposition point on the Sheriff Courts (Scotland) Bill was one of drafting only[11] but another Committee point – concerning the relationship between the Executive and the Judiciary – received further examination. The Government put down an amendment to ensure that when the Secretary

[1] 820 H.C. Deb., cols 215–8. [2] *Ibid.*, cols 237–8. [3] *Ibid.*, cols 238–41.
[4] *Ibid.*, cols 241–4. [5] *Ibid.*, cols 306–7. [6] *Ibid.*, cols 319–20.
[7] 808 H.C. Deb., cols 1281–3. [8] 817 H.C. Deb., cols 669–73.
[9] *Ibid.*, cols 679–81. [10] 812 H.C. Deb., cols 979–86.
[11] 817 H.C. Deb., cols 1409–10.

of State exercised his power to move a sheriff from one part of the country to another it should be done explicitly only for the purpose of securing the efficient organisation and administration of the sheriff courts and only after consultation with the Lord President of the Court of Session.[1]

To the Social Security Bill the Minister moved an amendment to increase from £2 (in the Bill as first drafted) to £3 the amount by which protected earnings were to exceed a former striker's supplementary benefit requirement. The Opposition had argued that the figure should be £4.[2] An amendment to the Investment and Building Grants Bill retained the right to grant of a person who on 26 October 1970 was entitled to the benefit of a contract for the construction of a new ship in certain circumstances.[3]

4.3.3. *Government reaction on report to defeat in committee*

1967–68 The Government were defeated eight times on substantive motions in committee.

In three cases the Government accepted their defeat. All were amendments successfully moved in committee by Government backbenchers for the deletion of sub-clauses. That of Mr English was clause 82(4) which concerned registered trade marks or designs in the Medicines Bill;[4] that of Mr Rose was clause 2(3) of the Race Relations Bill which made an important exception to unlawful discrimination;[5] and that of Mr Lyon concerned the exclusion of Crown liability under clause 25(4)(5) of the same bill.[6]

The other five cases were all reversed wholly or partially on report, two being the result of snap votes by the Opposition in committee. The first was the amendment of Mr Macmillan to exclude 'efficacy by comparison' as a matter for consideration under the Medicines Bill.[7] On report the Minister moved to delete the words inserted by the committee and to replace them with others the effect of which was in large part to meet Mr Macmillan's point but to make clear that where one drug was safer than another the fact that the other was equally efficacious did not mean that the Commission had to license it. The Opposition did not quarrel with this provision about safety, and the Minister's amendment was agreed to without a division.[8] The other was the Opposition amendment limiting the effectiveness of orders under the Prices and Incomes Bill.[9] This the Government wholly reversed on report after a division. Mr Carr said to do so was 'a shabby trick' and seemed to be saying that Government backbenchers had voted with the Opposition on this division in committee. This was not so.[10]

The Opposition amendment which enlarged the name of the Countryside Commission under the Countryside Bill to include National Parks[11] was

[1] *Ibid.*, cols 1406–8. [2] 820 H.C. Deb., col. 1639. [3] 819 H.C. Deb., cols 1357–63.
[4] See above, p. 100. [5] See above, pp. 100–1. [6] See above, p. 101.
[7] See above, p. 113. [8] 766 H.C. Deb., cols 1441–2. [9] See above, p. 113.
[10] 767 H.C. Deb., cols 628–36. [11] See above, pp. 113–4.

reversed on report. The Minister told the House that the day after the amendment was agreed to in committee the chairman of the National Parks Commission had written to him to say that the Commission had reconsidered the matter and now wished for the shorter title. Some of the Government backbenchers who voted against the Government in committee spoke against the Government on report but the reversal was agreed to without a division.[1]

In committee a clause in the Gaming Bill concerning the advertising of gaming was disagreed to on clause stand part.[2] On report the Secretary of State moved a new clause to reinstate it. Two Government backbenchers who voted for the removal of the clause in committee expressed their continued dislike of the clause. The new clause was read a second time after a division in which one of those two (Mr Paget) voted with the Government and the other (Mr Weitzman) abstained.[3]

Finally the Government backbench amendment requiring a local planning authority under the Town and Country Planning Bill to keep under review the relationship between the development of its area and that of the United Kingdom and its surrounding region was deleted on report without a division.[4]

1968–69 The Government were defeated twelve times on substantive matters in committee.

On report the Government accepted their defeat on two of these points. These were an amendment to the non-partisan Administration of Justice Bill concerning the obtaining of costs in the High Court in actions which could have been begun in the county court;[5] and the removal of the clause in the Education (Scotland) Bill repealing an earlier provision authorising the transfer to a local authority of certain denominational schools.[6] And considerable modifications were introduced by the Government following their defeat in committee on the Finance Bill.[7]

The other nine substantive Government defeats in committee were reversed on report. The provision in the Administration of Justice Bill that a leapfrog certificate could be granted only where all parties to the proceedings consented, was reinstated without a division.[8] A new clause had to be introduced in the Air Corporation Bill to reinstate the clause empowering the Board of Trade to provide for investment of public dividend capital in British European Airways; this also was agreed to without a division.[9] In the Children and Young Persons Bill, words were restored on report making clear that it was for the supervisor to decide whether, when, and in what way he exercised his power to give directions

[1] 762 H.C. Deb., cols 1255–66. [2] See above, p. 131.
[3] 766 H.C. Deb., cols 46–74. [4] 765 H.C. Deb., cols 241–53; see above, p. 100.
[5] See above, p. 104. [6] See above, pp. 133–4.
[7] 787 H.C. Deb., cols 532–4, 835–6, 898–903. See above, pp. 93–4, 174.
[8] 788 H.C. Deb., cols 808–12. See above, pp. 104–5.
[9] 786 H.C. Deb., cols 1089–108. See above, p. 134.

under a supervision order.[1] The Opposition divided the House on this amendment.

Clause 1 of the Decimal Currency Bill having been defeated in committee, a new clause was introduced on report which reinstated it with one alteration affecting the 50p piece. It was read a second time without a division. Then the Opposition moved an amendment to retain the sixpence and this was defeated on a division.[2]

The four substantive Government defeats in committee on the Development of Tourism Bill changed the name of the British Tourist Authority to British Travel Association; deleted a limitation restricting the payment of grants towards the provision of new hotels until after hotels were completed; reduced the size of hotels which were to be eligible to receive grants; and deleted the requirement that hotels to be eligible for grant should be those which provided an evening meal as well as breakfast. All these amendments were reversed on report and the bill restored to its original wording; only on the first was a division required.[3]

Finally, the amendment to the Horserace Betting Levy Bill limiting the discretion of the Secretary of State when determining a scheme for the bookmakers' levy or directing that the current scheme should continue, was deleted on report after a division.[4]

1970–71 The Government were defeated six times on substantive matters in committee.

On report, the Government accepted their defeat on four of these. On clause 7 of the National Insurance Bill in committee, I have referred above to a double defeat, the first of which (an amendment moved by Mrs Williams) was caught up in the second when the whole clause (unemployment benefit for occupational pensioners) was struck out.[5] The Government did not seek to reinstate the clause.[6] So also the Government accepted the major defeat on the Immigration Bill when the words 'or grandchild' were deleted from clause 2 on the right of abode.[7] The increase of the maximum fine for offences, increased in committee from £5000 to £50,000 by the Oil in Navigable Waters Bill 1970–71 was left untouched.[8]

Mr Foot's amendment to the Coal Industry Bill required the Secretary of State to submit for Parliamentary approval any directions given under clause 7(1)(2)(3) to the National Coal Board to which the Board objected. On report the Minister moved to delete that amendment and to insert a requirement that any direction given under clause 7(1)(2) should be laid in

[1] 784 H.C. Deb., cols 1126–32. See above, p. 115.

[2] 780 H.C. Deb., cols 1871–908. See above, p. 134.

[3] 785 H.C. Deb., cols 1237–52, 1341–52, 1353–60, 1360–8. See above, pp. 105, 115–6.

[4] 799 H.C. Deb., cols 563–90.

[5] See above, pp. 119, 136.

[6] See 819 H.C. Deb., cols 810–11. I have treated these as two defeats and two acceptances though they could also be interpreted as one defeat and one acceptance.

[7] See above, p. 110. [8] See above, p. 119.

draft before Parliament. Clause 7(3) empowered the Secretary of State to direct the Board to take specified steps with a view to altering the way in which the Board's activities were organised and its exclusion from the Minister's proposal was criticised by the Opposition. The Minister's amendment was agreed to without a division.[1]

The amendment in committee to the Mineral Workings Bill inserted a provision that the full rate of contribution by ironstone operators towards the Ironstone Restoration Fund should contain no charge for the cost of restoring land worked before 1 April 1971.[2] On report, the Under-Secretary of State moved to delete those words. He admitted that there had been some 'confusion' about the acreage of land involved with the result that 1082 acres which should have been brought into account were not. On a division the Government amendment was agreed to.[3]

The six substantive defeats were all on matters of some importance and the Government on report wholly reversed the decision in committee only once. In immediate effect the changes in the Immigration Bill and the deletion of the clause in the National Insurance Bill were considerable.

4.3.4 *Government backbench amendments negatived on report*

These must be looked at as possible rebellions that failed.

1967–68 Of the twenty-two amendments, fifteen were negatived without a division and seven were negatived on a division.

Four of the fifteen were amendments to the Race Relations Bill. The first, moved by Mr Rose, was a further attempt, after a long debate in committee, to diminish the effect of clause 8(2) which entitled an employer to discriminate in making appointments, or selecting persons to do work, if he acted in good faith to secure or preserve a reasonable balance between persons of different racial groups. Mr Rose wished to insert 'with prior approval of the Race Relations Board' after 'good faith'.[4] Secondly, under the bill, complaints to the Board or a conciliation committee had to be made within 2 months of the act, and an amendment was moved to extend this to 6 months.[5] Under the bill, complaints relating to employment, trade unions and organisations of employers were to be referred first to the Secretary of State for Employment and Productivity. The amendment sought to remove this requirement.[6] Fourthly, an amendment sought to empower the court to make an order requiring the defendant to place the person discriminated against as nearly as practicable in the position in which he would have been but for the unlawful act. The Attorney-General considered this would be objectionable in principle and that damages were the proper remedy.[7] In all four cases the Minister refused to budge.

[1] 812 H.C. Deb., cols 986–98; see above, pp. 118–9. [2] See above, p. 119.
[3] 821 H.C. Deb., cols 1177–208. [4] 768 H.C. Debs. cols 385–404.
[5] *Ibid.*, cols 409–12. [6] *Ibid.*, cols 412–17. [7] *Ibid.*, cols 437–40.

Three amendments negatived without division were to the Social Work (Scotland) Bill. Mr Willis moved a new clause to provide that children should not be finger-printed except in accordance with regulations made by the Secretary of State and approved by Parliament. The Secretary of State thought the question might be referred to a departmental committee that was about to be set up. But he made no promises and Mr Willis, who when a Minister of State in the Scottish Office had been concerned with this matter, did not ask leave to withdraw the clause.[1] To the clause in the bill dealing with the supervision and care of persons put on probation or released from prisons, etc., an amendment was moved to ensure that probation schemes made provision for co-operation between local authorities. Behind this lay concern about the Government's decision to designate large burghs was well as county councils as social work departments and also the question whether the probation service should be part of those departments.[2] Thirdly, an amendment was moved to empower a children's hearing to impose a fine on the child or his parents, to require repayment as restitution for damage, and to require an undertaking as to the child's future good behaviour. The Under-Secretary was sympathetic and regretted the matter had not been debated in committee; but he thought it was too late to act on report.[3]

Two technical proposals were made by Mr Alexander Lyon when he moved new clauses to the Civil Evidence Bill. One was to make an out-of-court statement by an employee admissible, but not conclusive, evidence against his employer although the employee had no authority to make an admission. The other was to render inadmissible evidence obtained by unauthorised intrusions into privacy. Both were recognised by the Solicitor-General to be important but he rejected both.[4] To the Countryside Bill, an amendment was moved to allow local authorities to receive grants in aid not only for tree planting but also for tree maintenance. The Minister was sympathetic but considered that the Government could not continue for an indefinite time with a supplementary grant.[5] Mr Peter Jackson also moved a second amendment to this bill on public rights of way when he tried unsuccessfully to persuade the Minister to extend from 28 days to 2 months the time within which objections could be made to revised maps and statements.[6] On that occasion the Minister admitted to feeling less than 'warm and responsive' at 3.30 a.m. Another Minister was no more responsive at 7.30 a.m. to an amendment to the Education Bill designed to deal with a constituency problem.[7] An attempt (previously debated at length in committee) more precisely to define the obligation of local authorities to take public sewers to points from which owners could connect drains at reasonable cost failed, the Minister not considering the amendment feasible.[8] Mr Rowlands moved an important amendment to

[1] 768 H.C. Deb., cols 1452–66. [2] *Ibid.*, cols 1485–502. [3] *Ibid.*, cols 1528–36.
[4] 769 H.C. Deb., col. 439–45. [5] 762 Deb., col. 1189–92. [6] *Ibid.*, col. 1318–20.
[7] 759 H.C. Deb., col. 1713–17.
[8] 762 H.C. Deb., col. 1453–7 (Sewerage (Scotland) Bill).

the Town and Country Planning Bill (repeating a long committee debate) to seek to enable purchase notices to be served not only when indicated in a structure plan in force but also when indicated in a proposed structure plan. Neither the mover nor the opposition spokesman was satisfied with the Minister's reply.[1] The Trade Descriptions (No. 2) Bill provided that in any proceedings for an offence under the Bill it should be a defence to prove, *inter alia*, that the commission of the offence was due to reliance on information supplied to him. Mr Gardner moved to omit this defence on the grounds that it would 'let through almost any unscrupulous trader who has good legal advice'.[2] Other somewhat wider but similar amendments were grouped for discussion. The Parliamentary Secretary acknowledged the importance of all these proposals but accepted none.[3]

Two of the seven amendments negatived on division were to the Prices and Incomes Bill. The first, moved by Mr Park, sought to exclude the continuance in force of sections 13 to 22 of the Prices and Incomes Act 1966 and in particular to delete section 16(4) which in the opinion of the mover 'subjects trade unions and trade unionists to legal penalties for carrying out the policies and purposes for which trade unions exist'.[4] The controversy over this bill, as over its predecessor of 1966, split the Government backbenchers in committee[5] and now Mr Park was supported in speeches by Messrs Heffer, Foot, Mikardo, Ted Fletcher, Mendelson, Paget and Orme. The debate continued for more than 3 hours and the Government's majority fell to eighteen, with twenty-two Government backbenchers crossvoting.[6] The second amendment was moved by Mr Mikardo who was refused leave to withdraw and who voted against the motion.[7] To the Agriculture (Miscellaneous Provisions) Bill the amendment was to protect a few individuals on whom notice to quit had been served before 26 January 1968, and who could not therefore challenge the notice. The mover was refused leave to withdraw and abstained, the Liberal members alone voting in favour of the amendment.[8] Mrs Butler sought to remove from the Pharmaceutical Society the duty under the Medicines Bill of enforcing certain regulations and a stronger Opposition motion to a similar effect was also discussed. In the division the mover abstained.[9] Mr A. H. Macdonald moved a new clause to the Town and Country Planning Bill on an old topic: the need to publicise planning applications by putting up notices on the land. The matter had been debated at length in committee and the Minister found no new arguments. In the division, the mover and one other Government backbencher voted with the Opposition.[10] To the Trade Descriptions Bill Mr Gardner sought to

[1] 765 H.C. Deb., cols 716–25. [2] 764 H.C. Deb., col. 509.
[3] 764 H.C. Deb., cols 507–21.
[4] 767 H.C. Deb., col. 343. This amendment was not at first selected: see cols 259–67, 297–8 and above, pp. 157–8.
[5] See above, pp. 96–9. [6] 767 H.C. Deb., cols 343–403. [7] *Ibid.*, cols 840–56.
[8] 759 H.C. Deb., cols 549–68. [9] 767 H.C. Deb., cols 97–106.
[10] 765 H.C. Deb., cols 116–42.

include price within the definition of trade description and so to apply the general provisions of the bill to false or misleading statements about price. This also had been discussed at length in committee and, with an Opposition amendment, was discussed on report for $1\frac{1}{2}$ hours before being defeated, the mover abstaining.[1] Finally a small technical amendment to the Transport Bill moved by Mr Carol Johnson seems to have stumbled into a division after a few minutes' debate of which one Member said he did not hear a single word of the mover and did not understand a single word of the Minister's reply.[2] The mover abstained.

These seven instances where divisions took place on amendments moved by Government backbenchers included therefore only one genuine revolt: on the continuance in force of the penal clauses of the Prices and Incomes Act 1966. On four occasions the mover abstained. On one occasion he voted against his own motion. And on one occasion he voted against the Government with one colleague in his support.

1968–69 Of seven such amendments, five were negatived without a division. Three of these were to the Housing Bill and all were moved by Mr Rowlands. The first was to require local authorities to survey the wishes and needs of residents before declaring an area to be a general improvement area.[3] The second was to leave out clause 33(1) which dealt with the mutual exclusion of general improvement areas and clearance areas. He was objecting to the division as being arbitrary.[4] The third was to extend the period for the payment of a higher level of compensation for unfit houses purchased or demolished. The Joint Parliamentary Secretary thought the question could best be looked at under a later amendment.[5]

Mr Stan Newens moved the second reading of a new clause to the Post Office Bill. This was for the establishment of local joint management committees representative of workers and of the Minister for the management of local post offices. The debate, interrupted by two divisions on the 10 o'clock adjournment and the motion that the question be now put, lasted $2\frac{1}{2}$ hours before the second reading was negatived.[6] To the Vehicle and Driving Licences Bill, Mr Arthur Lewis also unsuccessfully moved a new clause to strengthen the penalties for the evasion of vehicle excise duty.[7]

The two occasions where amendments were negatived on division occurred during the debates on the Housing Bill and the Post Office Bill. On the first Mr Arthur Lewis moved the second reading of a new clause to increase the financial assistance given by the Minister of Housing and Local Government to local authorities for strengthening high tower blocks. The debate was on the Ronan Point disaster of the previous year. He was supported by Opposition spokesmen. The motion was lost by 164 votes to

[1] 764 H.C. Deb., cols 440–72. [2] 765 H.C. Deb., cols 1983–90.
[3] 785 H.C. Deb., cols 1761–7. [4] *Ibid.*, cols 1777–9.
[5] *Ibid.*, col. 1855–7. [6] 782 H.C. Deb., cols 1527–76.
[7] 778 H.C. Deb., cols 1166–82.

131. Mr Lewis voted for his motion but the other five of his colleagues who spoke in his support abstained.[1] Mr Hugh Jenkins moved the second reading of a new clause to the Post Office Bill requiring the Minister to answer Parliamentary questions 'on all matters concerning the Post Office other than those of day to day administration'. The debate began just before 9.30 p.m.; after a division on the 10 o'clock adjournment it continued until a suspension motion was carried at 11.30 p.m. The debate resumed the next day at a morning sitting beginning at 10 a.m. and was marked by obstruction and filibustering, Mr Arthur Lewis speaking from 10.45 a.m. until 12.45 p.m. much encouraged and helped by interruptions. At 2 p.m. the debate was adjourned and resumed at 3.50 p.m. The closure was successfully moved shortly after 4 p.m. on a division and the new clause rejected on a division by 206 votes to 201 at 4.16 p.m., two Government backbenchers (Mr Hugh Jenkins and Mr Mikardo) acting as tellers for the Ayes and being supported by others in the lobby. Dislike of morning sittings was more strongly manifested than particular enthusiasm for the new clause.[2]

1970–71 There were nine occasions, five amendments being negatived without a division and four on a division.

Two of the five were on the Finance Bill. Mr W. H. K. Baker moved a new clause to exempt, from income tax, allowances paid to members of lifeboat crews for time spent saving life at sea. Such a provision had been urged in 1950 and in 1967. The relief would be to the Royal National Life-Boat Institution. The Chief Secretary asked the House to reject the clause, and he was supported by a former Financial Secretary on the Opposition benches, on this principle, as the latter put it: 'Every time a deserving exception is made it gives rise to other deserving exceptions and the whole progression never stops'.[3] Mr Hordern moved an amendment to the clause on annuities for the self-employed to permit unallowed amounts to be carried to the next year and added to the qualifying premium for that year and so on for succeeding years until fully relieved. The Government had extended relief for such persons in the bill in other ways and were not prepared to go further.[4]

Another two negatived without a division were to the Immigration Bill. Mr Powell moved an amendment, summarised by the Minister: 'The effect of the Amendment would be to remove from a Commonwealth or Irish citizen who had received a sentence of less than six months, or had been sentenced for even one day, the exemption from deportation which he already has'.[5] Mr Mawby moved an amendment which had been discussed in committee. It concerned the power of an immigration officer when refusing a person entry to require the captain of the ship or aircraft, or the

[1] 785 H.C. Deb., cols 557–606.
[2] 782 H.C. Deb., cols 1278–320, 1331–406, 1447–60.
[3] 820 H.C. Deb., cols 1081–91. [4] *Ibid.*, cols 1275–9.
[5] 819 H.C. Deb., cols 571–2.

owners or agents, to remove that person from the United Kingdom. Mr Mawby's amendment was to give protection to the captain, the owners or agents, when the falsity of the documents of the person was not reasonably apparent. The Minister was unable to accept the proposal.[1]

The fifth case was an attempt by Mr Turton to replace procedure by negative prayer to orders under clause 2 of the Water Resources Bill by affirmative resolution. As generally happens with such attempts, it was unsuccessful.[2]

None of these was more than an attempt by a backbencher to change the bill on a matter of detail, not of principle. Nor did any question of rebelling against Government policy arise.

Amendments moved by Government backbenchers and pressed to a division look more serious at first sight. To the contentious clause 7 of the Coal Industry Bill, Mr Stainton moved an amendment empowering the Secretary of State to direct the National Coal Board that any sums arising from the disposal of any part of their undertaking or assets should be applied to a Disposal Proceeds Reserve Fund, which Fund should be available to the Board for application in the general financing of its activities. The mover wanted to know where the proceeds from the sale of hived-off Board undertakings would go. It was not his intention that the money should go to the Board but he had been forced by the need to keep within the Money Resolution to allow his amendment to be truncated. Mr Skinner suggested various highly unlikely ways in which the proceeds might be used and Mr Stainton left the chamber in what another member called 'rather a huff'. So when the House proceeded to a Division, no Member being willing to act as Teller for the Ayes, the Deputy Speaker declared that the Noes had it. What had looked serious at first sight became mildly farcical.[3]

To the Finance Bill Mr Allason moved an amendment to clause 2 which subjected gas fuel for road vehicles (the first motor gas station outside London had been established in his constituency) to the equivalent rate of fuel tax as was charged on petrol. But for a car to be able to use gas or petrol it had to be converted at a cost of about £120. The amendment sought to take into account this cost when fixing the rate of tax. Mr Allason was supported from the Opposition frontbench and by others. The matter had been gone over in committee.[4] On the ground of fiscal equity, the Minister resisted the amendment which was defeated by 211 votes to 187. Of those who spoke in support of the amendment from the Government backbenches, Mr Allason, Mr Crouch and Mr Cooke abstained while Sir Brandon Rhys Williams and Mr M. McNair-Wilson voted with the Ayes.[5]

Mrs Oppenheim also moved an amendment to the Finance Bill to increase tax allowance for single women with elderly or infirm female dependants. This was one of those occasions when the mover could remind

[1] 819 H.C. Deb., cols 714–18.
[2] 817 H.C. Deb., cols 673–9.
[3] 812 H.C. Deb., cols 998–1014.
[4] See Standing Committee H, cols 35–69.
[5] 820 H.C. Deb., cols 1214–38.

Ministers that when in Opposition they had moved a similar amendment. She was supported from the Opposition benches. The Financial Secretary undertook that the matter would be 'firmly reviewed' before the next Finance Bill. Whether or not the mover then tried to withdraw the amendment is not clear but, in any event, Members shouted No and the division followed wherein the amendment was defeated by 190 votes to 170. Mrs Oppenheim and the three Government backbenchers who spoke in her support all abstained.[1]

Mr Sutcliffe moved an amendment to the Investment and Building Grants Bill which would have empowered the Secretary of State to make grants, despite the provisions of the bill, for mining in certain circumstances. In committee he had unsuccessfully moved an amendment with the similar purpose of helping Cleveland Potash.[2] He was supported by Opposition Members but the amendment was comprehensively defeated by 160 votes to 68. Five Government backbenchers spoke in support of the amendment. One of them (Mr Nott) joined Mr Sutcliffe in the Aye lobby; three voted with the Noes and one abstained.[3]

[1] 820 H.C. Deb., cols 1247–68. [2] See above, p. 108.
[3] 819 H.C. Deb., cols 1333–58.

CHAPTER FIVE

THIRD READING IN THE HOUSE OF COMMONS

The amount of discussion on third reading debates has recently perhaps been greater than the matter warrants. The table set out above[1] shows that the percentage of time spent on this stage of the consideration of bills has, for 1967–68, 1968–69 and 1970–71, been, respectively, 1·7, 1·9 and 2·8 per cent. If this represented a true rate of progression there might be some cause for concern but it is doubtful whether any useful comparisons can be drawn from those figures.[2]

The most recent history begins with a recommendation by the Select Committee on Procedure, reporting in 1967, that debate on the third reading of a bill should be permitted only if an amendment against it or a motion calling for a debate was signed by at least six Members.[3] This was adopted in 1967 and appears as Standing Order No. 56(2).

This recommendation impliedly rejected the view of the Clerk of the House that no debate should be permitted. In 1971 the Clerk pointed out to the Select Committee that his proposal would have saved 4½ days but that the Standing Order had saved only 1½ days.[4] The experiment has been a failure because it had been hoped that very few third reading debates would be asked for whereas in practice the Opposition frequently calls for a debate 'to show that they were interested in the Bill'.[5] The former Speaker was for abolition[6] – 'The war is over at third reading' – but the present Speaker preferred to continue the existing arrangements.[7] A variant sometimes argued is that third reading debate should be abolished only on unamended bills; and Sir Harry Legge-Bourke favoured abolition so long as, on report, a debate on clause stand part was allowed on amended clauses.[8]

Arguments favouring third reading debates are not often advanced – except that they provide an opportunity for compliments to be exchanged

[1] See p. 17.

[2] Compare these figures with those for private Members' and Government Bills in H.C. 538 of 1970–71, Appendix 1, Annex B, and the extremely dubious conclusions drawn by the Select Committee from those figures in its *Report* (*ibid.*, para 37). See below, p. 193.

[3] H.C. 539 of 1966–67, *Report* para 27.

[4] H.C. 538 of 1970–71, Q981.

[5] *Ibid.*, Q673 (Mr Whitelaw); and see Mr Mellish at Q863.

[6] *Ibid.*, Q328. [7] *Ibid.*, Q888. [8] *Ibid.*, Q584.

– but the Minister in charge of the Civil Aviation Bill 1967–68 did agree in committee that the debate on third reading should not be merely formal so as to give an opportunity for a debate on aircraft noise by the whole House and he undertook to put his name to the necessary motion.[1] And a debate of 40 minutes duly took place.[2]

The Select Committee on Procedure in 1971 concluded that the balance of advantage lay in the direction of abolition, and recommended 'that the question should be put forthwith on the motion for third reading of all bills'.[3] Nothing has resulted from this recommendation.

During three recent sessions the figures have been as shown in Table 5.1.

Table 5.1

	Number of Bills				
	Debated	Not debated under S.O. No. 56	Not debated under S.O. No. 93*	Not debated but divided on	Total
1967–68	23	36	3	1	63
1968–69	23	27	3	—	53
1970–71	30	40	4	2	76
Total	76	103	10	3	192

* This provides that Consolidated Fund and Appropriation Bills shall be read a third time without debate.

This table indicates that there is no movement towards change, the ratio of bills debated to bills not debated being very much the same. The Select Committee on Procedure in 1971 noted that between 1967–68 and 1969–70 the ratio (for all bills including private Members' bills which are excluded from my figures) decreased from 1 : 1·2 to 1 : 2·3 and the number of of hours spent on third reading from 25 to 11.[4] But any conclusion drawn from these figures is quite unreliable as the number of bills debated on third reading in 1969–70 was untypically low and 1970–71 saw a return to the norm.

The argument about third reading debates reflects, in microcosm, the central dilemma of Parliamentary debate on legislation. If the justification for debate is the extent to which change in the proposals may be effected, then third reading debates are of almost no value whatsoever. But if the justification is the giving of opportunities to Members to express their

[1] Standing Committee G, col. 232.
[2] 768 H.C. Deb., cols 1922–30; 769, cols 463–7.
[3] H.C. 538 of 1970–71, *Report* para 37.
[4] H.C. 538 of 1970–71, *Report* para 37, Appendix 1, Annex B.

views,[1] to criticise Ministers, to continue to draw Governments into the public arena, then they serve a limited purpose. The small amount of time taken in debates can be used at once as an argument for their abolition and for their retention.

[1] The motion for third reading of Government bills was divided on in 1967–68 on nine bills, in 1968–69 on two bills, and in 1970–71 on fourteen bills.

CHAPTER SIX

THE IMPACT OF THE HOUSE OF COMMONS

In seeking to make an evaluation of the impact that the Parliamentary process has on Government bills, it has been necessary to do two things. First, to see what quantities can tell us, how many amendments were moved or discussed, who put them down, and what was their fate. But since, under the procedure followed in our legislation, every amendment that is to be made must be brought before and approved by the two Houses or a committee thereof, so that a minor drafting improvement has the same status as the deletion of a whole group of sections, quantities will be helpful only in sketching the outlines of the evaluation. Secondly, therefore, having looked at the width, we have had to consider the quality of what has been done.

At this point another difficulty emerged. As already stated, it seemed a very dubious undertaking to use one man's judgement – my own – to determine what was important and what was not. Of course, at the extremes of the matter there could be no argument. Examples could easily be given of important amendments and of trivial or drafting amendments. But between these extremes lies a whole range of amendments of varying importance which could be separated from one another and put into groups with headings indicating their degrees of importance only on a highly personal view which would quickly become arbitrary.

No doubt the classification of amendments as trivial or drafting is also a matter of personal judgement about which there can be proper differences of opinion. And trivial or drafting amendments may acquire significance later when the courts interpret what has been enacted and surprise us all; or when unanticipated circumstances arise which give to the words a meaning which no one had intended them to bear. But this amount of imprecision is unavoidable.

The detailed treatment in earlier chapters has, I hope, enabled the reader to see what is the quality of the amendments moved. For what is considered to be important depends not only on the relative value of one amendment to another or of one amendment to the text of the bill but also on the conception which each man has of the functions of the Government and of Parliament in this legislative process. The point is not new. One who starts with the assumption that the function of legislating lies primarily with the two Houses of Parliament will consider relatively unimportant the changes which are effected as a result of debate. But one who starts with the assumption that the making of laws is primarily the responsibility of Governments who must, nevertheless, submit their proposals to the two Houses for consideration, will take a different view of the quality of the changes made, even though he also may think that the opportunity for making changes should be greater.

We may now consider the impact in committee and on report both quantitatively and qualitatively.

6.1 IN COMMITTEE

Quantitatively, the impact may first be assessed by seeing how many amendments in committees of the House of Commons were moved and discussed, how many were moved formally and how many were grouped and discussed. In the three sessions considered the figures were[1] as shown in Table 6.1. Those moved formally are, with very few exceptions, trivial

Table 6.1 AMENDMENTS IN COMMITTEES OF THE HOUSE OF COMMONS

Amendments	1967–68	%	1968–69	%	1970–71	%	Total	%
Moved and discussed	2161	72·1	1256	64·9	1000	78·3	4417	71·1
Moved formally*	837	27·9	678	35·1	278	21·7	1793	28·9
Total moved	2998	100	1934	100	1278	100	6210	100
Grouped and discussed	2013	—	1279	—	915	—	4207	—

* Some of these will have been grouped and discussed and so appear under that column also.

or drafting or wholly consequential amendments. The larger total number of amendments dealt with in 1967–68 was simply the result of this being the session when the greatest amount of legislation was introduced. It included the mammoth Transport Bill to which 1244 amendments were moved. If those moved formally are disregarded, we are still left with a total over the three sessions of 8624 amendments, the discussion of which represents a considerable amount of Parliamentary time.[2]

What was the success rate in committee of those amendments moved (see Table 6.2)? Throughout, 'amendments' includes new clauses.

To find that nearly half of the amendments dealt with were agreed to may be surprising. But if we again disregard those moved formally (all of which were agreed to) the percentage drops from 46·0 to 24·2. On the

[1] See Appendix 1. [2] For details of time spent, see above, p. 17.

Table 6.2 AMENDMENTS MOVED IN COMMITTEES OF THE HOUSE OF COMMONS

Amendments	1967–68	%	1968–69	%	1970–71	%	Total	%
Agreed to	1340	44·7	1019	52·7	511	40·0	2870	46·0
Withdrawn	925	30·9	465	24·0	407	31·8	1797	29·2
Negatived	733	24·4	450	23·3	360	28·2	1543	24·8
Total moved	2998	100	1934	100	1278	100	6210	100

other hand we must remember that not all those withdrawn are lost, some of them returning in similar form at the report stage.

As indications of the impact of the House of Commons on Government bills, these figures alone are seriously misleading. Table 6.3 shows who moved the amendments agreed to in committee.

Again, we must remember that all those amendments moved formally were agreed to and that all[1] were moved by Ministers. Nevertheless the figures point to the overwhelming dominance of Ministerial amendments (93·7 per cent) amongst those which were agreed to; and only one Ministerial amendment failed. The Opposition were successful in 4·3 per cent of the amendments they moved. Even this figure is inflated for of the 4207 amendments grouped and discussed but not selected to be moved, the great majority were tabled by Opposition Members so that their more accurate success rate is nearer 2 per cent.

In committee, Government amendments are not commonly the result of arguments advanced by members of the committee or indeed by Members of the House. Usually, they reflect later developments in the thinking of civil servants in the department, often reflecting pressures from interest groups. This being so, it would be wrong to attribute any but a few of these amendments to the impact on the Government of Parliament, of Members, or of the committee. Of course, Members may be leaning on the department either in support of interest groups or on their own or other initiative. But, for Government amendments at this stage, committee proceedings remain primarily the means by which amendments can be made not the reason why they are made.

So, in this somewhat limited sense, the committee has very little direct impact on bills, and the statistics support this. Indirectly the impact is stronger. This is because the committee provides an opportunity for argument, especially by the Opposition, to be deployed and developed, which may have an influence on the Minister and cause him to reconsider. These arguments may have been advanced during the debate on second

[1] This is not completely true but the exceptions are very few indeed. In this and other tables, the figure of 99·9 per cent is inaccurate as, to one place of decimals, it should be 100·0 per cent. But that would be more misleading.

Table 6.3 AMENDMENTS AGREED TO IN COMMITTEES OF THE HOUSE OF COMMONS

Moved by	1967–68			1968–69			1970–71			Total		
	Moved	Agreed to	% Agreed to	Moved	Agreed to	% Agreed to	Moved	Agreed to	% Agreed to	Moved	Agreed to	% Agreed to
Ministers	1276	1276	100	966	965	99·9	458	458	100	2700	2699	99·9
Government backbenchers	230	15	6·5	79	11	13·9	127	14	11·0	436	40	9·2
Opposition Members	1492	49	3·3	889	43	4·8	693	39	5·6	3074	131	4·3
Total	2998	1340	45·0	1934	1019	52·7	1278	511	40·0	6210	2870	46·0

reading and perhaps also, outside Westminster, in the press, in local authority circles, in party meetings. At this committee stage, as we have seen, the Opposition may, if they believe their chance of effecting some change in the Government's attitude is real, be content with the Minister's promise to 'look again' and so be willing to withdraw amendments. This must be analysed further when we consider the general impact on report.

The fate of amendments moved by Government backbenchers (see Table 6.4) and by Opposition Members (see Table 6.5) must be regarded more closely for it is in the activities of these two groups in committee rather than in the activities of Ministers that we can see both the quantity and the quality of the impact.[1]

Table 6.4 AMENDMENTS IN COMMITTEES OF THE HOUSE OF COMMONS MOVED BY GOVERNMENT BACKBENCHERS

	1967–68	1968–69	1970–71	Total
Withdrawn	160	45	89	294
Negatived without division	27	5	15	47
Negatived on division	28	18	9	55
Agreed to without division	10	8	13	31
Agreed to on division	5	3	1	9
Total	230	79	127	436

Of the forty-seven amendments moved by Government backbenchers and negatived without a division during the three sessions shown in Table 6.4, there were twelve instances where the mover was silent about his reasons for neither withdrawing nor pressing the matter to a division; ten where he was refused leave to withdraw or his request was nullified by subsequent speeches; two where he was absent at the close of the debate. In four cases, the mover seemed more or less satisfied with the Minister's reply but, in eleven, positive dissatisfaction seems to have been the reasons for refusals to withdraw. Five amendments were to the Finance Bill, being unsuccessful efforts by Conservative backbenchers to extract concessions for special cases. There were also three left-wing revolts against the Labour government: on the Prices and Incomes Bill and the Public Expenditure and Receipts Bill, both in 1967–68; and on the Housing Bill 1968–69.

Of the fifty-five such amendments negatived on a division, fifteen were caused by Opposition action either by refusing leave to withdraw or because a grouped Opposition amendment was involved. In two cases (Mr Maude on the Highways Bill 1970–71 and Mr Sutcliffe seeking exemption for

[1] The details of these amendments have been described above, see pp. 94–119.

Cleveland Potash from the Investment and Building Bill 1970–71) the movers from the Government side were dissatisfied with the Ministerial replies. Eight amendments were part of the attack on the Parliament (No. 2) Bill 1968–69; and one was another example of a Conservative backbencher seeking a special concession on the Finance Bill 1970–71. The remaining twenty-nine cases were major revolts.

Outstanding amongst the revolts were those coming from left-wing Labour backbenchers including eleven amendments moved by Mr Mikardo to the Prices and Incomes Bill 1967–68; one, on school milk, to the Public Expenditure and Receipts Bill 1967–68; and one to the Transport (London) Bill 1968–69. Others, not or not wholly associated with the left, were five to the Race Relations Bill 1967–68, one on SET to the Finance Bill 1967–68, three to the Commonwealth Immigrants Bill 1967–68, one to the Town and Country Planning Bill 1967–68, one to the Medicines Bill 1967–68, one to the Housing Bill 1968–69, one to the Representation of the People Bill 1968–69 (Mr Strauss's on voting age), and one to the Post Office Bill 1968–69.

All these amendments being negatived (with or without a division), none can be said to have had any direct impact on the bills to which they were directed. But the dimensions of revolt are themselves of some significance. The total number of amendments moved by Government backbenchers and negatived during these three sessions is 102. But the number of cases of genuine dissent, being more than the expression of dissatisfaction by one or two members, is small. The Prices and Incomes Bill 1967–68 attracted dissent from the left of the Labour party, expressed in twelve specific amendments; the Parliament (No. 2) Bill 1968–69 in ten amendments; the Commonwealth Immigrants Bill 1967–68 in three amendments; the Representation of the People Bill 1968–69 and the Housing Bill 1968–69 in two amendments. It is not surprising that these bills attracted protest from groups of Members; and worth noting that all these revolts were by Labour backbenchers against Labour Governments and that in 1970–71 when there was a Conservative Government there were effectively no comparable revolts represented by Government backbench amendments being negatived.

Amendments moved by Government backbenchers and agreed to without a division totalled thirty-one in these three sessions. These reflect Government acceptance of the proposals. Most were of minor importance effecting changes which amounted to some improvements of bills. Apart from six amendments to the Finance Bill 1970–71 where Conservative backbenchers successfully extracted concessions, two amendments to the Civil Aviation Bill 1970–71 moved by Mr Onslow, and one to the Highways Bill 1970–71 moved by Mr Maude, there were also, and of more importance, Mr Whitaker's amendment to the Race Relations Bill 1967–68 adding public authorities to the list of bodies subject to proceedings in respect of unlawful discrimination, and Mr Manuel's amendment to the Agriculture (Spring Traps) (Scotland) Bill 1968–69.

But amendments moved by Government backbenchers and carried on a division generally represent Government defeats and there were eight such defeats in the three sessions. Here we can see the impact of the House imposing itself on the Government. Two of these eight were to the Administration of Justice Bill 1968–69 which, as already noted, being a law reform bill, is traditionally regarded as being non-controversial between parties. Three others were to the Town and Country Planning Bill 1967–68, to the Medicines Bill 1967–68, and to the Development of Tourism Bill 1968–69 and were not of primary importance. But two to the Race Relations Bill 1967–68 by Mr Rose and Mr Lyon were of greater significance. And that moved by Mr Enoch Powell to the Immigration Bill 1970–71 was, of all the amendments successfully moved by Government backbenchers during the three sessions, that which most obviously changed a principle of Government policy.

Table 6.5 AMENDMENTS IN COMMITTEES OF THE HOUSE OF COMMONS MOVED BY OPPOSITION MEMBERS

	1967–68	1968–69	1970–71	Total
Withdrawn	765	420	318	1503
Negatived without division	188	180	92	460
Negatived on division	490	246	244	980
Agreed to without division	46	38	34	118
Agreed to on division	3	5	5	13
Total	1492	889	693	3074

From the analysis, therefore, some more precise answer can be given to the question how far amendments moved by Government backbenchers make an impact on legislation proposals, and some more precise meaning be given to evaluations of the greater or less importance to be attached to the effects of such amendments.

Whereas 9·2 per cent of Government backbench amendments (40 out of 436) were agreed to, only 4·3 per cent of Opposition amendments (131 out of 3074) were agreed to (see Table 6.5).

The debate on Opposition amendments that are negatived may, in a few cases, nevertheless persuade the Government to reconsider. But normally the amendment sought by the mover is sunk without trace. Opposition amendments that are withdrawn are more likely to result in subsequent concessions as we shall see.[1] And since no question of 'revolts' against the Government can arise from Opposition action (although Opposition backbenchers may revolt against their own front bench on

[1] See above, p. 119 *et seq.*; p. 167 *et seq.*

occasion) we must look to those Opposition amendments which are agreed to for any impact on Government bills.

During the three sessions, 118 Opposition amendments were agreed to without a division. As with Government backbench amendments, this normally signifies Government acceptance. Of the 118, I have classified (above) eighty-nine as drafting or clarificatory or very minor amendments and a further seventeen (all in 1970–71) as minor. The distinction between very minor and minor is little better than arbitrary but those seventeen set out give some indication of what I have classified as minor. Only twelve such amendments seem to me to be of some substance. Of these the three most important were Mr Turton's amendment to the Commonwealth Immigrants Bill 1967–68, Mr Macmillan's to the Medicines Bill 1967–68 (on misleading advertisements), and Mr Emery's to the Development of Tourism Bill 1968–69 (establishing the English Tourist Board). Three others worthy of special note were Mr Eldon Griffiths's amendment to the Race Relations Bill 1967–68, Dame Joan Vickers's to the Immigration Appeals Bill 1968–69, and Mr Millan's to the Civil Aviation Bill 1970–71.

Opposition amendments agreed to on divisions totalled thirteen in the three sessions. All but one were Government defeats, three only being brought about by crossvoting and one only (probably) by an abstention; the other eight resulted from absenteeism on the Government's side. Three stand out as being of some substance: Mr Macmillan's amendment excluding efficacy by comparison as a criterion under the Medicines Bill 1967–68; the limitation of the period of control under the Prices and Incomes Bill 1967–68; and the increase to £50,000 of the fine leviable under the Oil in Navigable Waters Bill 1970–71. Another two of note were the amendments to the Children and Young Persons Bill 1968–69 (on supervisory orders) and to the Coal Industry Bill 1970–71 (concerning Parliamentary supervision).

Of 3510 Government backbench and Opposition amendments moved during the three sessions, 171 were agreed to. Of those agreed to, only a very few can be said to be of any real substance.

I hope I have provided the evidence on which any reader can decide for himself what is the quality of the impact made on Government bills but I would select only nine amendments out of the 171 successfully moved as having real substance so that they could be said to have changed in part some principle of the bill. Nor is it surprising that four of these, moved by Messrs Whitaker, Rose, Lyon and Griffiths, were to the Race Relations Bill 1967–68;[1] one was Mr Turton's amendment to the Commonwealth Immigrants Bill 1967–68;[2] one was Dame Joan Vickers's amendment to Immigration Appeals Bill 1968–69;[3] and one was Mr Enoch Powell's amendment to the Immigration Bill 1970–71.[4] For it is in such contentious areas of social policy where party discipline is often weakest or where

[1] See above, pp. 100–2, 113. [2] See above, p. 112. [3] See above, pp. 114–5.
[4] See above, p. 110.

Governments are most sensitive that changes take place. The other two important amendments I would select were both moved by Mr Macmillan to the Medicines Bill 1967–68, on misleading advertisements,[1] and on efficacy by comparison.[2]

On seven occasions the negativing of the motion that the clause stand part was noteworthy. In 1967–68 the Minister's agreement to withdraw and reconsider clause 9 of the Civil Aviation Bill;[3] the Government defeat on clause 39 of the Gaming Bill;[4] and the withdrawal of clause 2 of the Family Allowances and National Insurance (No. 2) Bill[5] were all in this category. But the withdrawal of the whole of Part VI of the Transport Bill 1967–68 was, as we have seen, not the result of Parliamentary pressure.[6] In 1968–69, the two important instances were the rejections of clause 2 of the Air Corporations Bill,[7] and clause 1 of the Decimal Currency Bill.[8] In 1970–71, the Minister withdrew clause 9 of the Family Income Supplements Bill[9] and was forced to accept the negativing without a division of clause 7 of the National Insurance Bill.[10]

I am therefore suggesting that on only sixteen occasions during the three sessions was the Government of the day forced in committee, either by defeat in a division or by pressure there exerted, to modify a part of a principle. And if we consider such modification to be one of the main purposes of committee scrutiny of Government proposals, this surely represents a very small achievement. Looked at thus, the considerable expenditure of effort by non-Ministerial members of the committee in seeking modification seems not to be justified by the results. But such conclusions must not be come to until we have considered how far the Government on report stage were willing to modify their position further as a result of what took place in committee.

Finally we must again remember the one major defeat of the Government in these three sessions represented by the withdrawal of the Parliament (No. 2) Bill 1968–69. When emphasising the small impact that committee members make on the very large mass of legislation material put before them by Governments, we must also note that, as on that occasion, backbenchers when roused can triumph.

6.2 ON REPORT

The comparable table to that on the committee stage (see Table 6.1)[11] is Table 6.6. The much higher proportion of those moved formally – half of all amendments moved as compared with less than one-third in committee – reflects the large amount of drafting and consequential work involved in amendments made on report. The halving on report of the total number of amendments moved in committee results in part from the more stringent

1 See above, pp. 112–3.
2 See above, p. 113.
3 See above, p. 131.
4 *Ibid.*
5 See above, pp. 132–3.
6 See above, p. 132.
7 See above, p. 134.
8 *Ibid.*
9 See above, p. 136.
10 *Ibid.*
11 See also Appendix 2.

Table 6.6 AMENDMENTS ON REPORT IN THE HOUSE OF COMMONS

Amendments	1967–68	%	1968–69	%	1970–71	%	Total	%
Moved and discussed	672	45·3	466	50·3	415	59·8	1553	50·1
Moved formally	810	54·7	460	49·7	279	40·2	1549	49·9
Total moved	1482	100	926	100	694	100	3102	100
Grouped and discussed	795	—	576	—	568	—	1939	—

selection of amendments on report and in part from the fact that of the 192 bills considered in committee only ninety-two were considered on report.[1] In 1967–68, the Town and Country Planning Bill with 209 amendments moved, and the Transport Bill with 236, reflected the detailed nature of the consideration at this stage. In 1968–69 only the Finance Bill with 165 amendments dealt with was comparable. In 1970–71 most amendments were moved to the Finance Bill but these totalled only ninety-three.[2]

More significant of the differences between committee and report and of the impact of report on Government bills is the success rate of amendments moved (see Table 6.7). The percentage of amendments agreed to rises from forty-six in committee to seventy-nine on report; of the 2452 agreed to, 1549 were formally moved. The increased percentage reflects the dominance on report of Ministerial initiative and activity as Table 6.8 shows. Whereas in committee, Ministers moved 2700 out of 6210 amendments (43·5 per cent), on report they moved 2414 out of 3102

Table 6.7 AMENDMENTS ON REPORT IN THE HOUSE OF COMMONS

Amendments	1967–68	%	1968–69	%	1970–71	%	Total	%
Agreed to	1207	81·4	718	77·5	527	75·9	2452	79·0
Withdrawn	95	6·4	58	6·3	56	8·1	209	6·8
Negatived	180	12·2	150	16·2	111	16·0	441	14·2
Total moved	1482	100	926	100	694	100	3102	100

[1] See above, p. 147.

[2] Note, however, that 254 amendments were moved and discussed or grouped and discussed to the Industrial Relations Bill on report (see Appendix 2).

Table 6.8 AMENDMENTS AGREED TO ON REPORT IN THE HOUSE OF COMMONS

Moved by	1967–68			1968–69			1970–71			Total		
	Moved	Agreed to	% Agreed to	Moved	Agreed to	% Agreed to	Moved	Agreed to	% Agreed to	Moved	Agreed to	% Agreed to
Ministers	1189	1188	99·9	709	709	100	516	516	100	2414	2413	99·9
Government backbenchers	42	5	11·9	10	3	30·0	37	2	5·4	89	10	11·2
Opposition Members	251	14	5·6	207	6	2·9	141	9	6·4	599	29	4·8
Total	1482	1207	85·7	926	718	77·5	694	527	74·5	3102	2452	79·0

(77·5 per cent). And they were, of course, as successful on report as in committee, only one amendment not being agreed to but withdrawn by the Minister.

Of the thirty-nine amendments successfully moved by Opposition Members and Government backbenchers during these three sessions the most important was perhaps that gaining a concession under the Finance Bill 1970–71 for the severely disabled. A second of some importance was the blocking of the possibility of a national lottery under the Finance Bill 1967–68. Noteworthy were the technical amendments moved by Mr Patrick Jenkin to that bill; and the patents amendment to the Health Services and Public Health Bill 1967–68. Also of some importance were the amendments affecting the detention of aircraft under the Civil Aviation Bill 1967–68; enforcement notices under the Town and Country Planning (Scotland) Bill 1968–69; Mr Steel's amendment to the Immigration Bill 1970–71; public interest in relation to the withholding of information under the Civil Aviation Bill 1970–71; and the recovery of costs under that bill also.[1]

This total of nine amendments of more or of less importance is not impressive. A different assessment of relative importance might add two or three more to the list. None was of major significance. On no occasion was the Government either defeated or forced to make a tactical retreat. As in committee, the visible result of a great deal of Opposition and Government back-bench activity was very small indeed.

Moreover Governments do not take kindly to defeats in committee and in the three sessions, of the twenty-six defeats, the Government on report reversed fourteen of these, modified their position on three and accepted the change in nine only.

Though the direct impact of the House on Government proposals for legislation was unimpressive, the indirect impact shown by the positive response of Government to points made in committee was certainly deeper. On my estimate there were 365 occasions during these three sessions when Government amendments moved on report were traceable to committee points made by Government backbenchers and Opposition Members. And of these, I have classed one-third (125 in all) as important in varying degrees. This is not an inconsiderable number.

More significant than the counting of amendments is their weight and their effect on bills. Eleven bills, all of importance, were markedly affected by their passage through the House of Commons. In 1967–68 the Medicines Bill, the Race Relations Bill, and the Gaming Bill were changed in several important particulars; the Town and Country Planning Bill was reshaped and improved; and the Civil Aviation Bill emerged as a better and more coherent measure. In 1968–69 the Finance Bill was considerably amended in one important group of provisions, as were the Housing Bill and the Children and Young Persons Bill. In 1970–71, the widest range of amend-

[1] See above, pp. 160–6.

ments was to the Highways Bill while important limited amendments were made to the Finance Bill and to the Immigration Bill.

Against these achievements, must be set the long debates, the hundreds of aborted attempts at amendment, the scores of bills, including some of the greatest importance, which remained effectively unchanged despite the efforts of Opposition Members and, to a lesser extent, of Government backbenchers. But even when Members totally fail to persuade the Government to amend its proposals, other purposes of debate[1] may be fulfilled.

When we add the achievements of non-Ministerial Members in committee to those on report we are left with some sense of great effort making for little result and yet with a sense also that some slipshod thinking by Ministers, civil servants and draftsmen has been removed or clarified and that some bills look much better on third reading than they did on second, and that a few famous victories have been won. Whether this great effort is justified by those improvements is another matter; as is the question of the ways in which the effort might be made more effective.

[1] See below, pp. 232–4.

CHAPTER SEVEN

THE HOUSE OF LORDS

This chapter does not attempt a comprehensive assessment of the value of the House of Lords as a legislative assembly.[1] It seeks to analyse, in the manner of the preceding chapters, the impact made by the House of Lords on Government bills in two recent sessions, but with this limitation, that only bills originating in the House of Commons are looked at. Two sessions – and one of them the first of a Parliament – are too few to sustain any but tentative generalisations.[2]

Bills which are primarily financial (whether or not certified by the Speaker as 'money bills' under the Parliament Act 1911) are left alone, and many other bills, after being read a second time, are not further examined in committee because no amendments have been tabled.[3] Consideration on report takes place on bills yet further reduced in number. The third reading debate, on the other hand, has more significance in the Lords than it has in the Commons because amendments may be moved. Table 7.1 gives some recent figures.[4]

Usually, all bills that are committed are considered by committees of the whole House. In recent years, a few bills have been sent to public bill committees off the floor, and then re-committed to the whole. These are discussed below.[5]

We may now look in more detail at these two sessions remembering that in 1968–69 the Labour Government were faced with a House of Lords having its permanent Conservative majority not only amongst the totality of those entitled to sit in the House but also amongst those who are politically active; and that in 1970–71 the Conservative Government had the advantage of that majority.

[1] For another survey, see J. R. Vincent 'The House of Lords' in 19 *Parliamentary Affairs* 475 and 20 *Parliamentary Affairs* 178.

[2] With whatever modesty is considered appropriate, I would plead for much more detailed work of analysis to be done of what actually happens. 'The reform of the House of Lords' as a perennial subject of debate suffers greatly from a paucity of such analysis.

[3] 'There is a good tradition,' said the Clerk of Public Bills in the Lords in a note to me, 'that bills are not discussed merely for the sake of discussion'. House of Commons please copy.

[4] For detailed figures see Appendix 3.

[5] See below p. 226 *et seq*. References to committees of the whole House (as in Table 7.1) include bills re-committed to the whole.

Table 7.1 HOUSE OF LORDS – BILLS ORIGINATING IN HOUSE OF COMMONS

	1968–69		1970–71
	Committee of the whole House		Committee of the whole House
Number of bills	39		52
Committee negatived	8	Order of commitment discharged	16
Not debated	8		16
Debated	23		20
	Report		*Report*
Number of bills	39		52
Not debated	25		42
Debated	14		10
	Third reading		*Third reading*
Number of bills	39		52
Not debated	28		38
Debated	11		14

Table 7.2 shows that 45·7 per cent (512 out of 1119) of the amendments were moved by Ministers, 3·5 per cent by Government backbenchers, and 50·8 per cent by Opposition and Independent peers. The table also shows that all but one of the 512 amendments moved by Ministers were agreed to but that the success rate for all other movers was 12·3 per cent (75 out of 607).[1]

The higher number of Opposition amendments in 1970–71 is not accounted for by the greater number of statutes in that sessions, for fewer statutes were debated than in 1968–69. Moreover, fifty or more amendments were moved to four bills in 1968–69 and only to two bills in 1970–71. But those two bills were the Immigration Bill and the Industrial Relations Bill and to these 121 and 412 amendments were, respectively, moved. So of all amendments moved in committee of the whole House to House of Commons bills in 1970–71, 79·7 per cent were moved to those two bills. Of the 412 amendments to the Industrial Relations Bill, 234 were moved by Opposition Members (including twenty-two Liberal amendments). But 160 were moved by Ministers so that the large total is the result not only of the Opposition's antagonism to the bill but also of considerable Governmental activity; a large number of Government amendments in the Lords had originally been tabled for report stage in the Commons but were not moved there so as to reduce the number of divisions during the all-night sitting after the guillotine fell. But Ministers moved only nineteen of the 121 amendments to the Immigration Bill; sixty-two were moved by Labour, twenty-seven by Liberal and six by Independent peers (see Table 7.3).

[1] For details see Appendix 3. As throughout, 'amendments' includes new clauses.

Table 7.2 AMENDMENTS MOVED IN COMMITTEE OF THE WHOLE HOUSE (HOUSE OF COMMONS BILLS ONLY) SHOWING THOSE WITHDRAWN, NEGATIVED AND AGREED TO

	By Ministers				By Government backbenchers				By Opposition and Independent Peers				Total			
	Total	W	N	A	Total	W	N	A	Total	W	N	A	W	N	A	Grand total
1968–69	272	—	—	271	12	12	—	—	167	122	7	38	134	7	309	450
1970–71	241	1	—	240	26	20	—	6	402	247	124	31	268	124	277	669
Total	512	1	—	511	38	32	—	6	569	369	131	69	402	132	586	1119

Note: W means Withdrawn; N means Negatived (whether on division or not); A means Agreed to (whether on division or not).

Table 7.3 AMENDMENTS MOVED ON REPORT (HOUSE OF COMMONS BILLS ONLY)

	By Ministers				By Government backbenchers				By Opposition and Independent Peers				Total			Grand total
	Total	W	N	A	Total	W	N	A	Total	W	N	A	W	N	A	
1968–69	148	—	—	148	1	1	—	—	43	28	6	9	29	6	157	192
1970–71	249	1	—	248	1	—	1	—	225	110	71	44	111	72	292	475
Total	397	1	—	396	2	1	1	—	268	138	77	53	140	78	449	667

On report,[1] Ministers moved 59·5 per cent (397 out of 667) of the amendments while 0·3 per cent were moved by Government backbenchers and 40·2 per cent by Opposition and Independent peers. In 1968–69 the Children and Young Persons Bill (eighty-one amendments moved) and the Transport (London) Bill (forty-seven amendments) accounted for 66·6 per cent of all amendments moved at this stage. In 1970–71 the Industrial Relations Bill (316 amendments moved) and the Immigration Bill (sixty-three amendments) accounted for 79·8 per cent of the total moved. Ministers were wholly successful in the amendments they moved except for one which was withdrawn; Opposition and Independent peers were successful in 19·3 per cent of their amendments.

Unlike the practice in the House of Commons, no one is empowered to select amendments for debate in the House of Lords, either in committee or on report. But movers may invite the House to consider also other amendments in addition to the one or more being moved.[2]

On third reading[3] in 1968–69, all but one of the sixty-eight amendments were moved by Ministers, fifty-eight of them being to the Children and Young Persons Bill of which only three were of substance.[4] All were agreed to. In 1970–71 there were forty-one amendments of which twenty-eight were moved by Ministers and agreed to. None of the fourteen amendments moved by Opposition and Independent peers in the two sessions was agreed to. It is unusual for opposition to be made to the motion that the bill do now pass (which concludes the third reading)[5] but this happened in 1970–71 to the Civil Aviation (Declaratory Provisions) Bill.[6]

The direct impact of the House of Lords on Government bills may be seen first when amendments are successfully moved on a division against the Government's wish; secondly, when non-Ministerial amendments are agreed to without a division; and, thirdly, when Ministers move amendments in response to points made.

7.1 GOVERNMENT DEFEATS ON THE FLOOR OF THE HOUSE

It must not be too easily believed that the House of Lords, recognising the pre-eminence of the Commons, will yield to the wishes of the Government on all occasions. In 1968–69, the Labour Government were defeated

[1] For details, see Appendix 3.

[2] Again unlike the House of Commons, two or more consecutive amendments may be moved together in the Lords. The fact that there is no imposed selection of amendments or imposed grouping of amendments means that motions for amendments tabled but not moved have been *voluntarily* abandoned or withdrawn or discussed with other amendments (or, most exceptionally, ruled out of order).

[3] For details, see Appendix 3.

[4] 304 H.L. Deb., cols 1213–32, 1245–53.

[5] Whenever there are amendments on third reading, the final debate on the bill takes place not on the motion for third reading but on the motion that the bill do now pass, after the amendments have been disposed of.

[6] 315 H.L. Deb., cols 17–18. The reason seems to have been annoyance at the failure of the Government to give specific answers to questions raised.

in twenty divisions, including defeats which resulted in the failure to pass the House of Commons (Redistribution of Seats) (No. 2) Bill; in 1970–71, the Conservative Government were defeated in only two divisions. A Labour Opposition perforce relies more on filibustering than on voting down the Government when it wishes to obstruct. I will consider first the details of defeats in 1968–69.

The difficulties of legislating about the use of traps in Scotland have already been noticed.[1] As it reached the House of Lords, the Agriculture (Spring Traps) (Scotland) Bill removed from the Secretary of State, from 1 April 1973, the power to authorise the use of gin traps. During the second reading debate,[2] the Minister gave some encouragement to a proposal to forbid immediately the use of these traps for killing or taking otters. On report, an Opposition peer put down a new clause to this effect. The Salmon Net Fishing Association told the Minister that, if he accepted this, they would consider doing so a breach of faith, in view of the consultations which had taken place.[3] The Minister therefore reluctantly found himself unable to support the new clause but it was agreed to on a division.[4] The House of Commons, on a Government motion, agreed to all the Lords amendments.[5]

On a division, an Opposition amendment in the House of Commons to amend clause 1 of the Children and Young Persons Bill was defeated.[6] The same amendment was moved in committee in the Lords by an Opposition peer. Its effect was to authorise a court to make an order for the care of a child without the court having to be satisfied specifically that he was in need of care or control which he was otherwise unlikely to receive. The House agreed to the amendment on a division.[7] In the Commons, the Minister moved to disagree with this Lords amendment and this was carried on a division.[8] The Lords did not insist.[9]

The battle for the retention of the sixpenny piece[10] was continued in committee in the Lords on an Opposition amendment (to the Decimal Currency Bill) which was agreed to on a division.[11] But on report that amendment was struck out after another division.[12] Fee-charging schools in Scotland provided a struggle with reverberant echoes and another Opposition victory in committee in the Lords against the Government.[13] But in

[1] See above, p. 105.
[2] 299 H.L. Deb., cols 339–40.
[3] 300 H.L. Deb., cols 626.
[4] *Ibid.*, cols 626–30; on third reading the Minister moved two amendments consequential to the new clause: *ibid.*, cols 1142–3.
[5] 784 H.C. Deb., col. 1411.
[6] 784 H.C. Deb., cols 1020–50.
[7] 303 H.L. Deb., cols 796–820; a further consequential amendment was agreed to: *ibid.*, col. 819.
[8] 788 H.C. Deb., cols 415–56; the consequential amendment was also disagreed to: *ibid.*, col. 455.
[9] 304 H.L. Deb., cols 1628–9.
[10] See above, pp. 134, 184.
[11] 301 H.L. Deb., cols 947–59, 972–92.
[12] 302 H.L. Deb., cols 9–30.
[13] Education (Scotland) Bill, 303 H.L. Deb., cols 486–512.

the Commons this amendment was disagreed with on a division[1] and the Lords did not insist.[2]

There were three Government defeats when the Foreign Compensation Bill was in the Lords. This bill followed an agreement concluded with the Soviet Government and enabled assets in the United Kingdom formerly belonging to persons resident or carrying on business in the Baltic States to be used for the payment of compensation for losses suffered by British persons and interests in that area. In committee, after a bad-tempered debate, two amendments were carried against the Government.[3] And on report, the Government were defeated again.[4] On third reading, a Government amendment was agreed to without a division, which reversed one of the three amendments but in a form which was acceptable to the Opposition.[5] The second amendment was disagreed with by the Commons[6] and the Lords did not insist.[7] The third amendment was accepted by the Government.

In committee on the Housing Bill also, the Government were defeated three times. The first was on an amendment to advance by 8 months the date from which certain rent increases would be recoverable by landlords.[8] Two other associated amendments were agreed to without a division.[9] These were all disagreed with by the Commons[10] and the Lords did not insist.[11] The second defeat, with which two other amendments were linked, was similar being concerned with the period of delay until the full fair rent was reached. Again, on a division, the amendment was agreed to.[12] Again the Commons rejected it[13] and the Lords did not insist.[14] The third defeat was on the motion that clause 80, which was a clause concerned not with the principal subject matter of the Housing Bill but with the reform of the Leasehold Reform Act 1967, stand part of the bill; the motion was lost by 22 votes to 23.[15] On report the clause was reinstated, somewhat altered, after a division in which the Government were successful by 53 votes to 47.[16]

The Post Office Bill required the Post Office 'to provide (save in so far as the provision thereof is, in its opinion, impracticable or not reasonably practicable) such services for the conveyance of letters and such telephone services as satisfy all reasonable demands for them'. The Opposition amendment in committee to this less than onerous obligation was also mild. It proposed to require the Post Office to consult the Minister before deciding the impracticability of the provision of services. It was agreed to

[1] 787 H.C. Deb., cols 1659–66.
[2] 304 H.L. Deb., cols 1166–8; there were four consequential amendments.
[3] 299 H.L. Deb., cols 624–34, 640–54.
[4] 300 H.L. Deb., cols 349–82.
[5] 300 H.L. Deb., cols 1369–71. [6] 782 H.C. Deb., cols 1703–36.
[7] 302 H.L. Deb., cols 213–9. [8] 304 H.L. Deb., cols 342–50.
[9] *Ibid.*, col. 349. [10] 787 H.C. Deb., cols 2200–6.
[11] 304 H.L. Deb., cols 1187–93. [12] 304 H.L. Deb., cols 349–54.
[13] 787 H.C. Deb., cols 2215–20. [14] See above, note 11.
[15] 304 H.L. Deb., cols 401–16. [16] *Ibid.*, cols 861–76.

on a division.[1] The Commons disagreed with the amendment, on a division,[2] and the Lords did not insist.[3] The purpose of the second amendment in committee, with which another was associated, was to preserve the status quo of relay services until a review of all present arrangements for broadcasting had taken place.[4] In the Commons, the Postmaster-General accepted the principal amendment, but not that associated with it which was rejected on a division.[5] On report in the Lords, the Government were twice again defeated. First on an amendment moved by an Independent peer[6] which sought to make the Minister's consent necessary not only for the grant of licences but also for their refusal and for the attachment of conditions.[7] Again this was rejected by the Commons on a division.[8] And secondly on an amendment to render immune from suit, except at the instance of the Post Office, those acting on behalf of the Post Office in cases where the Post Office was itself immune.[9] The Government accepted this.[10]

A new clause was proposed to the Representation of the People Bill by which a person would be qualified for election to and membership of a local authority provided that for twelve preceding months he had a principal place of work within the area of the authority.[11] The clause was agreed to on a division. A second defeat was on a motion, which was agreed to, to delete from the bill the provision that was to alter the closing hour of the poll at Parliamentary elections from 9 p.m. to 10 p.m.[12] The Commons rejected both these amendments[13] and the Lords did not insist.[14]

An Opposition amendment to the Transport (London) Bill sought, by re-phrasing the general powers clause, to restrict the powers of the Executive to operate outside Greater London. On a division the amendment was agreed to as was a consequential amendment.[15] The House of Commons rejected it.[16] The next Opposition amendment sought to restrict the manufacturing powers of the Executive by requiring the Executive, before exercising them, to be satisfied that what was to be manufactured could not be satisfactorily obtained by any other means. As the left wing of the Labour party in the Commons sought to extend similar powers so the Conservative Opposition in the Lords sought to curtail them. As the Minister in the Lords said, 'This is yet another of our old friends and . . . I will spare the Committee the philosophical arguments that we had over many years'.[17] For certain functions, the bill provided that the Executive should act as if it were a company engaged in a commercial enterprise. And the Minister promised to put down an amendment on report to apply

[1] 303 H.L. Deb., cols 10–18. [2] 787 H.C. Deb., cols 1628–34.
[3] 304 H.L. Deb., cols 1193–5. [4] 303 H.L. Deb., cols 37–50.
[5] 787 H.C. Deb., cols 1636–44. [6] Lord Helsby. [7] 303 H.L. Deb., cols 944–60.
[8] 787 H.C. Deb., cols 1645–56. [9] 303 H.L. Deb., cols 959–70.
[10] 787 H.C. Deb., col. 1655. [11] 299 H.L. Deb., cols 245–84.
[12] *Ibid.*, cols 342–70. [13] 780 H.C. Deb., cols 1836–52, 1854–68.
[14] 301 H.L. Deb., cols 15–33. [15] 304 H.L. Deb., cols 7–18.
[16] 787 H.C. Deb., cols 2190–2. [17] 304 H.L. Deb., col. 19.

this principle also to the manufacturing powers.[1] So the Opposition amendment was withdrawn.

At this point, affairs began to go wrong. Lord Winterbottom had had charge of the bill during its earlier stages as a hybrid bill when it had been committed to a Select Committee and then to the Committee on Unopposed Bills. But he fell ill and so Lord Shepherd took over the bill in committee, on recommitment, and gave the undertaking referred to. It was a bill which, Lord Shepherd said, had 'nothing whatsoever to do with my Ministerial duties'[2] and he had received it on the Friday before the Monday when the committee stage had begun. Still he had had his brief over the weekend and based his undertaking on his reading of it. He seems, however, not to have fully understood it and so on report had to admit that he could not fulfil his undertaking though he made what amends he could by tabling other amendments. The Opposition found too difficult to resist the opportunity to make the most of these mishaps. The amendment in the terms of the undertaking was moved and pressed successfully to a division.[3] But the Commons disagreed with the amendments[4] and the Lords did not insist.[5]

Finally and famously, in 1968–69, the House of Lords struck down the House of Commons (Re-distribution of Seats) (No. 2) Bill, the subject matter of which, on a narrow view, was not in its field of concern. But the view taken both in the Commons and in the Lords was not narrow. The Opposition considered that the Government's failure to implement in full and without delay the recommendations of the Boundary Commission was, to quote the reasoned amendment on second reading in the Commons, a 'deliberate and flagrant breach' of statutory duties and violated constitutional arrangements agreed by all parties.[6] The bill did not reach the Lords until 15 July 1969 and the committee stage was taken on 21 July. Lord Brooke for the Opposition moved the first of a group of three amendments – which proposed to suspend action on the recommendations of the Boundary Commissions only to the end of that session – and suggested that what the Americans had done on the Moon was no more important to American history than the creation and maintenance of a fair and just democratic system of Parliamentary elections was to British history.[7] The debate on that amendment – in effect another second reading debate – lasted for over 3 hours and was agreed to by 270 votes to 96, a very considerable turnout for the Lords in committee. The connected amendments were agreed to and so was clause 1 as amended. Then clauses 2 and 3 and schedules 1 and 2 were disagreed to and the title was amended.[8] The report

[1] 304 H.L. Deb., cols 20–1.

[2] *Ibid.*, col. 808. He was Minister of State in the Foreign and Commonwealth Office; for that matter, Lord Winterbottom was Parliamentary Under-Secretary of State for Defence for the Royal Air Force.

[3] 304 H.L. Deb., cols 807–22.

[4] 787 H.C. Deb., cols 2192–3; one other was consequential.

[5] 304 H.L. Deb., cols 1195–8.

[6] 786 H.C. Deb., col. 460.

[7] 304 H.L. Deb., col. 657.

[8] *Ibid.*, cols 657–729.

stage and the third reading were taken formally and the bill as amended returned to the Commons on 23 July.[1] On 25 July the Commons adjourned until 13 October and they considered the Lords' amendments the next day after their return. The Government moved to agree with the first of the Lords' amendments 'for reasons of which their Lordships would thoroughly disapprove',[2] and to disagree with the others. Motions to disagree were carried after three divisions,[3] and the bill returned to the Lords. On 16 October the Lords considered the Commons' amendments. The usual motion that the House agreed with the Commons and did not insist on the Lords' amendments was put. It was comprehensively defeated by 229 votes to 78[4] and the bill returned to the Commons.[5] The session ended on 22 October and the bill fell.

Disregarding consequential amendments the Government were thus defeated in divisions on eighteen occasions in the House of Lords in 1968–69, apart from the House of Commons (Re-distribution of Seats) (No. 2) Bill. On that bill, only one division was taken in committee and the Government were defeated. But four motions that two clauses and two schedules stand part were negatived (without divisions), and three other amendments moved by the Opposition spokesman were agreed to – all associated with that first defeat. In addition there was the vote when the Lords insisted on their amendment. So there were two Government defeats in divisions on that bill and twenty during the whole session. Of these, two defeats in committee were reversed on report in the Lords and one on third reading.[6] The Government accepted the defeats on three occasions and reversed the Lords' decision on thirteen occasions; the other occasion was the Lords' insistence on their amendments on re-distribution of seats.

In contrast with these many excitements, the Lords voted down the Government only twice in 1970–71. In committee on the Housing Bill, Lord Derwent (Conservative) moved an amendment to alter the period prescribed by the bill for the beginning and ending of works eligible for improvement grants. On a division the amendment was agreed to by 66 votes to 62.[7] The Government accepted this but re-drafted it on report; and moved four other consequential amendments.[8] The second defeat for the Government was on the Immigration Bill. Lord Wade (Liberal) moved to add to the general principles clause a provision to declare that nothing in the bill should have the effect of taking away any right hitherto enjoyed by a resident Commonwealth citizen or should adversely affect his status. Against official Government opposition the amendment was agreed to by 93 votes to 79.[9] On report the Government moved two principal (and two consequential) amendments to replace Lord Wade's amendments while

[1] *Ibid.*, col. 981. [2] 788 H.C. Deb., cols 234–5. [3] *Ibid.*, cols 339–48.
[4] 304 H.L. Deb., cols 1543–96. [5] *Ibid.*, col. 1604.
[6] The third reading reversal of an amendment to the Foreign Compensation Bill was in effect an acceptance by the Government.
[7] 323 H.L. Deb., col. 812–24. [8] *Ibid.*, col. 1006–9.
[9] 322 H.L. Deb., cols 660–86.

preserving its principle. These amendments were acceptable to Lord Wade and his supporters.[1]

In the event, therefore, no amendment moved by a member of the official Labour Opposition and divided on during the session 1970–71 in the House of Lords was agreed to.

7.2 AMENDMENTS MOVED BY OPPOSITION PEERS, INDEPENDENTS AND GOVERNMENT BACKBENCHERS ON THE FLOOR OF THE HOUSE AND AGREED WITHOUT A DIVISION (HOUSE OF COMMONS BILLS ONLY), 1968–69 AND 1970–71

The numbers of such amendments in 1968–69 and 1970–71 were as shown in Table 7.4. No such amendments were agreed to on third reading in either session.

Table 7.4

	Opposition Members	Independents	Government backbenchers	Total
Committee of the whole House				
1968–69	23	2	Nil	25
1970–71	24	6	5	35
Report				
1968–69	4	Nil	Nil	4
1970–71	35	9	Nil	44
Total	86	17	5	108

Of the twenty-three amendments moved in committee by Opposition Members in 1968–69 and agreed to without a division, fourteen were consequential on Government defeats or on other accepted amendments. Seven of these were to the Education (Scotland) Bill, four to the Housing Bill, and one each to the Children and Young Persons Bill, the Post Office Bill and the Transport (London) Bill. Three amendments were those which followed, but were not consequential in the sense of being logically connected with, the Government defeat on the House of Commons (Re-distribution of Seats) (No. 2) Bill.

Of the remaining six separate amendments, two were to the Development of Tourism Bill. The first empowered Tourist Boards to establish advisory committees. The Minister said that to provide specifically for this was 'quite unnecessary' as the power was inherent but he gave way 'in order to get on to the more important parts of the Bill'.[2] The second was to require Tourist Boards before disposing of shares in a company to consult that

[1] 324 H.L. Deb., cols 209–15, 239–42, 408.

[2] 304 H.L. Deb., cols 886–90.

company. Again the Minister thought they would obviously do so in any event but agreed to insert the requirement.[1] An amendment to the Education (Scotland) Bill enabled local education authorities to increase their representation on governing bodies of schools where this was agreed with those bodies. The Minister accepted this as a 'useful change'.[2] Another amendment to this bill was merely to bring its wording into line with the Social Work (Scotland) Act.[3] The other two amendments were to the Post Office Bill. The first of these was to improve drafting and to prevent 'the actual abuse of the English language';[4] and the second (similarly) was to avoid the use of the phrase 'the next but one following section'.[5]

The two amendments moved by an Independent peer were to the Horserace Betting Levy Bill. The second was consequential on the first which Lord Goodman suggested was 'one of the least controversial amendments ever to be introduced into either House of Parliament'. Before the amalgamation of the Jockey Club and the National Hunt Committee, the Club had two members on the Levy Board and the Committee had one. The amendment proposed that the amalgamated body should have three members. It was, he said, 'incontrovertible in logic and in arithmetic'.[6]

In 1968–69 four amendments were successfully moved by Opposition peers on report. The first was to the Children and Young Persons Bill and increased the maximum recognisance payable by a parent or guardian on an order of the court from £25 to £50.[7] Two amendments to the Housing Bill moved by Lord Brooke in committee were clarificatory about compulsory purchase power; their intention was accepted by the Minister and they were withdrawn. On report Lord Brooke moved improved versions.[8] He also moved an amendment to the Representation of the People Bill to legalise postal voting at elections for rural district councils which had hitherto been excluded from this privilege. The Minister accepted the proposal but perhaps Lord Brooke was protesting a little too much when he welcomed this by saying: 'I should also like to put on record that here is a case where your Lordships' House, the non-elected Chamber, is able to be instrumental in bringing about a material improvement in the system of democratic election for the country'.[9]

As the table shows,[10] Opposition peers successfully moved twenty-four amendments in 1970–71 in committee without a division. Eighteen of these were to the Industrial Relations Bill of which fifteen were moved by Labour peers and three by Liberal peers. Six amendments were to

[1] *Ibid.*, cols 896–8. [2] 303 H.L. Deb., cols 519–20. [3] *Ibid.*, col. 533.
[4] *Ibid.*, cols 9–10. [5] *Ibid.*, col. 35. [6] 300 H.L. Deb., cols 1132–4.
[7] 304 H.L. Deb., cols 605–6.
[8] 304 H.L. Deb., cols 855–6, 331. He was given versions drafted by Parliamentary counsel.
[9] 299 H.L. Deb., cols 1221–5. [10] See above, p. 218.

correct printing and drafting errors, or were purely technical;[1] two substituted 'worker' for 'person' in clause 9;[2] another required regulations under clause 145 to be laid in draft and approved by resolution;[3] another removed the requirement that the Chief Registrar be a lawyer;[4] two required that the offence of making a false statement in connection with the notification of procedure agreements should be punishable only if it was false 'in a material particular';[5] another gave a right of legal or other representation before an industrial tribunal, a provision which the Government had intended to include in regulations.[6] Five of these eighteen amendments were of greater significance. Three made an important amendment for the protection of freelance unions (such as the Writers' Guild, the Musicians Union, the ACTT and the National Union of Journalists) in relation to negotiations.[7] Lord Brown moved an amendment to modify a condition about which the Industrial Court had to be satisfied before designating a procedure agreement in relation to dismissals. This condition was that the procedures provided included a right to arbitration or adjudication by an independent body in appropriate cases. The amendment was to delete 'appropriate cases' and to insert 'in cases where (by reason of an equality of votes or for any other reason) a decision cannot otherwise be reached'. The intention of the amendment was to help the solution of problems at a lower level and to put a 'small hurdle' in the way of those seeking to use the services of the external independent body.[8]

Finally, Lord Hoy moved an amendment to clause 5(1)(a) of the Industrial Relations Bill which as introduced provided 'Every worker shall, as between himself and his employer have . . . the right, *if he so desires*, to be a member of such trade union as he may choose'. The amendment was to delete the words italicised by me. The issue of the closed shop raised by this clause was hotly debated in the Commons on an amendment to the same effect as Lord Hoy's;[9] there it was negatived. Now in the Lords it was accepted. While the effect of the deletion of those words may be negligible, the opponents of the bill considered that an important principle had been restated.[10]

Four of the remaining six amendments moved by Opposition peers in committee were to the Immigration Bill. One improved the language of the bill;[11] another removed an anomaly in relation to the period of residence before registration;[12] one resulted from the Government acceptance of a right of appeal in the case of family deportations;[13] and one ensured rights to legal representation for appellants generally.[14] To the Civil Aviation Bill,

[1] 318 H.L. Deb., cols 576–9, 579–80, 1315; 319, cols 197–9, 1069; 320, cols 288–9.
[2] 318 H.L. Deb., cols 687–8, 690. [3] 320 H.L. Deb., col. 372.
[4] 319 H.L. Deb., cols 593–4. [5] 319 H.L. Deb., cols 441–2.
[6] 320 H.L. Deb., cols 48–9. [7] 318 H.L. Deb., cols 786–9, 815.
[8] 318 H.L. Deb., cols 1510–13. [9] 810 H.C. Deb., cols 591–610.
[10] 318 H.L. Deb., cols 196–204. [11] 322 H.L. Deb., cols 1027–9.
[12] *Ibid.*, col. 813. [13] 323 H.L. Deb., cols 937–8.
[14] *Ibid.*, col. 951 (Hansard is defective in this column).

Lord Kennet moved an amendment which had the effect of empowering the Secretary of State to control noise and vibration in small as well as large airports.[1] And Lord Gardiner administered the *coup de grâce* to the Expiring Laws Continuance Bill.[2]

Six amendments were moved by Independent peers and agreed to. Five of these were to the Industrial Relations Bill. Three concerned the same drafting point[3] and two required regulations to be laid in draft and subject to affirmative procedure.[4] The sixth amendment was to the Immigration Bill to enable Christian Scientists to produce evidence other than a medical certificate. But this was an amendment to an amendment and the principal amendment was withdrawn.[5]

The five successful amendments moved by Government backbenchers were to the Immigration Bill and the Industrial Relations Bill. Three to the Immigration Bill were on the same point. The proposal was to substitute 'parent' for 'father' in relation to the right of abode to cover the case of a child born to a mother who had died momentarily before the child was born (as might be the case in a birth by Caesarian section). The Minister was inclined to pooh-pooh the idea because it was 'inconceivable' that a court would draw such fine distinctions. But that roused Lord Gardiner to support the amendment; 'If I may say so, as a result of a long life, I am always unhappy when people say it is inconceivable a court may do something. In my experience there is nothing a court could not conceivably do.' And the Minister gave way.[6] Lord Thorneycroft moved an amendment to the Industrial Relations Bill about arrangements for the ballot on an agency shop agreement.[7] The other amendment was a technical point of drafting.[8]

On report in 1970–71, forty-four non-Ministerial amendments were agreed to, of which thirty-five were moved by Opposition peers. Twenty-nine of these were to the Industrial Relations Bill. Of these, fifteen were moved by Lord Gardiner to insert 'knowingly' into such phrases as 'knowingly induce'.[9] A further ten were clarificatory or to correct drafting or printing errors or were purely consequential.[10] Four were of some substance. The first changed the general principles clause by leaving out 'and responsibly conducted' and inserting 'conducted on behalf of workers and employers and with due regard to the general interests of the community'.[11] The second concerned the clause dealing with dismissals in connection with a strike or other industrial action. As the bill stood,

[1] 323 H.L. Deb., cols 773–4. [2] 313 H.L. Deb., cols 781–5.

[3] 318 H.L. Deb., cols 472–3, 473, 1017. [4] 319 H.L. Deb., cols 1391–2, 1395.

[5] 322 H.L. Deb., cols 710–14. [6] 322 H.L. Deb., cols 1008–11.

[7] 318 H.L. Deb., cols 817–21. [8] 320 H.L. Deb., col. 465 (Amendment 290F).

[9] 321 H.L. Deb., cols 515–16, 534, 790–1, 957, 958; 322, cols 112, 153. On third reading Lord Drumalbyn said 'knowingly' had been inserted seventeen times but I cannot find the other two.

[10] 321 H.L. Deb., cols 1069–70, 1167; 322, cols 33–4, 79, 84, 84–5, 473–6, 499–506, 526–7, 563.

[11] 321 H.L. Deb., cols 159–68.

before an employee could establish his claim that he had been unfairly dismissed because he took part in a strike, he had to show that he was dismissed when others were not because he took part in the activities of his union. But a proviso still prevented him from establishing his claim if those activities consisted in taking part in the strikes after the strikes had begun. Lord Stow Hill moved to leave out the proviso as offending article 1 of an ILO recommendation of June 1971 and on its own demerits. The Lord Chancellor accepted this.[1] The third amendment concerned the general duty of employers to disclose information. The bill (clause 56) imposed this duty 'for the purposes of collective bargaining'. Lord Diamond proposed it should read 'all stages of collective bargaining' because different information might be needed at different stages of negotiation. The Government said this was their intention.[2] Fourthly, the Government accepted an amendment to delete clause 121 which empowered the Commission to initiate action.[3]

Of the other six amendments moved by Opposition Members, four were to the Highways Bill, 'inspired by the County Councils' Association', and concerned with the draining of highways.[4] One was a drafting amendment to the Misuse of Drugs Bill.[5] And one was the deletion of a paragraph in schedule 2 of the Oil in Navigable Waters Bill on the understanding that the Government would introduce a modified version on third reading.[6]

Nine amendments were successfully moved on report in 1970–71 by Independent peers. Seven of these were moved by Lord Crowther to the Fire Preventions Bill. The principal amendment on which all the others were dependent was a new clause replacing that in the bill on the powers of inspectors. In preparing this new clause Lord Crowther had had 'the benefit of the expertise and drafting skill of the officials of the Home Office'.[7] Essentially the changes introduced by the new clause were intended to protect the rights of individuals, to shift the balance 'between the extent and exercise of powers by officials in the interests of the public good and the rights of the individual to privacy and not to be intimidated by officials', as the Minister put it.[8] The Government accepted the new clause and the other amendments.[9] The other amendments moved by an Independent were to the Industrial Relations Bill; both were primarily clarificatory.[10]

As a footnote, one negatived amendment is worth mentioning. Revolts and rebellions by backbenchers in the House of Lords are not often given public demonstration. In 1968–69 and 1970–71, I know of only one instance on a Government bill where a Government backbencher divided the House on an amendment in the face of Ministerial disapproval. The

[1] *Ibid.*, cols 757–60. [2] 321 H.L. Deb., cols 1058–60.
[3] 322 H.L. Deb., cols 260–1. [4] 319 H.L. Deb., cols 735–6, 736–7, 744, 744–5.
[5] 316 H.L. Deb., cols 40–1.
[6] 315 H.L. Deb., cols 1196–200; 316 H.L. Deb., cols 181–2,
[7] 319 H.L. Deb., col. 299. [8] *Ibid.*, col. 318.
[9] *Ibid.*, cols 299–301, 306–20. [10] 321 H.L. Deb., cols 454–5, 682–4.

Earl of Cork and Orrery moved a group of amendments to the Immigration Bill on report to provide that while any Commonwealth citizen could apply for United Kingdom citizenship after 5 years' residence, a citizen of a reciprocal country could apply after 2 years' residence. And a reciprocal country was any Commonwealth country 'that takes from us more immigrants than we take from them'.[1] The amendment was negatived on a division by 118 votes to 21.[2]

7.3 GOVERNMENT AMENDMENTS MOVED IN THE HOUSE OF LORDS TO MEET POINTS RAISED, 1968–69 AND 1970–71

As in the Commons, Ministers give undertakings in the House of Lords during the course of debates that they will at least 'look again'; and they may thereafter introduce amendments or accept amendments moved by others.

In 1968–69, the Transport (London) Bill was very closely examined by Opposition peers. On six occasions in committee, the Minister promised to draft amendments for the report stage which would meet the purpose of the amendments.[3] On seven other occasions, he promised to look again.[4] The only other bill during that session which was comparable in treatment was the Children and Young Persons Bill where Ministers gave promises on six occasions to look again.[5] On report, on the Transport (London) Bill, the firm undertakings were honoured, with one notable exception[6] and other concessions were made.[7] So also on the Children and Young Persons Bill, several Government amendments were moved on report to meet points made in committee;[8] as also on the Mines and Quarries (Tips) Bill on two occasions.[9]

In 1970–71, the House of Lords dealt with a considerable number of Ministerial amendments put down on report to deal with points made in committee in the Lords. The Industrial Relations Bill and the Immigration Bill dominated the scene but other bills were also significantly amended. Ministerial amendments to meet points made in committee were agreed to on report on twenty-two occasions during the report stage on the Industrial Relations Bill. Of these, thirteen were matters of drafting or were clarificatory, or consequential or trivial.[10] Four introduced new clauses: new clause 112 on applications to Industrial Court for declarations with respect to collective agreements; new clause 136 on general restrictions

[1] 324 H.L. Deb., cols 264. [2] 324 H.L. Deb., cols 263–84.
[3] 304 H.L. Deb., cols 17–21, 28–30, 64–5, 69–70, 115, 116. This was a hybrid bill.
[4] *Ibid.*, cols 76–7, 77–9, 79–82, 91–2, 100–1, 101–2, 105.
[5] 303 H.L. Deb., cols 829–31, 834–8, 864–8, 872–80, 1115–25, 1152–8.
[6] See above, pp. 215–6.
[7] 304 H.L. Deb., cols 821, 827–8, 832–3, 833, 833–4, 847, 848, 848–9, 850–1, 851.
[8] *Ibid.*, cols 600–7, 612–14, 634–41.
[9] 299 H.L. Deb., cols 767–8, 803–8, 1027–8, 1028–30.
[10] 321 H.L. Deb., cols 486, 551–3, 713–18, 919–20, 946–7; 322, cols 78–9, 109, 177, 230, 303, 325–7, 542, 544–5.

on the jurisdiction of the Industrial Court; new clause 156 on the winding up of trade unions, employers' associations and certain other organisations; and new clause 160 on the review of ballot taken under Part II or III of the bill.[1] A new section on time limits for complaints under sections 101 and 102 was added to schedule 3.[2] Other amendments of substance were the requirement to publish the advice given by the Commission in relation to the draft code of practice;[3] an additional provision defining discrimination by employers against workers;[4] a provision permitting an automatic deduction of the appropriate contribution from wages or salaries of non-union members in agency shop situations;[5] and a provision to make 'absolutely clear' that the onus of proof on the reason for dismissal rests 'fairly and squarely' on the employer.[6]

To the Immigration Bill, Ministers tabled amendments on report to meet committee points on five occasions. Of these the most important was a group which provided that a citizen of an independent Commonwealth country who was patrial because his mother was born in the United Kingdom was entitled to be registered as a citizen of the United Kingdom and Colonies on completion of 5 years' residence.[7] On the clause providing for the payment of expenses for those who wished to leave the United Kingdom a provision was added to make clear that this concerned only those who wished to leave voluntarily.[8] Another amendment provided that a Commonwealth or Irish citizen ordinarily resident in the United Kingdom was exempt from deportation if he had been continuously resident for the preceding five years.[9] The other amendments were of much less importance.[10]

To the Civil Aviation Bill a number of amendments were made to meet points made in public bill committee.[11] Nine amendments (of which four were consequential) were made to the Misuse of Drugs Bill in response to committee points – and often in response to pressure from the expert opinion of Lady Wootton.[12] So were five of the six amendments moved on the third reading of the Oil in Navigable Waters Bill;[13] and six amendments to the Fire Precautions Bill on report.[14]

[1] 322 H.L. Deb., cols 224–9, 330, 483–5, 527–31; the new clause numbers are those of the sections as they appear in the Act.

[2] *Ibid.*, cols 297–303. [3] 321 H.L. Deb., col. 237. [4] *Ibid.*, cols 274–6.

[5] *Ibid.*, cols 293–8. [6] *Ibid.*, cols 744–6. [7] 324 H.L. Deb., cols 709–11.

[8] 324 H.L. Deb., cols 407–8. [9] *Ibid.*, cols 381–2. [10] *Ibid.*, cols 402–4, 412.

[11] 323 H.L. Deb., cols 765–7, 767–70, 777–83, 785–6; for public bill committees see below, p. 226 *et seq*.

[12] 316 H.L. Deb., cols 14–23, 39.

[13] *Ibid.*, cols 177–82. In committee on this bill, the Minister moved a new clause to empower the Government to destroy vessels in certain circumstances outside territorial waters. This amendment would probably have been inadmissible in the Commons as being beyond the scope of the bill. But the rule about admissibility is less strict in the Lords (see 315 H.L. Deb., cols 47–58). Compare introduction (in the Lords) by Government into Immigration Appeals Bill 1968–69 of new clause requiring dependants to have entry certificates (301 H.L. Deb., cols 1098–142).

[14] 319 H.L. Deb., cols 301–5.

All these Government amendments dealt with matters raised in committee in the Lords. Far less frequent was the making of amendments to meet points made in the Commons. When the Children and Young Persons Bill 1968–69 was considered on report in the Lords, a group of amendments was moved to provide that a person who ceased to maintain foster children temporarily but expected to receive them back within 27 days would not be required to notify the local authority of this temporary absence unless he abandoned his intention to have the children back within that period or the period expired before the children came back. This was to meet an Opposition point raised in committee in the Commons.[1] On report in the Commons on the Housing (Scotland) Bill 1968–69, the Minister had promised to look again at the drafting of clause 50(3). This concerned the right of an applicant for a qualification certificate to appeal, if refused, to the sheriff. The amendment was to make clear that the sheriff would take into account any change in the state of the dwelling since the refusal. And the same applied where the tenant was appealing against the issue of a certificate.[2] An important amendment to the Immigration Appeals Bill 1968–69 originated in a speech made by an Opposition Member on second reading in the Commons. Where the disclosure of matters relevant to an appeal would be contrary to the interests of national security or might reveal methods of detection of forged documents, it was provided that those matters might be presented privately to the adjudicator or Tribunal and in the absence of the appellant and others.[3] An important if remote point for candidates, affecting their expenses, at elections where the poll is countermanded or abandoned because of the death of a candidate was dealt with in the Lords after being first raised in the Commons on the Representation of the People Bill 1968–69.[4] Also important to a small group of people affected by the Transport (London) Bill 1968–69 was a provision to allay fears expressed both in committee and on report in the Commons that local authorities' powers of inspection of the records which car park licensees were required to keep could be used to examine operators' general profit and loss accounts which they might be keeping for their own private business purposes.[5]

And, of course, the House of Lords is useful to meet late representations from outside interests affected by the legislation. Thus children's officers were responsible for late amendment to the Children and Young Persons Bill 1968–69 enabling a court to make an order to protect other children in a household where one child has been ill-treated.[6] And amendments were made on the third reading of the same bill at the instance of the Justices' Clerks Society.[7] Scottish local authority associations were behind the making of an amendment to the procedure for the calculation and application of the representative rate of interest on which Government subsidy under section 2 of the Housing (Financial Provisions) (Scotland)

[1] 304 H.L. Deb., cols 1028–9. [2] *Ibid.*, cols 134–5.
[3] 301 H.L. Deb., cols 1059–64. [4] 299 H.L. Deb., cols 238–41.
[5] 304 H.L. Deb., cols 61–2. [6] *Ibid.*, cols 588–92. [7] *Ibid.*, cols 1218–19.

Act 1968 was based. The change in the meaning of 'financial year' for this purpose was made in the Housing (Scotland) Bill 1968–69.[1] The Greater London Council and other local authorities, in the Vehicle and Driving Licences Bill 1968–69, obtained a definition of the phrase 'keeping a vehicle on a public road' to reverse an interpretation put on those words by the courts'[2] But these are examples only of the continuous pressure by outside bodies, both public and private, to obtain changes in legislation.

7.4 PUBLIC BILL COMMITTEES

The earlier history of the use by the House of Lords of committees for the examination of bills off the floor of the House has been recounted by Borthwick.[3] The idea was revived in the mid-sixties but not favoured by the Select Committee on Procedure because of the difficulty of obtaining party political balance and of persuading peers to attend. The idea, said the select committee, 'would be likely to meet the same fate as the unsuccessful experiment of 1889–1910'.[4] However, the Gaming Bill 1967–68 was so committed and adjudged by the select committee to have been a success.[5] In 1968–69, the Development of Tourism Bill, and in 1970–71 the Civil Aviation and Highways Bills were sent to public bill committees.

Public bill committees consist of the chairman of committees (or one of the deputy chairmen) and about twelve peers. The procedure is required to be, so far as possible, that of a committee of the whole House, with the same degree of formality. Bills which go to public bill committees are recommitted to the whole House and the bill before the committee of the whole House is the bill as reported from the public bill committee.

Table 7.5 summarises the amendments moved, and their fate, in the three bills recently committed.

The number of non-Ministerial amendments agreed to (fifteen) is 21·1 per cent of those moved (seventy-one) which is a high proportion. Six of these were agreed to on divisions and represent Government defeats.[6]

Standing Orders provide that a peer who is not a member of a committee may attend and speak but not vote.[7] Thirty-six peers used this right during the ten sittings on these three bills and attended once or more; nine of them moved a total of seventeen amendments including two moved on behalf of Ministers.

The present use of public bill committees can hardly be acclaimed as dramatic. Because of the Lords' practice of giving detailed consideration

[1] *Ibid.*, cols 135–8. [2] 300 H.L. Deb., cols 1041–2.

[3] Borthwick, R L., 'An early experiment with standing committees in the House of Lords', 25 *Parliamentary Affairs*, p. 80 (1971–72).

[4] H.L. (17) of 1965–66.

[5] H.L. (67) of 1968–69; see also H.L. (131) of 1970–71.

[6] Four of these defeats were on the Development of Tourism Bill where also the Government were defeated once on Clause stand part. The other two defeats were on amendments to the Civil Aviation Bill.

[7] S.O. No. 62.

Table 7.5 AMENDMENTS MOVED IN PUBLIC BILL COMMITTEES 1968–69, 1970–71

Bill	Moved by Ministers				Moved by Government backbenchers				Moved by Independent Peers				Moved by Opposition Peers				Total			Grand total
	Total	W	N	A	Total	W	N	A	Total	W	N	A	Total	W	N	A	W	N	A	
Development of Tourism 1968–69	—	—	—	—	—	—	—	—	4	1	3	—	31	22	3	6	23	6	6	35
Civil Aviation 1970–71	19	—	—	19	6	4	—	2	3	3	—	—	11	5	5	1	12	5	22	39
Highways 1970–71	19	—	—	19	11	8	—	3	—	—	—	—	5	2	—	3	10	—	25	35
Total	38	—	—	38	17	12	—	5	7	4	3	—	47	29	8	10	45	11	53	109

only to relatively few bills, shortage of time on the floor of the House is not a crucial factor. And so there is little pressure to debate bills outside the chamber. A chief whip in the Lords who was persuaded of the merits of such debate could no doubt divert more bills into these committees. But it is not obvious why he should be so persuaded. Almost certainly more total time is expended on bills sent to public bill committees and then re-committed to the whole House than would be expended if those same bills were committed directly to the whole House. Perhaps the extra time is often well spent. But to be well spent, the Minister in charge of the bill in public bill committee must be competent in the task and this means that he probably should be a former Member of the House of Commons. Simply on the internal evidence provided by the debates on these three bills, Lord Sandford made a success of the experiment whereas Lord Brown showed far less Parliamentary skill.

7.5 CONCLUSION

In seeking to assess the impact of the Second Chamber on Government bills first introduced in the House of Commons, it is important to re-emphasise that much of that legislation goes through on the nod. Table 7.6 shows the total length of time these bills were considered in committee of the whole House, on report and on third reading. The figures therefore exclude the proceedings in the joint committee on consolidation bills and the proceedings in public bill committees.

Table 7.6

	Number of bills*		
Time spent, hr	1968–69	1970–71	Total
Less than 1	9	9	18
1–2	2	6	8
2–3	3	1	4
3–4	2	2	4
4–5	1	—	1
5–6	1	1	2
6–7	1	—	1
7–8	2	—	2
8–9	1	1	2
9–10	—	1	1
11–12	1	—	1
15–16	1	—	1
More than 16	—	2	2
Total	24	23	47

* In 1968–69 one bill, and in 1970–71 three bills, were not debated in committee but were debated on third reading.

In 1970–71, 'more than 16' hours conceals more than it reveals. These two bills were the Industrial Relations Bill which was considered for 219¼ hours, and the Immigration Bill which was considered for 46¾ hours. As the total number of hours for which Government bills originating in the Commons were considered in the Lords in 1970–71 was 312, these two bills accounted for 85·3 per cent of the whole. In 1968–69, the total number of hours was 81¾.

The table shows that in 1968–69 nearly half of the bills were, apart from the second reading debates, considered for not more than 2 hours; and that in 1970–71, the proportion was more than half. Only ten bills out of forty-seven were considered for more than 6 hours.

The House of Lords is commonly spoken of as a revising chamber but three different kinds of activity lie within that phrase. Simply in terms of the quantity of amending material inserted in bills in the Lords, by far the greatest part of this revision is tidying up, that is, making changes of drafting and technical changes. When the Minister was moving the third reading of the Children and Young Persons Bill 1968–69 she said of the fifty-eight Government amendments that only three were of substance and they modified amendments made in committee and on report; the remainder were drafting and technical amendments. And she disposed of all fifty-eight in 49 minutes.[1] There were seventy-five Government amendments to the Post Office Bill 1968–69 in committee and of these sixty-seven were dealt with in about 38 minutes.[2] Of the twenty Government amendments to the Sea Fisheries Bill 1968–69 in committee (there were no other amendments tabled) only one had substance.[3]

But secondly, as will have been seen, the Lords also engage in genuine amendment where the changes made are not trivial. Amongst the important amendments were those made to the Industrial Relations Bill 1970–71 about freelance unions, about the closed shop, about the ILO recommendation; and also the four new clauses to this bill.

Undoubtedly in these two sessions the greatest impact made on the Government by the House of Lords was on the Immigration Bill 1970–71. In moving that the bill do now pass,[4] Lord Windlesham, the Minister in charge of the bill in the Lords, listed the more important amendments made in that House. He referred amongst others to the amendment on clause 1, made on the initiative of Lord Wade, making clearer the safeguards for existing residents (including rights of entry for the wives and children of Commonwealth citizens) who were already settled in the United Kingdom before the bill came into force; to the amendment on clause 2 making the acquisition of patriality easier for the citizen of the United Kingdom and Colonies; to the amendment of clause 7, on the initiative of Lord Brockway safeguarding certain existing residents from possible deportation; to the introduction of full rights of appeal in family deportation cases; to the

[1] 304 H.L. Deb., cols 1213–32.
[2] 303 H.L. Deb., cols 55–72.
[3] 298 H.L. Deb., cols 654–61.
[4] 324 H.L. Deb., cols 434–5.

amendment on clause 22, on the initiative of Lord Gardiner, so that appellants in statutory immigration appeals should have the right to be represented legally; to the amendment on clause 29 making explicit that any use of the powers to contribute towards the expenses of those who wished to return elsewhere would be conditional on its being demonstrated that it was in that person's interests to leave the United Kingdom and that he wished to do so. This influence on the Government is shown in the statistics of amendments agreed to.[1] In committee, twenty-eight amendments were agreed to, nineteen of which were moved by Ministers. On report, forty amendments were agreed to, all moved by Ministers.

Lord Windlesham's list did not include what many regarded as perhaps the most important concession of all. As first drafted the bill empowered immigration officers to require Commonwealth citizens, as well as aliens, to register with the police on arrival. This was strongly objected to both inside and outside Parliament. In committee in the Lords, the Minister, bowing to pressure from, amongst others, Lord Boyd (a former Conservative Secretary of State for the Colonies) and Lord Perth (a former Conservative Minister of State in the Colonial Office) assured the House that the Government would consider the matter 'very carefully indeed'.[2] On report, the Minister announced that police registration was not to be extended to Commonwealth citizens.[3] This change was to be made in the immigration rules so the bill remained unamended.

These changes to the Immigration Bill persuaded even Lord Brockway, who must be accounted a reluctant peer, to say that he was 'inclined now to think that we need a revising body independent of another place.'[4] His view was perhaps, in the context, more impressive than that of Lord Drumalbyn who thought that the proceedings in the Lords on the Industrial Relations Bill 'illustrated in striking colours the importance of a Revising Chamber'.[5]

Thirdly, the House of Lords gives the opportunity for new material to be introduced although there is clearly a danger to representative government if this is taken too far. Amendment 88G to the Industrial Relations Bill 1970–71 was first introduced by the Government in the House of Lords and provided that the Industrial Court should not be bound by the ordinary rules of evidence. It was welcomed by Lord Stow Hill.[6] It might perhaps have been scrutinised more closely, unless it had fallen under the guillotine, had it been before the Commons earlier.[7]

A similar value which the existence of a Second Chamber gives is that of time. If campaigns are to be mounted, they need time and many will not be altered until provisions appear in bills presented to the Commons. One striking example of this value was seen in the campaign to persuade the

[1] See Appendix 3. [2] 322 H.L. Deb., col. 1104. [3] 324 H.L. Deb., col. 289
[4] *Ibid.*, col. 449. [5] 322 H.L. Deb., col. 932. [6] 322 H.L. Deb., col. 265–8.
[7] But perhaps not. It was put forward as helping to make the Court 'a plain man's court' with 'discretionary' powers and much 'informality' and 'flexibility' and such words have great persuasive force.

Government not to require Commonwealth immigrants to register with the police. And the House of Lords was a valuable forum for this at an opportune time. The debate in the Lords on this question also exemplified well how difficult it is for Governments to withstand a heavy weight of opinion expressed by senior statesmen having direct Ministerial experience, especially if they belong to the party in office.

In committee of the House of Commons, Government backbenchers and Opposition Members moved 1788 amendments in 1968–69 and 1970–71 and of these 107 were agreed to – a success rate of 6·0 per cent. On report, 309 such amendments were moved and twenty were agreed to – a success rate of 5·1 per cent.[1] The comparable success rates, as we have seen, for the House of Lords were 12·3 and 19·3 per cent.[2] When all allowance has been made for the dangers of using such statistics, the difference is not only considerable but also confirms the impression given by reading the debates in the Lords: that Ministers in the Lords are more willing to accept amendments than they are in the Commons. Partly this may be because the details of a House of Commons Bill are much more settled and firm by the time it arrives in committee in the Lords so that the effect of amendments can be more clearly seen. But partly it may be because the less contentious, less partisan, atmosphere in the Lords makes amendments moved by those who are not Ministers more likely to be accepted.

In one respect, the House of Lords seems to play in practice a much less important role than is supposed. I mean the function of the Lords as a chamber for implementing undertakings given in the Commons. This happened, in these two sessions, only rarely.[3]

Finally, because it should have a paragraph to itself, it is necessary not to forget the rôle of the House of Lords in defeating the House of Commons (Re-distribution of Seats) (No. 2) Bill 1968–69. From time to time the Lords rise in their Conservative anger and strike Labour Governments on party political issues. Whatever the merits or demerits of that bill, the advantage to a Conservative Opposition in the Commons of having a final weapon is obvious.[4]

A case can always be made out for a second, third or fourth look at any proposal, whether legislative or other. And it is no part of my present task to argue the case for unicameral or bicameral legislatures. What is clear is that, with pressures as they are and with the House of Commons and Government Departments functioning as they do, legislation sometimes leave the Commons in a state unfit to be let loose on the public. Some kind of reviewing is necessary. And the House of Lords is presently the best reviewing body we have.

[1] See above, pp. 93, 159.

[2] See above, pp. 209, 212. These are for House of Commons bills only and exclude amendments in public bill committees. [3] See above, p. 225.

[4] In the opposite direction, Baroness Bacon successfully moved an amendment to the Local Government Bill 1971–72 to move the urban district of Rothwell from the metropolitan district of Wakefield to the metropolitan district of Leeds, against the Government's wish and vote (335 H.L. Deb., cols 1603–14).

CHAPTER EIGHT

PARLIAMENTARY SCRUTINY OF GOVERNMENT BILLS

If the debates and proceedings on a Government bill as it passed through the Houses of Parliament had one purpose, it would be easier to answer questions about the efficiency of the process. But this is not so. And criticism of a part of the process on the ground that it badly serves one purpose may miss the point that it has evolved to serve another.

Three principal purposes are achieved by the scrutiny. The first is the examination of the bill and its amendment. The second is the examination of the Minister in charge of the bill and of his departmental colleagues. The third is the examination of the Government and of its policies both as reflected in the bill and more generally.

The nature and extent of the examination and amendment of the bill have been considered in detail in the preceding pages of this book. And we shall consider below how far the process is defective and could be improved. The examination of Ministers and of Governments needs more emphasis.

One of the most important aspects of Parliamentary democracy in the United Kingdom, and certainly one of the most valuable, is the extent to which Ministers are subjected to scrutiny. To say that a Minister is a first-class administrator but a poor House of Commons man is to say, with very few exceptions, that he is not likely to attain high Ministerial rank or even perhaps to remain a Minister for long. One does not have to have been a Minister or even a Member of Parliament to realise that both the floor of the House and the Committee rooms upstairs are uncomfortable places to be under attack especially for Ministers who cannot properly defend themselves. And the Minister who is in charge of a bill which is either complex or controversial (and some are both) is subjected to an examination of his ability which is likely to be intense and thorough. This does not mean that Ministers are unable to slide past difficult questions. Only that if the procedure were such that that were impossible, their examination would be even stricter.

On the floor of the House, in committee, the size of the chamber and the large number of empty seats protect the Minister to some extent. The proceedings look and seem remote and the atmosphere is inevitably more relaxed. But upstairs, especially in the smaller committee rooms, the Minister is face to face with his critics at close range. And on a bill of some importance, the Minister will be physically present, with little relief, for 20 or 40 or 60 hours in all and sometimes, during evening sittings, for many hours at one stretch. However adequate his brief, however helpful the civil servants who are within reach, he must seek to remain alert and intelligent. And those who face him on the Opposition benches will have a general understanding of the subject matter of the bill probably as great, and quite possibly greater, especially if they were recently in office, as himself. If he is a senior Minister he will have learnt the trick of handling a committee, of defending himself, of not losing his head, of presenting a knowledgeable appearance even when his brief and his own experience suddenly seem insufficient. But even then he will be under pressure. If he is less experienced he will be tried in the fires. Reputations are frequently made and lost in standing committee. Many Ministers have become so because they have shown themselves expert in the much easier task of leading for the Opposition there. And many junior Ministers have been promoted or have sunk, leaving only an oily mark on the surface, because of their performance in standing committee. For the purpose of putting Ministers through the hoop, although there are (as I shall seek to show) changes that would make the gymnastics even more testing, the present procedures are undoubtedly effective.

The same exercise that examines Ministers and forces them in public to defend themselves and their bills, also enables the Opposition to attack the Government itself. But for this function committees – certainly standing committees – are not very effective. Governments suffer from attacks to the extent that these are made public. If a Member vividly and with accuracy castigates a Minister in the House itself, especially on a big occasion, publicity will follow. If a Government blunders and is exposed in the House, the press will carry the news to the electorate. But as the press rarely reports the proceedings of standing committees the most brilliant and critical speech will gain immortality, along with the dullest, only in the pages of Committee Hansard. True, a committee member may send his marked copy to his constituency newspaper. And that newspaper may reproduce excerpts from the Member's speech. True also, particular groups who have persuaded the Member to try his best to change the bill in their interests will wish to know how he has done his job. And the views of both of these groups of readers may affect the reputation of the Government. But this is remote stuff.

Committee proceedings on bills on important social issues, then, partake of challenges to the Government's fundamental attitudes. They are not concerned primarily to improve the bill or even, in ordinary language, to examine it. The debates on the Immigration Bill 1970–71, for example, in committee resembled debates on a white paper on immigration policy far more than they resembled standing committees debates on an important administrative measure. On the other hand committees on specialised or technical bills are often less effective because the purpose of the occasion, that is the detailed examination of the bill in an attempt to extract small concessions from the Minister, is ill-served by the formal antagonistic procedure.

In addition to the three principal purposes which the legislative process achieves – examining bills, examining Ministers, and providing a forum for policy debates – there are others of less importance. These include the representation of the interests of outside groups (who will also be in direct contact with the Department but using Members as additional pressures on the Minister); the informing of public opinion, partly, for those particularly concerned, by the publishing of the proceedings in committee and elsewhere, and partly by the mere holding of debates which, through the press and other media, remind the interested public that the matter has now reached this stage; and with information goes the education of that part of the public who are concerned but not so knowledgeable as the organised groups.

The achievement of the three principal purposes is less complete than it could be because of two major weaknesses. These are, first, the inadequacy of the information made available to those who are not Minister; secondly, and partly as a consequence of the first, the superficiality of the examination.

8.1 INADEQUACY OF INFORMATION

A bill represents some part of Government policy which will be well known or not depending on the importance of the subject matter. Generally, the more important the bill, the better known it will be because the longer and the more public will have been the preceding argument. Governments may sometimes, no doubt, launch into legislation in a situation that has taken them by surprise and their proposals may not sit easily with what their policy had been thought to be. The Commonwealth Immigrants Bill 1967–68 was not the obviously predictable Labour solution to that situation. Nor was the Rolls-Royce (Purchase) Bill 1970–71 what one would have guessed Mr Heath's Government to have supplied as a remedy to that state of affairs. But usually, in the main policy fields of housing, economic planning, defence, the health and welfare services and the rest, Government bills rarely, on publication, make the reader catch his breath with surprise.[1]

But although the policy may be well known, the detailed means adopted by the Government to effect it will not be, even if the bill has been preceded by a Government statement in the form of a white paper or otherwise. In the ordinary case, where there has been no preceding statement of detailed legislative intention, it would, I think, be natural to expect that the Government would begin the process by a full statement (long or short, depending on the complexity or otherwise of the bill) explaining

[1] The surprise at the European Communities Bill 1971–72 was over its form, not its substance.

what each clause of the bill was about and why that particular method had been adopted to arrive at the result sought after. Because only then could the examination of the bill proceed intelligently. What happens, however, is not like that at all. The Minister makes his first speech on second reading explaining the purpose of the bill in general terms and touching on a few of the more important clauses. And the Opposition replies either castigating the Government for bringing forward so unjust or unnecessary or ill-designed a measure, or more cautiously indicating that while in principle they have no objection to much of the bill there are parts they dislike and will seek to change; or simply welcoming the bill. Thence into committee.

On small, inoffensive or simple bills, this may be all that is needed. But on large, controversial or complex bills, the consequence of this almost total lack of specific information[1] (the explanatory and financial memorandum is on the level of a child's guide) is that only Ministers have any idea, at the beginning of the committee, what the details of the particular social, economic or political factors look like. The Housing Finance Bill 1971–72 is perhaps the best modern example despite the fact that it was preceded by a white paper. It was obvious that the Department had done many calculations on various hypotheses to arrive at the financial provisions in the bill. And indeed one such document fell into the hands of a Member of the Opposition. But the Government held its calculations close to its chest, occasionally releasing a quantity orally during debates. Mr Crosland protested in the early hours of 21 January 1972:

> 'When replying to our debates the Minister is sometimes hard to follow because he goes rapidly. At this time of night, on such a complicated subject, I did not find his argument altogether easy to follow. I am not saying that it was wrong. It is a commentary on how Governments, of either complexion, conduct affairs in the House of Commons that we are discussing at 4.45 a.m., an extremely intricate point affecting large numbers of people who are receiving supplementary benefit payments. I have not the faintest idea whether what the Minister said was satisfactory.'[2]

The point is not party political. There is no reason to believe that a Labour Government would have been more forthcoming in like circumstances. The system of secrecy is advantageous to all Governments and disadvantageous to all Opposition parties.

In March 1968, the Opposition protested during the debates on the Industrial Expansion Bill 1967–68: 'We cannot make speeches if we do not have the facts.'[3] And the Parliamentary Secretary replied:

[1] Many Members will have considerable knowledge of the subject matter of a bill but what is needed is a detailed spelling-out of the Government's intentions.

[2] Standing Committee E, col. 866.

[3] Standing Committee E, col. 380 (Mr Higgins).

'I appreciate the anxiety of hon. Gentlemen opposite to have the fullest facts relating to the position of Beagle and the Government's interest in it. I have endeavoured to set these out and the Government will endeavour to answer any questions that hon. Members may ask. However, I remind the Committee that if the giving of information leads, not to an objective appraisal of the economic and industrial prospects of the company but rather to an unseemly and irrelevant dog fight, then it is no encouragement to the Government – and this would apply to the Government of any party – to disclose fully the position regarding industrial activities in future.'[1]

An Opposition Member complained that the procedures of the House were 'thoroughly archaic when it comes to evaluating this sort of proposition'[2] and the argument continued.

But although the procedures of the House may be archaic, the real difficulty is deeper. It lies in the philosophy of government which is traditional in this country and which assumes that Governments will part with information only when it suits them or when they have no alternative or when their opponents manage to prise it from them by making the continued withholding less politically advantageous than its release. This arrogant philosophy was well exemplified by Dr Bray in the quotation above.

From time to time, Ministers do release information to committees in the form of circularised documents, and members always express their considerable gratitude in terms which suggest they are genuinely thankful rather than trying by irony to be provided with a proper service.

The point need not be laboured because all those who have had contact with Government will be familiar with this attitude, which I have perhaps glorified with the name of a philosophy, and will either approve or disapprove of it. Speaking of the Committee on National Expenditure during the war, Mr Woodburn has said that it

'found itself in trouble because people sent in information, which upset the Minister. However, it was able to save millions of man hours during the war by discovering and exposing waste. In the end, Sir John Anderson came along and said that no Civil Servants could give any information to the Committee unless the Minister authorised it and that rather put a stop to all the inside information the Committee received.'[3]

This need for more information and so more influence lies behind the present demand for pre-legislation committees. The Second Clerk Assistant described to the Select Committee on Procedure, comprehensively and at length, the story of select committees in relation to public bills.[4] He

[1] *Ibid.*, cols 380–1 (Dr Bray).

[2] *Ibid.*, cols 381–2 (Mr David Price) and see cols 398–9 (Mr Nott); the Minister expressed sympathy and later made available 'a short background note' (Mr Benn, cols 406, 426); and see, on report 762 H.C. Deb., cols 377–80.

[3] H.C. 410 of 1968–69, Q144.

[4] H.C. 538 of 1970–71, Appendix I, Part IV.

distinguished two ways in which a select committee might be used: first, to enquire into a public matter with a view to making recommendations on the scope of future legislation on that matter – known as a pre-legislation committee; secondly, to consider bills committed to a select committee after second reading.

Nineteen pre-legislation select committees of the House of Commons between 1900 and 1970 resulted in identifiable legislation[1] and twenty-two such committees did not. Of the nineteen, all except one were set up on a Government motion; seven were set up since 1945. Four of these seven concerned the armed forces (between 1951 and 1956); the other three were select committees on the House of Commons Members' Fund (1946–47), on the Rev J. G. Macmanaway's election (1950), and on obscene publications (1957–58). In addition a joint committee of both Houses on the censorship of stage plays in 1966–67 resulted in the Theatres Act 1968.[2]

The Select Committee on Procedure in 1966–67 considered there was considerable scope for the increased use of *ad hoc* Committees to consider the desirability of legislation in particular fields.[3] The then Leader of the House supported the idea when applied to the kind of social and moral questions often left to private Members' bills.[4] With this sort of bill, remote from the mainstream of Parliamentary legislation there might be relatively few problems. But the Select Committee tried to raise the level by saying:

> 'Although questions of party political controversy, subjects that have to be kept secret until legislation is introduced, and matters that need urgent Government action will usually be outside the scope of such Committees, matters of policy such as the Regional Employment Premium, and the rating system, are ones that could very usefully be canvassed before a Committee of Members.'

And they recommended the regular use in future of such committees.[5] They also expressed their belief that the House should be brought in at an earlier point in the legislative process so as to allow discussion by Parliament of subjects and details of potential legislation before the Government finally prepared a bill.[6]

In 1970–71 the Select Committee on Procedure also recommended that regular use should be made of such committees. They emphasised that 'the subject of the enquiry should be at the discretion of the Government and that the [pre-legislation] Select Committee would be considering specific matters which might subsequently form the basis for legislation'.[7] Further, the Select Committee on Procedure went on:

[1] *Ibid*, Annex G. The figures omit committees on tax matters.

[2] The resulting bill was introduced by a private Member, as was that for obscene publications.

[3] H.C. 539 of 1966–67, *Report* para 14. [4] *Ibid.*, Q251.

[5] *Ibid.*, para 14; and see Q24–8, 186, 198–202, 246A–58, 280–1, 286–304, 308–15.

[6] *Ibid.*, para 11. [7] H.C. 538 of 1970–71, *Report* para 8.

'If it was considered that certain matters of basic Party controversy would not be suitable for consideration by the Committee, they could nevertheless examine the less controversial aspects of a controversial proposal. . . . The appointment of these Committees need, therefore, not result in any delay in the legislative programme of the Government, since their work would be done before a draft Bill was in contemplation and perhaps one or two years before any legislation based on their report was introduced.'[1]

In talking of pre-legislation committees it is crucial to distinguish between types of legislative proposals. If we are considering the kinds of moral and social questions which are often the subject of Private Members' Bills, then the referral to an *ad hoc* committee of the House of such a question is feasible and indeed happens from time to time. A choice may have to be made between a Royal Commission, a departmental or other committee, one of the Law Commissions, and a select committee of the House. Such questions may be generally controversial but not on party lines; their resolution is not an immediate necessity and they do not, therefore, figure in any legislative programme present or future. Such a committee would report, with or without appending a draft bill, and the Government would decide whether or not to legislate. *Ad hoc* committees of this kind could also be used for other matters, not of a social or moral kind, which the department foresaw might have to be dealt with in a few years.

When, however, other types of legislation (including ordinary departmental administrative legislation in the major fields of policy) are considered, especially on matters which are controversial between the parties, *ad hoc* pre-legislation committees may be unworkable and even dangerous.[2] They are unworkable because it is impossible to see how they could be fitted in to the timetable which Governments have to adopt. We may assume that the discussions on what shall go into the legislative programme for 1972–73 proceed during 1971–72 and are effectively concluded by the summer or early autumn of 1972. There is little time between the making of these decisions and the second reading of the bills especially when the weeks of the summer recess have been extracted.[3] But in any event, what is to be put to the *ad hoc* committee? The whole question? a tentative Government answer to the whole question? a specific series of questions? Inevitably the matter is one on which the Government is in the process of making up its mind so that the Committee cannot deal with a concrete proposal. This leads on to the point of danger. For if the House of Commons on matters of Governmental policy allows itself to become

[1] H.C. 538 of 1970–71, *Report* para 8.

[2] A select committee on corporation tax which was not controversial between the parties worked well (H.C. 622 of 1970–71); but another on tax credit was less successful (H.C. 341 of 1972–73).

[3] Exceptionally a Government may make a firm announcement fairly early that legislation on a particular matter is to be introduced 'next session'.

involved, whether efficiently or inefficiently, in the process of policy formation at this level, its major Parliamentary role and function will be diminished. It is one thing, and wholly proper, for all non-Ministerial Members to seek to persuade the Government to take certain general courses of action and to abstain from others. And in this way to seek to affect policy. But it is another for Members to seek to be *directly* involved in the *immediate* policy-making process while it is embryonic. The danger of this latter activity is that it can easily blunt the edge of criticism. It is well known that Her Majesty's Opposition are often reluctant to be taken into the secret confidence of Government because this may inhibit them. Similarly, all non-Ministerial Members need to keep clear of collaboration with Government in the making of policy. If Members argue their views, publicly or privately, with Ministers in the hope of persuading Ministers to adopt a certain line, no danger arises. But if the involvement goes to the extent of reaching a compromise solution with Ministers, then criticism of that compromise becomes impossible.

All this is to say no more than that it is the function of Governments to govern and of other Members to scrutinise and to criticise or to applaud what Governments propose to do or have done.

Mr S. C. Silkin, in his evidence to the Select Committee on Procedure in 1970–71, took the opposing view in his proposals for the establishment of select committees with comprehensive powers and duties. He said:

> 'These Committees would operate, in conjunction with Ministers and civil servants, in a continuing process. They would examine the adequacy of existing legislative provision; initiate new legislation; guide its policy; supervise its translation into statutory provision; supervise consequential delegated legislation, directive and Ministerial circular and policy; review the workings of the legislation, including any necessary feed-back of judicial interpretation; and, where necessary, initiate new or amending legislation.'[1]

He accepted that this would involve 'a radical change from our present Parliamentary system.'

We have seen that the select committee emphasised that, under their proposals, 'the subject of the enquiry should be at the discretion of the Government' and that they recognised that controversial legislation or parts of such legislation might have to be excluded.[2] These two provisions would mean that matters referred to pre-legislation committees would not be from the central stream of Government legislation.

It would be a pity if arguments for devices like pre-legislation committees diverted attention from the need to make the present legislative procedures (which are highly unlikely to be replaced in the foreseeable future) more effective for the purpose of examining Government bills and from the

[1] H.C. 538 of 1970–71, p. 126. [2] See above, pp. 237–8.

need specifically to require Governments to provide more information relating to such bills so that criticism may be better directed.

The role of special committees also arises when the scrutiny of taxation is discussed. But first it is necessary to put the matter in its existing context.

Table 8.1 shows the time taken on Finance Bills in the 10 years from 1960–61.[1]

Table 8.1

Session	(1) Time spent in standing committee, hr	(2) Time spent in committee of whole House, hr	(3) Time spent on report, hr	(4) Total (2)+(3)	(5) Total (1)+(2)+(3)
1960–61	—	77	13	90	90
1961–62	—	62	20	82	82
1962–63	—	55¼	20	75¼	75¼
1963–64	—	33¾	8¼	42	42
1964–65 (1964)	—	28	5	33	33
No. 2 (1965)	—	156¼	38¼	194½	194½
1966–67 (1966)	—	98½	18½	117	117
No. 2 (1967)	—	51	3¼	54¼	54¼
1967–68	119¾	17¼	22	39¼	159
1968–69	46¼	29¼	26½	55¾	102
1969–70	—	15¾	¾	16½	16½
1970–71	47¾	26	22¼	48¼	96

In terms of the impact made by the debates on the bill, in three recent sessions, Table 8.2 relates.

With the exception of one defeat in standing committee in 1968–69,[2] all Ministerial amendments were agreed to. Of seventy-seven amendments moved by Government backbenchers, eight were agreed to. Of 363 Opposition amendments, fourteen were agreed to. These last two sets of figures represent 'success' rates of 1 in 9·6 and 1 in 25·9. The total number of amendments moved by Government backbenchers in committee and on report to all Government bills in those three sessions was 504 of which fifty were agreed to, a success rate of 1 in 10·1. For Opposition amendments the figures were 3773 and 160, a success rate of 1 in 23·6. The success rate on those Finance Bills was very similar to the overall rate. This is surprising for it would be easy to assume that the Finance Bill, above all others, was that on which the Government were least likely to feel able to meet the

[1] For 1960–61 to 1969–70 see H.C. 538 of 1970–71, Appendix 1, Annex C.
[2] See above, p. 93.

Table 8.2

	Number of amendments (including new clauses) moved to Finance Bill				Moved by Ministers			Moved by Government backbenchers			Moved by Opposition Members		
	By Min. (1)	By Govt BB (2)	By Opp. (3)	Total (1)–(3) (4)	W (5)	N (6)	A (7)	W (8)	N (9)	A (10)	W (11)	N (12)	A (13)
1967–68													
Standing Cttee	18	5	124	147	—	—	18	2	3	—	58	62	4
Recommitted to CWH	—	1	11	12	—	—	—	1	—	—	2	9	—
Report	25	—	20	45	—	—	25	—	—	—	5	13	2
Total	43	6	155	204	—	—	43	3	3	—	65	84	6
1968–69													
Standing Cttee	84	1	109	194	—	1	83	—	—	1	39	63	7
CWH	2	1	16	19	—	—	2	—	1	—	5	11	—
Report	53	—	28	81	—	—	53	—	—	—	8	19	1
Total	139	2	153	294	—	1	138	—	1	1	52	93	8
1970–71													
Standing Cttee	32	50	39	121	—	—	32	36	8	6	20	19	—
CWH	—	2	6	8	—	—	—	2	—	—	—	6	—
Report	32	17	10	59	—	—	32	12	4	1	3	7	—
Total	64	69	55	188	—	—	64	50	12	7	23	32	—
Grand total	246	77	363	686	—	1	245	53	16	8	140	209	14

proposals from its own backbenchers or from Opposition Members.[1] It is also sometimes said that the position of the two principal parties differs in that Conservatives are more likely to look for reductions in taxation and Labour members for imposing taxes for redistributive purposes and that as only the Government can initiate new taxation, Labour's opportunities when in Opposition to effect changes it thinks desirable are more limited. On this basis we would expect to see Conservative backbenchers at least more active and perhaps more successful under a Conservative Government than Labour backbenchers under a Labour Government. The figures tell us nothing significant about successes but there is a striking difference in activity as indicated by the moving of amendments. In 1967–68 and 1968–69, taken together, only eight amendments were moved by Labour backbenchers, whereas in 1970–71, Conservative backbenchers moved sixty-nine amendments to the Conservative Finance Bill. And, as a corollary, the Conservative Opposition moved 155 and 153 amendments in the first 2 years while the Labour Opposition moved only fifty-five amendments in 1970–71. Three sessions may, however, be too few to generalise from.

Special committees for financial (especially taxation) matters were considered by the Select Committee on Procedure in 1968–69 which made a report to the House on the scrutiny of public expenditure and administration but postponed the making of recommendations on taxation.[2] In 1969–70, the Select Committee took evidence (which they published) on the question but then Parliament was dissolved.[3] In 1970–71 the Select Committee published their views.[4] Their fourth recommendation was that sufficient members should be added to the Expenditure Committee[5] to form a sub-committee on taxation and finance. Their fifth was that the order of reference of the Expenditure Committee should be amended to include the consideration of the existing system of taxation, proposals for major changes in the structure of existing taxes and proposals for new forms of taxation; and the consideration of the economic implications of different forms of taxation.[6] Again in 1971–72, the Select Committee considered the question of taxation scrutiny[7] especially as the view (not necessarily final) of the Chief Secretary of the Treasury had been that the Government believed that a permanent taxation committee was inappropriate because it would inevitably become involved in political controversy into which officials were liable to be dragged. At that time – the Budget Debate in April 1971 – the Chief Secretary envisaged the

[1] Mr J. P. Mackintosh, MP, has said, rather obliquely, that 'it may be felt that the Commons has more control over or influence on taxation than on most other forms of legislation' and he finds the reasons for this belief in the inability of Governments to consult outside interests on tax proposals. See 'The House of Commons and Taxation', in 42 *Political Quarterly*, p. 75.

[2] H.C. 410 of 1968–69. [3] H.C. 123 and 302 of 1969–70.

[4] H.C. 276 of 1970–71. [5] Set up in January 1971 (see Cmnd. 4507).

[6] H.C. 276 of 1970–71, *Report* para 43(4)(5). [7] H.C. 449 of 1971–72.

possibility of an *ad hoc* select committee being set up to study the Green Paper on the corporation tax which had just been published.[1] This *ad hoc* committee was set up and the majority of their recommendations were embodied in the Finance Bill 1972.[2] At the same time the Chief Secretary said that as the Government were not willing to delay the abolition of selective employment tax and the introduction of value-added tax and so intended to introduce a bill soon after the start of the next session, there would be no time for a select committee to consider and report before the bill was prepared.[3]

With the support of the then chairman of the Expenditure Committee[4] who 'disagreed strongly' with the Chief Secretary's opinion that a taxation committee would 'inevitably' become involved in political controversy, the Select Committee of 1971–72 expressed its view that the case for a sub-committee or a select committee on tax had been firmly established and called for a debate.[5]

The disagreement between the Select Committee on Procedure and the Government in mid-1972 was between the committee's wish for a 'permanent' select committee or sub-committee and the Government's willingness to appoint *ad hoc* committees from time to time. The Chairman of the Expenditure Committee thought that 'particular *ad hoc* subjects of enquiry are almost like throwing the dog a bone'.[6] Mr Mackintosh clarified that Chairman's view of the function of the proposed committee when he asked: 'It would not be normal for a Select Committee to make a recommendation on a change of taxation. It would be laughed out of court, because it is the function of the House or of the Government to do this. But is it its function to find out the facts on which the House and the Government would take a stand?' And received the answer: 'That, as I see it, would be its chief value, of course – the detailed research work and the publication of it.'[7]

Two factors are common to the discussion about pre-legislation committees and about the scrutiny of taxation. The first is the question of timing and the second is the question of the limits of function. Budget secrecy makes impossible the reference to a select committee of immediate taxation proposals. But what can be put to a select committee are questions like those on corporation tax or the tax credit scheme. In other words, both for taxation and for other matters, what can be put forward in a Green Paper can be considered by a select committee. And without doubt, more Green Papers could be issued. The question of the function of the committee has two aspects. First, should it initiate enquiries into matters which might require legislation? There are precedents for doing so. The

[1] 815 H.C. Deb., cols 48–9, 52–4.

[2] The Chancellor of the Exchequer also announced in his Budget of 1972 that the Green Paper to be published on the Tax Credit Scheme would be referred to a Select Committee.

[3] 815 H.C. Deb., col. 51.

[4] H.C. 449 of 1971–72, *Report* paras 11, 12.

[5] *Ibid.*, Q11.

[6] *Ibid.*, Q14.

[7] Mr E. du Cann, now (1973) Chairman of the 1922 Committee.

difficulty might be that Ministers and departments, if not themselves presently seised of the matter, might not be greatly forthcoming with information. Certainly, if the committee were kept busy on matters referred to them by Ministers – and these were matters on which the Government's intention to contemplate legislation was genuine – they would be more usefully employed on these matters. Secondly, what should these committees be seeking to achieve? Primarily they should be seeking information. Possibly that is all they should be seeking. If they so limited themselves, the conflict and the dangers of confusing government with criticism of government would not arise. But the ammunition would be provided in readiness for the committee stage of the bill. But again, it must be repeated that, especially as it is unlikely that the pre-legislation committees would often consider more controversial legislation, this does not lessen the need for more departmental information to be given to Members and especially to members of standing committees on Government bills not referred to pre-legislation committees.

8.2 THE SUPERFICIALITY OF THE EXAMINATION

The procedure in standing committee and even more in committee of the whole House is much less efficient than it might be. The procedure enables the Minister too easily to slide past the questions put to him and this largely because the method of examination is essentially that of the chamber. Formal speech follows formal speech and really to penetrate the Minister's armour, to make him shift his ground, is made most difficult. This is not to say that Ministers and their supporters invariably stonewall. But that is their natural posture and all the analysis shows what every Parliamentarian knows so well, how, in the overwhelming mass of contentious issues (as distinct from those on which Members seek only assurances) the best that can be hoped for is the Minister's promise to look again. Mr Roy Jenkins has written of:

> 'one vital difference between speechmaking in Opposition and in Government. In Government most public presentation is of a defensive nature. This does not, of course, mean that it should be put forward apologetically. It means that a policy exists, that attacks and questions are made and asked around it. For a Government a drawn battle is in effect a victory. For the Opposition it is a defeat.'[1]

A different system might not produce a situation in which the Minister could come to a decision at the time when he is challenged. But a different system might enable members of the committee to pursue questions consistently, not by the exchange of formal speeches, but by genuine probing of the Minister's intentions and of the meaning of the bill's provisions.

[1] *The Observer*, p. 9 (20 June 1971).

To take one example of the weakness of procedure for the detailed examination of a bill. Typically a front-bench Opposition spokesman moves an amendment by which he hopes to discover what is the department's thinking on the particular matter. Another member of the committee on the same side makes a back-up speech in which he may or may not make additional points. The Minister replies. Further speeches follow from both sides in support of each. The Minister speaks again, followed by the mover of the amendment who may withdraw or press the amendment to a division. The first time the Minister speaks, he reads from his departmental brief which, if it is thorough, enables him to reply to the points made by the mover. The brief may or may not cover all or some of the other points. The brief will, let us assume, tell the Minister he should resist the amendment but that he could, if pressed, make a small concession, as indicated.

The Minister, when he comes to reply to the debate as a whole, may, and often does, totally ignore speakers' arguments because he has heard them before and had taken them into account when, with his advisers, he or they took their stand in relation to the amendment. To describe the scene thus is not to be critical except of the whole way of proceeding. What is done and what is not done follows the rules of the game that is played and understood.

Back-up speeches by Opposition backbenchers are important (though it often does not matter what they say) when a debate is deliberately made to run on so that the Minister, in order to make progress, promises to look again at the matter or makes a small concession. But that is as far as the Minister will or can go. Woe betide the Minister who gives undertakings or accepts amendments that are not set down in his brief. He may have to wear a white sheet on report.[1]

Now and again this description is a travesty of what takes place in committee. On important social issues, like race relations or immigration or housing, the atmosphere in committee may be lively, even intense. There the nature of the debates is different from that in the mass of committees where the tediousness of the proceedings is manifested in the attitude of members. For debates in those few committees are not directed primarily to the examination of the details of bills with a view to their understanding and improvement. The *method* is still that of the examination of this phrase and that, for that is dictated by the procedure which requires speeches to be made principally on particular amendments. But the examination is, in reality, of the principles that lie behind such legislation – which is why so many debates in such committees resemble the discussion on second reading.

A considerable amount of time is spent, especially in committee, on the making of speeches (mostly in support of front benches), which make little or no impact on the debate or on the bill and which (deliberate time-

[1] See, for example, above, p. 216.

wasting apart) often perform no function other than that of advancing or retarding the personal reputation of the speaker. This is a function of debate but it is one which must be kept within bounds. Speeches in the chamber to thirty or so Members, most of whom at least give the impression of not paying the keenest attention to what is being said, use the time of the House often to no discernible profit at all. And speeches in standing committee to one-third of that number are generally of even less value.

We have seen[1] the proportion that these back-up speeches bore to speeches made by front-bench spokesmen in committee of the House of Commons in 1967–68. Out of 9980 speeches, movers of amendments accounted for 2161. It would be generous to allow 2500 speeches as being replies from the principal spokesman on the other side of the committee for many amendments are accepted on the nod. That leaves over 5300 back-up speeches (of which about four-fifths were made by Opposition Members).

The front benches do not have a monopoly of wisdom or truth. And in any event a working democracy entails the right of elected representatives to speak irrespective of the value of what they say. Nevertheless, in an appreciable number of instances when one sits and listens to a committee of the House discussing a bill, one is forced to ask of some backbench speaker: 'Who is he talking to and why is he talking?' Sometimes satisfaction is expressed by speakers who have participated in what they call 'an interesting discussion' although it has not resulted and was not intended or expected to result in any consequence whatsoever.

The answer to the question posed in the last paragraph is sometimes said to be: 'He is talking to his own side. It is a morale-building exercise'. So perhaps it is but it also seems to include a great deal of pure rôle-playing for its own sake. The Member, being a Member and believing that this is what Members normally do, speaks; and speaks in a particular way and tone as preachers speak in a particular way and tone. It is a form of self-justification, *apologia pro vita sua*. The disease is no doubt one we all suffer from. But in the House of Commons it sometimes reaches epidemic, even epic, proportions and creates in committee rooms an atmosphere of boredom and a lack of interest which are crushing in their effect.

8.3 THE POSSIBILITIES FOR REFORM

The relationship between Governmental powers and the critical examination of those powers and of their exercise determines the nature of every constitution. In practice, the dangers of Governments being ineffective because of excessive critical opportunity are in modern industrial society not serious. Rather, Governments lean in the direction of tyranny and the need is to enlarge the area of criticism.

[1] See above, p. 40.

Nevertheless any proposal to enlarge that area within a system that already provides for critical opposition must satisfy two tests if it is to be considered: it must not make government ineffective, and it must be politically realistic.

Two reforms of the legislative process in Parliament are here suggested. They are both directed to making more information available and so to making the examination of bills, of Ministers, and of Governments more effective. Neither is, in its general provisions, novel. Both could be put into operation without unduly weakening the essential functioning of Governments. The first would require Governments to publish more information at an early stage in the Parliamentary process; the second would change the committee stage on bills. The first can be set out simply and shortly. The second requires much more elaboration.

8.3.1 *Documentary information*

I suggest that when a bill is first published, it should be accompanied by a document that would set out, in a general introduction, the history of the proposal and the need for the bill. The document would then deal clause by clause with the contents of the bill giving enough information to enable Members and other interested persons to understand the purpose of each clause and why (this being particularly important) the particular means used by the clause to achieve that purpose had been adopted. The document would also be accompanied by appendices setting out relevant statistical and other background material.

The purpose of this document – and this could be used as a yardstick to determine whether or not to include or exclude material – would be to ensure that Members and others were as well-informed as the Minister, no more and no less. The additional departmental work involved in producing such a document would be slight as the information needed would all be most easily and readily to hand in the process of building up the brief from which the Minister presently speaks. The size of the document would be determined by the size of the bill. I would expect that a bill of thirty clauses and schedules would require a document (with introduction and appendices) of about fifty to eighty pages.

8.3.2 *Committee and report stages*

Discussion about reform of the legislative process in the House of Commons centres on the committee and report stages. I have touched on the matter of second reading committees and on the abolition or otherwise of third reading debates. But neither of these is of much significance.

The detailed analysis and description of debates on Government bills during the three sessions 1967–68, 1968–69 and 1970–71, show the scale of the impact made by proceedings in the House of Commons and, to a lesser extent, in the House of Lords.

As we have seen, bills are so various in content and so varied in importance that in any instance, one or two of the three purposes of examination[1] is likely to predominate over the other or others. And the problem is how to devise systems which will enable these different functions to be fulfilled. There is a further difficulty: that although these three functions are broadly distinguishable, it is well nigh impossible to classify bills accordingly and so allot bills to different systems.

To the Select Committee on Procedure in 1970–71, Miss Norma Percy and I put forward a tentative proposal for a reform of the procedure in standing committee which envisaged a division of that stage into three parts.[2] The first part was to be a number of meetings of the whole committee which would debate a number of amendments tabled by the Opposition and selected by the Chairman as raising important matters of principle. The second part was to be a number of meetings where the number of members would be limited to three from each side; the proceedings were to be less formal than normal committee proceedings and would cover specific points on specific clauses; departmental advisers were to play a more direct rôle in the discussions. The third part was to be a further number of meetings of the whole committee for which Ministers and others could table amendments.

This proposal was designed to enable committees more flexibly to fulfil the first and second purposes, with the third purpose being fulfilled throughout. It was anticipated that on a more 'party political' bill, the first part would be lengthy while on a less controversial, more technical, bill the second part would predominate. There are two principal difficulties in this proposal. The first flows directly from it and is inevitable. It is that, to quote the Select Committee, 'backbenchers who wished to debate technical or detailed issues . . . would be excluded from such discussions at the second part of the proceedings'; and on this ground the Select Committee rejected the proposal.[3] The second difficulty is that of separating 'matters of principle' – the debate of which would be apt for the first part – and 'specific points on specific clauses' – which would be dealt with in the second part.

This second difficulty arises not primarily because of the inherent problem of deciding what is principled and what is specific (for the Opposition were to select the matters of principle) but because so often matters of principle emerge, often unexpectedly, from highly specific details. Furthermore, the first part as proposed would almost certainly develop into little more than a series of second reading debates which would be repetitious both of these debates and of themselves.

In considering reform of the legislative process it is necessary always to keep in mind the essential dimensions of the situation. I have shown above[4]

[1] I.e. the examination of bills, the examination of Ministers and the examination of Government policy, see above, p. 232 *et seq.*

[2] H.C. 538 of 1970–71, Appendix 9 para 39.

[3] *Ibid.*, *Report* para 26.

[4] See above, p. 15.

how many Government bills are dealt with quickly because they do not present any considerable problems. With all stages in the House of Commons included, only seventeen bills in 1967–68, fourteen bills in 1968–69 and sixteen bills in 1970–71 (out of a total for all three sessions of 183[1] bills) were debated for more than 20 hours. Some of the bills debated for between 20 and 30 hours in all are hardly entitled to be called major measures but even this sessional total of fourteen to seventeen bills is a small proportion of the total number and yet represents the most important part of the Government's legislative programme.

It is idle to expect Ministers voluntarily to change their ways, to cease being defensive, to become more generous in their supply of information, simply by demonstrating that backbenchers wish it so. There is a tradition of government to be, if not overcome, at least changed in direction.

One feasible alternative – feasible because already in existence in another form – is to subject the Minister and his bill to some adaptation of the select committee procedure. The idea of so doing is by no means new and, as we have seen,[2] has been applied to the legislative process in different ways in the past.

In 1970–71 the Second Clerk Assistant and the Clerk of Public Bills submitted to the Select Committee on Procedure a memorandum, already referred to, which in part considered select committees in relation to public bills.[3] I am here concerned only with the memorandum so far as it dealt with the submission of public bills to select commmittees after second reading, not with pre-legislation committees. The memorandum summarises the position thus:

'The procedure in a Select Committee to which a public bill has been committed after Second Reading differs according to whether a Bill is Hybrid or not. In the case of the majority of Bills which are not Hybrid, procedure follows a standard pattern. The Committees concerned are given power to send for persons, papers and records, and this power enables the Committee to take evidence on the Bill. When the evidence has been concluded the clauses of the Bill are considered. The rules which govern the admissibility of amendments are the same as those in a Committee of the whole House or a Standing Committee, but the Chairman does not have the power of selecting amendments nor of accepting closure. Proceedings on the Bill form part of the deliberations of the Committee and are not open to the public; nor are speeches for or against amendments recorded (as they are in Standing Committee) though the decision on each amendment is recorded in the minutes in the same manner as in Standing Committee Minutes. After the Committee have gone through the Bill, it is open to them to consider and agree to a special report informing the House of any matters in relation to the Bill,

[1] Excluding nine Consolidated Fund and Appropriation Bills.

[2] See above, p. 236 *et seq*.

[3] H.C. 538 of 1970–71, Appendix 1 paras 87–114.

to which it is thought the attention of the House should be drawn; in recent years it has been customary for Select Committees to make a special report of this nature, though there is no obligation upon them to do so.'[1]

It has not been the practice to refer to select committees bills which form the principal part of the Government's legislative programme. I wish to consider the feasibility of so doing. I assume that the major measures which are, for the reasons discussed above, usually sent to a committee of the whole House, would continue to be sent there. I assume the same for the minor measures which are similarly committed and indeed their number might well be increased. What I am therefore considering is the replacement of standing committee procedure (including that part of the Finance Bill usually so committed) by a new procedure.

Under this new procedure, the bills sent to select committee after second reading would be, in large or small part, controversial between the parties. The atmosphere would often be partisan and votes would need to be taken from time to time. The select committee would therefore need to be composed, as standing committees are at present, of members in numbers reflecting the party strengths in the House. The select committee would usually be composed of ten to twelve members.

I envisage the proceedings of this committee as falling into two distinct stages. In the first stage, its function would be to take evidence on the bill clause by clause. Throughout the bill the principal witnesses would be the Minister in charge of the bill, or a junior Minister deputising for him; the departmental advisers; and the draftsman of the bill. Ministers would not, therefore, at this stage, be members of the committee. Any member of the committee might ask questions of any witness and request the production of any document or of any other information. These powers would require controls to prevent abuse. It would be necessary for the chairman of the committee to act not as the chairman of a select committee normally acts (that is, as its leader), but as the chairman of a standing committee acts (that is, as a neutral). He would be empowered to refuse to allow questions to be put, as falling outside the scope of the clause under discussion or as being repetitious or as otherwise being out of order. He would also be empowered to refuse to put the request for the production of particular documents or the calling of particular witnesses on the ground of their prima facie irrelevance or the likelihood that they would merely duplicate other witnesses. Moreover the Minister (who, or whose deputy, would be entitled to be present throughout the proceedings), would be permitted to instruct any departmental adviser who gave evidence not to answer a particular question but to answer it himself or to refuse to do so.[2]

The select committee would have power to call for written or oral

[1] H.C. 538 of 1970–71, Appendix 1 para 89.

[2] For a discussion of these and other matters in another context see M. Rush, *Committees in the Canadian House of Commons*.

evidence from any other person or body; and any person or body might submit written evidence to the select committee.

The chairman would have power to accept or not to accept a closure motion to end discussion on a clause. In order to reduce the likelihood of one or two committee members taking an undue length of time in questioning a witness, the chairman would normally invite members alternately from the majority and minority members of the committee to put their questions. To prevent or limit obstruction, the guillotine would be available.

The proceedings would normally be open to the public and would be recorded in Committee Hansard, as would the documents and information submitted unless they were classified and the Minister requested that they be not published. No amendments would be moved at this stage of the proceedings. At the end of the first stage, the Minister might, if he thought fit, amend the bill and, if he did, the bill would be reprinted as amended, with a detailed explanatory memorandum on these amendments.

The second stage of the committee would be conducted by the same committee except that the Minister or Ministers would now be added members, an equal number of Opposition Members being added. Amendments might be tabled and the whole process would follow that of standing committees with the following modifications. The chairman's power to select amendments would be exercised more forcefully than at present and in particular he would be empowered not to select amendments that in his opinion were designed to probe matters already adequately probed during the first stage. So also where amendments were tabled which raised matters of principle already adequately discussed during the first stage, the chairman would have power either to select them for a division only, or to curtail discussion, much more strictly than at present, in particular by ruling that he would permit only two or three speeches (including the reply of the mover of the amendments) from each side of the committee. He might also need to use his power to accept closure motions more freely.

The justification for this increased control by the chairman at the second stage is, of course, that Opposition speakers in particular would already have had opportunities to raise with the Minister and his departmental advisers many of the questions that they would normally put in standing committee. The great majority of those amendments presently withdrawn because of the Minister's explanation or undertaking to look again would not need to be put again because the Minister would have answered those questions in that vein during the first stage; or because the Minister at this second stage would put forward amendments to meet the suggestions made, thus enabling this second stage in part to function as a report stage. Indeed it is obvious that since this proposal adds a new stage to the procedure, there would have to be closer control by the chairman of the committee on both stages to ensure that business was done within the available time. If this control were exercised it should be possible to ensure that the two stages together took no longer than the present single stage.

The principal saving in time would come from the reduction of the number of back-up speeches on both sides in the second stage. But this need not mean that backbenchers participated less than at present as their main opportunity would come during the first stage.

The committee stage on a bill has always to be thought of in connection with the report stage. Opinion is united that consideration of the bill on report, in some form or another, is essential where a bill has been amended in standing committee and usually desirable where it has been amended in committee of the whole House.

The main reform sought to be introduced has been that the consideration of a bill on report should be possible in committee – either the standing committee to which it had been sent for the committee stage or some differently composed committee. Such a scheme was proposed by the Clerk of the House in 1945–46,[1] and again in 1958–59[2] and was rejected on both occasions. On the third occasion, in 1966–67, the Select Committee on Procedure recommended that bills sent to second reading committees or to the Scottish Grand Committee might be considered on report by that same committee. This was adopted with the amendment that, instead of the second reading committee, the report committee should be a standing committee specially appointed; and the procedure could be blocked if twenty Members opposed it.[3]

This extremely modest experiment has been an almost total failure. Only one bill – the Water Resources Bill 1967–68 – has had its report stage taken in standing committee. Two reasons are usually given for the failure – they are also the reasons used to defeat the earlier proposals. One is the formal objection that not to take the report stage on the floor involves a departure from the principle that the whole House assumes responsibility for the details of legislation.[4] The other – or rather another version of the same – is that 'the House is jealous of its rights and feels that by giving things to a Committee it may be losing some of its rights to that Committee'.[5] Disregarding the anthropomorphic sentimentality, Members do no doubt feel that they would like to be able to intervene in some way on a bill, after or in addition to the opportunity on second reading.[6]

Mr Silkin also told the Select Committee on Procedure in 1970–71: 'the Report stage following a Standing Committee upstairs very rarely has anyone talking on it other than the original Members of the Committee. It is very noticeable. It does happen from time to time, perhaps with very controversial Bills, but it is not all that frequent'.[7] On the basis of a count made during one recent session, that statement is far too sweeping.

[1] H.C. 189 of 1945–46, *Report* para 11 (Sir Gilbert Campion).

[2] H.C. 92–I, *Report* para 10 (Sir Edward Fellowes).

[3] H.C. 539 of 1966–67, *Report* para 26; S.O. No. 73.

[4] H.C. 92–I of 1958–59, *Report* para 10.

[5] H.C. 538 of 1970–71, Q514 (Mr John Silkin).

[6] A more practical reason for the failure is that the bills which go to second reading committees are non-controversial and rarely need a report stage.

[7] See above, note 5.

For 1967–68 the figures were as shown in Table 8.3.

Table 8.3

Report stage	Backbenchers on standing committee	Backbenchers not on the standing committee	Total
Number of speeches made	690	419	1109
Percentage	62·2	37·8	100
Number of amendments moved	228	65	293
Percentage	77·8	22·2	100

While backbenchers on the committee are clearly more active than those not on the committee, the difference is not so considerable as Mr Silkin suggests.

The almost complete inability to use the standing order enabling bills sent to second reading committees to be considered on report in committee, and the significant participation in debates on report of those who were not committee members, make futile at the present time any further efforts to persuade Members to consider bills on report elsewhere than on the floor of the House. Moreover the arguments for the present practice are strong in themselves. There are those – like Mr Michael Foot and Mr Enoch Powell – who are always reluctant to allow debate to pass from the floor to committees, believing that the strength of the House as an institution lies in its function, in the old phrase, as the grand forum of the nation. Such apologists accept the necessity for legislative committees but consider every removal of debate from the floor as requiring clear and forceful justification. This view seems to me to be highly persuasive. If the House of Commons is not only to retain but to enlarge its scrutiny of Government bills then three things are necessary. The first is that that scrutiny shall be well-informed; the second is that it shall be detailed; and the third is that it shall be open to all Members not only on second reading but also when the Government has considered to what extent it should modify its legislative proposals in the light of the discussion in committee.[1] If the House allows its examination to be too fragmented, to be entrusted to a few people to the exclusion of the many, the scrutiny is likely over the years to diminish in effectiveness.

Minor reforms can be urged to the proceedings on report. That stage does suffer from being repetitious – though to some extent that is inherent in the idea of a delegate body giving an account of itself to its parent body; minor amendments could surely be listed and passed formally unless challenged; the Speaker could be made more accountable for his selection

[1] This also ensures greater publicity.

of amendments. But the general arguments for removing the report stage from the floor seem unconvincing.

8.4 CONCLUSION

The impulse behind movements for reform of the procedure of the House of Commons is to enable the House to perform its functions more efficiently. But what is 'efficient' for the Government may not appear 'efficient' to a Member of the Opposition. Lord Maybray-King told the Select Committee on Procedure in 1971:

> 'When you strive for greater efficiency, you are interfering with the right of an Opposition, which is to delay. To achieve a balance between the two is beyond anyone's comprehension. . . . Most of the delays that we complain about are the rightful delays of free people in a free society using the instruments that we fashioned for them (a) to get the business through swiftly (b) to get it through as unswiftly as possible.'[1]

When considering reform of the legislative process in the House of Commons, the purpose must be to improve the means whereby Members 'have ample opportunity of considering Bills in detail'[2] while still ensuring that Governments get their bills in the end. Many Members have concluded that debates in Parliament mean less than they did, perhaps because, as Mr Crossman has said, 'the real debate is taking place outside'.[3] Although he was not speaking of legislative committees, his next words are apposite and may be applied, without perversion, to the idea of select committees for bills:

> 'Here we come back to our whole procedural argument. I believe that we have consciously to revive the authority of Parliament. This is why I believe that you may well find that the debate and the discussion in specialist committee and the cross-examination of witnesses may in future be of greater interest and more central to the House than a normal staged debate on a Second Reading; and I have a great belief that that is because the specialist committee will be doing something of great importance, which is not done in a formal battledore and shuttlecock debate.'[4]

I have emphasised, as have others, the great need for more detailed information to be obtained by Members both by requiring Ministers to produce written detailed explanations of the bills they introduce and by subjecting Ministers and departmental advisers to questioning in select committees for legislation. There are many other sources of information which Members may, and often do, look to – including affected interests and the Universities. But it is detailed information about Ministerial aims and methods that is crucial.

[1] H.C. 538 of 1970–71, Q340, 345.
[2] *Ibid.*, Q234 (Sir David Renton).
[3] H.C. 539 of 1966–67, Q277.
[4] *Ibid.*

To achieve reforms of this kind is not easy and this for three associated reasons. First, there is a community of interest between Ministers and shadow Ministers not to favour reforms which will make more difficult the business of government. Secretiveness on the part of departments of state is not some traditional habit which only the conservatism of institutions perpetuates. It is deep in self-interest, for the less that is known the more difficult is the mounting of criticism. Secondly, there is the very strong hold that the Executive in this country exercises over the representative body. This is in part traditional but is even more the consequence of two-party politics and the anxiety of every Opposition to make the greatest party political capital out of every lapse or apparent lapse of the Government. This anxiety forces Government backbenchers into postures of support for the Government which they do not always feel or do not feel with the intensity they show. Thirdly, control by the party leadership is strong. The system of promotion from non-Ministerial Membership of the House to Ministerial office is dependent on the goodwill of the party leaders and in particular of the Prime Minister who also exercises many other forms of patronage. In the extreme case, the threat of the withdrawal of the whip has the almost certain consequence, if the withdrawal persists, of non-re-election. And the amount of effective alliance between backbenchers on opposite sides on matters which affect them in common as Members is very limited.

This dominance of the Executive is such that Members accept Ministerial decisions concerned not only with Government policy but with the procedures which Governments follow. Towards the end of 1970 the Select Committee on Procedure approached the Civil Service Department for views on a proposed study to be carried out on behalf of the Select Committee of a number of bills of the previous session. In particular, the study was intended to examine the extent to which and the ways in which Government had formal consultations with outside bodies during the earlier stages of the legislative process. This practice is well known to anyone, in or out of Parliament, who has studied the process but no systematic survey had been made of a number of bills in a session. The department refused the request for information on which the survey could be based. But even more remarkable than the fact of the refusal was its wording and its tone. The Parliamentary Secretary said that he and other Ministers considered the detailed study of the process of initiating legislation as described by the Select Committee as attaching far too much weight to formal consultations; that their experience, and that of the officials consulted, indicated that this was a much less important element than the Select Committee, '*no doubt because of incomplete information*',[1] seemed to have believed. He concluded by telling the Select Committee, which was composed of Members of Parliament of considerable political experience, that some bills originated in a political decision or an election manifesto;

[1] This is adding insult to injury with a vengeance.

or in the process of ordinary administration; or out of consultation with local authority associations; or were derived from white papers or other published reports.

The puerility of this Ministerial reply to the request of a select committee of the House of Commons reflects, in admittedly extreme fashion, the attitude too often shown by civil servants to elected representatives. The House of Commons in its attempts at reform which touch the governmental, rather than the Parliamentary, process is not infrequently treated with an indifference unthinkable in many other countries, not least the United States of America. And the Select Committee on Procedure in this case seems not to have reacted – at least not publicly – at all. Constitutionally, a select committee cannot compel a Minister or a Government department to produce documents unless the House passes a motion to that effect.[1] And the whips would no doubt be put on to prevent this happening. And the whip would be effective. So the wheel comes full circle.

If Members are to break out of this circle, they will have to break the habit not of their lifetime only but of the lifetime of their predecessors also. They will have to be willing, as backbenchers, to combine in their common interest and to force Governments by the pressure of their united opinion to adopt a much more open attitude, to be willing to give information which might be used against them. The cry for more open government is an old cry and the promises of political parties seeking election are old promises and are never fulfilled. Yet if 'the authority of Parliament' is to be revived and if, specifically, the full and detailed examination of the proposals of Governments is ever to be achieved, only backbench Members of Parliament can force the issue by requiring Governments to yield up, not their secrets, but their processes of thought and the documents which support, together with the documents which do not support, their conclusions. At present, there seems to be not the slightest possibility that this will happen.

The detailed analysis of the middle chapters of this book can be *said* to show that, despite the very great power which Governments exercise and despite the comprehensiveness of their control over the House of Commons, the impact of Parliament on Government bills is by no means negligible. And to this may be added the undoubted importance of the legislative process in giving publicity to the intentions of Governments, in forcing Ministers to defend their policies and themselves, and in other ways.

All this is true and yet it begs the most vital question of all: have Governments too much power, too much control over the House of Commons? Within the rules of the game as presently played, Governments do yield, are flexible. But they do so very largely on their own terms or, very rarely, when the opposition to some part of their proposals is strong and widespread.

[1] Erskine May, *op. cit.*, p. 632; and see H.C. 303 of 1964–65, Q136–43.

What must be criticised – how often is this said in how many contexts – is the excessive secrecy of Governments so that too often much of the information and many of the basic assumptions on which legislative proposals are based can be extracted (if at all) only by continuous and time-consuming pressure.

This secrecy is founded on a fear of effective criticism. And this is why the secrecy is dangerous. The danger is that the pressures of party loyalty and of party politics will increasingly reinforce and strengthen the position of Governments so that the machinery of Parliament and of the legislative process spins more and more smoothly to less and less effect.

APPENDICES

NOTES ON TABLES

1. The figures in these tables have had to be counted by turning the pages of the Official Report as neither the notices of amendments nor the minutes of committee proceedings yield the full information. The possibility of human error cannot therefore be eliminated but is thought to be not significant.

2. W means withdrawn; N means negatived; A means agreed to.

Appendices 1 and 2

3. New clauses or amendments which are not moved but are grouped for discussion *and* divided on are treated as moved and are included in cols (1)–(19) and not in col. (20).

4. Some of those included in col. (21) will have been grouped and discussed and so appear in col. (20) also.

APPENDIX ONE

COMMITTEE STAGE IN THE HOUSE OF COMMONS

Table A1.1 COMMITTEE H. OF C., 1967–68

Bill	Number of NC/amends moved				Moved by Minister [col. (1)]					Moved by Government backbencher [col. (2)]					Moved by Opposition [col. (3)]					Grpd and dis-cussed	Moved form-ally and agreed to	Div. on clause stand part	Total cols (4) and (20)	Number of NC/ amends tabled
	By Min	By Gvt BB	By Opp	Total cols 1–3	W/O div.			On div.		W/O div.			On div.		W/O div.			On div.						
					W	N	A	N	A	W	N	A	N	A	W	N	A	N	A					
	(1)	(2)	(3)	(4)	(5)	(6)	(7)	(8)	(9)	(10)	(11)	(12)	(13)	(14)	(15)	(16)	(17)	(18)	(19)	(20)	(21)	(22)	(23)	(24)
Administration of Justice	—	4	—	4	—	—	—	—	—	4	—	—	—	—	—	—	—	—	—	1	1	—	5	6
Agriculture Misc. Provs	36	1	51	88	—	—	35	—	1	1	—	—	—	—	38	3	3	7	—	44	21	—	132	135
Air Corporations	—	—	—	—	—	—	—	—	—	—	—	—	—	—	—	—	—	—	—	—	—	—	—	—
British Standard Time	1	—	5	6	—	—	1	—	—	—	—	—	—	—	2	—	—	3	—	13	1	1	19	22
Capital Allowances	—	—	2	2	—	—	—	—	—	—	—	—	—	—	—	2	—	—	—	1	—	—	3	3
Civil Aviation	13	—	7	20	—	—	13	—	—	—	—	—	—	—	3	3	—	1	—	21	17	—	41	73
Civil Evidence	7	—	3	10	—	—	7	—	—	—	—	—	—	—	3	—	—	—	—	6	4	—	16	17
Coal Industry	—	2	8	10	—	—	—	—	—	2	—	—	—	—	5	1	—	2	—	11	—	—	21	58
Commonwealth Immigrants	—	5	8	13	—	—	—	—	—	2	—	—	3	—	3	3	1	1	—	19	—	1	32	59
Commonwealth Telecommunications	—	—	—	—	—	—	—	—	—	—	—	—	—	—	—	—	—	—	—	—	—	—	—	—
Consolidated Fund	—	—	—	—	—	—	—	—	—	—	—	—	—	—	—	—	—	—	—	—	—	—	—	—
C.F. (No. 2)	—	—	—	—	—	—	—	—	—	—	—	—	—	—	—	—	—	—	—	—	—	—	—	—
C.F. (Apprp.)	—	—	—	—	—	—	—	—	—	—	—	—	—	—	—	—	—	—	—	—	—	—	—	—
Consular Relations	1	—	—	1	—	—	1	—	—	—	—	—	—	—	—	—	—	—	—	—	—	—	1	13
Countryside	15	52	138	205	—	—	15	—	—	44	3	4	1	—	119	4	4	10	1	92	22	2	297	366
Courts-Martial (Appeals)	—	—	—	—	—	—	—	—	—	—	—	—	—	—	—	—	—	—	—	—	—	—	—	2
Criminal Appeal	—	—	—	—	—	—	—	—	—	—	—	—	—	—	—	—	—	—	—	—	—	—	—	2
Criminal Appeal (N. Ireland)	—	—	—	—	—	—	—	—	—	—	—	—	—	—	—	—	—	—	—	—	—	—	—	1
Customs Duties (Dumping and Subsidies) Amendment	—	1	1	2	—	—	—	—	—	1	—	—	—	—	1	—	—	—	—	3	—	—	5	6
Education	2	—	6	8	—	—	1	—	1	—	—	—	—	—	6	—	—	—	—	1	1	—	9	9
Education No. 2	1	—	—	1	—	—	1	—	—	—	—	—	—	—	—	—	—	—	—	2	2	—	3	3
Erskine Bridge Tolls	—	—	4	4	—	—	—	—	—	—	—	—	—	—	4	—	—	—	—	1	—	—	5	5
Expiring Laws Continuance	—	—	1	1	—	—	—	—	—	—	—	—	—	—	1	—	—	—	—	1	—	—	2	3
Export Guarantees	—	—	—	—	—	—	—	—	—	—	—	—	—	—	—	—	—	—	—	—	—	—	—	1
Family Allowances and National Insurance	—	—	2	2	—	—	—	—	—	—	—	—	—	—	—	2	—	—	—	27	—	—	29	35

F.A. and N.I. (No. 2)	—	—	1	1	—	—	—	—	—	—	—	—	—	—	—	—	—	1	—	15	5	—	16	30
Finance (Standing)	18	5	124	147	—	—	17	—	1	2	1	—	2	—	58	13	4	49	—	177	18	20	324	636
(CWH)	—	1	11	12	—	—	—	—	—	1	—	—	—	—	2	2	—	7	—	24	—	3	36	275
Firearms	—	—	—	—	—	—	—	—	—	—	—	—	—	—	—	—	—	—	—	—	—	—	—	4
Gaming	34	17	53	104	—	—	34	—	—	15	1	—	1	—	40	6	3	4	—	87	146	1	191	326
Gas and Electricity	—	—	6	6	—	—	—	—	—	—	—	—	—	—	2	1	—	3	—	7	—	—	13	19
Health Services and Public Health	12	5	39	56	—	—	12	—	—	1	4	—	—	—	11	15	—	13	—	24	14	—	80	107
Housing (Fin. Provs) (Sc.)	—	—	—	—	—	—	—	—	—	—	—	—	—	—	—	—	—	—	—	—	—	—	—	—
Hovercraft	1	—	17	18	—	—	1	—	—	—	—	—	—	—	11	1	—	5	—	16	—	—	34	35
Industrial Expansion	3	3	29	35	—	—	3	—	—	3	—	—	—	—	8	1	—	20	—	19	10	5	54	70
International Monetary Fund	—	—	—	—	—	—	—	—	—	—	—	—	—	—	—	—	—	—	—	—	—	—	—	—
International Organisations	1	—	—	1	—	—	1	—	—	—	—	—	—	—	—	—	—	—	—	—	—	—	1	1
Justices of the Peace	10	2	1	13	—	—	10	—	—	—	—	2	—	—	—	—	—	1	—	35	10	—	48	48
Law Reform (Misc. Provs) (Scotland)	1	—	14	15	—	—	1	—	—	—	—	—	—	—	7	4	—	3	—	11	1	5	26	31
Legitimation (Scotland)	4	—	—	4	—	—	4	—	—	—	—	—	—	—	—	—	—	—	—	11	11	—	15	17
London Cab	1	5	2	8	—	—	1	—	—	4	1	—	—	—	1	—	—	1	—	7	—	—	15	21
Mauritius Independence	1	—	—	1	—	—	1	—	—	—	—	—	—	—	—	—	—	—	—	—	—	—	1	1
Medicines	27	38	88	153	—	—	27	—	—	28	7	—	2	1	50	9	8	20	1	116	18	2	269	305
National Loans	8	—	23	31	—	—	8	—	—	—	—	—	—	—	19	2	—	2	—	9	19	—	40	64
New Towns (Scotland)	—	—	—	—	—	—	—	—	—	—	—	—	—	—	—	—	—	—	—	—	—	—	—	—
Overseas Aid	2	—	1	3	—	—	2	—	—	—	—	—	—	—	1	—	—	—	—	2	2	—	5	6
Prices and Incomes	—	16	56	72	—	—	—	—	—	2	2	1	11	—	7	7	—	41	1	72	—	10	144	206
Provisional Collection of Taxes	—	—	1	1	—	—	—	—	—	—	—	—	—	—	—	1	—	—	—	—	—	—	1	1
Public Expenditure and Receipts	1	4	—	5	—	—	1	—	—	1	2	—	1	—	—	—	—	—	—	20	2	2	25	73
Race Relations	10	16	48	74	—	—	8	—	2	8	—	1	5	2	26	—	1	21	—	177	63	3	251	363
Rent	2	—	1	3	—	—	2	—	—	—	—	—	—	—	—	1	—	—	—	—	—	—	3	11
Restrictive Trade Practices	3	1	23	27	—	—	3	—	—	1	—	—	—	—	8	5	1	9	—	31	1	1	58	61
Revenue (No. 2)	—	1	7	8	—	—	—	—	—	—	1	—	—	—	2	1	—	4	—	13	4	1	21	23
Sewerage (Scotland)	30	14	61	105	—	—	30	—	—	13	1	—	—	—	36	5	10	10	—	77	36	3	182	200
Social Work	67	4	48	119	—	—	66	—	1	3	1	—	—	—	26	13	3	6	—	88	62	3	207	244
Swaziland Independence	—	—	—	—	—	—	—	—	—	—	—	—	—	—	—	—	—	—	—	—	—	—	—	—
Teachers Superannuation (Scotland)	—	1	2	3	—	—	—	—	—	—	—	—	1	—	—	1	—	1	—	—	—	—	3	3
Theft	6	—	12	18	—	—	6	—	—	—	—	—	—	—	9	1	—	2	—	7	17	—	25	42
Town and Country Planning	42	16	160	218	—	—	41	—	1	13	1	—	1	1	98	22	4	36	—	176	44	8	394	457
Trade Descriptions (No. 2)	10	5	34	49	—	—	10	—	—	5	—	—	—	—	16	11	—	7	—	35	8	1	84	99
Transport	67	11	386	464	—	—	59	—	8	6	2	2	—	1	141	48	3	194	—	508	272	47	972	2529
Transport Holding Company	—	—	6	6	—	—	—	—	—	—	—	—	—	—	—	—	—	6	—	2	—	—	8	13
Trustees Savings Banks	—	—	2	2	—	—	—	—	—	—	—	—	—	—	1	—	1	—	—	1	1	—	3	4
Water Resources	2	—	—	2	—	—	2	—	—	—	—	—	—	—	—	—	—	—	—	3	4	—	5	6
Total	439	230	1492	2161	—	—	424	—	15	160	27	10	28	5	765	188	46	490	3	2013	837	119	4174	7150

Table A1.2 COMMITTEE H. OF C., 1968–69

	Number of NC/amends moved				Moved by Minister [col. (1)]					Moved by Government backbencher [col. (2)]					Moved by Opposition [col. (3)]									
					W/O div.			On div.		W/O div.			On div.		W/O div.			On div.		Grpd and dis-cussed	Moved form-ally and agreed to	Div. on clause stand part	Total cols (4) and (20)	Number of NC/ amends tabled
	By Min	By Gvt BB	By Opp	Total cols 1–3	W	N	A	N	A	W	N	A	N	A	W	N	A	N	A					
Bill	(1)	(2)	(3)	(4)	(5)	(6)	(7)	(8)	(9)	(10)	(11)	(12)	(13)	(14)	(15)	(16)	(17)	(18)	(19)	(20)	(21)	(22)	(23)	(24)
Administration of Justice	7	4	4	15	—	—	7	—	—	2	—	—	—	2	1	—	—	3	—	15	13	—	30	39
Age of Majority (Scotland)	2	—	3	5	—	—	2	—	—	—	—	—	—	—	1	2	—	—	—	3	3	—	8	9
Agric. (Spring Traps) (Scotland)	—	1	1	2	—	—	—	—	—	—	—	1	—	—	—	—	—	1	—	6	—	—	8	8
Air Corporations	1	—	6	7	—	—	1	—	—	—	—	—	—	—	5	—	—	1	—	2	—	1	9	14
Army Reserve	—	—	1	1	—	—	—	—	—	—	—	—	—	—	—	1	—	—	—	—	—	—	1	1
Children and Young Persons	7	14	61	82	—	—	7	—	—	12	—	—	2	—	36	11	1	12	1	51	96	—	133	240
Consolidated Fund	—	—	—	—	—	—	—	—	—	—	—	—	—	—	—	—	—	—	—	—	—	—	—	—
C.F. (No. 2)	—	—	—	—	—	—	—	—	—	—	—	—	—	—	—	—	—	—	—	—	—	—	—	—
C.F. (Apprp.)	—	—	—	—	—	—	—	—	—	—	—	—	—	—	—	—	—	—	—	—	—	—	—	—
Customs Duties (Dumping and Subsidies)	—	—	1	1	—	—	—	—	—	—	—	—	—	—	—	1	—	—	—	—	—	—	1	1
Customs (Import Deposits)	2	1	24	27	—	—	2	—	—	—	—	—	1	—	4	9	—	11	—	63	2	—	90	151
Decimal Currency	3	3	13	19	—	—	2	—	1	3	—	—	—	—	9	2	—	2	—	24	1	1	43	54
Development of Tourism	4	7	69	80	—	—	4	—	—	6	—	—	—	1	31	9	2	24	3	97	31	—	177	223
Education (Scotland)	12	2	18	32	—	—	12	—	—	1	—	1	—	—	12	3	—	3	—	24	12	6	56	68
Electricity (Scotland)	—	—	1	1	—	—	—	—	—	—	—	—	—	—	—	—	—	1	—	1	—	1	2	2
Expiring Laws Continuance	—	—	1	1	—	—	—	—	—	—	—	—	—	—	1	—	—	—	—	1	—	—	2	3
Family Law Reform	11	—	13	24	—	—	10	—	1	—	—	—	—	—	6	3	—	4	—	19	3	1	43	55
Finance (Standing)	84	1	109	194	—	—	83	1	—	—	—	1	—	—	39	43	7	20	—	215	61	2	409	640
(CWH)	2	1	16	19	—	—	2	—	—	—	—	—	1	—	5	—	—	11	—	51	2	1	70	142
Foreign Compensation	—	—	1	1	—	—	—	—	—	—	—	—	—	—	—	—	—	1	—	—	—	—	1	3
Genocide	—	—	—	—	—	—	—	—	—	—	—	—	—	—	—	—	—	—	—	—	—	—	—	5
Horserace Betting Levy	5	—	9	14	—	—	5	—	—	—	—	—	—	—	4	2	—	2	1	7	1	—	21	24
Housing	6	10	133	149	—	—	6	—	—	3	1	4	2	—	51	34	6	42	—	124	11	4	273	364
Housing (Scotland)	37	3	31	71	—	—	36	—	1	3	—	—	—	—	21	2	4	4	—	69	57	—	140	173
Immigration Appeals	10	—	9	19	—	—	10	—	—	—	—	—	—	—	4	2	1	2	—	66	11	—	85	90
Iron and Steel	—	1	11	12	—	—	—	—	—	1	—	—	—	—	2	2	—	7	—	8	—	5	20	28
Late Night Refreshment Houses	1	—	—	1	—	—	1	—	—	—	—	—	—	—	—	—	—	—	—	1	—	—	2	2
Law of Property	4	—	16	20	—	—	4	—	—	—	—	—	—	—	9	4	—	3	—	14	3	1	34	43

Local Gvt Grants (Social Need)	—	—	—	—	—	—	—	—	—	—	—	—	—	—	—	—	—	—	—	—	—	—	—	—
Medical	—	—	3	3	—	—	—	—	—	—	—	—	—	—	—	2	—	1	—	2	—	1	5	9
Mines and Quarries (Tips)	3	—	23	26	—	—	3	—	—	—	—	—	—	—	15	4	1	3	—	13	6	—	39	42
Misc. Financial Provisions	—	—	—	—	—	—	—	—	—	—	—	—	—	—	—	—	—	—	—	—	—	—	—	—
Nat. Ins. (No. 2)	1	—	9	10	—	—	1	—	—	—	—	—	—	—	4	—	—	5	—	2	1	—	12	16
National Insurance, etc.	—	—	—	—	—	—	—	—	—	—	—	—	—	—	—	—	—	—	—	—	—	—	—	—
National Theatre	—	—	—	—	—	—	—	—	—	—	—	—	—	—	—	—	—	—	—	—	—	—	—	—
New Towns	—	—	3	3	—	—	—	—	—	—	—	—	—	—	3	—	—	—	—	—	—	—	3	3
Nuclear Installations	1	—	—	1	—	—	1	—	—	—	—	—	—	—	—	—	—	—	—	—	—	—	1	1
Nurses	1	3	4	8	—	—	1	—	—	2	—	—	1	—	1	1	1	1	—	7	1	—	15	18
Overseas Resources Development	—	—	—	—	—	—	—	—	—	—	—	—	—	—	—	—	—	—	—	—	—	—	—	1
Pensions (Increase)	2	—	8	10	—	—	2	—	—	—	—	—	—	—	3	3	—	2	—	2	—	—	12	18
Post Office	20	10	82	112	—	—	20	—	—	9	—	—	1	—	49	4	3	26	—	100	261	4	212	513
Redundancy Rebates	—	—	3	3	—	—	—	—	—	—	—	—	—	—	—	1	—	2	—	2	—	—	5	9
Redundant Churches etc.	—	—	—	—	—	—	—	—	—	—	—	—	—	—	—	—	—	—	—	—	—	—	—	—
Representation of the People	5	2	23	30	—	—	5	—	—	—	1	—	1	—	11	3	1	8	—	38	2	1	68	80
Sea Fisheries	6	—	4	10	—	—	6	—	—	—	—	—	—	—	4	—	—	—	—	2	5	—	12	19
Shipbuilding Industry	—	—	—	—	—	—	—	—	—	—	—	—	—	—	—	—	—	—	—	—	—	—	—	1
Statute Law (Repeals)	—	—	—	—	—	—	—	—	—	—	—	—	—	—	—	—	—	—	—	—	—	—	—	—
Tanzania	—	—	—	—	—	—	—	—	—	—	—	—	—	—	—	—	—	—	—	—	—	—	—	—
Town and Country Planning (Scotland)	25	2	72	99	—	—	25	—	—	1	—	1	—	—	46	11	8	7	—	61	51	1	160	199
Trustee Savings Banks	—	—	2	2	—	—	—	—	—	—	—	—	—	—	—	1	1	—	—	1	—	—	3	3
Transport (London)	14	2	70	86	—	—	13	—	1	1	—	—	1	—	32	15	2	21	—	69	20	—	155	183
Vehicle and Driving Licences	12	—	17	29	—	—	10	—	2	—	—	—	—	—	11	4	—	2	—	32	24	—	61	81
Govt. bills which did not receive R.A.																								
Parliament (No. 2)	—	12	9	21	—	—	—	—	—	1	3	—	8	—	—	1	—	8	—	49	—	5	70	293
House of Commons Redistribution of Seats) (No. 2)	—	—	6	6	—	—	—	—	—	—	—	—	—	—	—	—	—	6	—	38	—	1	44	82
Total	288	79	889	1256	—	—	281	1	6	45	5	8	18	3	420	180	38	246	5	1279	678	36	2535	3953

Table A1.3 COMMITTEE H. OF C., 1970–71

	Number of NC/amends moved				Moved by Minister [col. (1)]					Moved by Government backbencher [col. (2)]					Moved by Opposition [col. (3)]					Grpd and dis-cussed	Moved form-ally and agreed to	Div. on clause stand part	Total cols (4) and (20)	Number of NC/ amends tabled
					W/O div.			On div.		W/O div.			On div.		W/O div.			On div.						
	By Min	By Gvt BB	By Opp	Total cols 1–3	W	N	A	N	A	W	N	A	N	A	W	N	A	N	A					
Bill	(1)	(2)	(3)	(4)	(5)	(6)	(7)	(8)	(9)	(10)	(11)	(12)	(13)	(14)	(15)	(16)	(17)	(18)	(19)	(20)	(21)	(22)	(23)	(24)
Air Corporations	—	—	—	—	—	—	—	—	—	—	—	—	—	—	—	—	—	—	—	—	—	—	—	—
Anguilla	—	—	—	—	—	—	—	—	—	—	—	—	—	—	—	—	—	—	—	—	—	—	—	—
Animals	—	2	3	5	—	—	—	—	—	2	—	—	—	—	2	—	—	1	—	2	—	—	7	12
Armed Forces	2	—	—	2	—	—	2	—	—	—	—	—	—	—	—	—	—	—	—	2	2	—	4	6
Atomic Energy Authority	—	2	4	6	—	—	—	—	—	1	1	—	—	—	4	—	—	—	—	2	—	—	8	8
Attachment of Earnings	1	—	—	1	—	—	1	—	—	—	—	—	—	—	—	—	—	—	—	—	1	—	1	2
Civil Aviation	19	14	91	124	—	—	19	—	—	12	—	2	—	—	61	3	10	17	—	108	34	—	232	268
Civil Aviation (Decl. Provs)	—	—	—	—	—	—	—	—	—	—	—	—	—	—	—	—	—	—	—	—	—	1	—	—
Coal Industry	—	—	23	23	—	—	—	—	—	—	—	—	—	—	8	—	1	13	1	21	—	3	44	64
Coinage	—	—	—	—	—	—	—	—	—	—	—	—	—	—	—	—	—	—	—	—	—	—	—	—
Consolidated Fund	—	—	—	—	—	—	—	—	—	—	—	—	—	—	—	—	—	—	—	—	—	—	—	—
C.F. (No. 2)	—	—	—	—	—	—	—	—	—	—	—	—	—	—	—	—	—	—	—	—	—	—	—	—
C.F. (Apprp.)	—	—	—	—	—	—	—	—	—	—	—	—	—	—	—	—	—	—	—	—	—	—	—	—
C.F. (Apprp.) (No. 2)	—	—	—	—	—	—	—	—	—	—	—	—	—	—	—	—	—	—	—	—	—	—	—	—
Contingencies Fund	—	—	—	—	—	—	—	—	—	—	—	—	—	—	—	—	—	—	—	—	—	—	—	—
Courts	25	4	38	67	—	—	25	—	—	4	—	—	—	—	19	8	5	6	—	63	100	2	130	216
Criminal Damage	2	1	1	4	—	—	2	—	—	1	—	—	—	—	1	—	—	—	—	3	2	—	7	7
Diplomatic and Other Privileges	—	—	—	—	—	—	—	—	—	—	—	—	—	—	—	—	—	—	—	—	—	—	—	—
Education (Handicapped Children)	—	—	—	—	—	—	—	—	—	—	—	—	—	—	—	—	—	—	—	—	—	—	—	—
Education (Milk)	1	—	9	10	—	—	1	—	—	—	—	—	—	—	1	2	—	6	—	11	1	1	21	36
Education (Scotland)	—	—	51	51	—	—	—	—	—	—	—	—	—	—	13	3	—	35	—	15	—	1	66	83
Expiring Laws (Continuance)	—	—	1	1	—	—	—	—	—	—	—	—	—	—	1	—	—	—	—	—	—	—	1	2
Family Income Supplements	3	—	24	27	—	—	3	—	—	—	—	—	—	—	11	3	2	8	—	26	1	1	53	76
Fiji Independence	—	—	—	—	—	—	—	—	—	—	—	—	—	—	—	—	—	—	—	—	—	—	—	—
Finance (Standing)	32	50	39	121	—	—	32	—	—	36	5	6	3	—	20	9	—	10	—	111	17	—	232	379
(CWH)	—	2	6	8	—	—	—	—	—	2	—	—	—	—	—	1	—	5	—	3	—	1	11	23
Fire Precautions	7	7	20	34	—	—	7	—	—	6	—	1	—	—	15	4	—	1	—	58	22	—	92	95
Friendly Societies	11	—	2	13	—	—	11	—	—	—	—	—	—	—	1	1	—	—	—	12	9	—	25	26
Guardianship of Minors	—	—	—	—	—	—	—	—	—	—	—	—	—	—	—	—	—	—	—	—	—	—	—	—

Harbours (Amendment)	—	—	—	—	—	—	—	—	—	—	—	—	—	—	—	—	—	—	—	—	—	—	—	—
Highways	8	3	35	46	—	—	8	—	—	—	1	1	1	—	28	2	4	1	—	28	15	—	74	83
Hijacking	—	—	—	—	—	—	—	—	—	—	—	—	—	—	—	—	—	—	—	—	—	—	—	—
Hospital Endowments (Scotland)	—	—	23	23	—	—	—	—	—	—	—	—	—	—	19	—	2	2	—	6	—	—	29	39
Housing	1	—	5	6	—	—	1	—	—	—	—	—	—	—	3	1	—	1	—	7	—	—	13	31
Hydrocarbon Oil (Customs and Excise)	1	—	1	2	—	—	1	—	—	—	—	—	—	—	—	1	—	—	—	11	—	—	13	13
Immigration	—	14	71	85	—	—	—	—	—	6	5	1	1	1	25	21	2	23	—	74	1	6	159	249
Income and Corporation Taxes (No. 2)	—	—	2	2	—	—	—	—	—	—	—	—	—	—	2	—	—	—	—	—	—	—	2	4
Industrial Relations	12	8	50	70	—	—	5	—	7	5	2	1	—	—	1	8	1	40	G	99	20	91	169	950
Industry	1	—	10	11	—	—	1	—	—	—	—	—	—	—	5	1	—	4	—	3	—	2	14	15
International Monetary Fund	—	—	—	—	—	—	—	—	—	—	—	—	—	—	—	—	—	—	—	—	—	—	—	—
Investment and Building Grants	—	2	4	6	—	—	—	—	—	1	—	—	1	—	2	—	—	2	—	1	—	1	7	9
Land Commission (Dissolution)	3	—	5	8	—	—	3	—	—	—	—	—	—	—	4	—	—	1	—	3	1	1	11	18
Land Reg/ion and Land Charges	1	—	1	2	—	—	1	—	—	—	—	—	—	—	1	—	—	—	—	—	1	—	2	4
Law Reform (Jdn. in Delict) (Scotland)	—	—	1	1	—	—	—	—	—	—	—	—	—	—	—	—	1	—	—	—	—	—	1	1
Licensing (Abol. of State Man.)	—	—	27	27	—	—	—	—	—	—	—	—	—	—	7	6	—	13	1	35	1	3	62	86
Local Authys (Qualifcn Members)	3	—	16	19	—	—	2	—	1	—	—	—	—	—	7	—	—	9	—	32	5	1	51	64
Medicines	—	—	—	—	—	—	—	—	—	—	—	—	—	—	—	—	—	—	—	—	—	—	—	—
Merch. Shipping (Oil Pollution)	4	—	5	9	—	—	4	—	—	—	—	—	—	—	—	—	—	5	—	6	4	—	15	20
Mineral Workings	—	—	5	5	—	—	—	—	—	—	—	—	—	—	2	1	—	1	1	5	—	—	10	13
Mineral Wkgs (Offshore Instalns)	4	—	10	14	—	—	4	—	—	—	—	—	—	—	9	—	—	1	—	19	2	—	33	33
Mines Management	—	—	1	1	—	—	—	—	—	—	—	—	—	—	1	—	—	—	—	3	—	—	4	4
Mr Speaker King's Rtmt	—	—	—	—	—	—	—	—	—	—	—	—	—	—	—	—	—	—	—	—	1	—	—	1
Misuse of Drugs	9	—	11	20	—	—	9	—	—	—	—	—	—	—	7	2	1	1	—	46	16	1	66	72
National Insurance	5	—	14	19	—	—	5	—	—	—	—	—	—	—	2	5	—	6	1	10	5	—	29	33
National Insurance (Old Persons' and Widows, etc.)	1	2	7	10	—	—	1	—	—	1	—	—	1	—	3	2	—	2	—	8	—	—	18	19
National Savings Bank	—	—	—	—	—	—	—	—	—	—	—	—	—	—	—	—	—	—	—	—	—	—	—	—
Oil in Navigable Waters	6	2	8	16	—	—	6	—	—	2	—	—	—	—	5	—	—	2	1	5	4	—	21	24
Pensions (Increase)	2	—	7	9	—	—	2	—	—	—	—	—	—	—	2	2	—	3	—	10	—	—	19	22
Pool Competitions	1	—	1	2	—	—	1	—	—	—	—	—	—	—	1	—	—	—	—	—	—	—	2	2
Prevention of Oil Pollution	—	—	—	—	—	—	—	—	—	—	—	—	—	—	—	—	—	—	—	—	—	—	—	—
ating	1	2	18	21	—	—	1	—	—	1	—	1	—	—	8	3	—	7	—	18	1	1	39	61

Table A1.3 (*continued*)

Bill	Number of NC/amends moved				Moved by Minister [col. (1)]					Moved by Government backbencher [col. (2)]					Moved by Opposition [col. (3)]					Grpd and dis- cussed	Moved form- ally and agreed to	Div. on clause stand part	Total cols (4) and (20)	Number of NC/ amends tabled
	By Min	By Gvt BB	By Opp	Total cols 1–3	W/O div. W	W/O div. N	W/O div. A	On div. N	On div. A	W/O div. W	W/O div. N	W/O div. A	On div. N	On div. A	W/O div. W	W/O div. N	W/O div. A	On div. N	On div. A					
	(1)	(2)	(3)	(4)	(5)	(6)	(7)	(8)	(9)	(10)	(11)	(12)	(13)	(14)	(15)	(16)	(17)	(18)	(19)	(20)	(21)	(22)	(23)	(24)
Recog. of Divorces and Legal Sepns	2	—	4	6	—	—	2	—	—	—	—	—	—	—	2	—	1	1	—	5	2	—	11	11
Redemption of Standard Securities (Scotland)	—	—	—	—	—	—	—	—	—	—	—	—	—	—	—	—	—	—	—	—	—	—	—	—
Rent (Scotland)	1	—	—	1	—	—	1	—	—	—	—	—	—	—	—	—	—	—	—	—	—	—	1	1
Rolls-Royce (Purchase)	—	1	2	3	—	—	—	—	—	—	1	—	—	—	—	—	—	2	—	1	—	—	4	5
Rural Water Supplies and Sewerage	—	—	—	—	—	—	—	—	—	—	—	—	—	—	—	—	—	—	—	—	—	—	—	—
Sheriff Courts (Scotland)	6	2	13	21	—	—	6	—	—	2	—	—	—	—	11	—	1	1	—	15	5	—	36	40
Shipbuilding Industry	—	—	—	—	—	—	—	—	—	—	—	—	—	—	—	—	—	—	—	—	—	—	—	—
Social Security	2	—	21	23	—	—	2	—	—	—	—	—	—	—	3	2	2	14	—	14	4	6	37	47
Statute Law (Repeals)	—	—	—	—	—	—	—	—	—	—	—	—	—	—	—	—	—	—	—	—	—	—	—	—
Teaching Council (Scotland)	—	—	—	—	—	—	—	—	—	—	—	—	—	—	—	—	—	—	—	—	—	—	—	—
Town and Country Planning	3	—	—	3	—	—	3	—	—	—	—	—	—	—	—	—	—	—	—	—	—	—	3	10
T. and C.P. Regs (London) (Indemnity)	—	—	—	—	—	—	—	—	—	—	—	—	—	—	—	—	—	—	—	—	—	—	—	—
Tribunals and Inquiries	—	—	—	—	—	—	—	—	—	—	—	—	—	—	—	—	—	—	—	—	—	—	—	—
Vehicles (Excise)	—	—	—	—	—	—	—	—	—	—	—	—	—	—	—	—	—	—	—	—	—	1	—	—
Water Resources	—	7	2	9	—	—	—	—	—	5	—	—	2	—	1	—	1	—	—	8	1	1	17	16
Wild Creatures and Forest Laws	—	2	1	3	—	—	—	—	—	2	—	—	—	—	—	1	—	—	—	6	—	—	9	12
Total	180	127	693	1000	—	—	172	—	8	89	15	13	9	1	318	92	34	244	5	915	278	125	1915	3315

APPENDIX TWO

REPORT STAGE IN THE HOUSE OF COMMONS

Table A2.1 REPORT H. OF C., 1967–68

Bill	Number of NC/amends moved				Moved by Minister [col. (1)]					Moved by Government backbencher [col. (2)]					Moved by Opposition [col. (3)]					Grpd and dis-cussed	Moved form-ally and agreed to	Total cols (4) and (20)	Number of NC/ amends tabled
					W/O div.			On div.		W/O div.			On div.		W/O div.			On div.					
	By Min	By Gvt BB	By Opp	Total cols 1–3	W	N	A	N	A	W	N	A	N	A	W	N	A	N	A				
	(1)	(2)	(3)	(4)	(5)	(6)	(7)	(8)	(9)	(10)	(11)	(12)	(13)	(14)	(15)	(16)	(17)	(18)	(19)	(20)	(21)	(22)	(23)
Agriculture Misc. Provs	13	1	7	21	—	—	12	—	1	—	—	—	1	—	3	2	—	2	—	23	16	44	48
British Standard Time	1	—	—	1	—	—	1	—	—	—	—	—	—	—	—	—	—	—	—	2	2	3	10
Civil Aviation	3	—	14	17	—	—	3	—	—	—	—	—	—	—	—	13	1	—	—	10	2	27	36
Civil Evidence	2	2	2	6	—	—	2	—	—	—	2	—	—	—	1	1	—	—	—	1	1	7	8
Commonwealth Immigrants	1	—	—	1	—	—	1	—	—	—	—	—	—	—	—	—	—	—	—	—	—	1	1
Consular Relations	1	—	2	3	—	—	1	—	—	—	—	—	—	—	1	—	1	—	—	8	3	11	11
Countryside	27	4	23	54	1	—	26	—	—	2	2	—	—	—	14	4	—	5	—	75	32	129	150
Education	—	1	—	1	—	—	—	—	—	—	1	—	—	—	—	—	—	—	—	—	—	1	2
Erskine Bridge Tolls	—	—	1	1	—	—	—	—	—	—	—	—	—	—	—	—	1	—	—	—	—	1	1
Finance	25	—	20	45	—	—	25	—	—	—	—	—	—	—	5	3	1	10	1	46	100	91	416
Gaming	49	—	10	59	—	—	47	—	2	—	—	—	—	—	5	2	1	2	—	79	72	138	163
Health Services and Public Health	9	2	3	14	—	—	9	—	—	1	—	—	—	1	—	3	—	—	—	8	20	22	47
Hovercraft	—	—	2	2	—	—	—	—	—	—	—	—	—	—	1	—	—	1	—	—	—	2	6
Industrial Expansion	4	1	13	18	—	—	4	—	—	1	—	—	—	—	3	1	2	7	—	9	1	27	65
Justices of the Peace	1	1	1	3	—	—	1	—	—	—	—	1	—	—	—	—	—	1	—	26	1	29	29
Law Reform (Misc. Provs) (Scotland)	1	—	2	3	—	—	1	—	—	—	—	—	—	—	—	1	—	1	—	4	1	7	10
Legitimation (Scotland)	—	—	1	1	—	—	—	—	—	—	—	—	—	—	1	—	—	—	—	1	—	2	2
London Cab	2	—	1	3	—	—	2	—	—	—	—	—	—	—	—	1	—	—	—	2	2	5	6
Medicines	26	4	13	43	—	—	26	—	—	1	—	2	1	—	6	3	—	4	—	69	46	112	120
National Loans	5	—	1	6	—	—	5	—	—	—	—	—	—	—	—	1	—	—	—	5	2	11	18
Prices and Incomes	9	2	24	35	—	—	8	—	1	—	—	—	2	—	—	13	—	11	—	31	6	66	164
Race Relations	17	8	8	33	—	—	17	—	—	4	4	—	—	—	4	1	—	3	—	54	40	87	131
Restrictive Trade Practices	11	—	3	14	—	—	11	—	—	—	—	—	—	—	2	1	—	—	—	2	2	16	20
Sewerage (Scotland)	25	2	2	29	—	—	25	—	—	1	1	—	—	—	2	—	—	—	—	39	29	68	77
Social Work (Scotland)	59	4	4	67	—	—	59	—	—	1	3	—	—	—	—	1	2	1	—	67	127	134	201
Teachers Superannuation (Scotland)	—	—	1	1	—	—	—	—	—	—	—	—	—	—	—	1	—	—	—	—	—	1	1
Theft	7	1	4	12	—	—	7	—	—	1	—	—	—	—	2	2	—	—	—	15	16	27	31
Town and Country Planning	38	5	44	87	—	—	35	—	3	2	1	1	1	—	18	14	4	8	—	133	122	220	273
Trade Descriptions (No. 2)	10	2	7	19	—	—	10	—	—	—	1	—	1	—	1	2	—	4	—	13	4	32	32
Transport	33	2	38	73	—	—	22	—	11	1	—	—	1	—	10	8	—	20	—	73	163	146	596

Table A2.2 REPORT H. OF C., 1968–69

Bill	Number of NC/amends moved: By Min	By Gvt BB	By Opp	Total cols 1–3	Moved by Minister [col. (1)]: W/O div. W	W/O div. N	W/O div. A	On div. N	On div. A	Moved by Government backbencher [col. (2)]: W/O div. W	W/O div. N	W/O div. A	On div. N	On div. A	Moved by Opposition [col. (3)]: W/O div. W	W/O div. N	W/O div. A	On div. N	On div. A	Grpd and dis-cussed	Moved form-ally and agreed to	Total cols (4) and (20)	Number of NC/ amends tabled
	(1)	(2)	(3)	(4)	(5)	(6)	(7)	(8)	(9)	(10)	(11)	(12)	(13)	(14)	(15)	(16)	(17)	(18)	(19)	(20)	(21)	(22)	(23)
Administration of Justice	4	—	4	8	—	—	4	—	—	—	—	—	—	—	2	1	—	1	—	9	7	17	18
Agric. (Spring Traps) (Scotland)	1	—	—	1	—	—	1	—	—	—	—	—	—	—	—	—	—	—	—	—	4	1	5
Air Corporations	1	—	—	1	—	—	1	—	—	—	—	—	—	—	—	—	—	—	—	—	2	1	3
Children and Young Persons	28	—	21	49	—	—	26	—	2	—	—	—	—	—	5	10	2	4	—	64	59	113	135
Customs (Import Deposits)	—	—	2	2	—	—	—	—	—	—	—	—	—	—	1	1	—	—	—	—	—	2	2
Decimal Currency	3	—	3	6	—	—	3	—	—	—	—	—	—	—	—	1	—	2	—	2	1	8	14
Development of Tourism	10	—	12	22	—	—	8	—	2	—	—	—	—	—	1	4	—	7	—	74	17	96	182
Education (Scotland)	16	—	8	24	—	—	13	—	3	—	—	—	—	—	1	2	—	5	—	35	29	59	59
Family Law Reform	2	—	2	4	—	—	1	—	1	—	—	—	—	—	2	—	—	—	—	2	—	6	13
Finance	53	—	28	81	—	—	50	—	3	—	—	—	—	—	8	10	1	9	—	141	84	222	398
Foreign Compensation	1	—	—	1	—	—	1	—	—	—	—	—	—	—	—	—	—	—	—	2	1	3	3
Horserace Betting Levy	1	—	—	1	—	—	—	—	1	—	—	—	—	—	—	—	—	—	—	—	—	1	1
Housing	36	4	33	73	—	—	36	—	—	—	3	—	1	—	3	10	—	20	—	83	47	156	211
Housing (Scotland)	4	1	13	18	—	—	4	—	—	—	—	1	—	—	9	—	1	3	—	10	6	28	39
Immigration Appeals	5	—	1	6	—	—	5	—	—	—	—	—	—	—	—	1	—	—	—	2	2	8	8
Iron and Steel	—	—	5	5	—	—	—	—	—	—	—	—	—	—	2	2	—	1	—	4	—	9	36
Law of Property	5	—	7	12	—	—	5	—	—	—	—	—	—	—	—	6	1	—	—	4	11	16	29
Mines and Quarries (Tips)	5	—	7	12	—	—	5	—	—	—	—	—	—	—	2	2	1	2	—	13	13	25	32
National Insurance (No. 2)	—	—	—	—	—	—	—	—	—	—	—	—	—	—	—	—	—	—	—	—	—	—	2
National Theatre	—	—	1	1	—	—	—	—	—	—	—	—	—	—	1	—	—	—	—	—	—	1	1
Nuclear Installations	—	—	1	1	—	—	—	—	—	—	—	—	—	—	1	—	—	—	—	2	—	3	5
Nurses	1	—	—	1	—	—	1	—	—	—	—	—	—	—	—	—	—	—	—	6	6	7	7
Pensions (Increase)	—	—	2	2	—	—	—	—	—	—	—	—	—	—	1	1	—	—	—	—	—	2	6
Post Office	26	2	23	51	—	—	23	—	3	—	1	—	1	—	8	6	—	9	—	50	77	101	264
Representation of the People	12	—	3	15	—	—	12	—	—	—	—	—	—	—	2	—	—	1	—	42	37	57	63
Town and Country Planning (Scotland)	8	2	13	23	—	—	8	—	—	—	—	2	—	—	6	2	—	5	—	10	9	33	43
Transport (London)	14	—	13	27	—	—	14	—	—	—	—	—	—	—	1	12	—	—	—	21	13	48	60
Vehicle and Driving Licences	13	1	5	19	—	—	13	—	—	—	1	—	—	—	2	3	—	—	—	—	35	19	59
Total	249	10	207	466	—	—	234	—	15	—	5	3	2	—	58	74	6	69	—	576	460	1042	1698

Table A2.3 REPORT H. OF C., 1970–71

Bill	Number of NC/amends moved				Moved by Minister [col. (1)]					Moved by Government backbencher [col. (2)]					Moved by Opposition [col. (3)]					Grpd and dis-cussed	Moved form-ally and agreed to	Total cols (4) and (20)	Number of NC/ amends tabled
	By Min	By Gvt BB	By Opp	Total cols 1–3	W/O div. W	W/O div. N	W/O div. A	On div. N	On div. A	W/O div. W	W/O div. N	W/O div. A	On div. N	On div. A	W/O div. W	W/O div. N	W/O div. A	On div. N	On div. A				
	(1)	(2)	(3)	(4)	(5)	(6)	(7)	(8)	(9)	(10)	(11)	(12)	(13)	(14)	(15)	(16)	(17)	(18)	(19)	(20)	(21)	(22)	(23)
Animals	2	1	—	3	—	—	2	—	—	1	—	—	—	—	—	—	—	—	—	1	—	4	5
Attachment of Earnings	1	—	—	1	—	—	1	—	—	—	—	—	—	—	—	—	—	—	—	—	1	1	2
Civil Aviation	11	3	11	25	—	—	11	—	—	2	—	1	—	—	—	3	4	4	—	27	22	52	61
Coal Industry	3	1	6	10	—	—	3	—	—	—	—	—	1	—	4	—	—	2	—	9	1	19	30
Courts	18	3	10	31	—	—	18	—	—	3	—	—	—	—	1	6	2	1	—	38	27	69	80
Criminal Damage	—	—	2	2	—	—	—	—	—	—	—	—	—	—	—	2	—	—	—	2	—	4	4
Education (Milk)	—	1	7	8	—	—	—	—	—	1	—	—	—	—	—	3	—	4	—	40	—	48	82
Education (Scotland)	4	—	2	6	—	—	3	—	1	—	—	—	—	—	—	1	—	1	—	6	1	12	29
Family Income Supplements	—	—	10	10	—	—	—	—	—	—	—	—	—	—	1	—	—	9	—	13	—	23	28
Finance	32	17	10	59	—	—	32	—	—	12	2	1	2	—	3	1	—	6	—	45	34	104	181
Fire Precautions	8	—	3	11	—	—	8	—	—	—	—	—	—	—	3	—	—	—	—	8	4	19	28
Friendly Societies	—	—	—	—	—	—	—	—	—	—	—	—	—	—	—	—	—	—	—	—	4	—	4
Highways	25	1	3	29	—	—	25	—	—	1	—	—	—	—	1	2	—	—	—	69	62	98	101
Hospital Endowments (Scotland)	11	—	—	11	—	—	11	—	—	—	—	—	—	—	—	—	—	—	—	2	2	13	13
Housing	—	—	1	1	—	—	—	—	—	—	—	—	—	—	—	1	—	—	—	1	—	2	2
Immigration	16	3	21	40	—	—	15	—	1	1	2	—	—	—	9	6	1	5	—	76	43	116	166
Industrial Relations	70	—	16	86	—	—	2	—	68	—	—	—	—	—	—	—	1	15	—	168	5	254	370
Industry	—	—	1	1	—	—	—	—	—	—	—	—	—	—	—	1	—	—	—	—	—	1	1
Investment and Building Grants	2	2	—	4	—	—	2	—	—	1	—	—	1	—	—	—	—	—	—	4	4	8	8
Land Commission (Dissolution)	—	—	1	1	—	—	—	—	—	—	—	—	—	—	—	1	—	—	—	—	—	1	5
Land Reg/ion and Land Charges	1	—	—	1	—	—	1	—	—	—	—	—	—	—	—	—	—	—	—	1	1	2	2
Licensing (Abol. of State Man.)	1	—	6	7	—	—	1	—	—	—	—	—	—	—	—	—	—	6	—	9	1	16	39
Local Authys (Qualifcn of Members)	4	—	1	5	—	—	4	—	—	—	—	—	—	—	—	—	—	1	—	8	8	13	17
Merch. Shipping (Oil Pollution)	1	—	2	3	—	—	1	—	—	—	—	—	—	—	—	2	—	—	—	4	2	7	9
Mineral Workings	3	—	—	3	—	—	2	—	1	—	—	—	—	—	—	—	—	—	—	2	2	5	5
Mineral Wkgs (Offshore Instalns)	3	—	1	4	—	—	3	—	—	—	—	—	—	—	—	1	—	—	—	—	29	4	34
Misuse of Drugs	1	3	8	12	—	—	1	—	—	3	—	—	—	—	6	1	1	—	—	17	14	29	32
National Insurance	3	—	2	5	—	—	3	—	—	—	—	—	—	—	—	2	—	—	—	—	3	5	9
Oil in Navigable Waters	1	—	4	5	—	—	1	—	—	—	—	—	—	—	—	4	—	—	—	—	2	5	9
Pensions (Increase)	1	—	2	3	—	—	1	—	—	—	—	—	—	—	—	2	—	—	—	5	—	8	18
Rating	4	1	2	7	—	—	4	—	—	1	—	—	—	—	1	1	—	—	—	3	1	10	14
Recog. of Divorces Legal Sepns	—	—	2	2	—	—	—	—	—	—	—	—	—	—	—	2	—	—	—	1	—	3	3
Rent (Scotland)	1	—	—	1	—	—	1	—	—	—	—	—	—	—	—	—	—	—	—	—	—	1	1
Sheriff Courts (Scotland)	5	—	—	5	—	—	5	—	—	—	—	—	—	—	—	—	—	—	—	4	2	9	9
Social Security	2	—	7	9	—	—	2	—	—	—	—	—	—	—	1	—	—	6	—	2	1	11	20
Water Resources	3	1	—	4	—	—	3	—	—	—	1	—	—	—	—	—	—	—	—	3	3	7	11
Total	237	37	141	415	—	—	166	—	71	26	5	2	4	—	30	42	9	60	—	568	279	983	1432

APPENDIX THREE

HOUSE OF LORDS

Table A3.1 COMMITTEE H. OF L., 1968–69

	Number of NC/amends moved				Moved by Minister [col. (1)]					Moved by Government backbencher [col. (2)]					Moved by Opposition and Independent Peers [col. (3)]					Div. on clause stand part	Number of NC/ amends tabled
					W/O div.			On div.		W/O div.			On div.		W/O div.			On div.			
	By Min	By Gvt BB	By Opp	Total cols 1–3	W	N	A	N	A	W	N	A	N	A	W	N	A	N	A		
Bill	(1)	(2)	(3)	(4)	(5)	(6)	(7)	(8)	(9)	(10)	(11)	(12)	(13)	(14)	(15)	(16)	(17)	(18)	(19)	(20)	(21)
Agric. (Spring) Traps) (Sc.)	—	—	1	1	—	—	—	—	—	—	—	—	—	—	—	1	—	—	—	—	2
Children and Young Persons	30	6	19	55	—	—	30	—	—	6	—	—	—	—	17	—	1	—	1	—	64
Decimal Currency	—	—	3	3	—	—	—	—	—	—	—	—	—	—	1	1	—	—	1	—	3
Development of Tourism	9	—	10	19	—	—	9	—	—	—	—	—	—	—	7	—	2	1	—	—	25
Education (Sc.)	9	—	18	27	—	—	9	—	—	—	—	—	—	—	8	—	9	—	1	—	30
Foreign Compensation	—	—	7	7	—	—	—	—	—	—	—	—	—	—	5	—	—	—	2	—	14
Horserace Betting Levy	3	—	3	6	—	—	3	—	—	—	—	—	—	—	1	—	2	—	—	—	6
Housing	31	—	23	54	—	—	31	—	—	—	—	—	—	—	16	1	4	—	2	1	59
Housing (Sc.)	10	—	1	11	—	—	10	—	—	—	—	—	—	—	1	—	—	—	—	—	11
Immigration Appeals	19	3	5	27	—	—	18	—	1	3	—	—	—	—	5	—	—	—	—	—	27
Iron and Steel	—	—	1	1	—	—	—	—	—	—	—	—	—	—	1	—	—	—	—	—	1
Mines and Quarries (Tips)	—	—	14	14	—	—	—	—	—	—	—	—	—	—	14	—	—	—	—	—	14

Nat. Ins. (No. 2)	—	—	2	2	—	—	—	—	—	—	—	—	—	—	2	—	—	—	—	—	2
Pensions (Increase)	—	—	1	1	—	—	—	—	—	—	—	—	—	—	1	—	—	—	—	—	1
Post Office	75	3	6	84	—	—	75	—	—	3	—	—	—	—	1	—	3	—	2	—	87
Redundancy Rebates	—	—	2	2	—	—	—	—	—	—	—	—	—	—	2	—	—	—	—	—	2
Representation of the People	19	—	6	25	—	—	19	—	—	—	—	—	—	—	4	—	—	—	2	—	35
Sea Fisheries	20	—	—	20	—	—	20	—	—	—	—	—	—	—	—	—	—	—	—	—	20
Transport (London)	14	—	36	50	—	—	14	—	—	—	—	—	—	—	32	—	1	2	1	—	79
Vehicle and Driving Licences	32	—	5	37	—	—	32	—	—	—	—	—	—	—	4	1	—	—	—	—	38
House of Commons (Redistribution of Seats) (No. 2)	—	—	4	4	—	—	—	—	—	—	—	—	—	—	—	—	3	—	1	—	6
Total	271	12	167	450	—	—	270	—	1	12	—	—	—	—	122	4	25	3	13	1	526

Table A3.2 REPORT H. OF L., 1968–69

	Number of NC/amends moved				Moved by Minister [col. (1)]					Moved by Government backbencher [col. (2)]					Moved by Opposition and Independent Peers [col. (3)]					Div. on clause stand part	Number of NC/ amends tabled
					W/O div.			On div.		W/O div.			On div.		W/O div.			On div.			
	By Min	By Gvt BB	By Opp	Total cols 1–3	W	N	A	N	A	W	N	A	N	A	W	N	A	N	A		
Bill	(1)	(2)	(3)	(4)	(5)	(6)	(7)	(8)	(9)	(10)	(11)	(12)	(13)	(14)	(15)	(16)	(17)	(18)	(19)	(20)	(21)
Agric. (Spring Traps) (Sc.)	—	—	1	1	—	—	—	—	—	—	—	—	—	—	—	—	—	—	1	—	1
Children and Young Persons	68	1	12	81	—	—	68	—	—	1	—	—	—	—	10	—	1	1	—	—	83
Decimal Currency	1	—	3	4	—	—	—	—	1	—	—	—	—	—	3	—	—	—	—	—	4
Development of Tourism	1	—	—	1	—	—	1	—	—	—	—	—	—	—	—	—	—	—	—	—	1
Education (Sc.)	2	—	4	6	—	—	2	—	—	—	—	—	—	—	4	—	—	—	—	—	7
Foreign Compensation	3	—	2	5	—	—	3	—	—	—	—	—	—	—	—	—	—	1	1	—	6
Housing	3	—	4	7	—	—	2	—	1	—	—	—	—	—	2	—	2	—	—	—	9
Housing (Sc.)	1	—	—	1	—	—	1	—	—	—	—	—	—	—	—	—	—	—	—	—	1
Immigration Appeals	1	—	2	3	—	—	1	—	—	—	—	—	—	—	2	—	—	—	—	—	4
Mines and Quarries (Tips)	3	—	—	3	—	—	3	—	—	—	—	—	—	—	—	—	—	—	—	—	3
Post Office	10	—	6	16	—	—	10	—	—	—	—	—	—	—	4	—	—	—	2	—	16
Representation of the People	11	—	1	12	—	—	11	—	—	—	—	—	—	—	—	—	1	—	—	—	12
Transport (London)	41	—	6	47	—	—	41	—	—	—	—	—	—	—	1	3	—	1	1	—	48
Vehicle and Driving Licences	3	—	2	5	—	—	3	—	—	—	—	—	—	—	2	—	—	—	—	—	6
Total	148	1	43	192	—	—	146	—	2	1	—	—	—	—	28	3	4	3	5	—	201

Table A3.3 THIRD READING, H. OF L., 1968–69

Bill	Number of NC/amends moved				Moved by Minister [col. (1)]					Moved by Government backbencher [col. (2)]					Moved by Opposition and Independent Peers [col. (3)]					Div. on clause stand part	Number of NC/ amends tabled
	By Min	By Gvt BB	By Opp	Total cols 1–3	W/O div. W	W/O div. N	W/O div. A	On div. N	On div. A	W/O div. W	W/O div. N	W/O div. A	On div. N	On div. A	W/O div. W	W/O div. N	W/O div. A	On div. N	On div. A		
	(1)	(2)	(3)	(4)	(5)	(6)	(7)	(8)	(9)	(10)	(11)	(12)	(13)	(14)	(15)	(16)	(17)	(18)	(19)	(20)	(21)
Agric. (Spring Traps) (Sc.)	2	—	—	2	—	—	2	—	—	—	—	—	—	—	—	—	—	—	—	—	2
Children and Young Persons	58	—	—	58	—	—	58	—	—	—	—	—	—	—	—	—	—	—	—	—	58
Education (Sc.)	1	—	1	2	—	—	1	—	—	—	—	—	—	—	1	—	—	—	—	—	2
Foreign Compensation	1	—	—	1	—	—	1	—	—	—	—	—	—	—	—	—	—	—	—	—	2
Representation of the People	5	—	—	5	—	—	5	—	—	—	—	—	—	—	—	—	—	—	—	—	5
Total	67	—	1	68	—	—	67	—	—	—	—	—	—	—	1	—	—	—	—	—	69

Table A3.4 COMMITTEE H. OF L., 1970–71

	Number of NC/amends moved				Moved by Minister [col. (1)]					Moved by Government backbencher [col. (2)]					Moved by Opposition and Independent Peers [col. (3)]					Div. on clause stand part	Number of NC/ amends tabled
					W/O div.			On div.		W/O div.			On div.		W/O div.			On div.			
	By Min	By Gvt BB	By Opp	Total cols 1–3	W	N	A	N	A	W	N	A	N	A	W	N	A	N	A		
Bill	(1)	(2)	(3)	(4)	(5)	(6)	(7)	(8)	(9)	(10)	(11)	(12)	(13)	(14)	(15)	(16)	(17)	(18)	(19)	(20)	(21)
Anguilla	—	—	1	1	—	—	—	—	—	—	—	—	—	—	1	—	—	—	—	—	1
Atomic Energy Authority	1	—	2	3	—	—	1	—	—	—	—	—	—	—	2	—	—	—	—	—	3
Civil Aviation (on re-commitment)	14	2	5	21	—	—	13	—	1	2	—	—	—	—	3	—	1	1	—	—	22
Civil Aviation (Dect. Provs)	—	—	1	1	—	—	—	—	—	—	—	—	—	—	—	—	—	1	—	—	1
Coal Industry	—	—	8	8	—	—	—	—	—	—	—	—	—	—	2	2	—	4	—	1	12
Education (Milk)	—	—	8	8	—	—	—	—	—	—	—	—	—	—	—	5	—	3	—	—	13
Education (Scotland)	—	—	3	3	—	—	—	—	—	—	—	—	—	—	1	1	—	1	—	—	5
Expiring Laws (Continuance)	—	—	1	1	—	—	—	—	—	—	—	—	—	—	—	—	1	—	—	—	1
Fire Precautions	—	8	7	15	—	—	—	—	—	8	—	—	—	—	6	1	—	—	—	—	26
Highways (on re-commitment)	38	—	—	38	—	—	38	—	—	—	—	—	—	—	—	—	—	—	—	—	38
Housing	—	1	3	4	—	—	—	—	—	—	—	—	—	1	2	1	—	—	—	—	5
Immigration	19	7	95	121	—	—	19	—	—	4	—	3	—	—	76	3	5	10	1	—	222
Indus. Rels	160	4	248	412	1	—	155	—	4	2	—	2	—	—	140	29	23	56	—	31	700
Licensing (Abol. State Man.)	—	—	3	3	—	—	—	—	—	—	—	—	—	—	—	2	—	1	—	—	31

Misuse of Drugs	—	2	13	15	—	—	—	—	—	2	—	—	—	—	10	1	—	2	—	—	61
Nat. Insurance	—	—	1	1	—	—	—	—	—	—	—	—	—	—	1	—	—	—	—	—	2
Oil in Navigable Waters	4	—	—	4	—	—	4	—	—	—	—	—	—	—	—	—	—	—	—	—	4
Rating	3	1	1	5	—	—	3	—	—	1	—	—	—	—	1	—	—	—	—	—	6
Sheriff Courts (Scotland)	2	1	—	3	—	—	2	—	—	1	—	—	—	—	—	—	—	—	—	—	3
Social Security	—	—	2	2	—	—	—	—	—	—	—	—	—	—	2	—	—	—	—	—	8
Total	241	26	402	669	1	—	235	—	5	20	—	5	—	1	247	45	30	79	1	32	1164

Table A3.5 REPORT H. OF L., 1970–71

	Number of NC/amends moved				Moved by Minister [col. (1)]					Moved by Government backbencher [col. (2)]					Moved by Opposition and Independent Peers [col. (3)]					Div. on clause stand part	Number of NC/ amends tabled
					W/O div.			On div.		W/O div.			On div.		W/O div.			On div.			
	By Min	By Gvt BB	By Opp	Total cols 1–3	W	N	A	N	A	W	N	A	N	A	W	N	A	N	A		
Bill	(1)	(2)	(3)	(4)	(5)	(6)	(7)	(8)	(9)	(10)	(11)	(12)	(13)	(14)	(15)	(16)	(17)	(18)	(19)	(20)	(21)
Atomic Energy Authority	2	—	—	2	—	—	2	—	—	—	—	—	—	—	—	—	—	—	—	—	2
Coal Industry	—	—	6	6	—	—	—	—	—	—	—	—	—	—	1	2	—	3	—	—	9
Fire Precautions	15	—	7	22	—	—	15	—	—	—	—	—	—	—	—	—	7	—	—	—	22
Highways	25	—	4	29	—	—	25	—	—	—	—	—	—	—	—	—	4	—	—	—	30
Housing	5	—	—	5	—	—	5	—	—	—	—	—	—	—	—	—	—	—	—	—	5
Immigration	40	1	22	63	—	—	40	—	—	—	—	—	1	—	13	4	—	5	—	—	98
Industrial Relations	137	—	179	316	—	—	137	—	—	—	—	—	—	—	92	13	31	43	—	—	419
Licensing (Abol. State Man.)	—	—	1	1	—	—	—	—	—	—	—	—	—	—	—	1	—	—	—	—	1
Misuse of Drugs	14	—	1	15	1	—	13	—	—	—	—	—	—	—	—	—	1	—	—	—	15
Oil in Navigable Waters	11	—	5	16	—	—	9	—	2	—	—	—	—	—	4	—	1	—	—	—	21
Total	249	1	225	475	1	—	246	—	2	—	—	—	1	—	110	20	44	51	—	—	622

Table A3.6 THIRD READING, H. OF L., 1970–71

	Number of NC/amends moved				Moved by Minister [col. (1)]					Moved by Government backbencher [col. (2)]					Moved by Opposition and Independent Peers [col. (3)]					Div. on clause stand part	Number of NC/ amends tabled
					W/O div.			On div.		W/O div.			On div.		W/O div.			On div.			
	By Min	By Gvt BB	By Opp	Total cols 1–3	W	N	A	N	A	W	N	A	N	A	W	N	A	N	A		
Bill	(1)	(2)	(3)	(4)	(5)	(6)	(7)	(8)	(9)	(10)	(11)	(12)	(13)	(14)	(15)	(16)	(17)	(18)	(19)	(20)	(21)
Civil Aviation	7	—	1	8	—	—	7	—	—	—	—	—	—	—	1	—	—	—	—	—	8
Education (Milk)	—	—	1	1	—	—	—	—	—	—	—	—	—	—	—	—	—	1	—	—	4
Education (Scotland)	—	—	3	3	—	—	—	—	—	—	—	—	—	—	1	1	—	1	—	—	4
Immigration	6	—	—	6	—	—	6	—	—	—	—	—	—	—	—	—	—	—	—	—	6
Industrial Relations	8	—	7	15	—	—	8	—	—	—	—	—	—	—	2	2	—	3	—	—	20
Misuse of Drugs	1	—	1	2	—	—	1	—	—	—	—	—	—	—	—	—	—	1	—	—	2
Oil in Navigable Waters	6	—	—	6	—	—	6	—	—	—	—	—	—	—	—	—	—	—	—	—	6
Total	28	—	13	41	—	—	28	—	—	—	—	—	—	—	4	3	—	6	—	—	50

INDEX

INDEX